BEGINNING
IPAD™ APPLICATION DEVELOPMENT

Continues

BEGINNING

iPad™ Application Development

BEGINNING

iPad™ Application Development

Wei-Meng Lee

Wiley Publishing, Inc.

Beginning iPad™ Application Development

Published by
Wiley Publishing, Inc.
10475 Crosspoint Boulevard
Indianapolis, IN 46256
www.wiley.com

ISBN: 978-0-470-64165-1

ISBN: 978-0-470-88690-8 (ebk)

ISBN: 978-0-470-88700-4 (ebk)

ISBN: 978-0-470-88702-8 (ebk)

Manufactured in the United States of America

10 9 8 7 6 5 4 3 2 1

For general information on our other products and services please contact our Customer Care Department within the United States at (877) 762-2974, outside the United States at (317) 572-3993 or fax (317) 572-4002.

Wiley also publishes its books in a variety of electronic formats. Some content that appears in print may not be available in electronic books.

Library of Congress Control Number: 2010924556

To my family:

Thanks for the understanding and support while I worked on getting this book ready! I love you all!

ABOUT THE AUTHOR

WEI-MENG LEE is a technologist and founder of Developer Learning Solutions (`www.learn2develop.net`), a technology company specializing in hands-on training for the latest Microsoft and Mac OS X technologies. He is also an established author with Wrox and O'Reilly.

Wei-Meng first started the iPhone programming course in Singapore and it has since received much positive feedback. His hands-on approach to iPad/iPhone programming makes understanding the subject much easier than reading books, tutorials, and documentation from Apple.

Contact Wei-Meng at `weimenglee@learn2develop.net`.

ABOUT THE TECHNICAL EDITOR

TRENT SHUMAY is the founder and Chief Architect at Finger Food Studios Inc. in the Vancouver, BC area. After graduating from the UBC Computer Science program, Trent spent thirteen years in the gaming and interactive entertainment space, where handheld gaming devices ignited his passion for mobile development. Today, Finger Food Studios focuses on developing media-rich, interactive mobile and Web applications. You can reach Trent directly at `trent@fingerfoodstudios.com`.

CREDITS

ACQUISITIONS EDITOR
Scott Meyers

PROJECT EDITOR
Ami Frank Sullivan

TECHNICAL EDITOR
Trenton Shumay

PRODUCTION EDITOR
Kathleen Wisor

COPY EDITOR
Maryann Steinhart

EDITORIAL DIRECTOR
Robyn B. Siesky

EDITORIAL MANAGER
Mary Beth Wakefield

**ASSOCIATE DIRECTOR
OF MARKETING**
David Mayhew

PRODUCTION MANAGER
Tim Tate

**VICE PRESIDENT AND
EXECUTIVE GROUP PUBLISHER**
Richard Swadley

VICE PRESIDENT AND EXECUTIVE PUBLISHER
Barry Pruett

ASSOCIATE PUBLISHER
Jim Minatel

PROJECT COORDINATOR, COVER
Lynsey Stanford

COMPOSITOR
Craig Woods, Happenstance Type-O-Rama

PROOFREADER
Word One, New York

INDEXER
Johnna VanHoose Dinse

COVER DESIGNER
Michael E. Trent

COVER IMAGE
© Thomas Perkins/istockphoto

ACKNOWLEDGMENTS

ON THE MORNING OF 27TH JANUARY 2010, Steve Jobs announced the iPad, a device that has long been rumored to be the next killer device from Apple. Now that it is official, developers are flocking to see what next killer applications they can build.

Having just finished writing my iPhone book, this was a natural progression for me to take. Since the iPad is based on the iPhone OS, writing one on iPad development shouldn't be that difficult, right? Well, no matter how familiar you are with a topic, writing a book is always a huge commitment, and this book is no exception. Now that this book is finally done, I would like to take this chance to thank the many people who made this a reality.

First, I want to thank Scott Meyers, who had faith in me when he signed me up for this book: I know that you have been under tremendous stress to get this book out into the bookstores, and I hope I have not disappointed you. Thank you, Scott!

Next, a huge thanks to Ami Sullivan, my editor, who is always a pleasure to work with. I deeply appreciate her patience with me, for without her, this book would not be in your hands now. For that, please accept my sincere thanks, Ami! And thanks for the guidance!

I should not forget the heroes behind the scene: copy editor Maryann Steinhart and technical editor Trenton Shumay. They have been eagle-eye editing the book, making sure that every sentence makes sense — both grammatically as well as technically. Thanks, Maryann and Trent!

Last, but not least, I want to thank my parents, and my wife, Sze Wa, for all the support they have given me. They have selflessly adjusted their schedules to accommodate my busy schedule when I was working on this book. My wife has also stayed up with me on numerous nights as I was furiously working to meet the deadlines, and for this I would like to say to her and my parents: "I love you all!" Finally, to our lovely dog, Ookii, thanks for staying by our side. Now that the book is done, we can look forward to an earlier night.

CONTENTS

INTRODUCTION

ON JANUARY 27, 2010, APPLE ANNOUNCED a magical and revolutionary product: the iPad. The iPad is a tablet computer that is based on the iPhone OS. What this means is that overnight, there were instantly more than 150,000 applications that can run on the iPad. Programming on the iPad is very similar to programming for the iPhone, with the addition of a few new features specifically designed for the iPad, including the following:

1. The introduction of the new Split View-based Application template and the new Popoverview, both of which are covered in Chapter 4.

2. The new Gesture Recognizers, covered in Chapter 12.

When I first started learning about iPhone and iPad development, I went through the same journey that most developers go through: Write a Hello World application, mess with Interface Builder, try to understand what the code is doing, and repeat that process. I was also overwhelmed by the concept of a View Controller and wondered why it was needed if I simply wanted to display a view. My background in developing for Windows Mobile and Android did not help much, and I had to start working with this concept from scratch.

This book was written to help jumpstart beginning iPad developers. It covers the various topics in such a manner that you will progressively learn without being overwhelmed by the details. I adopt the philosophy that the best way to learn is by doing, hence the numerous Try It Out sections in all the chapters, which first show you how to build something and then explain how things work.

Although iPad programming is a huge topic, my aim for this book is to get you started with the fundamentals, help you understand the underlying architecture of the SDK, and appreciate why things are done certain ways. It is beyond the scope of this book to cover everything under the sun related to iPad programming, but I am confident that after reading this book (and doing the exercises), you will be well equipped to tackle your next iPad programming challenge.

WHO THIS BOOK IS FOR

This book is for the beginning iPad developer who wants to start developing iPad applications using the Apple iPhone SDK. To truly benefit from this book, you should have some background in programming and at least be familiar with object-oriented programming concepts. If you are totally new to the Objective-C language, you might want to jump straight to Appendix D, which provides an overview of the language. Alternatively, you can use Appendix D as a quick reference while you tackle the various chapters, checking out the syntax as you try the exercises. Depending on your learning pattern, one of those approaches may work best for you.

NOTE *All the examples discussed in this book were written and tested using the iPhone SDK 3.2 beta 3. Even though Apple continues to call it the iPhone SDK, it can be used to develop iPhone, iPod touch, and iPad applications. At the time of writing (March 2010), Apple continues to use the term "iPhone Simulator" to refer to the simulator that allows you to simulate both an iPhone and iPad. While every effort has been made to ensure that the screen shots are as up to date as possible, the actual screen that you see may differ when the iPhone SDK is out of beta.*

WHAT THIS BOOK COVERS

This book covers the fundamentals of iPad programming using the iPhone SDK. It is divided into 18 chapters and four appendices.

Chapter 1: Getting Started with iPad Programming covers the various tools found in the iPhone SDK and explains their uses in iPad development.

Chapter 2: Write Your First Hello World! Application gets you started with Xcode and Interface Builder to build a Hello World application. The focus is on getting your hands dirty. More details on the various parts and components are covered in subsequent chapters.

Chapter 3: Views, Outlets, and Actions covers the fundamental concepts of iPad programming: outlets and actions. You learn how outlets and actions allow your code to interact with the visual elements in Interface Builder and why they are an integral part of every iPad application. You will also learn about the various UI widgets known as views that make up the user interface of your iPad application.

Chapter 4: View Controllers discusses the various view controllers available in the iPhone SDK. You will learn how to develop different types of iPad applications — View-based, Window-based, Split View-based, as well as Tab Bar applications.

Chapter 5: Keyboard Inputs shows you how to deal with the virtual keyboard in your iPad. You see how to hide the keyboard on demand and how to ensure that your views are not blocked by the keyboard when it is displayed.

Chapter 6: Screen Rotations demonstrates how you can reorient your application's UI when the device is rotated. You learn about the various events that are fired when the device is rotated. You also learn how to force your application to display in a certain orientation.

Chapter 7: Using the Table View explores one of the most powerful views in the iPhone SDK — the Table view. The Table view is commonly used to display rows of data. In this chapter, you also learn how to implement search capabilities in your Table view.

Chapter 8: Application Preferences discusses the use of application settings to persist application preferences. Using application settings, you can access preferences related to your application through the Settings application available on the iPad.

Chapter 9: File Handling shows how you can persist your application data by saving the data to files in your application's sandbox directory. You also learn how to access the various folders available in your application sandbox.

Chapter 10: Database Storage Using SQLLite3 covers the use of the embedded SQLite3 database library to store your data.

Chapter 11: Simple Animations provides an overview of the various techniques you can use to implement simple animations on the iPad. You also learn about the various affine transformations supported by the iPhone SDK.

Chapter 12: Recognizing Gestures provides an overview of the various gesture recognizers available in the iPhone SDK to help your device interpret user's input gestures.

Chapter 13: Accessing the Accelerometer shows how you can access the accelerometer that comes with every iPad. You will also learn how to detect shakes to your device.

Chapter 14: Web Services teaches you how to consume Web services from within your iPad application. You will learn the various ways to communicate with Web services — SOAP, HTTP GET, and HTTP POST. You will also learn how to parse the returning XML result returned by the Web service.

Chapter 15: Bluetooth Programming explores the use of the Game Kit framework for Bluetooth programming. You will learn how to get two iPads to communicate using a Bluetooth connection. You will also learn how to implement voice chatting over a Bluetooth connection.

Chapter 16: Bonjour Programming shows how you can publish services on the network using the Bonjour protocol.

Chapter 17: Apple Push Notification Services explains how you can implement applications that use push notifications. The APNs allows your applications to constantly receive status updates from a service provider even though the application may not be running.

Chapter 18: Displaying Maps shows how to build location-based services application using the Map Kit framework. You will also learn how to obtain geographical locations data and use them to display a map.

Appendix A: Answers to Exercises contains the solutions to the end-of-chapter exercises found in every chapter except Chapter 1.

Appendix B: Getting Around in Xcode provides a quick run-through of the many features in Xcode.

Appendix C: Getting Around in Interface Builder provides an overview of the many features of Interface Builder.

Appendix D: Crash Course in Objective-C provides a crash course in Objective-C. Readers who are new to this language should read this chapter before getting started.

HOW THIS BOOK IS STRUCTURED

This book breaks down the task of learning iPad programming into several smaller chunks, allowing you to digest each topic before delving into a more advanced topic. In addition, there are a few chapters that cover topics already discussed in the previous chapter. That's because there is usually more than one way of doing things in Xcode and Interface Builder, and hence this approach allows you to learn the different techniques in developing iPad applications.

If you are a total beginner to iPad programming, start with Chapters 1 and 2. Once you have gotten things moving, head on to the appendixes to read more about the tools and language you are using. Once you are ready, you can now continue with Chapter 3 and gradually move into more advanced topics.

A feature of this book is that all the code samples in each chapter are independent of those discussed in previous chapters. That way, you have the flexibility to dive into the topics that interest you and start working on the Try It Out projects.

WHAT YOU NEED TO USE THIS BOOK

Most of the examples in this book run on the iPhone Simulator (which comes as part of the iPhone SDK). For exercises that access the hardware (such as the accelerometer), you need a real iPad. In general, to get the most out of this book, having a real iPad device is not necessary (although it is definitely required for testing if you plan to deploy your application on the AppStore).

CONVENTIONS

To help you get the most from the text and keep track of what's happening, we've used a number of conventions throughout the book.

TRY IT OUT   These Are Exercises or Examples for You to Follow

The Try It Out exercises appear once or more per chapter as exercises to work through as you follow the text in the book.

1.   They usually consist of a set of numbered steps.

2.   Follow the steps through with your copy of project files.

How It Works

After each Try It Out, the code you've typed is explained in detail.

As for other conventions in the text:

➤ New terms and important words are *highlighted* in italics when first introduced.

➤ Keyboard combinations are treated like this: Control-R.

➤ Filenames, URLs, and code within the text are treated like so: `persistence.properties`.

➤ Code is presented in two different ways:

```
We use a monofont type with no highlighting for most code examples.
```

```
We use bolding to emphasize code that is of particular importance in the
present context.
```

 WARNING *Boxes like this one hold important, not-to-be forgotten information that is directly relevant to the surrounding text.*

 NOTE *Notes, tips, hints, tricks, and asides to the current discussion look like this.*

 COMMON MISTAKES *This feature, Common Mistakes, helps you avoid the obstacles that many new practitioners find themselves negotiating.*

SOURCE CODE

As you work through the examples in this book, you may choose either to type in all the code manually or to use the source code files that accompany the book. All the source code used in this book is available for download at www.wrox.com. When at the site, simply locate the book's title (use the Search box or one of the title lists) and click the Download Code link on the book's detail page to obtain all the source code for the book. Code that is included on the Web site is highlighted by the following icon and/or CodeNote, as shown following the icon:

**Available for
download on
Wrox.com**

Listings include the filename in the title. If it is just a code snippet, you'll find the filename in a CodeNote such as this:

code snippet filename

After you download the code, just decompress it with your favorite compression tool. Alternatively, go to the main Wrox code download page at `www.wrox.com/dynamic/books/download.aspx` to see the code available for this book and all other Wrox books.

ERRATA

We make every effort to ensure that there are no errors in the text or in the code. However, no one is perfect, and mistakes do occur. If you find an error in one of our books, such as a spelling mistake or faulty piece of code, we would be very grateful for your feedback. By sending in errata, you may save another reader hours of frustration and at the same time help us provide even higher-quality information.

To find the errata page for this book, go to `www.wrox.com` and locate the title using the Search box or one of the title lists. Then, on the book details page, click the Book Errata link. On this page, you can view all errata that has been submitted for this book and posted by Wrox editors. A complete book list including links to each book's errata is also available at `www.wrox.com/misc-pages/booklist.shtml`.

 NOTE *Because many books have similar titles, you may find it easiest to search by ISBN; this book's ISBN is 978-0-470-64165-1.*

If you don't spot "your" error on the Book Errata page, go to `www.wrox.com/contact/techsupport.shtml` and complete the form there to send us the error you have found. We'll check the information and, if appropriate, post a message to the book's errata page and fix the problem in subsequent editions of the book.

P2P.WROX.COM

For author and peer discussion, join the P2P forums at `p2p.wrox.com`. The forums are a Web-based system for you to post messages relating to Wrox books and related technologies and interact with other readers and technology users. The forums offer a subscription feature to e-mail you topics of interest of your choosing when new posts are made to the forums. Wrox authors, editors, other industry experts, and your fellow readers are present on these forums.

At `http://p2p.wrox.com`, you will find a number of different forums that will help you not only as you read this book but also as you develop your own applications. To join the forums, just follow these steps:

1. Go to `p2p.wrox.com` and click the Register link.
2. Read the terms of use and click Agree.

3. Complete the required information to join as well as any optional information you want to provide and click Submit.

4. You will receive an e-mail with information describing how to verify your account and complete the joining process.

After you join, you can post new messages and respond to messages that other users post. You can read messages at any time on the Web. If you want to have new messages from a particular forum e-mailed to you, click the Subscribe to This Forum icon by the forum name in the forum listing.

For more information about how to use the Wrox P2P, be sure to read the P2P FAQs for answers to questions about how the forum software works as well as for many common questions specific to P2P and Wrox books. To read the FAQs, click the FAQ link on any P2P page.

PART I
Getting Started

1

Getting Started with iPad Programming

WHAT YOU WILL LEARN IN THIS CHAPTER:

➤ How to obtain the iPhone SDK

➤ The components included in the iPhone SDK

➤ The features of the development tools — Xcode, Interface Builder, iPhone Simulator

➤ The capabilities of the iPhone Simulator

➤ The architecture of the iPhone OS

➤ The frameworks of the iPhone SDK

➤ The limitations and characteristics of the iPad

Welcome to the world of iPad programming! That you are now holding this book shows that you are fascinated with the idea of developing iPad applications and want to join the ranks of those tens of thousands of developers whose applications are already deployed in the AppStore.

As the old Chinese adage says, "To accomplish your mission, first sharpen your tools." Successful programming requires you first of all to know your tools well. Indeed, this couldn't be more true for iPad programming — you need to know quite a few tools before you can even get started. Hence, the goal of this chapter is to show you the various relevant tools and information you need to jump on the iPad development bandwagon.

Without further ado, it's time to get down to work.

OBTAINING THE IPHONE SDK

To develop for the iPad, you first need to sign up as a Registered iPhone Developer at `http://developer.apple.com/iphone/program/start/register/`. The registration is free and provides you with access to the iPhone SDK (software development kit) and other resources that are useful for getting started.

 NOTE *The iPad uses the same operating system (OS) as the iPhone and iPod touch. So, although you are developing for the iPad, you will still use the iPhone SDK. Hence, throughout this book you will see the term "iPhone" used very often.*

After signing up, you can download the iPhone SDK (version 3.2; see Figure 1-1).

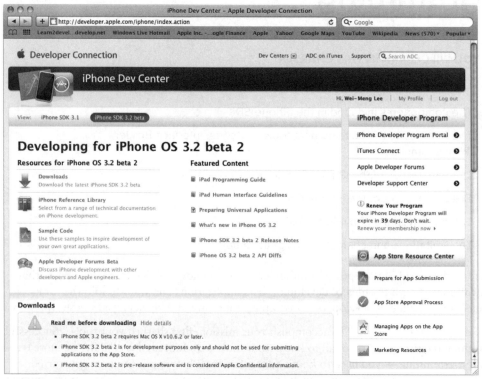

FIGURE 1-1

Before you install the iPhone SDK, make sure you satisfy the following system requirements:

➤ Only Intel Macs are supported, so if you have another processor type (such as the older G4 or G5 Macs), you're out of luck.

➤ You have updated your system with the latest Mac OS X release.

An actual iPad is highly recommended, although not strictly necessary. To test your application, you can use the included iPhone Simulator (which allows you to simulate an iPhone or an iPad). However, to test certain hardware features like GPS, the Accelerometer, and such, you need to use a real device.

When the SDK is downloaded, proceed with installing it (see Figure 1-2). Accept a few licensing agreements and then select the destination folder in which to install the SDK.

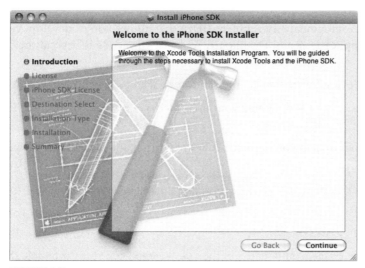

FIGURE 1-2

If you select the default settings during the installation phase, the various tools will be installed in the /Developer/Applications folder (see Figure 1-3).

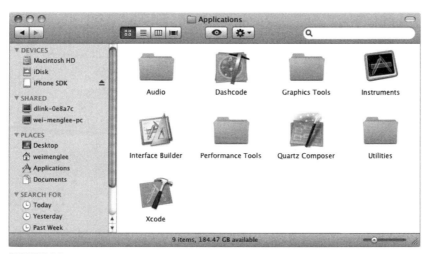

FIGURE 1-3

COMPONENTS OF THE IPHONE SDK

The iPhone SDK includes a suite of development tools to help you develop applications for your iPhone, iPod touch, and iPad. It includes:

➤ Xcode — Integrated development environment (IDE) that enables you to manage, edit, and debug your projects.

➤ Dashcode — Integrated development environment (IDE) that allows you to develop web-based iPhone and iPad applications and Dashboard Widgets. Dashcode is beyond the scope of this book.

➤ iPhone Simulator — Provides a software simulator to simulate an iPhone or an iPad on your Mac.

➤ Interface Builder — Visual editor for designing your user interfaces for your iPhone and iPad applications.

➤ Instruments — Analysis tool to help you optimize your application and monitor for memory leaks in real-time.

The following sections discuss each tool (except Dashcode) in more detail.

Xcode

To launch Xcode, double-click the Xcode icon (located in the `/Developer/Applications` folder; refer to Figure 1-3). Alternatively, go the quicker route and use Spotlight: simply type **Xcode** into the search box and Xcode should be in the Top Hit position.

Figure 1-4 shows the Xcode Welcome screen.

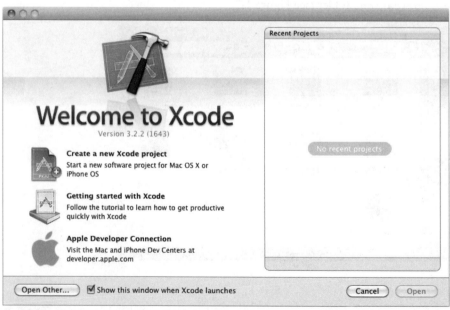

FIGURE 1-4

Using Xcode, you can develop different types of iPhone, iPad, and Mac OS X applications using the various project templates shown in Figure 1-5.

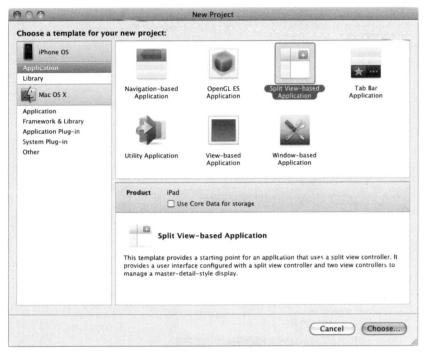

FIGURE 1-5

The IDE in Xcode provides many tools and features that make your development life much easier. One such feature is Code Completion (see Figure 1-6), which displays a pop-up list showing the available classes and members (such as methods, properties, and so on).

 NOTE *For a more comprehensive description of some of the most commonly used features in Xcode, refer to Appendix B.*

iPhone Simulator

The iPhone Simulator (see Figure 1-7) is a very useful tool that you can use to test your application without using your actual iPhone/iPod touch/iPad. The iPhone Simulator is located in the `/Developer/Platforms/iPhoneSimulator.platform/Developer/Applications` folder. Most of the time, you don't need to launch the iPhone Simulator directly — running (or debugging) your application in Xcode automatically brings up the iPhone Simulator. Xcode installs the application on the iPhone Simulator automatically.

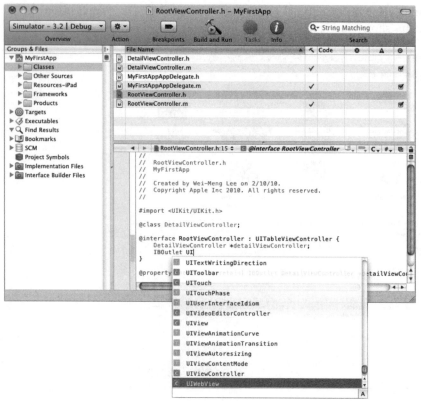

FIGURE 1-6

THE IPHONE SIMULATOR IS NOT AN EMULATOR

The iPhone Simulator is a simulator, not an emulator. So what is the difference? Well, a simulator tries to mimic the behavior of a real device. In the case of the iPhone Simulator, it simulates the real behavior of an actual iPhone/iPad device. However, the simulator itself uses the various libraries installed on the Mac (such as QuickTime) to perform its rendering so that the effect looks the same as an actual iPhone. Also, applications tested on the simulator are compiled into x86 code, which is the byte-code understood by the simulator.

In contrast, an emulator emulates the working of a real device. Applications tested on an emulator are compiled into the actual byte-code used by the real device. The emulator executes the application by translating the byte-code into a form that can be executed by the host computer running the emulator.

A good way to understand the subtle difference between simulation and emulation is this: Imagine you are trying to convince a child that playing with knives is dangerous. To *simulate* this, you pretend to cut yourself with a knife and groan in pain. To *emulate* this, you hold a knife and actually cut yourself.

The iPhone Simulator can simulate different versions of the iPhone OS (see Figure 1-8). This capability is useful if you need to support older versions of the platform as well as testing and debugging errors reported in the application on specific versions of the OS.

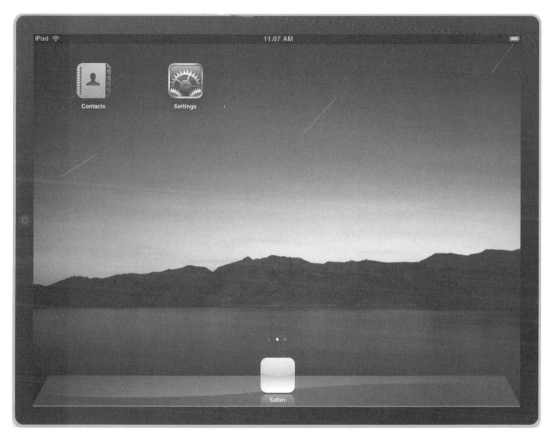

FIGURE 1-7

FIGURE 1-8

Features of the iPhone Simulator

The iPhone Simulator simulates various features of a real iPhone, iPod touch, or iPad device. Features you can test on the iPhone Simulator include:

➤ Screen rotation — left, top, and right

➤ Support for gestures:

    ➤ Tap

    ➤ Touch and Hold

    ➤ Double Tap

    ➤ Swipe

    ➤ Flick

    ➤ Drag

    ➤ Pinch

➤ Low-memory warning simulations

However, the iPhone Simulator, being a software simulator for the real device, does have its limitations. Features not available on the iPhone Simulator include:

➤ Making phone calls

➤ Accessing the Accelerometer

➤ Sending and receiving SMS messages

➤ Installing applications from the App Store

➤ Camera

➤ Microphone

➤ Several features of OpenGL ES

> **NOTE** In the previous version of the SDK (3.1.3), the iPhone Simulator supports location data by always returning a fixed coordinate, such as Latitude 37.3317 North and Longitude 122.0307 West. In the latest release of the SDK, the iPhone Simulator uses the location data of the Mac it is currently running on and returns the current location.

It is worth noting that the speed of the iPhone Simulator is more tightly coupled to the performance of your Mac instead of the actual device. Therefore, it is important that you test your application on a real device rather than rely exclusively on the iPhone Simulator for testing.

Although you have limitations with the iPhone Simulator, it is definitely a useful tool to get your applications tested. That said, testing your application on a real iPad is imperative before you deploy it on the AppStore.

Uninstalling Applications from the iPhone Simulator

The user domain of the iPhone OS file system for the iPhone Simulator is stored in the `~/Library/Application Support/iPhone Simulator/` folder.

 NOTE *The* `~/Library/Application Support/iPhone Simulator/` *folder is also known as the* `<iPhoneUserDomain>`.

All third-party applications are stored in the `<iPhoneUserDomain>/<version_no>/Applications/` folder. When an application is deployed onto the iPhone Simulator, an icon is created on the Home screen (shown on the left in Figure 1-9) and a file and a folder are created within the `Applications` folder (shown on the right in Figure 1-9).

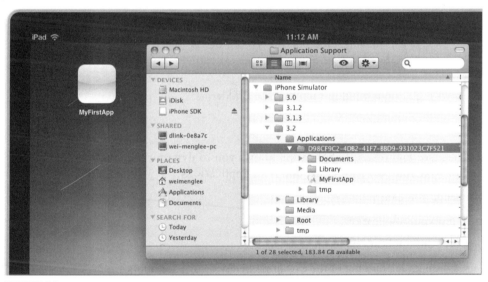

FIGURE 1-9

To uninstall (delete) an application, execute the following steps:

1. Click and hold the icon of the application on the Home screen until all the icons start wriggling. Observe that all the icons now have an X button displayed on their top left corners.

2. Click the X button (see Figure 1-10) next to the icon of the application you want to uninstall.

FIGURE 1-10

3. An alert window appears asking if you are sure you want to delete the icon. Click Delete to confirm the deletion.

> **WARNING** When the application is uninstalled, the corresponding files and folders in the Applications folder are deleted automatically.

The easiest way to reset the iPhone Simulator to its original state is to select iPhone Simulator ➪ Reset Content and Settings.

Interface Builder

Interface Builder is a visual tool that allows you to design your user interfaces for your iPad applications. Using Interface Builder, you drag and drop views on windows and then connect the various views with outlets and actions so that they can programmatically interact with your code.

> **NOTE** Outlets and actions are discussed in more detail in Chapter 3 and Appendix C discusses Interface Builder in more detail.

Figure 1-11 shows the various windows in Interface Builder.

Instruments

The Instruments (see Figure 1-12) application allows you to dynamically trace and profile the performance of your Mac OS X, iPhone, and iPad applications.

Using Instruments, you can:

➤ Stress test your applications.

➤ Monitor your applications for memory leaks.

➤ Gain a deep understanding of the executing behavior of your applications.

➤ Track difficult-to-reproduce problems in your applications.

> **NOTE** Covering the Instruments application is beyond the scope of this book. For more information, refer to Apple's documentation.

FIGURE 1-11

FIGURE 1-12

ARCHITECTURE OF THE IPHONE OS

Although this book doesn't explore the innards of the iPhone OS, understanding some of the important points of the iPhone OS is useful. Figure 1-13 shows the different abstraction layers that make up the Mac OS X and the iPhone OS (which is used by the iPhone, iPod touch, and iPad).

 NOTE *The iPhone OS is architecturally very similar to the Mac OS X except that the topmost layer is Cocoa Touch for iPhone instead of the Cocoa Framework.*

FIGURE 1-13

The bottom layer is the Core OS, which is the foundation of the operating system. It is in charge of memory management, the file system, networking, and other OS tasks, and it interacts directly with the hardware. The Core OS layer consists of components such as:

➤ OS X Kernel

➤ Mach 3.0

➤ BSD

➤ Sockets

➤ Security

➤ Power Management

➤ Keychain

➤ Certificates

➤ File System

➤ Bonjour

The Core Services layer provides an abstraction over the services provided in the Core OS layer. It provides fundamental access to iPhone OS services and consists of the following components:

➤ Collections

➤ Address Book

➤ Networking

➤ File Access

➤ SQLite

➤ Core Location

➤ Net Services

➤ Threading

➤ Preferences

➤ URL Utilities

The Media layer provides multimedia services that you can use in your iPad applications. It consists of the following components:

➤ Core Audio

➤ OpenGL

➤ Audio Mixing

➤ Audio Recording

➤ Video Playback

➤ JPG, PNG, TIFF

➤ PDF

➤ Quartz

➤ Core Animation

➤ OpenGL ES

The Cocoa Touch layer provides an abstraction layer to expose the various libraries for programming the iPad, such as:

➤ Multi-Touch events

➤ Multi-Touch controls

➤ Accelerometer

➤ View Hierarchy

➤ Localization

➤ Alerts

➤ Web Views

➤ People Picker

➤ Image Picker

➤ Controllers

The iPhone SDK consists of the frameworks shown in Table 1-1.

 NOTE *A framework is a software library that provides specific functionalities.*

TABLE 1-1: The Frameworks in the iPhone SDK

FRAMEWORK NAME	DESCRIPTION
AddressBook.framework	Provides access to the centralized database for storing a user's contacts.
AddressBookUI.framework	Provides the UI to display the contacts stored in the Address Book database.
AudioToolbox.framework	Provides low-level C APIs for audio recording and playback, as well as managing the audio hardware.
AudioUnit.framework	Provides the interface for iPhone OS-supplied audio processing plug-ins in your application.
AVFoundation.framework	Provides low-level C APIs for audio recording and playback, as well as for managing the audio hardware.
CFNetwork.framework	Provides access to network services and configurations, such as HTTP, FTP, and Bonjour services.
CoreAudio.framework	Declares data types and constants used by other Core Audio interfaces.
CoreData.framework	Provides a generalized solution for object graph management in your application.
CoreFoundation.framework	Provides abstraction for common data types, Unicode strings, XML, URL resource, and so on.
CoreGraphics.framework	Provides C-based APIs for 2D rendering; based on the Quartz drawing engine.
CoreLocation.framework	Provides location-based information using a combination of GPS, cell ID, and Wi-Fi networks.
ExternalAccessory.framework	Provides a way to communicate with accessories.

FRAMEWORK NAME	DESCRIPTION
Foundation.framework	Provides the foundation classes for Objective C, such as NSObject, basic data types, operating system services, and so on.
GameKit.framework	Provides networking capabilities to games; commonly used for peer-to-peer connectivity and in-game voice features.
IOKit.framework	Provides capabilities for driver development.
MapKit.framework	Provides an embedded map interface for your application.
MediaPlayer.framework	Provides facilities for playing movies and audio files.
MessageUI.framework	Provides a view-controller–based interface for composing e-mail messages.
MobileCoreServices.framework	Provides access to standard types and constants.
OpenAL.framework	Provides an implementation of the OpenAL specification.
OpenGLES.framework	Provides a compact and efficient subset of the OpenGL API for 2D and 3D drawing.
QuartzCore.framework	Provides ability to configure animations and effects and then render those effects in hardware.
Security.framework	Provides the ability to secure your data and control access to software.
StoreKit.framework	Provides in-app purchase support for applications.
SystemConfiguration.framework	Provides the ability to determine network availability and state on device.
UIKit.framework	Provides the fundamental objects for managing an application's UI.

SOME USEFUL INFORMATION BEFORE YOU GET STARTED

You now have a good idea of the tools involved in iPad application development. Before you go ahead and take the plunge, the following sections discuss some useful information that can make your journey more pleasant.

Versions of iPhone OS

At the time of writing, the iPhone OS is in its third revision — that is, version 3.2. Its major versions are as follows:

➤   1.0 — Initial release of iPhone

➤   1.1 — Additional features and bug fixes for 1.0

➤ 2.0 — Released with iPhone 3G; comes with App Store

➤ 2.1 — Additional features and bug fixes for 2.0

➤ 2.2 — Additional features and bug fixes for 2.1

➤ 3.0 — Third major release of the iPhone OS

➤ 3.1 — Additional features and bug fixes for 3.0

➤ 3.2 — This version release for iPad only; see the sidebar for what is new in iPhone OS 3.2

For a detailed description of the features in each release, check out `http://en.wikipedia.org/wiki/IPhone_OS_version_history`.

WHAT'S NEW IN IPHONE OS 3.2

In January 2010, Apple announced a new device based on the existing iPhone OS — the iPad. The iPad is a tablet computer that resembles an iPod touch, except that it has a much bigger screen. The iPad comes in six different editions, three with Wi-Fi and another three with Wi-Fi and 3G networks. The iPad will be released in three storage configurations: 16GB, 32GB, and 64GB.

Some of the important new features of iPhone OS 3.2 include:

➤ Support for existing iPhone applications by running them either in their original screen size or in pixel-doubled mode.

➤ New UI features such as Popovers, Split Views, and Custom Input Views.

➤ Support for external displays.

➤ Support for gestures detection using Gestures Recognizers.

➤ Improved Text support to allow applications to have more sophisticated text-handling capabilities.

➤ New File and Document support to facilitate building document-centric applications.

Testing on Real Devices

One of the most common complaints that beginning iPad programmers made was about the inability to test iPad applications they have developed on their actual devices. It seems odd that as the owner of the device, they can't even test their applications on it. Turns out that for security reasons, Apple requires all applications to be signed with a valid certificate, and for testing purposes, a developer certificate is required.

To test your applications on a device, you must sign up for the iPhone Developer program and request that a developer certificate be installed onto your device.

Screen Resolution

The iPad is a beautiful device with a high-resolution screen. At 9.7 inches (diagonally), the iPad screen supports multi-touch operation and allows a pixel resolution of 1024 x 768 at 132 ppi (see Figure 1-14). When designing your application, note that because of the status bar, the actual resolution is generally limited to 1004 x 768 pixels. Of course, you can turn off the status bar programmatically and gain access to the full 1024 x 768 resolution.

Also, be mindful that users may rotate the device to display your application in Landscape mode. You need to make provisions to your user interface so that the applications can still work properly in Landscape mode.

FIGURE 1-14

> **NOTE** *Chapter 6 discusses how to handle screen rotations. Unlike developing on the iPhone, applications running on the iPad must support different screen orientations.*

Single-Window Applications

If you are new to mobile programming, be aware that the limited screen real estate means that most mobile platforms support only single-window applications — that is, your application window occupies the entire screen. The iPad is no exception to this platform limitation. Overlapping windows that are so common in desktop operating systems (such as Mac OS X and Windows) are not supported on the iPad.

No Background Applications

One of the major challenges in programming mobile devices is power management. A badly written application can be a resource hog and will drain the battery of the device very quickly. Apple acknowledges this issue, and from reviewing experiences obtained from other platforms, decided that major culprits in hurting battery life and performance are background applications. For example, on platforms such as Windows Mobile, when an application remains in memory when it goes out of view (because of an incoming call, for instance), each background application retained in memory continues to take its toll on the device's performance and battery life.

Apple's solution to this problem is simple: Disallow applications to run in the background. Although this is an effective solution, it has irked a lot of developers. Many useful applications require background operation to function correctly. For example, a chatting application needs to be running to receive messages from other users. To overcome this limitation, Apple has developed its Push Notification Service, which feeds applications with data even when they are not running. This service was released with iPhone 3.0. Using push technology, a device is constantly connected to Apple's server through an IP connection. When a device needs attention, a notification is sent from Apple's server to the device, thereby alerting the specific application that needs to service that notification.

> **NOTE** *Push notification is discussed in Chapter 17, "Apple Push Notification Services."*

SUMMARY

This chapter offered a quick tour of the tools used for iPhone application development. You also learned some of the characteristics of iPad, such as the one-application limit and the support for existing iPhone applications. In the next chapter, you develop your first iPad application, and you will soon be on your way to iPad nirvana!

▶ **WHAT YOU LEARNED IN THIS CHAPTER**

TOPIC	KEY CONCEPTS
Obtaining the iPhone SDK	Register as an iPhone Developer at `http://developer.apple.com` first and download the free SDK.
iPhone Simulator	Most of the testing can be done on the iPhone Simulator. However, it is strongly recommended that you have a real device for actual testing.
Limitations of the iPhone Simulator	Access to hardware is generally not supported by the simulator. For example, the camera, Accelerometer, voice recording, and so on are not supported.
Frameworks in the iPhone SDK	The iPhone SDK provides several frameworks that perform specific functionalities on the iPad. You program your iPad applications using all these frameworks.
Background applications	The iPad does not support third-party background applications.
Screen resolution	1024 x 768 pixels (with status bar hidden). 1004 x 768 pixels (with status bar visible).
Single-window applications	All iPad applications are single-windowed — that is, all windows fill the entire screen and overlapping windows are not allowed.

Write Your First Hello World! Application

WHAT YOU WILL LEARN IN THIS CHAPTER:

➤ Create a new iPad project

➤ Build your first iPad application using Xcode

➤ Design the user interface (UI) of your iPad application using Interface Builder

➤ Write some simple code to allow the application to rotate its content based on the orientation of the device

➤ Add an icon to your iPad application

Now that you have set up all the tools and SDK, you are ready to start developing for the iPad! For programming books, it is customary to start the chapter by showing you how to develop a "Hello World!" application. This approach allows you to use the various tools quickly without getting bogged down with the details. It also provides you with instant gratification: You see for yourself that things really work, which can be a morale booster that inspires you to learn more.

GETTING STARTED WITH XCODE

Power up Xcode and you should see the Welcome screen, as shown in Figure 2-1.

 NOTE *The easiest way to start Xcode is to type* **Xcode** *in Spotlight and then press the Enter key to launch it.*

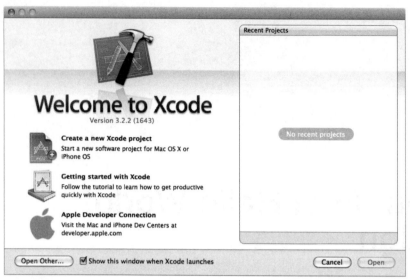

FIGURE 2-1

To create a new iPad project, choose File ➪ New Project. Figure 2-2 shows the different types of projects you can create using Xcode. You see the two primary categories — iPhone OS and Mac OS X — in the left panel. iPad uses the iPhone OS, so click the Application item listed under iPhone OS to view the different templates available for developing your iPad application.

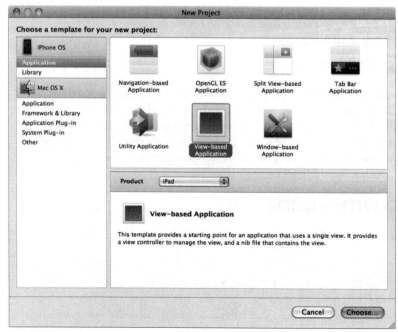

FIGURE 2-2

Although there are quite a few types of iPad applications you can create, for this chapter, select the View-based Application template and click the Choose button.

 NOTE *Subsequent chapters show you how to develop some of the other types of iPad applications, such as Tab Bar Application and Split View-based Application.*

Name the project `HelloWorld` and click Save. Xcode proceeds to create the project for the template you have selected. Figure 2-3 shows the various files and folders in your project.

FIGURE 2-3

The left panel of Xcode shows the groups in the project. You can expand on each group or folder to reveal the files contained in it. The right panel of Xcode shows the files contained within the group or folder you have selected on the left panel. To edit a particular file, select it from the list, and the editor at the bottom of the right panel opens the file for editing. If you want a separate window for editing, simply double-click the file to edit it in a new window.

Using Interface Builder

As yet, this project has had no UI. To prove this, simply press Command-R (or select Run ➪ Run), and your application is deployed to the included iPhone Simulator. Figure 2-4 shows the blank screen displayed on the iPhone Simulator. It's good to see this now, because as you go through the chapter you will see changes occur based on your actions.

iPad 📶   10:43 PM

FIGURE 2-4

Obviously, a blank screen is not very useful. So, it's time to try adding some views to the UI of your application. In the list of files in your project, you'll notice two files with the `.xib` extension — `MainWindow.xib` and `HelloWorldViewController.xib`. Files with `.xib` extensions are basically XML files containing the UI definitions of an application. You can edit `.xib` files by either modifying their XML content, or more easily (and more sanely), edit them using Interface Builder.

Interface Builder comes as part of the iPhone SDK and allows you to build the UI of iPad (and Mac) applications by using drag-and-drop.

Double-click the `HelloWorldViewController.xib` file to launch Interface Builder. Figure 2-5 shows Interface Builder displaying the content of `HelloWorldViewController.xib` (which is really empty at this moment). As you can see, the Library window shows the various views that you can add to the UI of your iPad application. The View window shows the graphical layout of your UI. You will see the use of the other windows shortly.

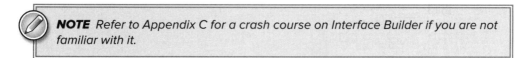

NOTE *Refer to Appendix C for a crash course on Interface Builder if you are not familiar with it.*

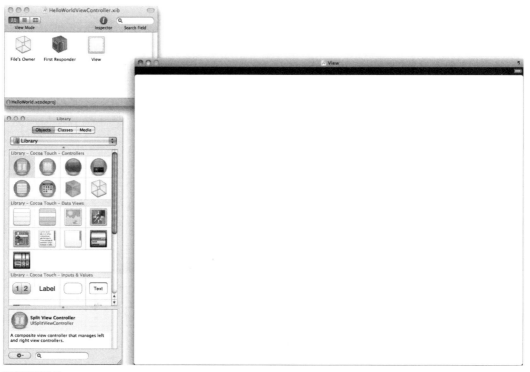

FIGURE 2-5

With the View window in Landscape mode (click on the arrow at the top-right corner of the window to switch the orientation if it is not already in Landscape mode), scroll down to the Label view in the Library pane and drag and drop a `Label` view onto the View window (see Figure 2-6).

After the Label view is added, select it and choose Tools ⇨ Attributes Inspector. Enter **Hello World!** in the Text field. Also, next to Layout, click the center Alignment type (see Figure 2-7).

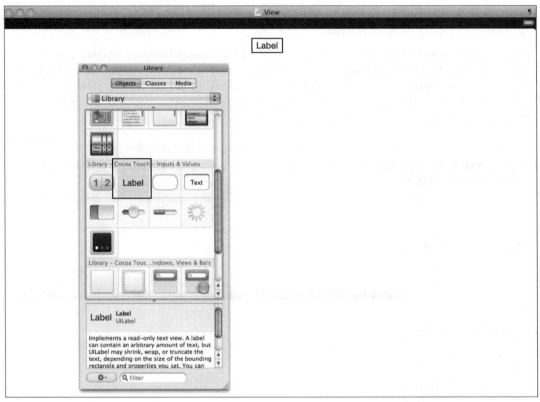

FIGURE 2-6

With the Label view still selected, press Command-T to invoke the Fonts window (see Figure 2-8). Set the font size to 64.

FIGURE 2-7

FIGURE 2-8

Next, from the Library window drag and drop a Text Field view to the View window, followed by a Round Rect Button view. Modify the attribute of the Round Rect Button view by entering **Click Me!** in the Title field (see Figure 2-9).

FIGURE 2-9

 NOTE *Rather than specify the* Text *or* Title *property of a view to make the text display in the view (for example, the Label and the Round Rect Button views), you can simply double-click the view itself and type the text directly. After you've done this, you can rearrange the views and resize them to suit your needs. Interface Builder provides you with alignment guidelines to help you arrange your controls in a visually pleasing layout.*

Save the `HelloWorldViewController.xib` file by pressing Command-S. Then, return to Xcode and run the application again by pressing `Command-R`. The iPhone Simulator now displays the modified UI (see Figure 2-10).

 NOTE *Always remember to save all your changes in Interface Builder before you run the application in Xcode.*

Tap the Text Field view and watch the keyboard automatically appear (see Figure 2-11).

Press the Home button on the iPhone Simulator, and you will see that your application has been installed on the simulator. To go back to the application, simply tap the HelloWorld icon (see Figure 2-12).

FIGURE 2-10

FIGURE 2-11

FIGURE 2-12

 NOTE *Only one application can run on the iPad at any time (except for some built-in applications by Apple). Hence, when you press the Home button on your iPad, your application exits. Tapping an application icon starts the application all over again.*

Changing Screen Orientations

The iPad Simulator also supports changes in view orientation. To change the view orientation mode, press the Command-→ or Command-← key combination. Figure 2-13 shows the iPhone Simulator in Portrait mode.

Notice that your application automatically flips upright when you change the orientation mode. This is controlled programmatically in one of the code files in your Xcode project.

In Xcode, edit the `HelloWorldViewController.m` file and look for the following code segment:

```
// Override to allow orientations other than the default portrait orientation.
- (BOOL)shouldAutorotateToInterfaceOrientation:(UIInterfaceOrientation)
interfaceOrientation {
    return YES;
}
```

FIGURE 2-13

Observe that this method returns a YES, indicating that all orientation modes are supported and that your application will automatically flip itself when the orientation mode changes.

NOTE *At this juncture, do not worry about the other files such as* HelloWorldAppDelegate.h *and* HelloWorldAppDelegate.m. *You learn more about them in later chapters.*

To restrict your application to only support certain orientation modes, you need to programmatically specify the mode(s) you want to support, such as the following:

```
// Override to allow orientations other than the default portrait orientation.
- (BOOL)shouldAutorotateToInterfaceOrientation:(UIInterfaceOrientation)
interfaceOrientation {

    //return YES;
    return (interfaceOrientation==UIInterfaceOrientationPortrait ||
            interfaceOrientation==UIInterfaceOrientationLandscapeLeft);
}
```

This code snippet indicates that your application will only flip itself upright when the screen is displayed in the Portrait or Landscape Left (when the Home Screen button is on the left side) mode. Figure 2-14 shows that when the screen is displayed in the Landscape Right mode, the application does not flip itself upright.

FIGURE 2-14

Chapter 6 discusses screen rotations in more detail.

 NOTE *It's important that iPad applications support all the Landscape and Portrait display modes. Hence, it is recommended that you return a* YES *in the* shouldAutorotateToInterfaceOrientation: *method. The preceding code snippet is only for your information.*

Views Repositioning

In the previous section, you saw that as the orientation changes, the size and positioning of the views remain. In the real world, this scenario is not desirable because it doesn't give the user a good experience while using your application. Ideally, you should reposition your views on the screen so that they change with the view orientation.

To resize your views, go to the Interface Builder, select Label view, and choose Tools ⇨ Size Inspector. Modify the Autosizing attribute of the view as shown in Figure 2-15 by clicking the various lines inside the two squares (observe carefully the various anchors that are set in the Autosizing section). This will cause the Label view to expand/contract as the view orientation changes. At the same time, the view will anchor to the top of the screen.

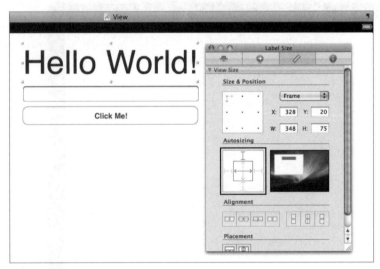

FIGURE 2-15

Likewise, modify the Autosizing attribute of the Text Field view as shown in Figure 2-16 by clicking the various lines inside the two squares.

Finally, modify the Autosizing attribute for the Round Rect Button control as shown in Figure 2-17 by clicking the line within the two squares. This time, you are not resizing the view when the view orientation changes. Instead, you are only anchoring it to the top of the screen.

FIGURE 2-16

FIGURE 2-17

That's it! In Interface Builder, click the arrow at the top-right corner (see Figure 2-18) of the screen to rotate the screen so that you can view the effect of the changes you have made immediately.

Go back to Xcode and run the application again. This time, notice that the controls reposition and resize themselves as you rotate the screen. Figure 2-19 shows the views displayed in Portrait mode.

FIGURE 2-18

Writing Some Code

By now you should be comfortable enough with Xcode and Interface Builder to write some code. That will give you a flavor of programming the iPad.

In the `HelloWorldViewController.h` file, add a declaration for the `btnClicked:` action:

```
#import <UIKit/UIKit.h>

@interface HelloWorldViewController : UIViewController {

}

-(IBAction) btnClicked:(id) sender;

@end
```

FIGURE 2-19

The bold statement creates an action (commonly known as an event handler) named btnClicked:. With the action declared, save the file and return to Interface Builder.

Earlier in this chapter, you saw a window labeled `HelloWorldViewController.xib`. Within this window are three components: File's Owner, First Responder, and View Control-click the Round Rect Button view in the View window and drag it to the File's Owner item in the `HelloWorldViewController.xib` window (see Figure 2-20). A small pop-up containing the `btnClicked:` action appears. Select the `btnClicked:` action. Basically, what you are doing here is linking the `Round Rect Button` view with the action (`btnClicked:`) so that when the user clicks the button, the action is invoked.

FIGURE 2-20

In the `HelloWorldViewController.m` file, add the code that provides the implementation for the `btnClicked:` action:

```
#import "HelloWorldViewController.h"

@implementation HelloWorldViewController

-(IBAction) btnClicked:(id) sender {
    //---display an alert view---
    UIAlertView *alert = [[UIAlertView alloc] initWithTitle:@"Hello World!"
                                                    message:@"iPad, here I come!"
                                                   delegate:self
                                          cancelButtonTitle:@"OK"
                                          otherButtonTitles:nil];
    [alert show];
    [alert release];
}
```

The preceding code displays an alert containing the sentence "`iPad, here I come!`"

That's it! Go back to Xcode and run the application again. This time, when you click the Button view, an alert view displays (see Figure 2-21).

CUSTOMIZING YOUR APPLICATION ICON

As you saw earlier, the application installed on your iPhone Simulator uses a default white image as an icon. It is possible, however, to customize this icon. When designing icons for your iPad applications, bear the following in mind:

➤ Design your icon to be 72 × 72 pixels. Larger size is all right because iPad automatically sizes it for you. For distribution through the App Store, you need to prepare a 512 × 512 pixel image.

➤ Use square corners for your icon image, because iPad automatically rounds them and adds a glossy surface (you can turn off this feature, though).

FIGURE 2-21

The following Try It Out shows you how to add an icon to your application so that the iPad will use it instead of the default white image.

To make your application more interesting, specify your own icon. Before you do so, note that icons for the iPad come in two sizes: 72 x 72 pixels (for the main screen) and 48 x 48 pixels (as shown in the Settings application). Figures 2-22 and 2-23 show the two possible sizes for the icon.

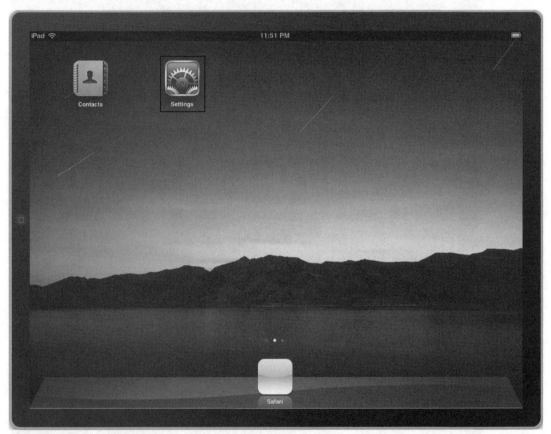

FIGURE 2-22

1. To add an icon to your application, drag and drop an image onto the Resources folder of your project (see Figure 2-24). You will be asked if you want to make a copy of the image you are dropping. Check this option so that a copy of the image will be stored in your project folder.

2. Select the `Info.plist` item (also located under the Resources-iPad folder). Select the Icon file item and set its value to the name of the icon (`app-icon.png`; see Figure 2-25). This specifies the name of the image to be used as the application icon.

3. Run the application and test it on the iPhone Simulator. Press the Home button to return to the (simulation of the) main screen of the iPad. You should see the newly added icon (see Figure 2-26).

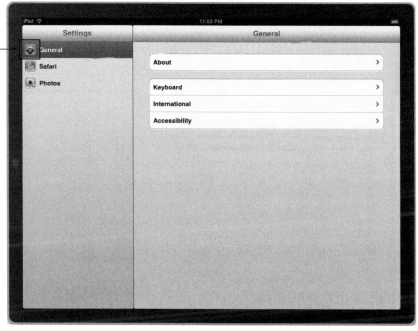

FIGURE 2-23

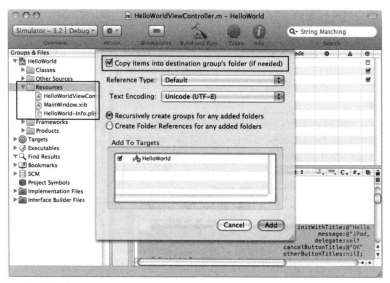

FIGURE 2-24

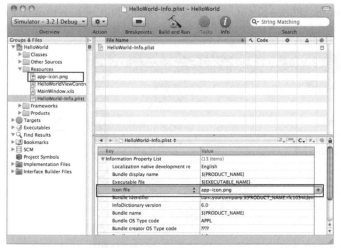

FIGURE 2-25

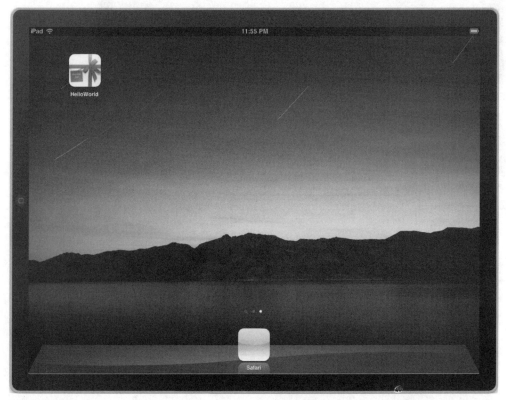

FIGURE 2-26

SUMMARY

This chapter was a whirlwind journey of developing your first iPad application. Although you may still have many questions, the aim of this chapter was to get you started. The next few chapters dive deeper into the details of iPad programming, and the secret of all those mysterious items working together is gradually revealed.

EXERCISES

1. You want to add an icon to your iPad project in Xcode. What is the size of the image that you should provide?

2. If your application wants to support a specific display orientation, what should you do?

3. When adding an image to the Resources folder in your Xcode project, why do you need to check the "Copy items into destination group's folder (If needed)" option?

Answers to the Exercises can be found in Appendix A.

▶ **WHAT YOU LEARNED IN THIS CHAPTER**

TOPIC	KEY CONCEPTS
Xcode	Create your iPad application project and write code that manipulates your application.
Interface Builder	Build your iPad UI using the various views located in the Library.
Repositioning views	Use the Autosizing feature in Interface Builder to ensure that the views resize when there is an orientation change.
Adding application icon	Add an image to the project and then specify the image name in Icon file property of the `info.plist` file.
Creating icons for your iPad applications	Icon size is 72 x 72 pixels (Home screen) and 48 x 48 pixels (Settings). For AppStore hosting, size is 512 x 512 pixels.

3

Views, Outlets, and Actions

WHAT YOU WILL LEARN IN THIS CHAPTER:

➤ How to declare and define outlets

➤ How to declare and define actions

➤ How to connect outlets and actions to the views in your View window

➤ How to use the `UIAlertView` to display an alert view to the user

➤ How to use the `UIActionSheet` to display some options to the user

➤ How to use the `UIPageControl` to control paging

➤ How to use the `UIImageView` to display images

➤ How to use the `UIWebView` to display Web content in your application

➤ How to add views dynamically to your application during runtime

In the previous chapter, you built a simple Hello World! iPad application without understanding much of the underlying details of how things work together. In fact, one of the greatest hurdles in learning iPad programming is the large number of details you need to learn before you can get an application up and running. This book aims to make the iPad programming experience both fun and bearable. Hence, this chapter starts with the basics of creating the user interface (UI) of an iPad application and how your code connects with the various graphical widgets.

OUTLETS AND ACTIONS

One of the first things you need to understand in iPad programming is outlets and actions. If you are familiar with traditional programming languages such as Java or C#, this is a concept that requires some time to get used to — the concepts are similar, just that it is a different way of doing things. At the end of this section, you will have a solid understanding of what outlets and actions are and how to create them, and be on your way to creating great iPad applications.

TRY IT OUT Creating Outlets and Actions

1. Using Xcode, create a View-based Application project and name it `OutletsAndActions`.

2. Edit the `OutletsAndActionsViewController.xib` file by double-clicking it to open it in Interface Builder. When Interface Builder is loaded, double-click on the View item in the `OutletsAndActionsViewController.xib` window to visually display the View window (see Figure 3-1). Populate the three views onto the View window — Label, TextField, and Button. Set the Label view with the text "Enter your name" by double-clicking on it. Also, set the Button with the "OK" string.

FIGURE 3-1

3. In Xcode, modify the `OutletsAndActionsViewController.h` file with the following statements shown in bold:

```
#import <UIKit/UIKit.h>

@interface OutletsAndActionsViewController : UIViewController {
    //---declaring the outlet---
    IBOutlet UITextField *txtName;
}
```

```
//---expose the outlet as a property---
@property (nonatomic, retain) UITextField *txtName;

//---declaring the action---
-(IBAction) btnClicked: (id) sender;

@end
```

4. In the `OutletsAndActionsViewController.m` file, define the following statements in bold:

```
#import "OutletsAndActionsViewController.h"

@implementation OutletsAndActionsViewController

//---synthesize the property---
@synthesize txtName;

//---displays an alert view when the button is clicked---
-(IBAction) btnClicked:(id) sender {

    NSString *str = [[NSString alloc]
                         initWithFormat:@"Hello, %@", txtName.text];
    UIAlertView *alert = [[UIAlertView alloc]
                             initWithTitle:@"Hello!"
                                   message:str delegate:self
                         cancelButtonTitle:@"Done"
                         otherButtonTitles:nil];
    [alert show];
    [str release];
    [alert release];
}

- (void)dealloc {
    //---release the outlet---
    [txtName release];
    [super dealloc];
}
```

5. In the `OutletsAndActionsViewController.xib` window, control-click and drag the File's Owner item to the TextField view (see Figure 3-2). A popup will appear; select the outlet named `txtName`.

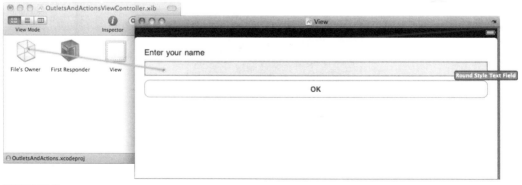

FIGURE 3-2

6. Control-click and drag the OK Button view to the File's Owner item (see Figure 3-3). Select the action named `btnClicked:`.

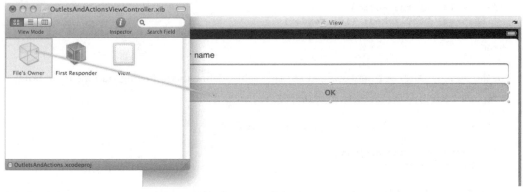

FIGURE 3-3

7. Right-click the OK Button view to display its events (see Figure 3-4). Notice that the Button view has several events, but one particular event — `Touch Up Inside` — is now connected to the action you specified (`btnClicked:`). Because the `Touch Up Inside` event is so commonly used, it is automatically connected to the action when you control-click and drag it to the File's Owner item. To connect other events to the action, simply click on the circle displayed next to each event and then drag it to the File's Owner item.

8. That's it! Press Command-R to test the application on the iPhone Simulator. Enter a name in the TextField and tap the OK button. An alert view displays a welcome message (see Figure 3-5).

FIGURE 3-4

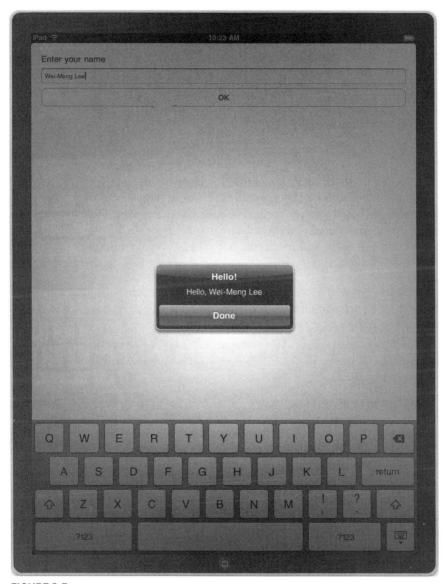

FIGURE 3-5

How It Works

In iPad, you use actions and outlets to connect your code to the various views in your UI. Think of actions as methods in the traditional object-oriented programming world and outlets as objects references. Actions are represented using the IBAction keyword while outlets use the IBOutlet keyword:

```
#import <UIKit/UIKit.h>

@interface OutletsAndActionsViewController : UIViewController {
```

```
    //---declaring the outlet---
    IBOutlet UITextField *txtName;
}

//---expose the outlet as a property---
@property (nonatomic, retain) UITextView *txtName;

//---declaring the action---
-(IBAction) btnClicked: (id) sender;

@end
```

The IBOutlet identifier is used to prefix variables so that Interface Builder can synchronize the display and connection of outlets with Xcode. The @property keyword indicates to the compiler that you want the txtName outlet to be exposed as a property. The nonatomic keyword indicates that there is no need to ensure that the property is used in a thread-safe manner because it is not used in multiple threads. The default behavior is atomic, and specifying nonatomic actually improves the performance of your application.

> **NOTE** The IBOutlet tag can also be added to the @property identifier. This syntax is common in the Apple documentation:
>
> ```
> @property (nonatomic, retain) IBOutlet UITextField *txtName;
> ```

> **NOTE** For the use of the nonatomic and retain identifiers, refer to Appendix D, where you can find an introduction to Objective-C, the language used for iPad programming. Also, the @synthesize keyword, discussed shortly, is explained in more detail there as well.

The IBAction identifier is used to synchronize action methods. An *action* is a method that can handle events raised by views (for example, when a button is clicked) in the View window. An outlet, on the other hand, allows your code to programmatically reference a view on the View window.

Once your actions and outlets are added to the header (.h) file of the View Controller, you then need to connect them to your views in Interface Builder.

When you control-click and drag the File's Owner item to the TextField view and select txtName, you essentially connect the outlet you have created (txtName) with the TextField view on the View window. In general, to connect outlets you control-click and drag the File's Owner item to the view on the View window.

> **WARNING** A quick tip: to connect outlets to the views, you drag the File's Owner item onto the required view in the View window.

To connect an action, you control-click and drag a view to the File's Owner item. Hence, for the OK Button view, you control-click and drag the OK Button view to the File's Owner item and then select the action named btnClicked:.

 WARNING *A quick tip: to connect actions, you drag from the view in the View window onto the File's Owner item.*

In the implementation file (.m), you use the @synthesize keyword to indicate to the compiler to create the getter and setter for the specified property:

 COMMON MISTAKES *Forgetting to add the* @synthesize *keyword is one of the most common mistakes that developers make. Remember to add this statement or else you will encounter a runtime error when the application is executed. Appendix D covers getter/setter in more details.*

```
#import "OutletsAndActionsViewController.h"

@implementation OutletsAndActionsViewController

//---synthesize the property---
@synthesize txtName;

//---displays an alert view when the button is clicked---
-(IBAction) btnClicked:(id) sender {

    NSString *str = [[NSString alloc]
                        initWithFormat:@"Hello, %@", txtName.text];
    UIAlertView *alert = [[UIAlertView alloc]
                            initWithTitle:@"Hello!"
                                message:str delegate:self
                            cancelButtonTitle:@"Done"
                            otherButtonTitles:nil];
    [alert show];
    [str release];
    [alert release];
}

- (void)dealloc {
    //---release the outlet---
    [txtName release];
    [super dealloc];
}
```

The `btnClicked:` action simply displays an alert view with a message containing the user's name. Note that it has a parameter sender of type `id`. The `sender` parameter allows you to programmatically find out who actually invokes this action. This is useful when you have multiple views connecting to one single action. For such cases, you often need to know which is the view that invokes this method and the sender parameter will contain a reference to the calling view.

USING VIEWS

So far, you have seen quite a number of views in action — Round Rect Button, TextField, and Label. All these views are quite straightforward, but they give you a good opportunity to understand how to apply the concepts behind outlets and actions.

To use more views, you can locate them from the Library window in Interface Builder (see Figure 3-6).

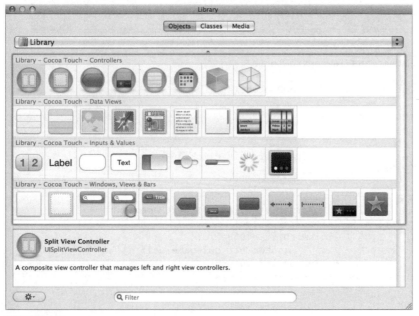

FIGURE 3-6

The Library is divided into sections:

➤ Controllers — Contains views that control other views, such as the View Controller, Tab Bar Controller, Navigation Controller, and so on

➤ Data Views — Contains views that display data, such as the Image View, Table View, Data Picker, Picker View, and so on

> ➤ Inputs and Values — Contains views that accept input from users as well as display values, such as the Label, Round Rect Button, Text Field, and so on

> ➤ Windows, Views and Bars — Contains views that display other, miscellaneous views, such as View, Search Bar, Toolbar, and so on

In the following sections, you learn how to use some of the views available in the Library. Although it is beyond the scope of this book to show the use of every view, you have the opportunity to see a number of views in action throughout the book. In this chapter, you learn some of the fundamental concepts of dealing with views so that you can use other views without problems.

Using the Alert View

One of the views not listed in the Library is the UIAlertView. The UIAlertView displays an alert view to the user and is usually created during runtime. Hence, you have to create it using code.

 NOTE *You actually saw the* UIAlertView *in Chapter 2. In this section, you see how it actually works.*

The UIAlertView is useful for cases in which you have to display a message to the user. In addition, it can serve as a quick debugging tool when you want to observe the value of a variable during runtime.

The following Try It Out explores the UIAlertView in more detail. Download the code as indicated.

TRY IT OUT **Using the Alert View**

codefile UsingViews.zip available for download at Wrox.com

1. Using Xcode, create a new View-based Application project and name it UsingViews.

2. In the UsingViewsViewController.m file, add the following bold code to the viewDidLoad method:

```
- (void)viewDidLoad {

    UIAlertView *alert = [[UIAlertView alloc]
                            initWithTitle:@"Hello"
                                message:@"This is an alert view"
                                delegate:self
                      cancelButtonTitle:@"OK"
                      otherButtonTitles:nil];
    [alert show];
    [alert release];
    [super viewDidLoad];
}
```

3. Press Command-R to test the application on the iPhone Simulator. When the application is loaded, you see the alert view shown in Figure 3-7.

FIGURE 3-7

4. In Xcode, modify the `otherButtonTitles` parameter by setting it with the value shown in bold:

```
UIAlertView *alert = [[UIAlertView alloc]
                        initWithTitle:@"Hello"
                             message:@"This is an alert view"
                             delegate:self
                      cancelButtonTitle:@"OK"
                      otherButtonTitles:@"Option 1", @"Option 2", nil];
```

5. In the `UsingViewsViewController.h` file, add the following line that appears in bold:

```
#import <UIKit/UIKit.h>

@interface UsingViewsViewController : UIViewController
    <UIAlertViewDelegate> {
}

@end
```

6. In the `UsingViewsViewController.m` file, add the following method:

```
- (void)alertView:(UIAlertView *)alertView
clickedButtonAtIndex:(NSInteger)buttonIndex {

    NSLog([NSString stringWithFormat:@"%d", buttonIndex]);

}
```

7. Press Command-R to test the application in the iPhone Simulator. Notice that there are now two buttons in addition to the OK button (see Figure 3-8).

8. Click any one of the buttons — Option 1, Option 2, or OK.

9. In Xcode, press Command-Shift-R to view the Debugger Console window. Observe the values printed. You can rerun the application a number of times, clicking the different buttons to observe the values printed. The values printed for each button clicked are as follows:

➤ OK button — 0

➤ Option 1 — 1

➤ Option 2 — 2

FIGURE 3-8

How It Works

To use `UIAlertView`, you first instantiate it and initialize it with the various arguments:

```
UIAlertView *alert = [[UIAlertView alloc]
                            initWithTitle:@"Hello"
                                message:@"This is an alert view"
                                delegate:self
                            cancelButtonTitle:@"OK"
                            otherButtonTitles:nil];
```

The first parameter is the title of the alert view, which you set to `"Hello"`. The second is the message, which you set to `"This is an alert view"`. The third is the delegate, which you need to set to an object that will handle the events fired by the `UIAlertView` object. In this case, you set it to `self`, which means that the event handler will be implemented in the current class, that is, the View Controller. The `cancelButtonTitle` parameter displays a button to dismiss your alert view. Last, the `otherButtonTitles` parameter allows you to display additional buttons if needed. If no additional buttons are needed, simply set this to `nil`.

To show the alert view modally, use the `show` method:

```
[alert show];
```

 COMMON MISTAKES *It is important to note that showing the alert view modally using the* `show` *method does not cause the program to stall execution at this statement. The subsequent statements after this line continue to execute even though the user may not have dismissed the alert.*

For simple use of the alert view, you don't really need to handle the events fired by it. Tapping the OK button (as set in the `cancelButtonTitle` parameter) simply dismisses the alert view.

If you want more than one button, you need to set the `otherButtonTitles` parameter, like this:

```
UIAlertView *alert = [[UIAlertView alloc]
                            initWithTitle:@"Hello"
                                message:@"This is an alert view"
                                delegate:self
                            cancelButtonTitle:@"OK"
                            otherButtonTitles:@"Option 1", @"Option 2", nil];
```

Note that you need to end the `otherButtonTitles` parameter with a `nil` or a runtime error will occur.

Now that you have three buttons, you need to be able to know which button the user pressed — in particular, whether Option 1 or Option 2 was pressed. To do so, you need to handle the event raised by the `UIAlertView` class. You do so by ensuring that your View Controller implements the `UIAlertViewDelegate` protocol:

```
@interface UsingViewsViewController : UIViewController
    <UIAlertViewDelegate> {
    //...
```

The `UIAlertViewDelegate` protocol contains several methods associated with the alert view. To know which button the user tapped, you need to implement the `alertView:clickedButtonAtIndex:` method:

```
- (void)alertView:(UIAlertView *)alertView clickedButtonAtIndex:
    (NSInteger)buttonIndex {

    NSLog([NSString stringWithFormat:@"%d", buttonIndex]);

}
```

The index of the button clicked will be passed in via the `clickedButtonAtIndex:` parameter.

 NOTE *Refer to Appendix D for a discussion of the concept of protocols in Objective-C.*

Using the Action Sheet

Although the Alert view can display multiple buttons, its primary use is still as a tool to alert users when something happens. If you need to display a message with multiple choices for the user to select, you should use an action sheet rather than the Alert view. An *action sheet* displays a collection of buttons among which the user can select one.

To use an action sheet, use the code snippet below:

```
UIActionSheet *action = [[UIActionSheet alloc]
                        initWithTitle:@"Title of Action Sheet"
                        delegate:self
                        cancelButtonTitle:@"OK"
                        destructiveButtonTitle:@"Delete Message"
                        otherButtonTitles:@"Option 1", @"Option 2", nil];
[action showInView:self.view];
[action release];
```

To handle the event fired by the action sheet when one of the buttons is tapped, implement the `UIActionSheetDelegate` protocol in your View Controller, like this:

```
#import <UIKit/UIKit.h>

@interface UsingViewsViewController : UIViewController
    <UIActionSheetDelegate> {

}
```

When a button is tapped, the `actionSheet:clickedButtonAtIndex:` event will be fired:

```
- (void)actionSheet:(UIActionSheet *)actionSheet
clickedButtonAtIndex:(NSInteger)buttonIndex{

    NSLog([NSString stringWithFormat:@"%d", buttonIndex]);

}
```

Figure 3-9 shows the action sheet when it is displayed.

Notice that the OK button (as specified in the `cancelButtonTitle:` part of the method name) is not shown. The value (`buttonIndex`) of each button is as follows:

FIGURE 3-9

➤ Delete Message — 0

➤ Option 1 — 1

➤ Option 2 — 2

When the user taps on an area outside of the action sheet, the action sheet is dismissed and the value of `buttonIndex` becomes 3. Interestingly, if you specified `nil` for the `cancelButtonTitle:` part, the value of `buttonIndex` would be –1 when the action sheet is dismissed.

Page Control and Image View

Near the bottom of iPad's Home screen is a series of dots (see Figure 3-10). A lighted dot represents the currently selected page. As you swipe the page to the next page, the next dot lights, and the first one dims. In the figure, the dots indicate that the third page is the active page. In the iPhone SDK, the series of dots is represented by the `UIPageControl` class.

FIGURE 3-10

In the following exercise, you learn to use the page control view within your own application to switch between images displayed in the ImageView.

TRY IT OUT   Using the Page Control and the Image View

1.   Using the `UsingViews` project created in the previous section, add five images to the Resources folder by dragging and dropping them from the Finder. Figure 3-11 shows the five images added to the project.

2.   Double-click the `UsingViewsViewController.xib file` to edit it using Interface Builder.

3.   Drag and drop two ImageViews onto the View window (see Figure 3-12). At this point, overlap them (but not entirely) as shown in the figure.

4.   With the first ImageView selected, open the Attributes Inspector window and set the `Tag` property to 0. Select the second ImageView and set the `Tag` property to 1 (see Figure 3-13).

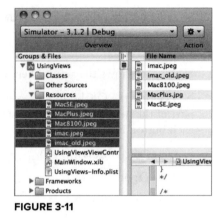

FIGURE 3-11

FIGURE 3-12

5. Drag and drop the Page Control view onto the View window and set its number of pages to five (see Figure 3-14).

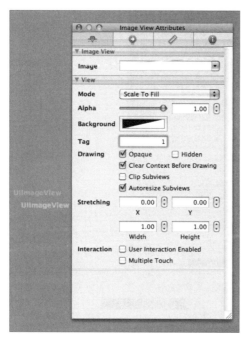

FIGURE 3-13

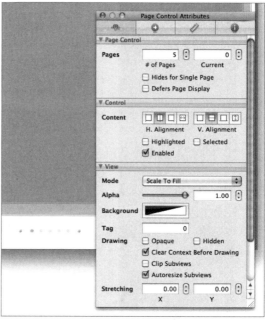

FIGURE 3-14

Ensure that you increase the width of the Page Control view so that all the dots are now visible.

6. Set the Background color of the View window to black so that the dots inside the Page Control are clearly visible (see Figure 3-15).

7. In Xcode, declare three outlets and two `UIImageView` objects in the `UsingViewsViewController.h` file:

```
#import <UIKit/UIKit.h>

@interface UsingViewsViewController : UIViewController {

    IBOutlet UIPageControl *pageControl;
    IBOutlet UIImageView *imageView1;
    IBOutlet UIImageView *imageView2;

    UIImageView *tempImageView, *bgImageView;
}

@property (nonatomic, retain) UIPageControl *pageControl;
@property (nonatomic, retain) UIImageView *imageView1;
@property (nonatomic, retain) UIImageView *imageView2;

@end
```

FIGURE 3-15

8. In Interface Builder, connect the three outlets to the views on the View window. Figure 3-16 shows the connections made for the `imageView1`, `imageView2`, and `pageControl` outlets.

9. You can now rearrange the ImageViews on the View window so that they overlap each other.

FIGURE 3-16

10. In Xcode, add the following statements that appear in bold to the `UsingViewsViewController.m` file:

```
#import "UsingViewsViewController.h"

@implementation UsingViewsViewController

@synthesize pageControl;
@synthesize imageView1, imageView2;

- (void)viewDidLoad {

    //---initialize the first ImageView to display an image---
    [imageView1 setImage:[UIImage imageNamed:@"iMac_old.jpeg"]];
    tempImageView = imageView2;

    //---make the first ImageView visible and hide the second---
    [imageView1 setHidden:NO];
    [imageView2 setHidden:YES];

    //---add the event handler for the page control---
    [pageControl addTarget:self
                    action:@selector(pageTurning:)
          forControlEvents:UIControlEventValueChanged];

    [super viewDidLoad];
}

//---when the page control's value is changed---
- (void) pageTurning: (UIPageControl *) pageController {

    //---get the page number you can turning to---
    NSInteger nextPage = [pageController currentPage];
    switch (nextPage) {
        case 0:
            [tempImageView setImage:
                [UIImage imageNamed:@"iMac_old.jpeg"]];
            break;
        case 1:
            [tempImageView setImage:
                [UIImage imageNamed:@"iMac.jpeg"]];
            break;
        case 2:
            [tempImageView setImage:
                [UIImage imageNamed:@"Mac8100.jpeg"]];
            break;
        case 3:
            [tempImageView setImage:
                [UIImage imageNamed:@"MacPlus.jpeg"]];
            break;
        case 4:
            [tempImageView setImage:
                [UIImage imageNamed:@"MacSE.jpeg"]];
            break;
```

```
        default:
            break;
    }

    //---switch the two ImageView views---
    if (tempImageView.tag == 0) { //---imageView1---
        tempImageView = imageView2;
        bgImageView = imageView1;
    }
    else {     //---imageView2---
        tempImageView = imageView1;
        bgImageView = imageView2;
    }

    //---animate the two views flipping---
    [UIView beginAnimations:@"flipping view" context:nil];
    [UIView setAnimationDuration:0.5];
    [UIView setAnimationCurve:UIViewAnimationCurveEaseInOut];
    [UIView setAnimationTransition:UIViewAnimationTransitionFlipFromLeft
                        forView:tempImageView
                          cache:YES];
    [tempImageView setHidden:YES];
    [UIView commitAnimations];

    [UIView beginAnimations:@"flipping view" context:nil];
    [UIView setAnimationDuration:0.5];
    [UIView setAnimationCurve:UIViewAnimationCurveEaseInOut];
    [UIView
        setAnimationTransition:UIViewAnimationTransitionFlipFromRight
                      forView:bgImageView
                        cache:YES];
    [bgImageView setHidden:NO];
    [UIView commitAnimations];

}

- (void)dealloc {
    [pageControl release];
    [imageView1 release];
    [imageView2 release];
    [super dealloc];
}
```

11. Press Command-R to test the application on the iPhone Simulator. When you tap the Page
Control located at the bottom of the screen, the image view flips to display the next one (see
Figure 3-17).

FIGURE 3-17

How It Works

When the View is first loaded, you get one of the ImageViews to display an image and then hide the other:

```
//---initialize the first ImageView to display an image---
[imageView1 setImage:[UIImage imageNamed:@"iMac_old.jpeg"]];
tempImageView = imageView2;

//---make the first ImageView visible and hide the second---
[imageView1 setHidden:NO];
[imageView2 setHidden:YES];
```

You then wire the Page Control so that when the user taps it, an event is fired and triggers a method. In this case, the `pageTurning:` method is called:

```
//---add the event handler for the page control---
[pageControl addTarget:self
                action:@selector(pageTurning:)
      forControlEvents:UIControlEventValueChanged];
```

In the `pageTurning:` method, you determine which image you should load based on the value of the Page Control:

```
//---when the page control's value is changed---
- (void) pageTurning: (UIPageControl *) pageController {
    //---get the page number you can turning to---
    NSInteger nextPage = [pageController currentPage];
    switch (nextPage) {
        case 0:
            [tempImageView setImage:
                [UIImage imageNamed:@"iMac_old.jpeg"]];
            break;
        case 1:
            [tempImageView setImage:
                [UIImage imageNamed:@"iMac.jpeg"]];
            break;
        case 2:
            [tempImageView setImage:
                [UIImage imageNamed:@"Mac8100.jpeg"]];
            break;
        case 3:
            [tempImageView setImage:
                [UIImage imageNamed:@"MacPlus.jpeg"]];
            break;
        case 4:
            [tempImageView setImage:
                [UIImage imageNamed:@"MacSE.jpeg"]];
            break;
        default:
            break;
    }
    //...
}
```

You then switch the two ImageViews and animate them by using the various methods in the `UIView` class:

```
//---switch the two ImageView views---
if (tempImageView.tag==0) { //---imageView1---
    tempImageView = imageView2;
    bgImageView = imageView1;
}
else {    //---imageView2---
    tempImageView = imageView1;
    bgImageView = imageView2;
}

//---animate the two views flipping---
```

```
[UIView beginAnimations:@"flipping view" context:nil];
[UIView setAnimationDuration:0.5];
[UIView setAnimationCurve:UIViewAnimationCurveEaseInOut];
[UIView setAnimationTransition:UIViewAnimationTransitionFlipFromLeft
                        forView:tempImageView
                          cache:YES];
[tempImageView setHidden:YES];
[UIView commitAnimations];

[UIView beginAnimations:@"flipping view" context:nil];
[UIView setAnimationDuration:0.5];
[UIView setAnimationCurve:UIViewAnimationCurveEaseInOut];
[UIView
    setAnimationTransition:UIViewAnimationTransitionFlipFromRight
                   forView:bgImageView
                     cache:YES];
[bgImageView setHidden:NO];
[UIView commitAnimations];
```

Specifically, you apply the flipping transitions to the ImageViews:

```
[UIView setAnimationTransition:UIViewAnimationTransitionFlipFromLeft
                        forView:tempImageView
                          cache:YES];
```

Using the Web View

To load Web pages from within your application, you can embed a Web browser in your application through the use of the UIWebView. Using the Web view, you can send a request to load Web content, which is very useful if you want to convert an existing Web application into a native application (such as those written using Dashcode). All you need to do is to embed all the HTML pages into your Resources folder in your Xcode project and load the HTML pages into the Web view during runtime.

 NOTE *Depending on how complex your Web applications are, you may have to do some additional work to port your Web application to a native application if it involves server-side technologies such as CGI, PHP, or others.*

The following Try It Out shows how to use the Web view to load a Web page.

TRY IT OUT Loading a Web Page Using the Web View

codefile UsingViews2.zip available for download at Wrox.com

1. Using Xcode, create a new View-based Application project and name it UsingViews2.

2. Double-click the UsingViews2ViewController.xib file to edit it using Interface Builder.

3. In the View window, add a Web view from the Library (see Figure 3-18). In the Attributes Inspector window for the Web view, check the `Scales Page to Fit` property.

FIGURE 3-18

4. In the `UsingViews2ViewController.h` file, declare an outlet for the Web view:

```
#import <UIKit/UIKit.h>

@interface UsingViews2ViewController : UIViewController {
    IBOutlet UIWebView *webView;
}

@property (nonatomic, retain) UIWebView *webView;

@end
```

5. In Interface Builder, connect the `webView` outlet to the Web view.

6. In the `UsingViews2ViewController.m` file, add the following statements that appear in bold:

```
#import "UsingViews2ViewController.h"
```

```
@implementation UsingViews2ViewController

@synthesize webView;

- (void)viewDidLoad {
    NSURL *url = [NSURL URLWithString:@"http://www.apple.com"];
    NSURLRequest *req = [NSURLRequest requestWithURL:url];
    [webView loadRequest:req];

    [super viewDidLoad];
}

- (void)dealloc {
    [webView release];
    [super dealloc];
}
```

7. Press Command-R to test the application on the iPhone Simulator. You should see the application loading the page from Apple.com (see Figure 3-19).

FIGURE 3-19

How It Works

To load the Web view with a URL, you first instantiate an NSURL object with a URL via the URLWithString method:

```
NSURL *url = [NSURL URLWithString:@"http://www.apple.com"];
```

You then create an NSURLRequest object by passing the NSURL object to its requestWithURL: method:

```
NSURLRequest *req = [NSURLRequest requestWithURL:url];
```

Finally, you load the Web view with the NSURLRequest object via the loadRequest: method:

```
[webView loadRequest:req];
```

ADDING VIEWS DYNAMICALLY USING CODE

Up to this point, all the UIs of your application have been created visually using Interface Builder. Although Interface Builder makes it relatively easy to build a UI using drag-and-drop, sometimes you are better off using code to create it. One such instance is when you need a dynamic UI, such as for games.

 NOTE *Interface Builder may be easy to use, but it can be confusing to some people. Because you often have more than one way of doing things in Interface Builder, it may create unnecessary complications. I know of developers who swear by creating their UIs using code.*

In the following Try It Out, you learn how to create views dynamically from code, which will help you understand how views are constructed and manipulated.

TRY IT OUT Creating Views from Code

codefile DynamicViews.zip available for download at Wrox.com

1. Using Xcode, create a View-based Application project and name it DynamicViews.

2. In the DynamicViewsViewController.m file, add the following statements that appear in bold:

```
#import "DynamicViewsViewController.h"

@implementation DynamicViewsViewController

- (void)loadView {
```

```
      //---create a UIView object---
      UIView *view =
          [[UIView alloc] initWithFrame:[UIScreen mainScreen].applicationFrame];
      view.backgroundColor = [UIColor lightGrayColor];

      //---create a Label view---
      CGRect frame = CGRectMake(10, 15, 300, 20);
      UILabel *label = [[UILabel alloc] initWithFrame:frame];
      label.textAlignment = UITextAlignmentCenter;
      label.backgroundColor = [UIColor clearColor];
      label.font = [UIFont fontWithName:@"Verdana" size:20];
      label.text = @"This is a label";
      label.tag = 1000;

      //---create a Button view---
      frame = CGRectMake(10, 70, 300, 50);
      UIButton *button = [UIButton buttonWithType:UIButtonTypeRoundedRect];
      button.frame = frame;

      [button setTitle:@"Click Me, Please!" forState:UIControlStateNormal];
      button.backgroundColor = [UIColor clearColor];
      button.tag = 2000;
      [button addTarget:self
                 action:@selector(buttonClicked:)
       forControlEvents:UIControlEventTouchUpInside];

      [view addSubview:label];
      [view addSubview:button];

      self.view = view;
      [label release];
  }

  -(IBAction) buttonClicked: (id) sender{
      UIAlertView *alert = [[UIAlertView alloc]
                              initWithTitle:@"Action invoked!"
                                    message:@"Button clicked!"
                                   delegate:self
                          cancelButtonTitle:@"OK"
                          otherButtonTitles:nil];
      [alert show];
      [alert release];
  }

  @end
```

3. Press Command-R to test the application in the iPhone Simulator. Figure 3-20 shows that the Label and Round Rect Button views are displayed on the view. Click the button to see an alert view displaying a message.

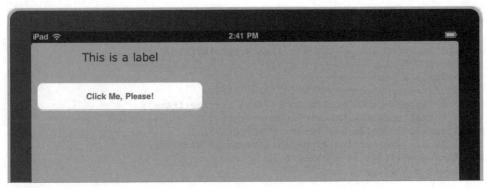

FIGURE 3-20

How It Works

You can use the `loadView` method defined in your View Controller to programmatically create your views. You implement this method only if you are generating your UI during runtime. This method is automatically called when the `view` property of your View Controller is called but its current value is `nil`.

The first view you create is the `UIView` object, which allows you to use it as a container for more views:

```
//---create a UIView object---
UIView *view =
    [[UIView alloc] initWithFrame:[UIScreen mainScreen].applicationFrame];

//---set the background color to lightgray---
view.backgroundColor = [UIColor lightGrayColor];
```

Next, you create a Label view and set it to display a string:

```
//---create a Label view---
CGRect frame = CGRectMake(10, 15, 300, 20);
UILabel *label = [[UILabel alloc] initWithFrame:frame];
label.textAlignment = UITextAlignmentCenter;
label.backgroundColor = [UIColor clearColor];
label.font = [UIFont fontWithName:@"Verdana" size:20];
label.text = @"This is a label";
label.tag = 1000;
```

Notice that you have also set the `tag` property, which is very useful for allowing you to search for particular views during runtime.

You also create a Button view by calling the `buttonWithType:` method with the `UIButtonTypeRoundedRect` constant. This method returns a `UIRoundedRectButton` object (which is a subclass of `UIButton`).

```
//---create a Button view---
frame = CGRectMake(10, 70, 300, 50);
UIButton *button = [UIButton buttonWithType:UIButtonTypeRoundedRect];
button.frame = frame;
```

```
[button setTitle:@"Click Me, Please!"
        forState:UIControlStateNormal];
button.backgroundColor = [UIColor clearColor];
button.tag = 2000;
```

You then wire an event handler for its `Touch Up Inside` event so that when the button is tapped, the `buttonClicked:` method is called:

```
[button AddTarget:Self
            action:@selector(buttonClicked:)
   forControlEvents:UIControlEventTouchUpInside];
```

Finally, you add the `label` and `button` views to the `view` you created earlier:

```
[view addSubview:label];
[view addSubview:button];
```

Finally, you assign the `view` object to the `view` property of the current View Controller:

```
self.view = view;
```

 WARNING *One important point to note here is that within the* `loadView` *method, you should not get the value of the* `view` *property (setting it is all right), like this:*

```
[self.view addSubView: label];   //---this is not OK---
self.view = view;                //---this is OK---
```

Trying to get the value of the `view` *property in this method will result in a circular reference and cause memory overflow.*

UNDERSTANDING VIEW HIERARCHY

As views are created and added, they are added to a tree data structure. Views are displayed in the order that they are added. To verify this, modify the location of the `UIButton` object you created earlier by changing its location to `CGRectMake(10, 30, 300, 50)`, as in the following:

```
//---create a Button view---
frame = CGRectMake(10, 30, 300, 50);
UIButton *button = [UIButton buttonWithType:UIButtonTypeRoundedRect];
button.frame = frame;
[button setTitle:@"Click Me, Please!"
        forState:UIControlStateNormal];
button.backgroundColor = [UIColor clearColor];
button.tag = 2000;
[button addTarget:self
            action:@selector(buttonClicked:)
   forControlEvents:UIControlEventTouchUpInside];
```

When you now run the application again, you will notice that the button overlaps the label control (see Figure 3-21) since the button was added last:

```
[view addSubview:label];
[view addSubview:button];
```

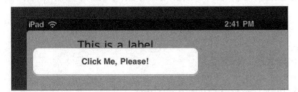

FIGURE 3-21

To switch the order in which the views are displayed after they have been added, use the `exchangeSubviewAtIndex:withSubviewAtIndex:` method, like this:

```
[self.view addSubview:label];
[self.view addSubview:button];

[self.view exchangeSubviewAtIndex:1 withSubviewAtIndex:0];

[label release];
```

The preceding statement in bold swaps the order of the Label and Button views. When the application is run again, the Label view will now appear on top of the Button view (See Figure 3-22).

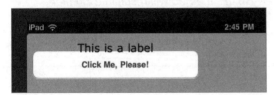

FIGURE 3-22

To learn the order of the various views already added, you can use the following code segment to print the value of the `tag` property for each view:

```
[self.view addSubview:label];
[self.view addSubview:button];
[self.view exchangeSubviewAtIndex:1 withSubviewAtIndex:0];

for (int i=0; i<[self.view.subviews count]; ++i) {
    UIView *view = [self.view.subviews objectAtIndex:i];
    NSLog([NSString stringWithFormat:@"%d", view.tag]);
}
```

The following method recursively prints out all the views contained in a `UIView` object:

```
-(void) printViews: (UIView *) view {
    if ([view.subviews count] > 0){
```

```
          for (int i=0; i<[view.subviews count]; ++i) {
              UIView *v = [view.subviews objectAtIndex:i];
              NSLog([NSString stringWithFormat:@"View index: %d Tag: %d",i, v.tag]);
              [self printViews:v];
          }
      } else
          return;
  }
```

To remove a view from the current view hierarchy, use the `removeFromSuperview` method of the view you want to remove. For example, the following statement removes the `label` view:

```
[label removeFromSuperview];
```

SUMMARY

This chapter explored the roles played by outlets and actions in an iPad application. Outlets and actions are the cornerstone of iPad development, so understanding their use is extremely important. Throughout this book, you will come across them frequently. You have also seen the use of some of the commonly used views in the Library.

In the next chapter, you learn how you can control the virtual keyboard that automatically pops up when the user tries to enter data into your application.

EXERCISES

1. Declare and define an outlet for a `UITextField` view using code.

2. Declare and define an action using code.

3. When do you use an Alert view and when do you use an action sheet?

4. Create a `UIButton` from code and wire its `Touch Up Inside` event to an event handler.

Answers to the Exercises can be found in Appendix A.

▶ **WHAT YOU LEARNED IN THIS CHAPTER**

TOPIC	KEY CONCEPTS
Action	An action is a method that can handle events raised by views (for example, when a button is clicked, etc.) in the View window.
Outlet	An outlet allows your code to programmatically reference a view on the View window.
Adding outlet using code	Use the `IBOutlet` keyword: `IBOutlet UITextField *nameTextField;`
Adding action using code	Use the `IBAction` keyword: `- (IBAction)btnClicked:(id)sender;`
Connecting actions	To link actions, you always drag from the view in the View window onto the File's Owner item.
Connection outlets	To link outlets, you always drag from the File's Owner item onto the required view in the View window.

Using the UIAlertView	`UIAlertView *alert = [[UIAlertView alloc]`
	`    initWithTitle:@"Hello"`
	`    message:@"This is an alert view"`
	`    delegate:self`
	`cancelButtonTitle:@"OK"`
	`otherButtonTitles:nil];`

Handling events fired by UIAlertView	Ensure that your View Controller conforms to the `UIAlertViewDelegate` protocol.

Using the UIActionSheet	`UIActionSheet *action =`
	`    [[UIActionSheet alloc]`
	`    initWithTitle:@"Title of Action Sheet"`
	`    delegate:self`
	`    cancelButtonTitle:@"OK"`
	`    destructiveButtonTitle:`
	`    @"Delete Message"`
	`    otherButtonTitles:@"Option 1",`
	`    @"Option 2", nil];`

Handling events fired by UIActionSheet	Ensure that your View Controller conforms to the `UIActionSheetDelegate` protocol.

Wiring up the events for the UIPageControl	`[pageControl addTarget:self`
	`    action:@selector(pageTurning:)`
	`    forControlEvents:UIControlEventValueChanged];`

TOPIC	KEY CONCEPTS
Using the UIImageView	```[imageView1 setImage:``` ``` [UIImage imageNamed:@"iMac_old.jpeg"]];```

Using the UIWebView	```NSURL *url =```
	``` [NSURL URLWithString:@"http://www.apple.com"];```
	```NSURLRequest *req =```
	``` [NSURLRequest requestWithURL:url];```
	```[webView loadRequest:req];```

View Controllers

WHAT YOU WILL LEARN IN THIS CHAPTER:

➤ Understand the structure of an iPad Application project

➤ How to create a Window-based Application and manually add a View Controller and a View window to it

➤ How to create views dynamically during runtime

➤ How to wire up events of views with event handlers via code

➤ How to switch to another view during runtime

➤ How to animate the switching of views

➤ How to create a Split View-based Application

➤ How to create a Tab Bar Application

So far you've dealt only with single-view applications — that is, applications with a single View Controller. The previous chapters all use the View-based Application template available in the iPhone SDK because it is the simplest way to get started in iPad programming. When you create a View-based Application, there is one View Controller (named *<project_name>*ViewController by the iPhone SDK) by default.

In real-life applications, you often need more than one View Controller, with each controlling a different view displaying different information. This chapter shows various types of projects you can create for your iPad and how each utilizes a different type of View Controller. You will also learn how to create multiple views in your application and then programmatically switch among them during runtime. In addition, you learn how to animate the switching of views using the built-in animation methods available in the iPhone SDK.

THE VIEW-BASED APPLICATION TEMPLATE

When you create a View-based Application project using Xcode, you automatically have a single view in your application. Until now, you have been using it without understanding much of the workings under the hood. In the following Try It Out, you dive into the details and unravel all the magic that makes your application work.

TRY IT OUT **Creating a View-based Application Project**

codefile viewBasedApp.zip available for download at Wrox.com

1. Using Xcode, create a View-based Application project and name it `viewBasedApp`.

2. Press Command-R to test the application on the iPhone Simulator. The application displays an empty screen as shown in Figure 4-1.

FIGURE 4-1

How It Works

What you have just created is a View-based Application. By default, the View-based Application template includes a single view, controlled by a View Controller class. So let's dissect the inner workings and see how all things gel together.

First, take a look at the files and folders created for your project in Xcode. In particular, observe the Classes and Resources folder listed under the project name (see Figure 4-2).

FIGURE 4-2

As you can see, many files are created for you by default when you create a new project. The iPhone SDK tries to make your life simpler by creating some of the items that you will use most often when you develop an iPad application. Table 4-1 describes the use of the various files created in the project.

 NOTE *The numbers and types of files created are dependent on the type of project you have selected. The View-based Application template is a good starting point to understanding the various files involved.*

TABLE 4-1: The Various Files Created in the Project

FILE	DESCRIPTION
`viewBasedApp.app`	The application bundle (executable), which contains the executable as well as the data that is bundled with the application.
`viewBasedApp_Prefix.pch`	Contains the prefix header for all files in the project. The prefix header is included by default in the other files in the project.
`viewBasedAppAppDelegate.h`	Headers file for the application delegate.
`viewBasedAppAppDelegate.m`	Implementations file for the application delegate.
`viewBasedAppViewController.h`	Headers file for a View Controller.
`viewBasedAppViewController.m`	Implementations file for a View Controller.
`viewBasedAppViewController.xib`	The XIB file containing the UI of a view.
`CoreGraphics.framework`	C-based APIS for low-level 2D rendering.
`Foundation.framework`	APIs for foundational system services such as data types, XML, URL, and so on.
`UIKit.framework`	Provides fundamental objects for constructing and managing your application's UI.
`viewBasedApp-Info.plist`	A dictionary file that contains information about your project, such as icon, application name, and others; information is stored in key/value pairs.
`main.m`	The main file that bootstraps your iPad application.
`MainWindow.xib`	The XIB file for the main window of the application.

The `main.m` file contains code that bootstraps your application, and you rarely need to modify it:

```
#import <UIKit/UIKit.h>

int main(int argc, char *argv[]) {

    NSAutoreleasePool * pool = [[NSAutoreleasePool alloc] init];
    int retVal = UIApplicationMain(argc, argv, nil, nil);
    [pool release];
    return retVal;
}
```

Most of the hard work is done by the `UIApplicationMain()` function, which examines the `viewBasedApp-Info.plist` file to obtain more information about the project. In particular, it looks at the main NIB file you will use for your project. Figure 4-3 shows the content of the viewBasedApp-Info.plist file. Notice that the Main nib file base name key is pointing to MainWindow, which is the name of the NIB file to load when the application is started.

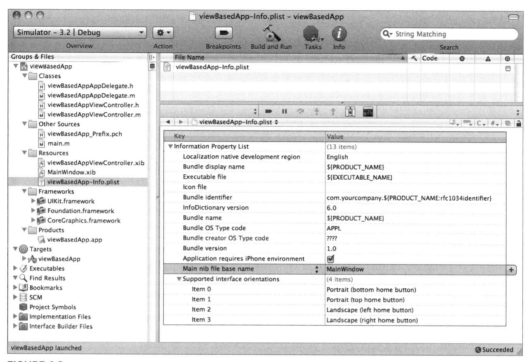

FIGURE 4-3

WHAT DO XIB AND NIB STAND FOR?

In iPad application development, you will always come across files with the .xib extension (sometimes also known as NIB files). So, what do the NIB and .xib stand for, exactly? Turns out that the current Mac OS X was built upon an operating system called NeXTSTEP, from a company known as NeXT (founded by Apple's cofounder, Steve Jobs, in 1985). The N in NIB stands for NeXTSTEP. As for .xib, the x in presumably stands for XML because its content is saved as an XML file. The IB stands for Interface Builder, the application that allows you to visually construct the UI for your application.

Editing XIB Files

Double-click the MainWindow.xib file to edit it using Interface Builder. As mentioned, the XIB file represents the UI of your application, and it is used almost exclusively by Interface Builder.

NOTE *An XIB file is actually an XML file. You can view and edit an XIB file using applications such as TextEdit. However, most of the time, to maintain your sanity you use Interface Builder to visually modify the UI of your applications.*

When the `MinWindow.xib` file is opened by Interface Builder, you see a window with the same title as the name of the file (see Figure 4-4).

This window contains five items:

➤ `File's Owner` — Represents the object that is set to the owner of the user interface (that is, the class responsible for managing the content of the XIB file).

➤ `First Responder` — Represents the object that the user is currently interacting with.

➤ `viewBasedApp App Delegate` — Points to the `viewBasedAppAppDelegate` class. You can see this when you select the `viewBasedApp App Delegate` item and view its Identity Inspector window (see Figure 4-5).

➤ `View Based App View Controller` — Points to a View Controller that you will be using to display your UI. In this case, it points to the `viewBasedAppViewController` class. You can see this when you select the `View Based App View Controller` item and view its Identity Inspector window (see Figure 4-6).

➤ `Window` — The screen that you will see when the application is launched.

FIGURE 4-4

FIGURE 4-5

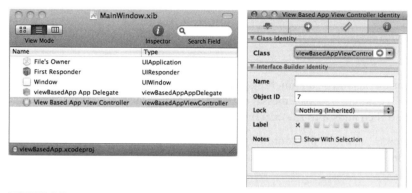

FIGURE 4-6

Application Delegate

The `viewBasedAppAppDelegate.m` file contains code that is typically executed after the application has finished loading, or just before it is being terminated. For this example, the content of it is as follows:

 NOTE When creating your project using Xcode, the filename of your application delegate will always be appended with the string `AppDelegate`. Hence, if the project name is `viewBasedApp`, then the application delegate will be called `viewBasedAppAppDelegate`.

```
#import "viewBasedAppAppDelegate.h"
#import "viewBasedAppViewController.h"

@implementation viewBasedAppAppDelegate

@synthesize window;
@synthesize viewController;

- (BOOL)application:(UIApplication *)application
didFinishLaunchingWithOptions:(NSDictionary *)
launchOptions {

    // Override point for customization after app launch
    [window addSubview:viewController.view];
    [window makeKeyAndVisible];

    return YES;
}

- (void)dealloc {
    [viewController release];
    [window release];
```

```
        [super dealloc];
    }

    @end
```

When the application has finished launching, it sends its delegate the `application:`
`DidFinishLaunchingWithOptions:` message. In the preceding case, it uses a View Controller to
obtain its view and then adds it to the current window so that it can be displayed.

The `viewBasedAppDelegate.h` file contains the declaration of the members of the
`viewBasedAppAppDelegate` class:

```
    #import <UIKit/UIKit.h>

    @class viewBasedAppViewController;

    @interface viewBasedAppAppDelegate : NSObject <UIApplicationDelegate> {
        UIWindow *window;
        viewBasedAppViewController *viewController;
    }

    @property (nonatomic, retain) IBOutlet UIWindow *window;
    @property (nonatomic, retain) IBOutlet viewBasedAppViewController
    *viewController;

    @end
```

Of particular interest is this line:

```
    @interface viewBasedAppAppDelegate : NSObject <UIApplicationDelegate> {
```

The `<UIApplicationDelegate>` statement specifies that the delegate class implement the
`UIApplicationDelegate` protocol. Put simply, it means that the delegate class will handle
events (or messages) defined in the `UIApplicationDelegate` protocol. Examples of events in
the `UIApplicationDelegate` protocol include the following:

➤ `Application:DidFinishLaunchingWithOptions:` (You saw this implemented in the
    `viewBasedAppAppDelegate.m` file.)

➤ `applicationWillTerminate:`

➤ `applicationDidDidReceiveMemoryWarning:`

The Application Delegate class is also a good place to put your global objects and functions, as they
are accessible from all the other classes in your project.

 NOTE *Protocols are discussed in more detail in Appendix D.*

Controlling Your UI Using View Controllers

In iPad programming, you typically use a View Controller to manage a view as well as perform navigation and memory management. In the project template for a View-based Application, Xcode automatically uses a View Controller to help you manage your *view*. Think of a view as a screen (or window) you see on your iPad.

Earlier in this chapter, you saw that the `MainWindow.xib` window contains the `View Based App View Controller` item. When you double-click the item, it shows a window of the same name (see Figure 4-7).

 NOTE *When creating your project using Xcode, the filename of your View Controller will always be appended with the string* `ViewController`. *Hence, if the project name is* `viewBasedApp`, *then the application delegate will be called* `viewBasedAppViewController`. *When the View Controller is displayed in Interface Builder, Interface Builder will examine the name and display the View Controller with spaces inserted whenever there is a change in capitalization; e.g.,* `viewBasedAppViewController` *now becomes* `View Based App View Controller`.

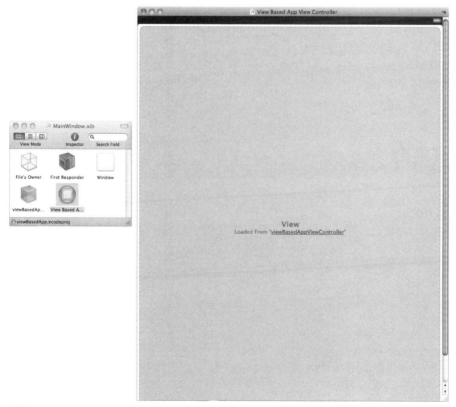

FIGURE 4-7

As you can see, the view says that it is loaded from `viewBasedAppViewController`, which refers to the name of the `viewBasedAppViewController.xib` file that's also in your project.

Now, double-click the `viewBasedAppViewController` `.xib` file to edit it in Interface Builder. As with the `MainWindow.xib` file, a few objects are contained inside the `viewBasedAppViewController.xib` window. In this case, it contains File's Owner, First Responder, and View.

You can right-click (or Control-click) the File's Owner item to view its properties (see Figure 4-8). Observe that the `view` outlet is connected to the `View` item.

The `View` item represents the screen that appears on your application. Double-click View to display it (see Figure 4-9).

FIGURE 4-8

FIGURE 4-9

When you select the File's Owner item and view its Identity Inspector window, you should see that the class is pointing to viewBasedAppViewController class (see Figure 4-10). This means that the View window is being controlled by the viewBasedAppViewController class.

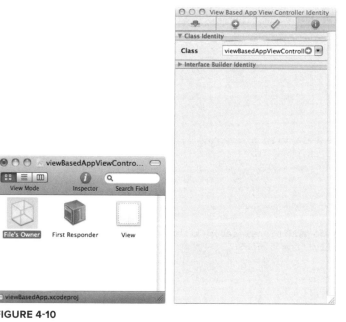

FIGURE 4-10

The viewBasedAppViewController class is represented by two files — viewBasedAppViewController.h and viewBasedAppViewController.m. The viewBasedAppViewController class is where you write your code to interact with the views of your application.

The content of the viewBasedAppViewController.h file looks like this:

```
#import <UIKit/UIKit.h>

@interface viewBasedAppViewController : UIViewController {

}

@end
```

Note that the viewBasedAppViewController class inherits from the UIViewController base class, which provides most of the functionalities available on a View window.

The content of the viewBasedAppViewController.m file looks like this:

```
#import "viewBasedAppViewController.h"

@implementation viewBasedAppViewController
```

```objc
/*
// The designated initializer. Override to perform setup that
// is required before the view is loaded.
- (id)initWithNibName:(NSString *)nibNameOrNil
              bundle:(NSBundle *)nibBundleOrNil {
    if ((self = [super initWithNibName:nibNameOrNil
        bundle:nibBundleOrNil])) {
        // Custom initialization
    }
    return self;
}
*/

/*
// Implement loadView to create a view hierarchy
// programmatically, without using a nib.
- (void)loadView {
}
*/

/*
// Implement viewDidLoad to do additional setup after
// loading the view, typically from a nib.
- (void)viewDidLoad {
    [super viewDidLoad];
}
*/

// Override to allow orientations other than the
// default portrait orientation.
- (BOOL)shouldAutorotateToInterfaceOrientation:
(UIInterfaceOrientation)interfaceOrientation {
    return YES;
}

- (void)didReceiveMemoryWarning {
// Releases the view if it doesn't have a superview.
    [super didReceiveMemoryWarning];
// Release any cached data, images, etc that aren't in use.
}

- (void)viewDidUnload {
// Release any retained subviews of the main view.
// e.g. self.myOutlet = nil;
}

- (void)dealloc {
    [super dealloc];
}

@end
```

THE WINDOW-BASED APPLICATION TEMPLATE

In this section, you discover another type of application template you can create using the iPhone SDK: the *Window-based Application* template. Unlike the View-based Application template, the Window-based Application template does not include a View Controller by default. Instead, it provides only the skeleton of an iPad application and leaves the rest to the developer — you need to add your own views and their respective View Controllers. Because of this, a Window-based Application presents a very good way for you to understand how View Controllers work and appreciate all the work needed to connect the View Controllers and XIB files. When you understand how View Controllers work, you will be on your way to creating more sophisticated applications.

To put first things first, execute the following Try it Out to write a Window-based Application and then progressively add a View Controller to it.

TRY IT OUT   Creating a Window-based Application

codefile windowBasedApp.zip available for download on Wrox.com

1.   Using Xcode, create a Window-based Application project and name it `windowBasedApp`. Observe the files created for this project type (see Figure 4-11). Apart from the usual supporting files, note that there is only one XIB file (`MainWindow.xib`) and two delegate files (`windowBasedAppAppDelegate.h` and `windowBasedAppAppDelegate.m`).

FIGURE 4-11

2.   Press Command-R to test the application. An empty screen is displayed on the iPhone Simulator. This is because the Window-based Application template provides only the skeleton structure for a simple iPad application — just a window and the application delegate.

3.   In Xcode, double-click `MainWindow.xib` to edit it in Interface Builder. Note that there are four items in the `MainWindow.xib` window (see Figure 4-12):

➤   File's Owner

➤   First Responder

➤   Window

➤   Window Based App App Delegate

FIGURE 4-12

4.   From the Library window, drag and drop a `View Controller` item onto the `MainWindow.xib` window (see Figure 4-13). You will connect this `View Controller` item to a view that you will add to the project in the next step.

FIGURE 4-13

5.   In Xcode, right-click the Classes group and add a new file (see Figure 4-14). In the New File window, click the Cocoa Touch Class item and select the `UIViewController` subclass template (see Figure 4-15). Ensure that the "Targeted for iPad" and "With XIB for user interface" checkboxes are checked. Click Next and name the item `HelloWorldViewController.m`. Xcode should now look like Figure 4-16. The two files (.h and .m) will serve as the `View Controller` class for the `View Controller` item you have added previously in Interface Builder. The `.xib` file serves as the UI for the view controller.

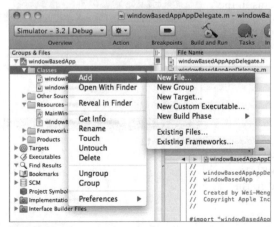

FIGURE 4-14

FIGURE 4-15

FIGURE 4-16

 NOTE *To keep things neat in your project, it is recommended that you drag the* `.xib` *file into the Resources folder.*

6. Double-click the `HelloWorldViewController.xib` file to edit it in Interface Builder.

7. Add a Round Rect Button to the View window and label the button as shown in Figure 4-17.

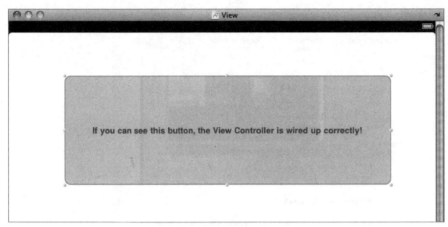

FIGURE 4-17

8. In Interface Builder, select the `View Controller` item in the `MainWindow.xib` window and view its Identity Inspector window. In the Class drop-down list, select `HelloWorldViewController` (see Figure 4-18). The name of the View Controller will now change to `Hello World View Controller`.

FIGURE 4-18

9. View the Attributes Inspector window for the `Hello World View Controller`, and for the NIB Name drop-down list, select `HelloWorldViewController` (see Figure 4-19).

FIGURE 4-19

10. Back in Xcode, insert the bold lines in the following code into the windowBasedAppAppDelegate.h file:

```
#import <UIKit/UIKit.h>

//---add a forward reference to the HelloWorldViewController class---
@class HelloWorldViewController;

@interface windowBasedAppAppDelegate :
    NSObject <UIApplicationDelegate> {
    UIWindow *window;

    //---create an instance of the view controller---
    HelloWorldViewController *viewController;
}

@property (nonatomic, retain) IBOutlet UIWindow *window;

//---expose the view controller as a property---
@property (nonatomic, retain) IBOutlet
    HelloWorldViewController *viewController;

@end
```

11. In the `windowBasedAppAppDelegate.m` file, insert the following code lines that appear in bold:

```
#import "windowBasedAppAppDelegate.h"
#import "HelloWorldViewController.h"

@implementation windowBasedAppAppDelegate

@synthesize window;

//---synthesize the property---
@synthesize viewController;

- (BOOL)application:(UIApplication *)application
didFinishLaunchingWithOptions:(NSDictionary *)launchOptions {

    // Override point for customization after application launch

    //---add the new view to the current window---
    [window addSubview:viewController.view];

    [window makeKeyAndVisible];

    return YES;
}

- (void)dealloc {
    [viewController release];
    [window release];
    [super dealloc];
}

@end
```

12. In the `MainWindow.xib` window, Control-click and drag the `Window Based App App Delegate` item to the `Hello World View Controller` item (see Figure 4-20). Select `viewController`. This will associate the window with the View Controller.

13. That's it! Press Command-R to test the application on the iPhone Simulator. The button appears on the main screen of the application (see Figure 4-21).

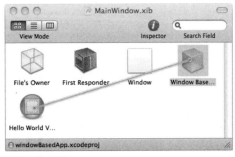

FIGURE 4-20

If you can see this button, the View Controller is wired up correctly!

FIGURE 4-21

How It Works

When you create an iPad project using the Window-based Application template, Xcode provides you with only the bare minimum number of items in your project — a MainWindow.xib file and the application delegate. You are supposed to add your own View Controller(s) and view(s).

In the preceding exercise, you first added a View Controller item to the MainWindow.xib window. You then added an instance of the UIViewController class (which you named HelloWorldViewController) so that it could be connected to the View Controller you just added. This controller class contains the code that you will write to handle the interactions between the view and the user.

When the application has finished launching, you add the View represented by the `HelloWorldViewController` object to the window so that it is visible using the `addSubview:` method of the `UIWindow` instance:

```
[window addSubview:viewController.view];
```

Adding a View Controller and Views Programmatically

Another commonly used technique is to programmatically create the views during runtime without using Interface Builder. This provides a lot of flexibility, especially when you are writing games for which the UI of the application is constantly changing.

In the following Try It Out, you learn how to create a View using an instance of the `UIViewController` class and then programmatically add views to it.

TRY IT OUT   Adding a View Controller and Views Programmatically

1. Using the `windowBasedApp` project, right-click the Classes group in Xcode and add a new file. Select the `UIViewController` subclass item and name it `MySecondViewController`. Ensure that the "With XIB for user interface" checkbox is unchecked. Xcode should now look like Figure 4-22.

FIGURE 4-22

2. In the `windowBasedAppAppDelegate.m` file, add the following bold code:

```
#import "windowBasedAppAppDelegate.h"
#import "HelloWorldViewController.h"

#import "MySecondViewController.h"

@implementation windowBasedAppAppDelegate

@synthesize window;
@synthesize viewController;
```

```
//---create an instance of the second view controller---
MySecondViewController *mySecondViewController;

- (BOOL)application:(UIApplication *)application
didFinishLaunchingWithOptions:(NSDictionary *)launchOptions {

    //---instantiate the second view controller---
    mySecondViewController = [[MySecondViewController alloc]
                                 initWithNibName:nil
                                        bundle:nil];

    //---add the view from the second view controller---
    [window addSubview:mySecondViewController.view];

    //---comment this out so that it doesn't load the viewController---
    //[window addSubview:viewController.view];
    [window makeKeyAndVisible];
    return YES;
}

- (void)dealloc {
    [mySecondViewController release];
    [viewController release];
    [window release];
    [super dealloc];
}
```

3. In the MySecondViewController.h file, insert the following bold lines of code:

```
#import <UIKit/UIKit.h>

@interface MySecondViewController : UIViewController {
    //---create two outlets - label and button---
    UILabel *label;
    UIButton *button;
}

//---expose the outlets as properties---
@property (nonatomic, retain) UILabel *label;
@property (nonatomic, retain) UIButton *button;

@end
```

4. In the MySecondViewController.m file, add the viewDidLoad() method and modify the dealloc method:

```
@synthesize label, button;
- (void)viewDidLoad {

    //---create a CGRect for the positioning---
    CGRect frame = CGRectMake(230, 10, 300, 50);

    //---create a Label view---
    label = [[UILabel alloc] initWithFrame:frame];
    label.textAlignment = UITextAlignmentCenter;
```

```
    label.font = [UIFont fontWithName:@"Verdana" size:20];
    label.text = @"This is a label";

    //---create a Button view---
    frame = CGRectMake(230, 100, 300, 50);
    button = [UIButton buttonWithType:UIButtonTypeRoundedRect];
    button.frame = frame;
    [button setTitle:@"OK" forState:UIControlStateNormal];
    button.backgroundColor = [UIColor clearColor];

    //---add the views to the View window---
    [self.view addSubview:label];
    [self.view addSubview:button];

    [super viewDidLoad];
}

- (void)dealloc {
    [label release];
    [button release];
    [super dealloc];
}
```

5. Press Command-R to test the application on the iPhone Simulator. The Label and Button views appear on the main screen of the application (see Figure 4-23).

How It Works

In contrast to the previous example, in which you added a View Controller item, an instance of the UIViewController class, and a XIB file to your project, this example simply creates an instance of the UIViewController class and adds the views programmatically to the main View window.

In the application delegate, after the application has finished launching, you create an instance of the UIViewController class that you have created:

```
    //---instantiate the second view controller---
    mySecondViewController = [[MySecondViewController alloc]
                            initWithNibName:nil
                                    bundle:nil];
```

You do not need an XIB file because the various views that you will be using will be added programmatically. Hence the initWithNibName: parameter can be set to nil.

To load the View window represented by the instance of the UIViewController class, you use the addSubview: method of the UIWindow instance:

```
    //---add the view from the second view controller---
    [window addSubview:mySecondViewController.view];
```

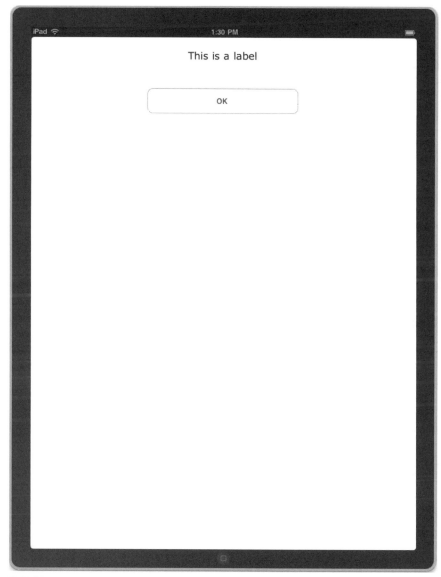

FIGURE 4-23

To programmatically create your views during runtime, you need to override the viewDidLoad()
method of the UIViewController class. Here, you create instances of the Label and Button views
programmatically, specifying their positions as well as their text captions. Finally, you add them to
the main View window:

```
- (void)viewDidLoad {
    //---create a CGRect for the positioning---
    CGRect frame = CGRectMake(10, 10, 300, 50);
```

```
    //---create a Label view---
    label = [[UILabel alloc] initWithFrame:frame];
    label.textAlignment = UITextAlignmentCenter;
    label.font = [UIFont fontWithName:@"Verdana" size:20];
    label.text = @"This is a label";

    //---create a Button view---
    frame = CGRectMake(10, 250, 300, 50);
    button = [UIButton buttonWithType:UIButtonTypeRoundedRect];
    button.frame = frame;
    [button setTitle:@"OK" forState:UIControlStateNormal];
    button.backgroundColor = [UIColor clearColor];

    //---add the views to the current View---
    [self.view addSubview:label];
    [self.view addSubview:button];

    [super viewDidLoad];
}
```

Creating and Connecting Actions

In the previous example, you saw how you can add a Label and Button view to the main View window. However, you need to handle the events raised by the Button view so that when the user presses it, you can perform some work. Chapter 3 covered using outlets and actions and how you connect your code to them using Interface Builder, but in the following Try it Out, the views are created using code, and hence you cannot use Interface Builder to connect the actions and outlets — you have to do it by code, too.

TRY IT OUT Linking Actions to Views

1. Continuing with the `windowBasedApp` project, declare the `buttonClicked:` action (shown in bold) in the `MySecondViewController.h` file as follows:

```
#import <UIKit/UIKit.h>

@interface MySecondViewController : UIViewController {
    //---create two outlets - label and button---
    UILabel *label;
    UIButton *button;
}

//---expose the outlets as properties---
@property (nonatomic, retain) UILabel *label;
@property (nonatomic, retain) UIButton *button;

//---declaring the IBAction---
-(IBAction) buttonClicked: (id) sender;

@end
```

2. In the `MySecondViewController.m` file, you provide the implementation for the `buttonClicked:` action:

```
-(IBAction) buttonClicked: (id) sender{
    UIAlertView *alert = [[UIAlertView alloc] initWithTitle:@"Action invoked!"
                                                    message:@"Button clicked!"
                                                   delegate:self
                                          cancelButtonTitle:@"OK"
                                          otherButtonTitles:nil];
    [alert show];
    [alert release];
}
```

3. To connect the relevant event (`Touch Up Inside`) of the Button view with the `buttonClicked:` action, add the following bold code to the `viewDidLoad()` method:

```
- (void)viewDidLoad {
    //---create a CGRect for the positioning---
    CGRect frame = CGRectMake(10, 10, 300, 50);

    //---create a Label view---
    label = [[UILabel alloc] initWithFrame:frame];
    label.textAlignment = UITextAlignmentCenter;
    label.font = [UIFont fontWithName:@"Verdana" size:20];
    label.text = @"This is a label";

    //---create a Button view---
    frame = CGRectMake(10, 250, 300, 50);
    button = [UIButton buttonWithType:UIButtonTypeRoundedRect];
    button.frame = frame;
    [button setTitle:@"OK" forState:UIControlStateNormal];
    button.backgroundColor = [UIColor clearColor];

    //---add the action handler and set current class as target---
    [button addTarget:self
        action:@selector(buttonClicked:)
        forControlEvents:UIControlEventTouchUpInside];

    //---add the views to the current View---
    [self.view addSubview:label];
    [self.view addSubview:button];

    [super viewDidLoad];
}
```

4. That's it! Press Command-R to test the application on the iPhone Simulator. Clicking the OK button displays an alert view (see Figure 4-24).

FIGURE 4-24

CONTROL EVENTS

The list of events you can use for control objects are:

➤ UIControlEventTouchDown

➤ UIControlEventTouchDownRepeat

➤ UIControlEventTouchDragInside

➤ UIControlEventTouchDragOutside

➤ UIControlEventTouchDragEnter

➤ UIControlEventTouchDragExit

➤ UIControlEventTouchUpInside

➤ UIControlEventTouchUpOutside

➤ UIControlEventTouchCancel

➤ UIControlEventValueChanged

➤ UIControlEventEditingDidBegin

➤ UIControlEventEditingChanged

➤ UIControlEventEditingDidEnd

➤ UIControlEventEditingDidEndOnExit

➤ UIControlEventAllTouchEvents

➤ UIControlEventAllEditingEvents

➤ UIControlEventApplicationReserved

➤ UIControlEventSystemReserved

➤ UIControlEventAllEvents

The use of each event is detailed at: http://developer.apple.com/iphone/
library/documentation/UIKit/Reference/UIControl_Class/Reference/
Reference.html#//apple_ref/doc/constant_group/Control_Events.

Switching to Another View

In real life, you often have a number of views, each representing different pieces of information.
Depending on the selections made by the user, you then switch to different views to perform different tasks.

Hence, in this section you learn how you can switch to another view depending on the selection
made by the user.

TRY IT OUT Switching Views

1. Using the same project created in the previous section, add the following bold code to the `MySecondViewController.m` file:

```
import "MySecondViewController.h"

#import "HelloWorldViewController.h"

@implementation MySecondViewController

//---create an instance of the view controller---
HelloWorldViewController *viewController;

-(IBAction) buttonClicked: (id) sender{

    //---add the view of the view controller to the current View---
    viewController = [[HelloWorldViewController alloc]
                        initWithNibName:@"HelloWorldViewController"
                                bundle:nil];
    [self.view addSubview:viewController.view];

    /*
    UIAlertView *alert = [[UIAlertView alloc] initWithTitle:@"Action invoked!"
                                                message:@"Button clicked!"
                                                delegate:self
                                      cancelButtonTitle:@"OK"
                                      otherButtonTitles:nil];
    [alert show];
    [alert release];
    */
}

- (void)dealloc {
    [viewController release];
    [label release];
    [button release];
    [super dealloc];
}
```

2. Declare a `btnClicked:` action in the `HelloWorldViewController.h` file:

```
#import <UIKit/UIKit.h>

@interface HelloWorldViewController : UIViewController {

}

-(IBAction) btnClicked:(id) sender;

@end
```

3. In the `HelloWorldViewController.m` file, define the `btnClicked:` action as follows:

```
-(IBAction) btnClicked:(id) sender{
    //---remove the current view; essentially hiding the view---
    [self.view removeFromSuperview];
}
```

4. Double-click the `HelloWorldViewController.xib` file to edit it in Interface Builder. Control-click and drag the Round Rect Button in the View window to the File's Owner item in the `HelloWorldViewController.xib` window and select `btnClicked:`.

5. In Xcode, press Command-R to test the application. Now when you click the OK button in the main View, you are brought to the Hello World View. To close the View, press the button.

How It Works

1. For this example, you simply add the View of the view controller (that you are switching to) to the current view using the `addSubview:` method:

```
//---add the view of the view controller to the current View---
viewController = [[HelloWorldViewController alloc]
                        initWithNibName:@"HelloWorldViewController"
                                bundle:nil];
[self.view addSubview:viewController.view];
```

2. To dismiss a view, you use the `removeFromSuperview:` method:

```
//---remove the current view; essentially hiding the view---
[self.view removeFromSuperview];
```

Animating the Switching of Views

The switching of Views that you have just seen in the previous section happens instantaneously — the two Views change immediately without any visual cues. One of the key selling points of the iPad is its animation capabilities. Therefore, for the switching of views, you can make the display a little more interesting by performing some simple animations, such as flipping one View window to reveal another. Here is how to do that.

TRY IT OUT Animating the Transitions

1. Using the same project, add the following bold code to the `MySecondViewController.m` file:

```
-(IBAction) buttonClicked: (id) sender{

    //---add the view of the view controller to the current View---
    viewController = [[HelloWorldViewController alloc]
                        initWithNibName:@"HelloWorldViewController"
                                bundle:nil];

    [UIView beginAnimations:@"flipping view" context:nil];
```

```
    [UIView setAnimationDuration:1];
    [UIView setAnimationCurve:UIViewAnimationCurveEaseInOut];
    [UIView setAnimationTransition: UIViewAnimationTransitionFlipFromLeft
                            forView:self.view cache:YES];

    [self.view addSubview:viewController.view];

    [UIView commitAnimations];
}
```

2. In the `HelloWorldViewController.m file`, add the following code that appears in bold:

```
-(IBAction) btnClicked:(id) sender{

    [UIView beginAnimations:@"flipping view" context:nil];
    [UIView setAnimationDuration:1];
    [UIView setAnimationCurve:UIViewAnimationCurveEaseIn];
    [UIView setAnimationTransition: UIViewAnimationTransitionFlipFromRight
        forView:self.view.superview cache:YES];

    [self.view removeFromSuperview];

    [UIView commitAnimations];
}
```

3. Press Command-R to test the application on the iPhone Simulator. Click the OK buttons on both Views and notice the direction in which the two Views flip to one another (see Figure 4-25 and Figure 4-26).

How It Works

First, examine the animation that is applied to the `MySecondViewController`. You perform the animation by first calling the `beginAnimations:` method of the `UIView` class to start the animation block:

```
    [UIView beginAnimations:@"flipping view" context:nil];
```

The `setAnimationDuration:` method specifies the duration of the animation in seconds. Here, you set it to one second:

```
    [UIView setAnimationDuration:1];
```

The `setAnimationCurve:` method sets the curve of the animating property changes within an animation:

```
    [UIView setAnimationCurve:UIViewAnimationCurveEaseInOut];
```

You can use the following constants for the curve of the animation:

➤ `UIViewAnimationCurveEaseInOut` — Causes the animation to begin slowly, accelerate through the middle of its duration, and then slow again before completing

➤ `UIViewAnimationCurveEaseIn` — Causes the animation to begin slowly and then speed up as it progresses

➤ `UIViewAnimationCurveEaseOut` — Causes the animation to begin quickly and then slow as it completes

➤ `UIViewAnimationCurveLinear` — causes an animation to occur evenly over its duration

The `setAnimationTransition:` method applies a transition type to be applied to a view during the animation duration.

```
[UIView setAnimationTransition: UIViewAnimationTransitionFlipFromLeft
       forView:self.view cache:YES];
```

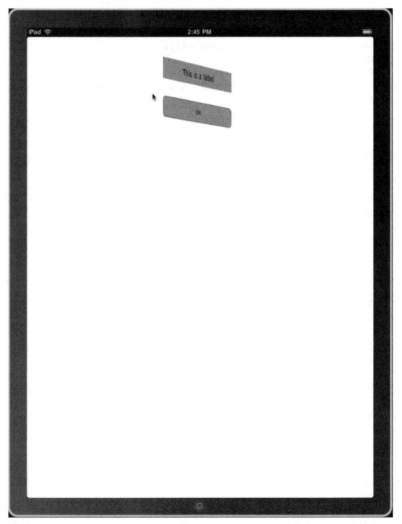

FIGURE 4-25

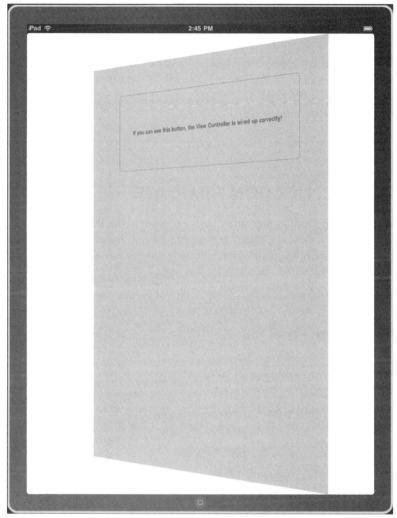

If you can see this button, the View Controller is wired up correctly!

FIGURE 4-26

The `cache:` parameter specifies whether the iPad should cache the image of the view and use it during the transition. Caching the image speeds up the animation process. The following constants can be used for the animation transition:

➤ `UIViewAnimationTransitionNone` — No transition

➤ `UIViewAnimationTransitionFlipFromLeft` —Flips a view around a vertical axis from left to right

➤ `UIViewAnimationTransitionFlipFromRight` — Flips a view around a vertical axis from right to left

➤ `UIViewAnimationTransitionCurlUp` — Curls a view up from the bottom

➤ `UIViewAnimationTransitionCurlDown` — Curls a view down from the top

To end the animation, call the `commitAnimations:` method:

```
[UIView commitAnimations];
```

The animation performed on the `HelloWorldViewController` is similar to that of the `MySecondViewController`, except that the view to animate must be set to `self.view.superview`:

```
[UIView setAnimationTransition: UIViewAnimationTransitionFlipFromRight
    forView:self.view.superview cache:YES];
```

THE SPLIT VIEW-BASED APPLICATION TEMPLATE

In the iPhone SDK 3.2, there is a new application template that is exclusive to the iPad: Split View-based Application. It allows you to create a split-view interface for your application, which is essentially a master-detail interface. The left side of the screen displays a list of selectable items while the right-side displays the details of the item selected.

To see how Split View-based Application works, take a look at the following Try It Out.

TRY IT OUT Creating a Split View-based Application

codefile splitViewBasedApp.zip available for download at Wrox.com

1. Using Xcode, create a new Split View-based Application project and name it `splitViewBasedApp` (see Figure 4-27).

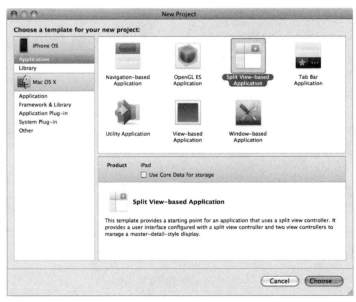

FIGURE 4-27

2. Observe the files created in the Classes and Resources folder (see Figure 4-28). Notice that there are now two View Controller classes (`RootViewController` and `DetailViewController`) as well as two XIB files.

3. Press Command-R in Xcode to test the application on the iPhone Simulator. Figure 4-29 shows the application when it is displayed in landscape mode. When you rotate the simulator to portrait mode, the application now looks like Figure 4-30.

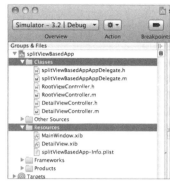

FIGURE 4-28

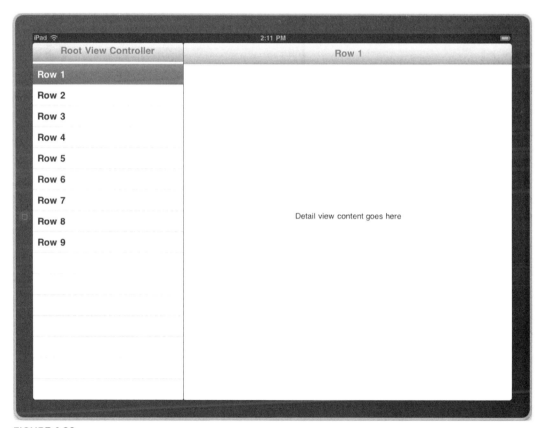

FIGURE 4-29

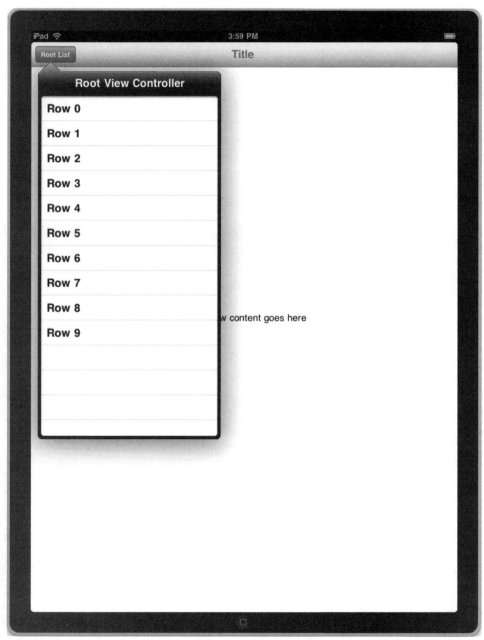

FIGURE 4-30

How It Works

The magic of a Split View-based Application lies in its transformation when the device is rotated. When in landscape mode, the application displays a list of rows on the left. When it is turned to portrait mode, the list of rows is now hidden in a Popover view. Let's see how this is done.

First, observe the content of the `splitViewBasedAppAppDelegate.h` file:

```
#import <UIKit/UIKit.h>

@class RootViewController;
@class DetailViewController;

@interface splitViewBasedAppAppDelegate : NSObject <UIApplicationDelegate> {

    UIWindow *window;

    UISplitViewController *splitViewController;

    RootViewController *rootViewController;
    DetailViewController *detailViewController;
}

@property (nonatomic, retain) IBOutlet UIWindow *window;

@property (nonatomic,retain) IBOutlet UISplitViewController *splitViewController;
@property (nonatomic,retain) IBOutlet RootViewController *rootViewController;
@property (nonatomic,retain) IBOutlet DetailViewController *detailViewController;

@end
```

Notice that it contains a view controller object of type `UISplitViewController`
(`splitViewController`) as well two view controllers (`rootViewController` and
`detailViewController`). The `UISplitViewController` is a container view controller that contains
two view controllers, allowing you to implement a master-detail interface.

Next, look at the content of the `splitViewBasedAppAppDelegate.m` file:

```
#import "splitViewBasedAppAppDelegate.h"

#import "RootViewController.h"
#import "DetailViewController.h"

@implementation splitViewBasedAppAppDelegate

@synthesize window, splitViewController, rootViewController, detailViewController;

- (BOOL)application:(UIApplication *)application
didFinishLaunchingWithOptions:(NSDictionary *)launchOptions {

    // Override point for customization after app launch

    // Add the split view controller's view to the window and display.
    [window addSubview:splitViewController.view];
    [window makeKeyAndVisible];

    return YES;
}

- (void)applicationWillTerminate:(UIApplication *)application {
```

```
        // Save data if appropriate
    }

    - (void)dealloc {
        [splitViewController release];
        [window release];
        [super dealloc];
    }

    @end
```

When the application is loaded, the view contained in the `splitViewController` object is added to the window.

Now, double-click on the `MainWindow.xib` file to edit it in Interface Builder. You'll see that the `MainWindow.xib` contains an item named Split View Controller (recall that for a View-based Application project, you had a View Controller item instead).

Switch the `MainWindow.xib` file to display in List view mode and observe the items located within the Split View Controller item (see Figure 4-31):

➤   Navigation Controller

➤   Detail View Controller

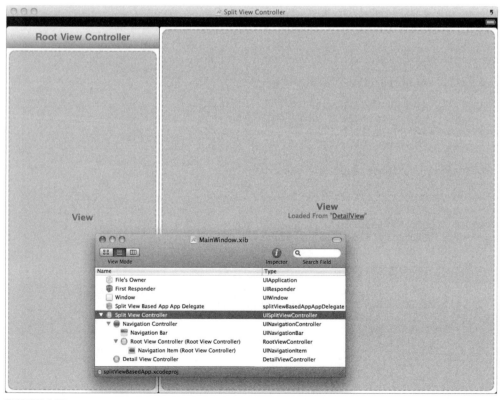

FIGURE 4-31

The Navigation Controller controls the left side of a split-view application. Figure 4-32 shows that it consists of a Navigation Bar as well as a Root View Controller.

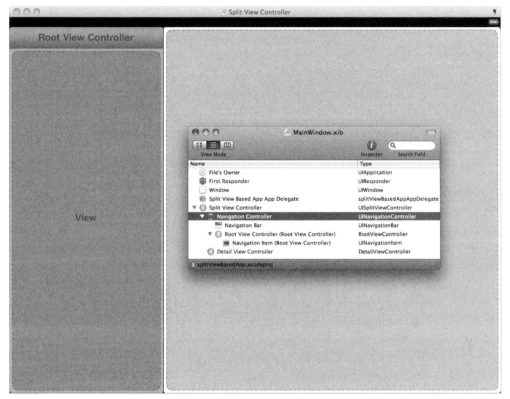

FIGURE 4-32

The Root View Controller is mapped to the `RootViewController` class (see Figure 4-33).

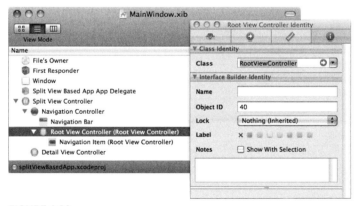

FIGURE 4-33

The Detail View Controller controls the right side of a split-view application (see Figure 4-34).

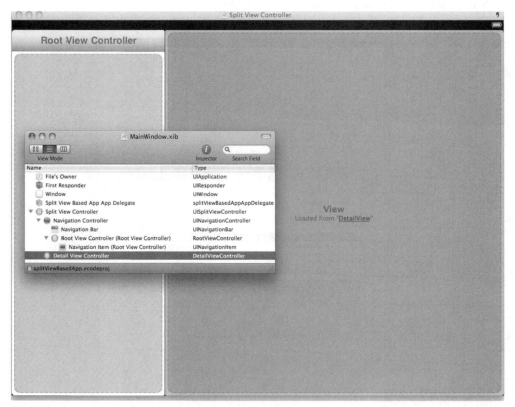

FIGURE 4-34

The Detail View Controller is mapped to the `DetailViewController` class (see Figure 4-35).

FIGURE 4-35

The application delegate is connected to the various view controllers, as you can see when you right-click on the Split View Based App App Delegate item (see Figure 4-36).

Let's examine the two view controllers that are contained within the Split View Controller: RootViewController and DetailViewController.

Observe the content of the RootViewController.h file:

```
#import <UIKit/UIKit.h>

@class DetailViewController;

@interface RootViewController : UITableViewController {
    DetailViewController *detailViewController;
}

@property (nonatomic, retain) IBOutlet DetailViewController *detailViewController;

@end
```

Note that the RootViewController class inherits from the UITableViewController class, not the UIViewController class you have seen earlier. The UITableViewController class is a subclass of the UIViewController class, providing the capability to display a table containing rows of data. (Chapter 7 discusses the Table view in more detail.)

The content of the RootViewController.m file looks like this:

```
#import "RootViewController.h"
#import "DetailViewController.h"


@implementation RootViewController

@synthesize detailViewController;

/*
    ---Other commented out code are omitted from this code listing---
```

```objc
*/

- (void)viewDidLoad {
    [super viewDidLoad];
    self.clearsSelectionOnViewWillAppear = NO;
}

// Ensure that the view controller supports rotation and
// that the split view can therefore show in
// both portrait and landscape.
- (BOOL)shouldAutorotateToInterfaceOrientation:
(UIInterfaceOrientation)interfaceOrientation {
    return YES;
}

// The size the view should be when presented in a popover.
- (CGSize)contentSizeForViewInPopoverView {
    return CGSizeMake(320.0, 600.0);
}

- (NSInteger)numberOfSectionsInTableView:(UITableView *)aTableView {
    // Return the number of sections.
    return 1;
}

- (NSInteger)tableView:(UITableView *)aTableView
numberOfRowsInSection:(NSInteger)section {
    // Return the number of rows in the section.
    return 10;
}

- (UITableViewCell *)tableView:(UITableView *)tableView
cellForRowAtIndexPath:(NSIndexPath *)indexPath {

    static NSString *CellIdentifier = @"CellIdentifier";

    // Dequeue or create a cell of the appropriate type.
    UITableViewCell *cell = [tableView
        dequeueReusableCellWithIdentifier:CellIdentifier];
    if (cell == nil) {
        cell = [[[UITableViewCell alloc]
            initWithStyle:UITableViewCellStyleDefault
            reuseIdentifier:CellIdentifier] autorelease];
        cell.accessoryType = UITableViewCellAccessoryNone;
    }

    // Configure the cell.
    cell.textLabel.text =
        [NSString stringWithFormat:@"Row %d", indexPath.row];
    return cell;
}

- (void)tableView:(UITableView *)aTableView
didSelectRowAtIndexPath:(NSIndexPath *)indexPath {
```

```
    /*
    When a row is selected, set the detail view controller's
    detail item to the item associated with the selected row.
    */
    detailViewController.detailItem =
        [NSString stringWithFormat:@"Row %d", indexPath.row];
}

- (void)didReceiveMemoryWarning {
    // Releases the view if it doesn't have a superview.
    [super didReceiveMemoryWarning];

    // Relinquish ownership any cached data, images,
    // etc that aren't in use.
}

- (void)viewDidUnload {
    // Relinquish ownership of anything that
    // can be recreated in viewDidLoad or on demand.
    // For example: self.myOutlet = nil;
}

- (void)dealloc {
    [super dealloc];
}

@end
```

While the content of the `RootViewController.m` file contains many methods related to the Table view, here is a quick summary of some of the important methods:

➤ `contentSizeForViewInPopoverView` — The size of the PopoverView to display.

➤ `numberOfSectionsInTableView:` — The number of sections to be displayed in the Table view.

➤ `tableView:numberOfRowsInSection:` — The number of rows to be displayed in the Table view.

➤ `tableView:cellForRowAtIndexPath:` — The data to populate for each row.

➤ `tableView:didSelectRowAtIndexPath:` — The row that was selected by the user.

Next, take a look at the `DetailsViewController.h` file:

```
#import <UIKit/UIKit.h>

@interface DetailViewController : UIViewController
    <UIPopoverControllerDelegate, UISplitViewControllerDelegate> {

    UIPopoverController *popoverController;
    UINavigationBar *navigationBar;

    id detailItem;
}

@property (nonatomic, retain) UIPopoverController *popoverController;
```

```
@property (nonatomic, retain) IBOutlet UINavigationBar *navigationBar;

@property (nonatomic, retain) id detailItem;

@end
```

Notice that the `DetailsViewController` class implements the following protocols:

➤ `UIPopoverControllerDelegate` — It implements this protocol so that if the PopoverView is about to be dismissed, you have a chance to be notified (so you can prevent its dismissal, for example).

➤ `UISplitViewControllerDelegate` — It needs to implement this protocol because when the iPad changes orientation, it needs to hide/display the PopoverView.

Examine the content of the `DetailsViewController.m` file:

```objc
#import "DetailViewController.h"
#import "RootViewController.h"

@implementation DetailViewController

@synthesize navigationBar, popoverController, detailItem;

/*
    ---Other commented out code are omitted from this code listing---
*/

/*
 When setting the detail item, update the view and dismiss
 the popover controller if it's showing.
*/
- (void)setDetailItem:(id)newDetailItem {
    if (detailItem != newDetailItem) {
        [detailItem release];
        detailItem = [newDetailItem retain];

        // Update the view.
        navigationBar.topItem.title = [detailItem description];
    }

    if (popoverController != nil) {
        [popoverController dismissPopoverAnimated:YES];
    }
}

- (void)splitViewController:(UISplitViewController*)svc
      willHideViewController:(UIViewController *)aViewController
           withBarButtonItem:(UIBarButtonItem*)barButtonItem
       forPopoverController:(UIPopoverController*)pc {

    barButtonItem.title = @"Root List";
    [navigationBar.topItem setLeftBarButtonItem:barButtonItem
                                       animated:YES];
```

```
        self.popoverController = pc;
    }


    // Called when the view is shown again in the split view,
    // invalidating the button and popover controller.
    - (void)splitViewController:(UISplitViewController*)svc
          willShowViewController:(UIViewController *)aViewController
      invalidatingBarButtonItem:(UIBarButtonItem *)barButtonItem {

        [navigationBar.topItem setLeftBarButtonItem:nil animated:YES];
        self.popoverController = nil;
    }

    // Ensure that the view controller supports rotation and that the
    // split view can therefore show in both portrait and landscape.
    - (BOOL)shouldAutorotateToInterfaceOrientation:
    (UIInterfaceOrientation)interfaceOrientation {
        return YES;
    }

    - (void)viewDidUnload {
        // Release any retained subviews of the main view.
        // e.g. self.myOutlet = nil;
        self.popoverController = nil;
    }

    - (void)dealloc {
        [popoverController release];
        [navigationBar release];

        [detailItem release];
        [super dealloc];
    }

    @end
```

There are two important events you need to handle in this controller (both events are defined in the `UISplitViewControllerDelegate` protocol):

➤ `splitViewController:willHideViewController:withBarButtonItem:forPopover-Controller:` — Fired when the iPad switches to portrait mode (where the PopoverView will be shown and the Table View will be hidden).

➤ `splitViewController:willShowViewController:invalidatingBarButtonItem:` — Fired when the iPad switches to landscape mode (where the PopoverView will be hidden and the Table View will be shown).

Displaying Some Items in the Split View-based Application

Now that you have seen a Split View-based Application in action, it is now time to make some changes to it and see how it is useful for the iPad. The following Try It Out shows a list of movies and when a movie is selected, a picture will be displayed on the detail view.

TRY IT OUT Displaying Some Items

1. Using the `splitViewBasedApp` project, double-click the `DetailView.xib` file to edit it in Interface Builder.

2. Add an ImageView to the View window and set its Mode to Aspect Fit in the Attributes Inspector window (see Figure 4-37).

FIGURE 4-37

3. In the Size Inspector window, set its Autosizing attribute as follows (see also Figure 4-38):

➤ X: 152

➤ Y: 163

➤ W: 463

➤ H: 644

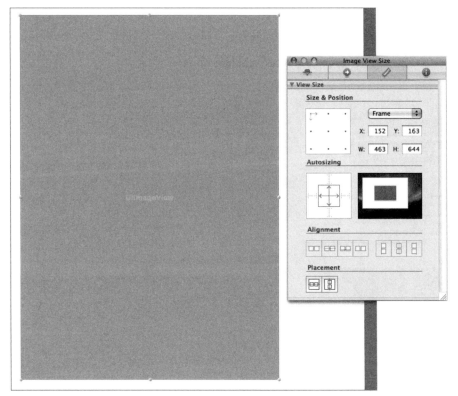

FIGURE 4-38

4. In Xcode, add the images shown in Figure 4-39 to the Resources folder (you can download the images together with this project from Wrox.com; see the section in the introduction titled "Source Code" for details).

5. In the `DetailViewController.h` file, insert the following bold statements:

```
#import <UIKit/UIKit.h>

@interface DetailViewController : UIViewController
    <UIPopoverControllerDelegate, UISplitViewControllerDelegate> {
```

```
        UIPopoverController *popoverController;
        UINavigationBar *navigationBar;

        id detailItem;

        IBOutlet UIImageView *imageView;
}

@property (nonatomic, retain) UIPopoverController *popoverController;
@property (nonatomic, retain) IBOutlet UINavigationBar *navigationBar;

@property (nonatomic, retain) id detailItem;

@property (nonatomic, retain) UIImageView *imageView;

@end
```

FIGURE 4-39

6. Control-click and drag the File's Owner item and drop it on the ImageView. Select imageView (see Figure 4-40).

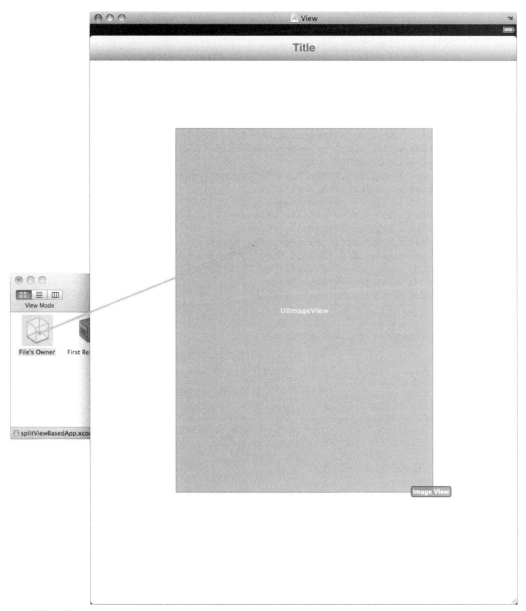

FIGURE 4-40

7. Add the following bold statements to the RootViewController.m file:

```
#import "RootViewController.h"
#import "DetailViewController.h"
```

```
@implementation RootViewController

@synthesize detailViewController;

NSMutableArray *listOfMovies;

- (void)viewDidLoad {
    //---initialize the array---
    listOfMovies = [[NSMutableArray alloc] init];
    [listOfMovies addObject:@"Training Day"];
    [listOfMovies addObject:@"Remember the Titans"];
    [listOfMovies addObject:@"John Q."];
    [listOfMovies addObject:@"The Bone Collector"];
    [listOfMovies addObject:@"Ricochet"];
    [listOfMovies addObject:@"The Siege"];
    [listOfMovies addObject:@"Malcolm X"];
    [listOfMovies addObject:@"Antwone Fisher"];
    [listOfMovies addObject:@"Courage Under Fire"];
    [listOfMovies addObject:@"He Got Game"];
    [listOfMovies addObject:@"The Pelican Brief"];
    [listOfMovies addObject:@"Glory"];
    [listOfMovies addObject:@"The Preacher's Wife"];

    //---set the title---
    self.navigationItem.title = @"Movies";

    [super viewDidLoad];
    self.clearsSelectionOnViewWillAppear = NO;
}

- (NSInteger)tableView:(UITableView *)aTableView
 numberOfRowsInSection:(NSInteger)section {
    // Return the number of rows in the section.
    //return 10;
    return [listOfMovies count];
}

- (UITableViewCell *)tableView:(UITableView *)tableView
        cellForRowAtIndexPath:(NSIndexPath *)indexPath {

    static NSString *CellIdentifier = @"CellIdentifier";

    // Dequeue or create a cell of the appropriate type.
    UITableViewCell *cell = [tableView
        dequeueReusableCellWithIdentifier:CellIdentifier];

    if (cell == nil) {
        cell = [[[UITableViewCell alloc
                initWithStyle:UITableViewCellStyleDefault
                reuseIdentifier:CellIdentifier] autorelease];
        cell.accessoryType = UITableViewCellAccessoryNone;
    }
```

```
        // Configure the cell.
        //cell.textLabel.text = [NSString stringWithFormat:@"Row %d", indexPath.row];
        cell.textLabel.text = [listOfMovies objectAtIndex:indexPath.row];

        return cell;
}

- (void)tableView:(UITableView *)aTableView
didSelectRowAtIndexPath:(NSIndexPath *)indexPath {

        /*
        When a row is selected, set the detail view controller's detail item to
        the item associated with the selected row.
        */
        //detailViewController.detailItem =
        //      [NSString stringWithFormat:@"Row %d", indexPath.row];

        detailViewController.detailItem =
            [NSString stringWithFormat:@"%@",
                [listOfMovies objectAtIndex:indexPath.row]];
}

- (void)dealloc {
        [listOfMovies release];
        [super dealloc];
}
```

8. Add the following bold statements to the `DetailViewController.m` file:

```
#import "DetailViewController.h"
#import "RootViewController.h"

@implementation DetailViewController

@synthesize navigationBar, popoverController, detailItem;

@synthesize imageView;


/*
 When setting the detail item, update the view and dismiss the
popover controller if it's showing.
 */
- (void)setDetailItem:(id)newDetailItem {
    if (detailItem != newDetailItem) {
        [detailItem release];
        detailItem = [newDetailItem retain];

        // Update the view.
        navigationBar.topItem.title = [detailItem description];

        NSString *imageName = [NSString
            stringWithFormat:@"%@.jpg",navigationBar.topItem.title];
```

```
        imageView.image = [UIImage imageNamed:imageName];
    }

    if (popoverController != nil) {
        [popoverController dismissPopoverAnimated:YES];
    }
}
```

9. Press Command-R to test the application on the iPhone Simulator. Figure 4-41 shows that when the simulator is in landscape mode, the application shows a list of movies on the left of the application. Selecting a movie displays the movie image. You can also switch to portrait mode and select the movies from the PopoverView (see Figure 4-42).

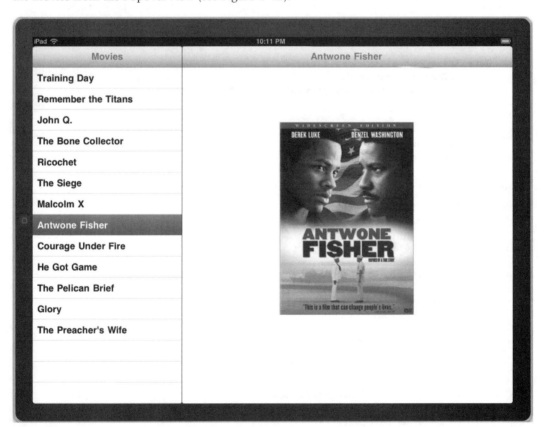

FIGURE 4-41

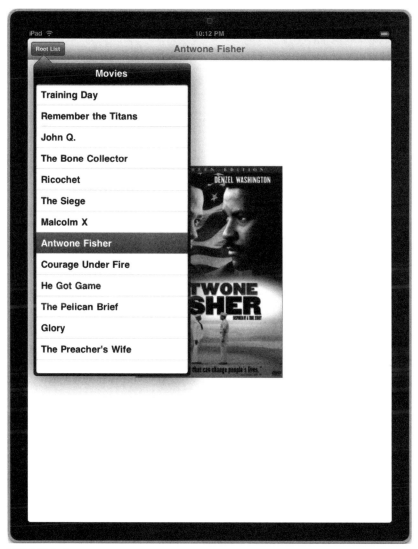

FIGURE 4-42

How It Works

First, you initialize a mutable array with list of movie names:

```
- (void)viewDidLoad {
    //---initialize the array---
    listOfMovies = [[NSMutableArray alloc] init];
    [listOfMovies addObject:@"Training Day"];
    [listOfMovies addObject:@"Remember the Titans"];
    [listOfMovies addObject:@"John Q."];
    [listOfMovies addObject:@"The Bone Collector"];
```

```
[listOfMovies addObject:@"Ricochet"];
[listOfMovies addObject:@"The Siege"];
[listOfMovies addObject:@"Malcolm X"];
[listOfMovies addObject:@"Antwone Fisher"];
[listOfMovies addObject:@"Courage Under Fire"];
[listOfMovies addObject:@"He Got Game"];
[listOfMovies addObject:@"The Pelican Brief"];
[listOfMovies addObject:@"Glory"];
[listOfMovies addObject:@"The Preacher's Wife"];

//---set the title---
self.navigationItem.title = @"Movies";

[super viewDidLoad];
self.clearsSelectionOnViewWillAppear = NO;
}
```

The value returned by the `tableView:numberOfRowsInSection:` method sets the number of rows to be displayed, and in this case it is the size of the mutable array:

```
- (NSInteger)tableView:(UITableView *)aTableView
numberOfRowsInSection:(NSInteger)section {
    // Return the number of rows in the section.
    //return 10;
    return [listOfMovies count];
}
```

The `tableView:cellForRowAtIndexPath:` method is fired for each item in the mutable array, thereby populating the Table view:

```
- (UITableViewCell *)tableView:(UITableView *)tableView
        cellForRowAtIndexPath:(NSIndexPath *)indexPath {

    static NSString *CellIdentifier = @"CellIdentifier";

    // Dequeue or create a cell of the appropriate type.
    UITableViewCell *cell = [tableView
        dequeueReusableCellWithIdentifier:CellIdentifier];

    if (cell == nil) {
        cell = [[[UITableViewCell alloc]
                initWithStyle:UITableViewCellStyleDefault
                reuseIdentifier:CellIdentifier] autorelease];
        cell.accessoryType = UITableViewCellAccessoryNone;
    }

    // Configure the cell.
    //cell.textLabel.text = [NSString stringWithFormat:@"Row %d", indexPath.row];
    cell.textLabel.text = [listOfMovies objectAtIndex:indexPath.row];

    return cell;
}
```

When an item is selected in the Table view, you pass the movie selected to the `DetailViewController` object via its `detailItem` property:

```
- (void)tableView:(UITableView *)aTableView
didSelectRowAtIndexPath:(NSIndexPath *)indexPath {

    /*
     When a row is selected, set the detail view controller's
     detail item to the item associated with the selected row.
    */
    //detailViewController.detailItem =
    //    [NSString stringWithFormat:@"Row %d", indexPath.row];

    detailViewController.detailItem =
        [NSString stringWithFormat:@"%@",
            [listOfMovies objectAtIndex:indexPath.row]];
}
```

In the `DetailViewController.m` file, you modified the `setDetailItem:` method (which is really a setter for the `detailItem` property) so that an image can be displayed. For the image name, you simply append a `.jpg` to the movie name:

```
- (void)setDetailItem:(id)newDetailItem {
    if (detailItem != newDetailItem) {
        [detailItem release];
        detailItem = [newDetailItem retain];

        // Update the view.
        navigationBar.topItem.title = [detailItem description];

        NSString *imageName = [NSString
            stringWithFormat:@"%@.jpg",navigationBar.topItem.title];
        imageView.image = [UIImage imageNamed:imageName];
    }

    if (popoverController != nil) {
        [popoverController dismissPopoverAnimated:YES];
    }
}
```

THE TAB BAR APPLICATION TEMPLATE

You have seen the use of three types of application templates provided by the iPhone SDK: View-based Application, Window-based Application, and Split View-based Application. A fourth type of application template exists for the iPad: The Tab Bar application template. The following Try it Out uses the Tab Bar Application template to create a project and shows what a Tab Bar application looks like. Download the necessary project files as indicated here.

Creating a Tab Bar Application

codefile TabBarApplication.zip available for download at Wrox.com

1. Using Xcode, create a new Tab Bar application project and name it `TabBarApplication`.

2. Examine the content of the project (see Figure 4-43). Besides the usual application delegate files, it also contains two View Controllers (`FirstViewController` and `SecondViewController`) and three XIB files: `MainWindow.xib`, `FirstView.xib`, and `SecondView.xib`.

FIGURE 4-43

3. Examine the content of the `TabBarApplicationAppDelegate.h` file, which is as follows:

```
#import <UIKit/UIKit.h>
@interface TabBarApplicationAppDelegate : NSObject
    <UIApplicationDelegate, UITabBarControllerDelegate> {
    UIWindow *window;
    UITabBarController *tabBarController;
}

@property (nonatomic, retain) IBOutlet UIWindow *window;
@property (nonatomic, retain) IBOutlet UITabBarController *tabBarController;

@end
```

Instead of the usual `UIViewController` class, you are now using the `UITabBarController` class, which inherits from the `UIViewController` class. A `TabBarController` is a specialized `UIViewController` class that contains a collection of view controllers.

4. When the application has finished loading, the current view of the `UITabBarController` instance is loaded, an occurrence that is evident in the `TabBarApplicationAppDelegate.m` file:

```
#import "TabBarApplicationAppDelegate.h"

@implementation TabBarApplicationAppDelegate
```

```
@synthesize window;
@synthesize tabBarController;

- (BOOL)application:(UIApplication *)application
didFinishLaunchingWithOptions:(NSDictionary *)launchOptions {

    // Add the tab bar controller's current view as a subview of the window
    [window addSubview:tabBarController.view];
    [window makeKeyAndVisible];

    return YES;
}
```

5. Double-click the `MainWindow.xib` file to edit it in Interface Builder. Observe the two Tab Bar Item views contained within the Tab Bar view shown at the bottom of the View.

6. Click the first Tab Bar Item labeled First (see Figure 4-44). In the Identify Inspector window, observe that this is a View Controller and that the implementing class is `FirstViewController`. If you view its Attributes Inspector window, you will see that it is linked to the `FirstView.xib` file (see Figure 4-45).

7. Click the second Tab Bar Item and view its Attributes and Identity Inspector windows. Like the first Tab Bar Item, it is pointing to the `SecondView.xib` file and `SecondViewController` class, respectively.

8. In Xcode, press Command-R to run the application on the iPhone Simulator (see Figure 4-46). You can now touch the Tab Bar Items at the bottom of the screen to switch between the two views.

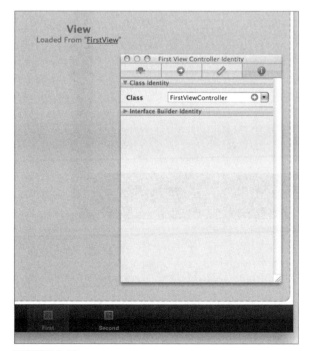

FIGURE 4-44

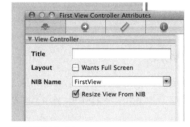

FIGURE 4-45

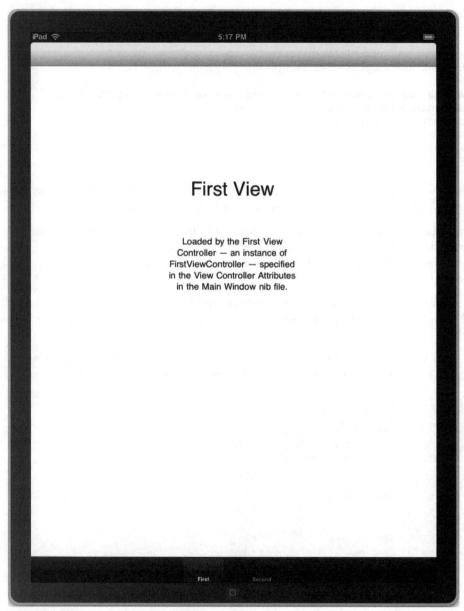

FIGURE 4-46

How It Works

Basically, the magic of a Tab Bar application is in the use of the `UITabBarController` class. Double-click the `MainWindow.xib` file; you'll see that it has a Tab Bar Controller item (see Figure 4-47).

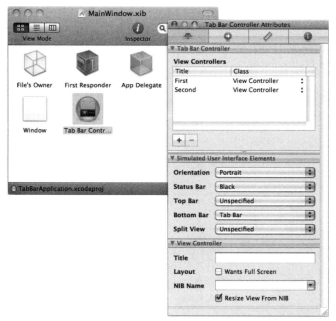

FIGURE 4-47

The Tab Bar Controller contains a collection of View Controllers. In this case, it has two view controllers. The first view controller inside the `UITabBarController` instance is always displayed when it is added to the current view:

```
- (BOOL)application:(UIApplication *)application
didFinishLaunchingWithOptions:(NSDictionary *)launchOptions {

    // Add the tab bar controller's current view as a subview of the window
    [window addSubview:tabBarController.view];
    [window makeKeyAndVisible];

    return YES;
}
```

When the user touches the Tab Bar Items, each corresponding view controller is loaded to display its view.

 NOTE *A Tab Bar Item actually is comprised of a View Controller and a Tab Bar Item object.*

By default, the Tab Bar application template includes only two Tab Bar Items, so in this section, you see how to add more Tab Bar Items to the existing Tab Bar.

Adding Tab Bar Items

1. Using the `TabBarApplication` project, in Interface Builder, drag and drop a Tab Bar Item from the Library onto the Tab Bar view (see Figure 4-48).

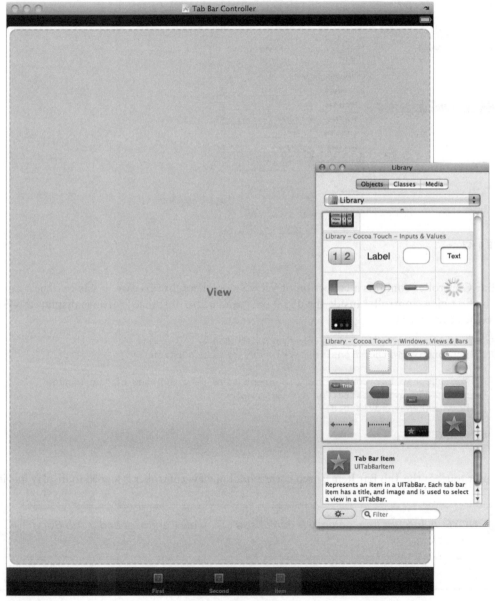

FIGURE 4-48

2. Select the newly added Tab Bar Item and view its Attributes Inspector window. Set the Badge property to 5 and the Identifier property to Search (see Figure 4-49). Observe the change in appearance of the Tab Bar Item. Be sure to click the center of the Tab Bar Item so that the Tab Bar Item can be selected; if you click the outside, the View Controller is selected.

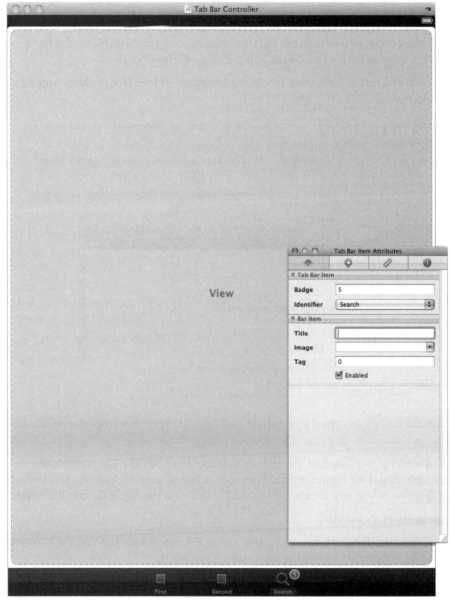

FIGURE 4-49

NOTE *The Badge property is a nifty way for you to set some numbers or other text on the Tab Bar Item so that it can serve as a quick visual cue to users to remind them of something.*

4. In Xcode, right-click the Classes folder in Xcode and choose Add ⇨ New File. Click the Cocoa Touch Classes category and select the `UIViewController` subclass. Name the file `SearchViewController.m` (check the "With XIB for user interface" option).

5. Double-click the newly created `SearchView.xib` file to open it in Interface Builder. Add a Label view to it (see Figure 4-50).

 NOTE *You won't be doing much in this `SearchView.xib` file. You're just adding a Label view so that you will see that this view loads successfully when the user taps on the Tab Bar Item.*

FIGURE 4-50

6. Back in `MainWindow.xib`, select the Tab Bar Item and view its Attributes Inspector window (see Figure 4-51). Set its NIB name to `SearchViewController`.

7. In the Identity Inspector window for the Search Tab Bar Item, set the Class name to `SearchViewController` (see Figure 4-52). This step is important; without it, you will get a runtime error later on when you create outlets and actions on the View Controller class.

8. Save the project in Interface Builder.

9. That's it! Press Command-R to test the application on the iPhone Simulator. You can now touch the third Tab Bar Item (Search) to view the label (see Figure 4-53).

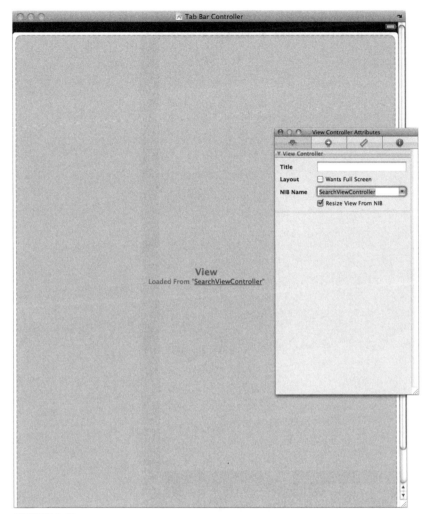

FIGURE 4-51

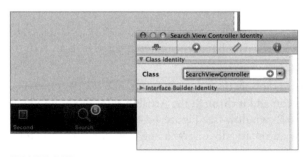

FIGURE 4-52

FIGURE 4-53

How It Works

In this example, you added a Tab Bar Item view to the Tab Bar view and connected it to an XIB file and its corresponding View Controller class.

Adding new Tab Bar Item views is straightforward: Simply drag the Tab Bar Item from the Library and drop it into the Tab Bar view. Alternatively, you can add it through the Attributes Inspector window for the Tab Bar Controller item in the `MainWindow.xib` window (see Figure 4-54). Click the + (plus) button to add new View Controllers, and the Tab Bar view automatically inserts a new Tab Bar Item view for you.

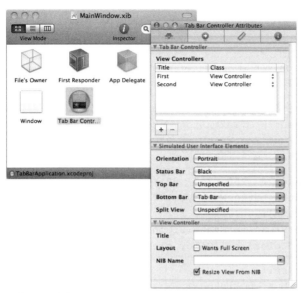

FIGURE 4-54

SUMMARY

This chapter provided a detailed look at the application templates provided by the iPhone SDK: View-based Application, Window-based Application, Split View-based Application, and Tab Bar Application. Each one uses a different type of View Controller. It is important that you have a good understanding of how the various pieces of an iPad project are put together — knowing that will allow you to build applications with sophisticated user interfaces.

EXERCISES

1. Write the code snippet that allows you to create a View Controller programmatically.

2. Write the code snippet that creates a view dynamically during runtime.

3. Write the code snippet that wires an event of a view with an event handler.

4. In the `windowBasedApp` project created earlier in this chapter, create an action to display an alert view when the button in the `HelloWorldViewController` class is pressed.

Answers to the Exercises can be found in Appendix A.

▶ **WHAT YOU LEARNED IN THIS CHAPTER**

TOPIC	KEY CONCEPTS
Types of iPad Applications	View-based Application, Window-based Application, Split View-based Application, and Tab Bar Application

Creating a `Label` view by code	```label = [[UILabel alloc] initWithFrame:frame];```
	```label.textAlignment = UITextAlignmentCenter;```
	```label.font = [UIFont fontWithName:@"Verdana" size:20];```
	```label.text = @"This is a label";```

Creating a `Button` view by code	```frame = CGRectMake(10, 250, 300, 50);```
	```button = [[UIButton buttonWithType:UIButtonTypeRoundedRect] initWithFrame:frame];```
	```[button setTitle:@"OK" forState:UIControlStateNormal];```
	```button.backgroundColor = [UIColor clearColor];```

Wiring up an event with an event handler	```button addTarget:self```
	```action:@selector(buttonClicked:)```
	```forControlEvents:```
	```UIControlEventTouchUpInside];```

Switching to another view	```//---instantiate the second view controller---```
	```mySecondViewController = [[MySecondViewController alloc]```
	``` initWithNibName:nil```
	``` bundle:nil];```
	```//---add the view from the second view controller---```
	```[window addSubview:mySecondViewController.view];```

Animating the view transition	```UIView beginAnimations:@"flipping view"```
	```context:nil];```
	```[UIView setAnimationDuration:1];```
	```[UIView```
	```setAnimationCurve:```
	```UIViewAnimationCurveEaseInOut];```
	```[UIView setAnimationTransition:```
	```UIViewAnimationTransitionFlipFromLeft```
	```forView:self.view cache:YES];```
	```[self.view addSubview:viewController.view];```
	```[UIView commitAnimations];```

5

Keyboard Inputs

WHAT YOU WILL LEARN IN THIS CHAPTER:

➤ How to customize the keyboard for different types of inputs

➤ The different ways to make the keyboard go away when you are done typing

➤ How to detect when a keyboard is visible or not

➤ How to shift views to make way for the keyboard

One of the controversial aspects of the iPad is the multi-touch keyboard that allows users to input data into their iPad. Critics of the iPad (as well as the iPhone) have criticized its lack of a physical keyboard for data entry (short of buying an external keyboard accessory for it), whereas ardent supporters of virtual keyboard swear by its ease of use.

What makes the iPad keyboard so powerful is its intelligence in tracking what you type, followed by suggestions for the word you are typing, and automatically correcting the spelling and inserting punctuation for you. What's more, the keyboard knows when to appear at the right time — it appears when you tap a TextField view, and it goes away automatically when you tap a non-input view. Also, it lets you input data in different languages.

For iPad application programmers, the key concern is how to integrate the keyboard into their applications. How do you make the keyboard go away naturally when it is no longer needed? And how do you ensure that the view the user is currently interacting with is not blocked by the keyboard? In this chapter, you learn various ways to deal with the keyboard programmatically.

USING THE KEYBOARD

In iPad programming, the views most commonly associated with the keyboard are the TextField view and the TextView view. When a TextField view is tapped (or clicked, if you are using the Simulator), the keyboard is automatically displayed. The data that the user taps on the keyboard is then inserted into the TextField view. The following Try It Out demonstrates this.

TRY IT OUT Using a TextField for Inputs

---

codefile KeyboardInputs.zip available for download at Wrox.com

---

1. Using Xcode, create a new View-based Application project and name it KeyboardInputs.

2. Double-click the KeyboardInputsViewController.xib file to edit it using Interface Builder.

3. Populate the View window with the Label and TextField views (see Figure 5-1). Set the Label view to display the text "Alphanumeric Input."

FIGURE 5-1

4. Save the `KeyboardInputsViewController.xib` file and press Command-R in Xcode to run the application on the iPhone Simulator. When the application is loaded, the keyboard is initially hidden, and when the user clicks the TextField view, the keyboard automatically appears (see Figure 5-2).

FIGURE 5-2

How It Works

The beauty of the iPad user interface is that when the system detects that the current active view is a TextField view, the keyboard automatically appears; you don't need to do anything to bring up the keyboard. Using the keyboard, you can enter alphanumeric data as well as numbers and special characters (such as symbols). The keyboard in iPad also supports characters of languages other than English, such as Chinese and Hebrew.

To hide the keyboard, click the button located at the bottom right of the keyboard.

CUSTOMIZING THE TYPE OF INPUTS

To learn more about the input behaviors, go to Interface Builder, select the TextField view, and view its Attributes Inspector window (choose Tools ➪ Attributes Inspector). Figure 5-3 shows that window. In particular, pay attention to the section labeled Text Input Traits.

The Text Input Traits section contains several items for you to use to configure how the keyboard handles the text entered.

FIGURE 5-3

➤ **Capitalize** — Allows you to capitalize the words, sentences, or all characters of the data entered via the keyboard.

➤ **Correction** — Lets you indicate whether you want the keyboard to provide suggestions for words that are not spelled correctly. You can also choose the Default option, which defaults to the user's global text correction settings.

➤ **Keyboard** — Allows you to choose the different types of keyboard for entering different types of data. Figure 5-4 shows (from top to bottom) the keyboard configured with the following Keyboard types: Email Address, Phone Pad/Number Pad, and URL.

➤ **Appearance** — Lets you choose how the keyboard should appear.

➤ **Return Key** — Allows you to show different types of Return key in your keyboard (see Figure 5-5). Figure 5-6 shows the keyboard set with the Google key serving as the Return key (the Return key appears as "Search").

➤ **Auto-Enable Return Key** check box — Indicates that if no input is entered for a field, the Return key will be disabled (grayed out). It will be enabled again if at least one character is entered.

➤ **Secure** check box — Indicates if the input will be masked (see Figure 5-7). This is usually used for password input.

FIGURE 5-4

FIGURE 5-5

FIGURE 5-6

FIGURE 5-7

Making the Keyboard Go Away

You know that the keyboard in the iPad automatically appears when a TextField view is selected. You have three ways to make the keyboard go away.

First, simply tapping the key located on the bottom right of the keyboard always dismisses the keyboard. This method requires no programming effort on your part.

Second, you can dismiss the keyboard by tapping the Return key on the keyboard. This method requires you to handle the `Did End on Exit` event of the TextField view that caused the keyboard to appear. This method is demonstrated in the following Try It Out.

Third, you can dismiss the keyboard when the user taps outside a TextField view. This method, which requires some additional coding, makes your application very user-friendly. The subsequent Try It Out illustrates this method.

TRY IT OUT   Dismissing the Keyboard (Technique 1)

1.   Using the `KeyboardInputs` project, edit the `KeyboardInputsViewController.h` file and add in the following bold statements:

```
#import <UIKit/UIKit.h>

@interface KeyboardInputsViewController : UIViewController {

}

-(IBAction) doneEditing:(id) sender;

@end
```

2.   Double-click the `KeyboardInputsViewController.xib` file to edit it in Interface Builder. Right-click the TextField view in the View window and then click the circle next to the `Did End on Exit` event and drag it to the File's Owner item (see Figure 5-8). The `doneEditing:` action you have just created should appear. Select it.

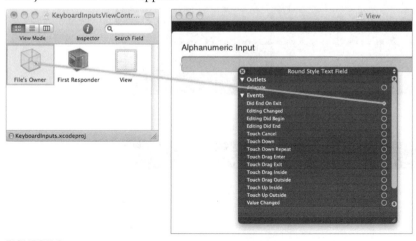

FIGURE 5-8

3. Save the `KeyboardInputsViewController.xib` file.

4. In the `KeyboardInputsViewController.m` file, provide the implementation for the
`doneEditing:` action:

```
#import "KeyboardInputsViewController.h"

@implementation KeyboardInputsViewController

-(IBAction) doneEditing:(id) sender{
    [sender resignFirstResponder];
}
```

5. Save the project and press Command-R to run the application on the iPhone Simulator.

6. When the application appears on the iPhone Simulator, tap the TextField view. The keyboard
should appear. Using the keyboard, type some text into the view and click the Return key when
you are done. The keyboard now goes away.

How It Works

What you have just done is connect the `Did End on Exit` event of the TextField view with the `done-
Editing:` action you have created. When you are editing the content of a TextField view using the key-
board, clicking the Return key on the keyboard fires the `Did End on Edit` event of the TextField view.
In this case, it invokes the `doneEditing:` action, which contains the following statement:

```
[sender resignFirstResponder];
```

The `sender` in this case refers to the TextField view, and `resignFirstResponder` asks the TextField
view to resign its First-Responder status. Essentially, it means that you do not want to interact with the
TextField view anymore and that the keyboard is no longer needed. Hence, the keyboard should hide itself.

> **NOTE** *The First Responder in a view always refers to the current view that the
> user is interacting with. In this example, when you click the TextField view, it
> becomes the First Responder and activates the keyboard automatically.*

An alternative way of hiding the keyboard is when the user taps an area outside of the TextField
view. This method is more natural and does not require the user to manually tap on the Return
key on the keyboard to hide the keyboard. The following Try It Out shows how this method can be
implemented.

TRY IT OUT   Dismissing the Keyboard (Technique 2)

1. Using the `KeyboardInputs` project, double-click the `KeyboardInputsViewController.xib` file to
edit it using Interface Builder.

2. Add a Round Rect Button view to the View window (see Figure 5-9).

FIGURE 5-9

3. With the Round Rect Button view selected, choose Layout ⇨ Send to Back. This makes the button appear behind the other controls.

4. Resize the Round Rect Button view so that it now covers the entire screen (see Figure 5-10).

FIGURE 5-10

5. In the Attributes Inspector window, set the Type of the Round Rect Button view to Custom (see Figure 5-11).

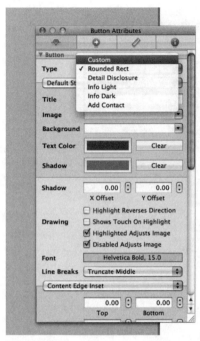

FIGURE 5-11

6. In Xcode, edit the `KeyboardInputsViewController.h` file and add the following bold statements:

```
#import <UIKit/UIKit.h>

@interface KeyboardInputsViewController : UIViewController {
    IBOutlet UITextField *textField;
}

@property (nonatomic, retain) UITextField *textField;

-(IBAction) doneEditing:(id) sender;

-(IBAction) bgTouched:(id) sender;

@end
```

7. In Interface Builder, Control-click and drag the File's Owner item onto the TextField view. The `textField` outlet should appear. Select it.

8. Control-click and drag the Round Rect Button view onto the File's Owner item in the `KeyboardInputsViewController.xib` window (see Figure 5-12). Select the `bgTouched:` action.

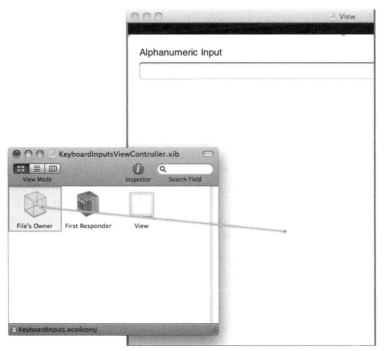

FIGURE 5-12

 NOTE *The* `Touch Up Inside` *event of the Round Rect Button view is wired to the* `bgTouched:` *action.*

9. Save the XIB file in Interface Builder.

10. In the `KeyboardInputsViewController.m` file, add the following statements highlighted in bold:

```
#import "KeyboardInputsViewController.h"

@implementation KeyboardInputsViewController

@synthesize textField;

-(IBAction) bgTouched:(id) sender{
    [textField resignFirstResponder];
}

-(IBAction) doneEditing:(id) sender{
    [sender resignFirstResponder];
}
```

11. That's it. Press Command-R in Xcode to deploy the application onto the iPhone Simulator. Then, try the following:

➤ Click the TextField view to bring up the keyboard.

➤ When you are done, click the Return key on the keyboard to dismiss it. Alternatively, click any of the empty spaces outside the TextField view to dismiss the keyboard.

How It Works

In this example, you added a Round Rect Button view to cover up all the empty spaces in the View window of your application. Essentially, the button acts as a net to trap all touches outside of the TextField view on the View window. So when the user clicks (or taps, on a real device) the screen outside the keyboard and the TextField view, the Round Rect Button fires the Touch Up Inside event, which is handled by the bgTouched: action. In the bgTouched: action, you explicitly asked textField to resign its First-Responder status, which causes the keyboard to disappear.

The technique used in this example applies even if you have multiple TextField views on your view. Suppose you have three TextField views, with outlets named textField, textField2, and textField3. In that case, the bgTouched: action looks like this:

```
-(IBAction) bgTouched:(id) sender{
    [textField resignFirstResponder];
    [textField2 resignFirstResponder];
    [textField3 resignFirstResponder];
}
```

So when the bgTouched: action is invoked, all three TextField views are asked to relinquish their First-Responder status. Calling the resignFirstResponder method on a view that is currently not the First Responder is harmless; hence, the preceding statements are safe and will not cause an exception during runtime.

UNDERSTANDING THE RESPONDER CHAIN

The prior Try It Out is a good example of the responder chain in action. In the iPad, events passed through a series of event handlers known as the *responder chain*. As you touch the screen of your iPad, the iPad generates events that get passed up the responder chain. Each object in the responder chain checks to see if it can handle the event. In the preceding example, when the user taps on the Label view, the Label view checks to see if it can handle the event. Because the Label event does not handle the Touch event, it is passed up the responder chain. The large background button that you have added is now next in line to examine the event. Because it handles the Touch Up Inside event, the event is consumed by the button.

In summary, objects higher up in the responder chain examine the event first and handle the event if it is applicable. Any object can then stop the propagation of the event up the responder chain, or pass the event up the responder chain if it only partially handles the event.

Automatically Displaying the Keyboard When the View Is Loaded

Sometimes you might want to straightaway set a TextField view as the active view and display the keyboard without waiting for the user to do so. In such cases, you can use the `becomeFirstResponder` method of the view. The following code shows that the TextField view will be the First Responder as soon as the View window is loaded:

```
- (void)viewDidLoad {
    [textField becomeFirstResponder];
    [super viewDidLoad];
}
```

DETECTING THE PRESENCE OF THE KEYBOARD

Up to this point, you have seen the various ways to hide the keyboard after you are done using it. However, there is one problem that you need to note. When the keyboard appears, it takes up a significant portion of the screen. If your TextField view is located at the bottom of the screen, it would be covered by the keyboard. As a programmer, it is your duty to ensure that the view is relocated to a visible portion of the screen. Surprisingly, this is not taken care of by the SDK; you have to do the hard work yourself.

 NOTE *The current keyboard in the iPad takes up 264 pixels in height when in Portrait mode, and 352 pixels when in Landscape mode.*

First, though, it is important for you to understand a few key concepts related to the keyboard:

➤ You need to be able to programmatically know when a keyboard is visible or hidden. To do so, your application needs to register `UIKeyboardWillShowNotification` and `UIKeyboardWillHideNotification`.

➤ You also need to know when and which TextField view is currently being edited so that you can relocate it to a visible portion of the screen. You can know these two pieces of information through the two delegate protocols — `textFieldDidBeginEditing:` and `textFieldDidEndEditing:` — available in the `UITextFieldDelegate` protocol.

Confused? Worry not; the following Try It Out makes it all clear.

TRY IT OUT Shifting Views

codefile ScrollingViews.zip available for download at Wrox.com

1. Using Xcode, create a new View-based Application project and name it `ScrollingViews`.

2. Populate the View with a ScrollView view (see Figure 5-13). Resize the ScrollView view so it covers the entire screen.

FIGURE 5-13

3. Add a Label view, TextField field and a Round Rect Button view onto the ScrollView (see Figure 5-14). Set the Label view to display the text "Enter some text here" and the Button to "OK."

Enter some text here

OK

FIGURE 5-14

4. In Xcode, type the following statements highlighted in bold into the
ScrollingViewsViewController.h file and save it:

```
#import <UIKit/UIKit.h>

@interface ScrollingViewsViewController : UIViewController
    <UITextFieldDelegate> {

    IBOutlet UIScrollView *scrollView;
    IBOutlet UITextField *textField;
```

```
        UITextField *currTextField;
}

@property (nonatomic, retain) UITextField *textField;
@property (nonatomic, retain) UIScrollView *scrollView;

@end
```

5. In Interface Builder, Control-click and drag the File's Owner item onto the TextField view (see Figure 5-15). Select `textField`.

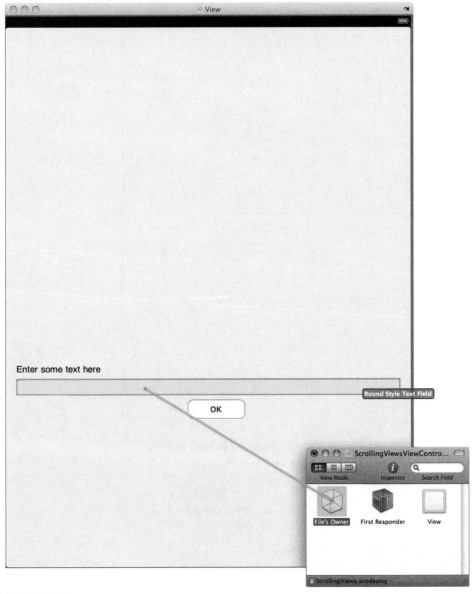

FIGURE 5-15

6. Control-click and drag the File's Owner item onto the ScrollView view (see Figure 5-16). Select `scrollView`.

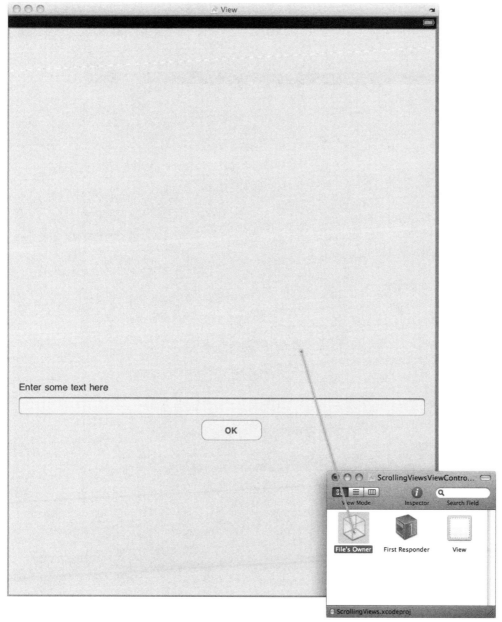

FIGURE 5-16

7. Control-click and drag the TextField view onto the File's Owner item (see Figure 5-17). Select `delegate`.

NOTE *Step 7 is important because it enables the delegate protocols* (`textFieldDidBeginEditing:` *and* `textFieldDidEndEditing:`) *to be handled by your View Controller.*

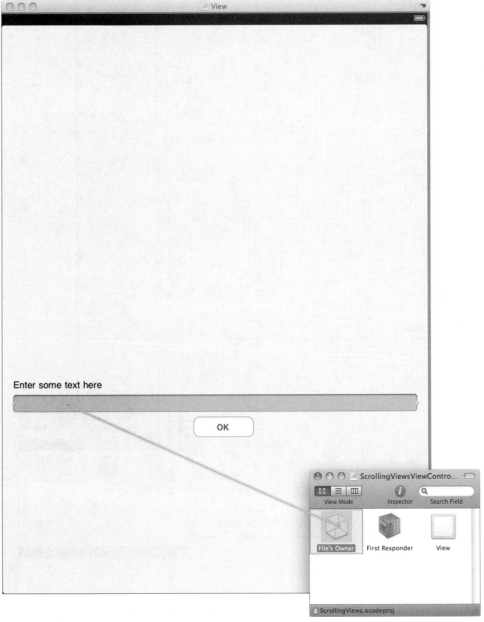

FIGURE 5-17

8.   Save the `ScrollViewsViewController.xib` in Interface Builder.

9.   Type the following statements **highlighted in bold** in the `ScrollingViewsViewController.m` file:

```
#import "ScrollingViewsViewController.h"

@implementation ScrollingViewsViewController

@synthesize textField;
@synthesize scrollView;

//---size of keyboard---
CGRect keyboardBounds;

//---size of application screen---
CGRect applicationFrame;

//---original size of ScrollView---
CGSize scrollViewOriginalSize;

-(void) moveScrollView:(UIView *) theView {

    //---get the y-coordinate of the view---
    CGFloat viewCenterY = theView.center.y;

    //---calculate how much visible space is left---
    CGFloat freeSpaceHeight =
        applicationFrame.size.height - keyboardBounds.size.height;

    //---calculate how much the scrollview must scroll---
    CGFloat scrollAmount = viewCenterY - freeSpaceHeight / 2.0;

    if (scrollAmount < 0)  scrollAmount = 0;

    //---set the new scrollView contentSize---
    scrollView.contentSize = CGSizeMake(applicationFrame.size.width,
                                        applicationFrame.size.height +
                                        keyboardBounds.size.height);

    //---scroll the ScrollView---
    [scrollView setContentOffset:CGPointMake(0, scrollAmount)
                        animated:YES];
}

//---when a TextField view begins editing---
-(void) textFieldDidBeginEditing:(UITextField *)textFieldView {
    currTextField = textFieldView;
}

//---when a TextField view is done editing---
-(void) textFieldDidEndEditing:(UITextField *) textFieldView {
    [UIView beginAnimations:@"back to original size" context:nil];
    scrollView.contentSize = scrollViewOriginalSize;
    [UIView commitAnimations];
}
```

```
//---when the keyboard appears---
-(void) keyboardWillShow:(NSNotification *) notification {
    //---gets the size of the keyboard---
    NSDictionary *userInfo = [notification userInfo];
    NSValue *keyboardValue =
        [userInfo objectForKey:UIKeyboardBoundsUserInfoKey];
    [keyboardValue getValue:&keyboardBounds];

    [self moveScrollView:currTextField];
}

//---when the keyboard disappears---
-(void) keyboardWillHide:(NSNotification *) notification {

}

-(void) viewWillAppear:(BOOL)animated {
    //---registers the notifications for keyboard---
    [[NSNotificationCenter defaultCenter]
        addObserver:self
            selector:@selector(keyboardWillShow:)
                name:UIKeyboardWillShowNotification
              object:self.view.window];

    [[NSNotificationCenter defaultCenter]
        addObserver:self
            selector:@selector(keyboardWillHide:)
                name:UIKeyboardWillHideNotification
              object:nil];
}

-(void) viewWillDisappear:(BOOL)animated {
    [[NSNotificationCenter defaultCenter]
        removeObserver:self
                  name:UIKeyboardWillShowNotification
                object:nil];

    [[NSNotificationCenter defaultCenter]
        removeObserver:self
                  name:UIKeyboardWillHideNotification
                object:nil];
}

-(void) viewDidLoad {
    scrollViewOriginalSize = scrollView.contentSize;
    applicationFrame = [[UIScreen mainScreen] applicationFrame];
    [super viewDidLoad];
}

-(BOOL) textFieldShouldReturn:(UITextField *) textFieldView {
    if (textFieldView == textField){
        [textField resignFirstResponder];
    }
```

```
        return NO;
}

-(void) dealloc {
    [textField release];
    [scrollView release];
    [super dealloc];
}
```

10. Save the project in Xcode and press Command-R to deploy the application onto the iPhone Simulator. Figure 5-18 shows that when you click the TextField view, the keyboard appears and the TextField view (along with other views) is scrolled to the center of the screen. To hide the keyboard, simply click the Return key, and the views are restored to their original positions.

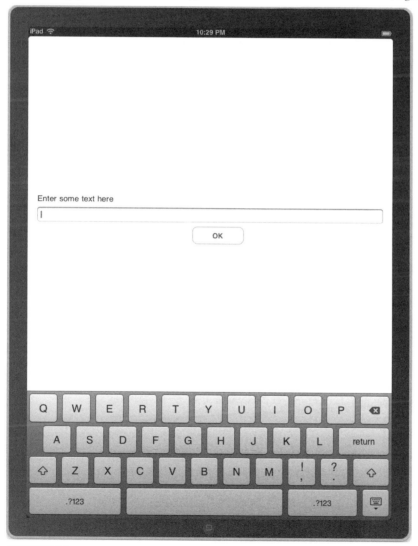

FIGURE 5-18

How It Works

This example demonstrates the various ways in which you can detect the presence of a keyboard and how the view involved can be relocated so that it is not covered by the keyboard.

First, you declare three private variables:

```
//---size of keyboard---
CGRect keyboardBounds;

//---size of application screen---
CGRect applicationFrame;

//---original size of ScrollView---
CGSize scrollViewOriginalSize;
```

The `keyboardBounds` is used to store the size of the keyboard (in particular, to obtain the height of the keyboard). Although you can always hard-code the height of the keyboard to be 264, I don't recommend doing so because the size of the keyboard may change at a later time. A better practice is to dynamically obtain the size of the keyboard during runtime.

The `applicationFrame` is used to store the size of the screen. As with the size of the keyboard, it is always better to obtain this figure dynamically during runtime.

The `scrollViewOriginalSize` is used to save the original size of the ScrollView view. Doing so allows you to restore the ScrollView to its original size after the user is done with the editing (at which time all the views need to be moved back to their original positions).

When the View is loaded, you first save the size of the ScrollView view as well as obtain the size of the screen:

```
-(void) viewDidLoad {
    scrollViewOriginalSize = scrollView.contentSize;
    applicationFrame = [[UIScreen mainScreen] applicationFrame];
    [super viewDidLoad];
}
```

In the `viewWillAppear:` event (this method is invoked before the View appears on-screen), you register for the two notifications — `UIKeyboardWillShowNotification` and `UIKeyboardWillHideNotification`. When the keyboard appears (`UIKeyboardWillShowNotification`), the `keyboardWillShow:` method is invoked. When the keyboard disappears, the `keyboardWillHide:` method is invoked:

```
-(void) viewWillAppear:(BOOL)animated {
    //---registers the notifications for keyboard---
    [[NSNotificationCenter defaultCenter]
        addObserver:self
           selector:@selector(keyboardWillShow:)
               name:UIKeyboardWillShowNotification
             object:self.view.window];

    [[NSNotificationCenter defaultCenter]
        addObserver:self
```

```
            selector:@selector(keyboardWillHide:)
                name:UIKeyboardWillHideNotification
              object:nil];
}
```

Before the View disappears, you remove the notifications you had previously set:

```
-(void) viewWillDisappear:(BOOL)animated {
    [[NSNotificationCenter defaultCenter]
        removeObserver:self
                  name:UIKeyboardWillShowNotification
                object:nil];

    [[NSNotificationCenter defaultCenter]
        removeObserver:self
                  name:UIKeyboardWillHideNotification
                object:nil];
}
```

When you tap a TextField view, the `textFieldDidBeginEditing:` method will first be invoked. With this method, you can know which TextField view is being edited:

```
//---when a TextField view begins editing---
-(void) textFieldDidBeginEditing:(UITextField *)textFieldView {
    currTextField = textFieldView;
}
```

Next, the `keyboardWillShow:` method is invoked. With this method, you try to obtain the size of the keyboard by passing a reference to the `keyboardBounds` variable. You are now ready to move the ScrollView view so that the TextField view can be centered in the remaining visible space not covered by the keyboard. You perform the scrolling by calling the `moveScrollView:` method, which you define next:

```
//---when the keyboard appears---
-(void) keyboardWillShow:(NSNotification *) notification {
    //---gets the size of the keyboard---
    NSDictionary *userInfo = [notification userInfo];
    NSValue *keyboardValue =
        [userInfo objectForKey:UIKeyboardBoundsUserInfoKey];
    [keyboardValue getValue:&keyboardBounds];

    [self moveScrollView:currTextField];
}
```

In the `moveScrollView:` method, you calculate the number of pixels to scroll and then get the ScrollView view to scroll the views contained within it until the TextField view currently being edited is at the center of the visible area of the screen:

```
-(void) moveScrollView:(UIView *) theView {
    //---get the y-coordinate of the view---
    CGFloat viewCenterY = theView.center.y;
```

```
    //---calculate how much visible space is left---
    CGFloat freeSpaceHeight =
        applicationFrame.size.height - keyboardBounds.size.height;

    //---calculate how much the scrollview must scroll---
    CGFloat scrollAmount = viewCenterY - freeSpaceHeight / 2.0;

    if (scrollAmount < 0)  scrollAmount = 0;

    //---set the new scrollView contentSize---
    scrollView.contentSize = CGSizeMake(applicationFrame.size.width,
                                applicationFrame.size.height +
                                keyboardBounds.size.height);

    //---scroll the ScrollView---
    [scrollView setContentOffset:CGPointMake(0, scrollAmount)
                        animated:YES];
}
```

When the TextField view resigns its First Responder status, the `textFieldDidEndEditing:` method will be invoked. At this point, you restore the ScrollView view to its original content size:

```
//---when a TextField view is done editing---
-(void) textFieldDidEndEditing:(UITextField *) textFieldView {
    [UIView beginAnimations:@"back to original size" context:nil];
    scrollView.contentSize = scrollViewOriginalSize;
    [UIView commitAnimations];
}
```

A noteworthy point here is that you use the `beginAnimations` method of the `UIView` class to animate the ScrollView view in the process of restoring to its original size. If you do not use this method, the ScrollView will very abruptly restore to its original size, causing a flicker.

Just before the keyboard disappears, the `keyboardWillHide:` method is invoked. In this case, you don't have much to do:

```
//---when the keyboard disappears---
-(void) keyboardWillHide:(NSNotification *) notification {

}
```

Finally, in the `dealloc` method, you release all the outlets you have created:

```
-(void) dealloc {
    [textField release];
    [scrollView release];
    [super dealloc];
}
```

HANDLING THE RETURN KEY OF THE KEYBOARD

Earlier, you saw how you can connect an IBAction with the Did End On Exit event of a TextField view to hide the keyboard when the user taps the Return key. Alternatively, you can also implement the textFieldShouldReturn: method (defined in the UITextFieldDelegate protocol). This method is invoked whenever the user taps the Return key on the keyboard:

```
-(BOOL) textFieldShouldReturn:(UITextField *) textFieldView {
    if (textFieldView == textField){
        [textField resignFirstResponder];
    }
    return NO;
}
```

SUMMARY

In this chapter, you learned the various techniques to deal with the keyboard in your iPad application. In particular, this chapter showed you how to make the keyboard go away when you are done with the data entry, how to detect the presence or absence of the keyboard, and how to ensure that views are not blocked by the keyboard.

EXERCISES

1. How do you hide the keyboard for a UITextField object?

2. How do you detect whether the keyboard is visible or not?

3. How do you get the size of the keyboard?

Answers to the Exercises can be found in Appendix A.

▶ **WHAT YOU LEARNED IN THIS CHAPTER**

TOPIC	KEY CONCEPTS
Making the keyboard go away	Use the `resignFirstResponder` method on a `UITextField` object to resign its First-Responder status.
Displaying the different types of keyboard displayed	Modify the keyboard type by changing the Text Input Traits of a `UITextField` object in the Attributes Inspector window.
Handling the return key of the keyboard	You either handle the `Did End on Exit` event of a `UITextField` object, or implement the `textFieldShouldReturn:` method in your view controller (remember to ensure that your view controller class is the delegate for the `UITextField` object).
Detecting when the keyboard appears or hides	Register for the two notifications — `UIKeyboardWillShowNotification` and `UIKeyboardWillHideNotification`.
Detecting which `UITextField` object has started editing	Implement the `textFieldDidBeginEditing:` method in your view controller.
Detecting which `UITextField` object has ended editing	Implement the `textFieldDidEndEditing:` method in your view controller.

Screen Rotations

➤ How to support the four different types of screen orientations

➤ The various events that are fired when a device rotates

➤ How to reposition the views on a View when the orientation of a device changes

➤ How to change the screen rotation dynamically during runtime

➤ How to set the orientation of your application before it is loaded

The Hello World! application in Chapter 2 showed you how your iPad application supports viewing in either the portrait or landscape mode. This chapter dives deeper into the topic of screen orientation. In particular, it demonstrates how to manage the orientation of your application when the device is rotated. You will also learn how to reposition your views when the device is rotated so that your application can take advantage of the change in screen dimensions.

RESPONDING TO DEVICE ROTATIONS

One of the features that modern mobile devices support is the capability to detect the current orientation — portrait or landscape — of the device. An application can take advantage of this to readjust the device's screen to maximize the use of the new orientation. A good example is Safari on the iPad. When you rotate the device to landscape orientation, Safari automatically rotates its view so that you have a wider screen to view the content of the page (see Figure 6-1).

In the iPhone SDK, there are several events that you can handle to ensure that your application is aware of changes in orientation. Check them out in the following Try it Out.

FIGURE 6-1

Supporting Different Screen Orientations

codefile ScreenRotations.zip available for download at Wrox.com

1. Using Xcode, create a new View-based Application project and name it ScreenRotations.

2. Press Command-R to test the application on the iPhone Simulator.

3. Change the iPhone Simulator orientation by pressing either the Command ⇨ (rotate it to the right) or Command ⇦ (rotate it to the left) key combination. Notice that the screen orientation of your application changes with the change in device orientation (see Figure 6-2 and Figure 6-3).

FIGURE 6-2

FIGURE 6-3

How It Works

By default, the iPad application project you created using Xcode supports all orientations — portrait as well as landscape modes. This is evident in the `ScreenRotationsViewController.m` file, where you have the `shouldAutorotateToInterfaceOrientation:` method:

```
- (BOOL)shouldAutorotateToInterfaceOrientation:
(UIInterfaceOrientation)interfaceOrientation {
    return YES;
}
```

> **NOTE** On the iPad, screen rotation is automatically handled by the OS. When the OS detects a change in screen orientation, it fires the `shouldAutorotate-ToInterfaceOrientation:` event; it is up to the developer to decide how the application should display in the target orientation.

The shouldAutorotateToInterfaceOrientation: method is called when the View is loaded and when orientation of the device changes. This method passes in a single parameter — the orientation that the device has been changed to. The returning value of this event determines whether the current orientation is supported. By default, your iPad application supports all screen orientations, hence it simply returns a YES.

This means that your application will rotate to all orientations (the status bar will always appear at the top) when the device is rotated.

To support specific orientations, simply perform an equality check to specify the orientation supported. For example, the following code snippet shows that only the landscape left orientation is supported.

```
- (BOOL)shouldAutorotateToInterfaceOrientation:
(UIInterfaceOrientation)interfaceOrientation {
    //return YES;
    return (interfaceOrientation ==
        UIInterfaceOrientationLandscapeLeft);
}
```

This means that your application will display upright only in landscape mode with the Home button on its left (hence the constant name UIInterfaceOrientationLandscapeLeft).

If the user rotates the device to portrait mode or landscape mode with the Home button on the right (UIInterfaceOrientationLandscapeRight), the application will not change its orientation.

While you can specify the orientation supported by your application, Apple has specifically indicated that your application should support all screen orientations.

NOTE *Here is one easy way to differentiate between* UIInterfaceOrientationLandscapeLeft *and* UIInterfaceOrientationLandscapeRight. *Just remember that* UIInterfaceOrientationLandscapeLeft *refers to the Home button positioned on the left and* UIInterfaceOrientationLandscapeRight *refers to the Home button positioned on the right.*

Different Types of Screen Orientations

You have a total of four constants to use for specifying screen orientations:

➤ UIInterfaceOrientationPortrait — Displays the screen in portrait mode

➤ UIInterfaceOrientationPortraitUpsideDown — Displays the screen in portrait mode but with the Home button at the top of the screen

➤ UIInterfaceOrientationLandscapeLeft — Displays the screen in landscape mode with the Home button on the left

➤ UIInterfaceOrientationLandscapeRight — Displays the screen in landscape mode with the Home button on the right

If your application supports multiple screen orientations, override the `shouldAutorotateTo-InterfaceOrientation:` method and then use the || (logical OR) operator to specify all the orientations it supports, like this:

```
- (BOOL)shouldAutorotateToInterfaceOrientation:
(UIInterfaceOrientation)interfaceOrientation {

    return (interfaceOrientation == UIInterfaceOrientationPortrait ||
            interfaceOrientation == UIInterfaceOrientationLandscapeRight);

}
```

The preceding code snippet enables your application to support both the portrait and landscape right modes.

Handling Rotations

The View Controller exposes several events that you can handle during the rotation of the screen. The capability to handle events fired during rotation is important because it allows you to reposition the views on the View, or you can stop media playback while the screen is rotating. The events that you can handle are:

➤   `willAnimateFirstHalfOfRotationToInterfaceOrientation:`

➤   `willAnimateSecondHalfOfRotationFromInterfaceOrientation:`

➤   `willRotateToInterfaceOrientation:`

➤   `willAnimateRotationToInterfaceOrientation:`

The following sections take a more detailed look at each of these events.

willAnimateFirstHalfOfRotationToInterfaceOrientation:

The `willAnimateFirstHalfOfRotationToInterfaceOrientation:` event is fired just before the rotation of the View starts. The method looks like this:

```
- (void)willAnimateFirstHalfOfRotationToInterfaceOrientation:
(UIInterfaceOrientation) toInterfaceOrientation
duration: (NSTimeInterval) duration {

}
```

The `toInterfaceOrientation` parameter indicates the orientation that the View is changing to, and the `duration` parameter indicates the duration of the first half of the rotation, in seconds.

In this event, you can insert your code to carry out tasks that you want to perform before the rotation starts, such as pausing media playback, pausing animations, and so on.

willAnimateSecondHalfOfRotationFromInterfaceOrientation:

The `willAnimateSecondHalfOfRotationFromInterfaceOrientation:` event is fired when the rotation is halfway through. The method looks like this:

```
- (void)willAnimateSecondHalfOfRotationFromInterfaceOrientation:
(UIInterfaceOrientation) fromInterfaceOrientation
duration: (NSTimeInterval) duration {

}
```

The `fromInterfaceOrientation` parameter indicates the orientation that it is changing from, whereas the `duration` parameter indicates the duration of the second half of the rotation, in seconds.

In this event, you typically perform tasks such as repositioning the views on the View, resuming media playback, and so on.

willRotateToInterfaceOrientation:

The previous two events are fired consecutively — first the `willAnimateFirstHalfOfRotationTo-InterfaceOrientation:`, followed by the `willAnimateSecondHalfOfRotationFromInterface-Orientation` event. If you do not need two separate events for handling rotation, you can use the simpler `willRotateToInterfaceOrientation:` event.

The `willRotateToInterfaceOrientation:` event is fired before the orientation starts. In contrast to the previous two events, this is a one-step process. Note that if you handle this event, the `willAnimateFirstHalfOfRotationToInterfaceOrientation:` and `willAnimateSecond-HalfOfRotationFromInterfaceOrientation:` events will still be fired.

The method looks like this:

```
- (void)willRotateToInterfaceOrientation:
(UIInterfaceOrientation) toInterfaceOrientation
duration: (NSTimeInterval) duration {

}
```

The `toInterfaceOrientation` parameter indicates the orientation that it is changing to, and the `duration` parameter indicates the duration of the rotation, in seconds.

willAnimateRotationToInterfaceOrientation:

The `willAnimateRotationToInterfaceOrientation:` event is fired before the animation of the rotation starts.

 NOTE *If you handle both the* `willRotateToInterfaceOrientation:` *and* `willAnimateRotationToInterfaceOrientation:` *events, the former will fire first, followed by the latter.*

The method looks like this:

```
- (void)willAnimateRotationToInterfaceOrientation:
(UIInterfaceOrientation) interfaceOrientation
duration: (NSTimeInterval) duration {

}
```

The `interfaceOrientation` parameter specifies the target orientation to which it is rotating.

 NOTE *If you handle this event, the* `willAnimateFirstHalfOfRotationTo-` `InterfaceOrientation:` *and* `willAnimateSecondHalfOfRotationFrom-` `InterfaceOrientation:` *events will not fire anymore.*

In the following Try It Out, you will reposition the views on your user interface (UI) when the device changes orientation.

TRY IT OUT   **Repositioning Views during Orientation Change**

1.   Using the project created earlier, double-click the `ScreenRotationsViewController.xib` file and add a Round Rect Button view to the View (see Figure 6-4).

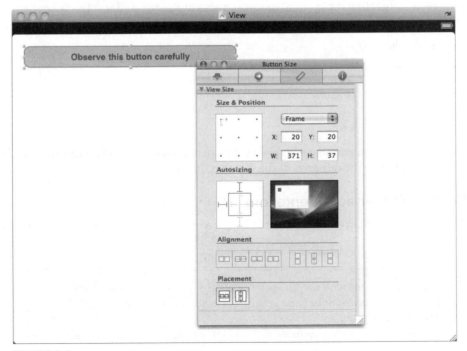

FIGURE 6-4

2. Observe its size and positioning by viewing the Size Inspector window. Here, its position is (20,20) and its size is 371 by 37 pixels.

3. Rotate the orientation of the View by clicking the arrow icon on the upper-right corner of the window.

4. Reposition the Round Rect Button view by relocating it to the bottom-right corner of the View window (see Figure 6-5). Also observe and take note of its position.

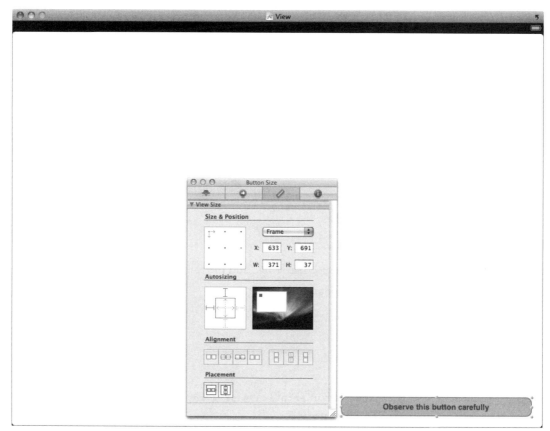

FIGURE 6-5

5. In the `ScreenRotationsViewController.h` file, add the following code shown in bold:

```
#import <UIKit/UIKit.h>

@interface ScreenRotationsViewController : UIViewController {
    IBOutlet UIButton *btn;
}

@property (nonatomic, retain) UIButton *btn;

@end
```

6. In Interface Builder, connect the outlet you have created by control-clicking the File's Owner item and dragging over to the Round Rect Button view (see Figure 6-6). Select `btn`.

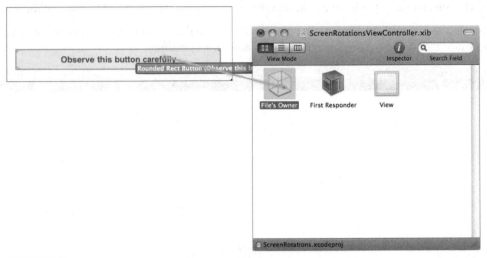

FIGURE 6-6

7. Save the project in Interface Builder.

8. In the `ScreenRotationsViewController.m` file, add the following bold code:

```
#import "ScreenRotationsViewController.h"

@implementation ScreenRotationsViewController

@synthesize btn;

-(void) positionViews {

    UIInterfaceOrientation destOrientation = self.interfaceOrientation;

    if (destOrientation == UIInterfaceOrientationPortrait ||
        destOrientation == UIInterfaceOrientationPortraitUpsideDown) {
        //---if rotating to portrait mode---
        btn.frame = CGRectMake(20, 20, 371, 37);
    } else {
        //---if rotating to landscape mode---
        btn.frame = CGRectMake(633, 691, 371, 37);
    }
}

- (void)willAnimateSecondHalfOfRotationFromInterfaceOrientation:
(UIInterfaceOrientation) fromInterfaceOrientation
duration: (NSTimeInterval) duration {
```

```
    [self positionViews];
}

- (void)viewDidLoad {
    [self positionViews];
    [super viewDidLoad];
}

- (void)dealloc {
    [btn release];
    [super dealloc];
}
```

9. Save the project and press Command-R in Xcode to deploy the application onto the iPhone Simulator.

10. Observe that when the iPhone Simulator is in portrait mode, the Round Rect Button view is displayed in the top-left corner. But when you change the orientation to landscape mode, it is repositioned to the bottom-right corner (see Figure 6-7).

FIGURE 6-7

How It Works

This project illustrates how you can reposition the views on your application when the device changes orientation. You first create an outlet and connect it to the Round Rect Button view on the View window.

When the device is being rotated, you handle the `willAnimateSecondHalfOfRotationFrom-InterfaceOrientation:` event because doing so allows you to know the destination orientations that the device is changing to. When this event is fired, you can obtain the destination orientation using the `interfaceOrientation` property of the current View (`self`), like this:

```
UIInterfaceOrientation destOrientation = self.interfaceOrientation;
```

Using this information, you position the view according to the destination orientation by altering its `frame` property via the `positionViews` method, which you have defined:

```
-(void) positionViews {

    UIInterfaceOrientation destOrientation = self.interfaceOrientation;

    if (destOrientation == UIInterfaceOrientationPortrait ||
        destOrientation == UIInterfaceOrientationPortraitUpsideDown) {
        //---if rotating to portrait mode---
        btn.frame = CGRectMake(20, 20, 371, 37);
    } else {
        //---if rotating to landscape mode---
        btn.frame = CGRectMake(633, 691, 371, 37);
    }
}
```

You should also call the `positionViews` method in the `viewDidLoad` method so that the Round Rect Button can be displayed correctly when the View window is loaded:

```
- (void)viewDidLoad {
    [self positionViews];
    [super viewDidLoad];
}
```

PROPERTIES FOR DEALING WITH POSITIONING OF VIEWS

In the previous example, you used the `frame` property to change the position of a view during runtime. The `frame` property defines the rectangle occupied by the view, with respect to its superview (the view that contains it). Using the `frame` property allows you to set the positioning and size of a view. Besides using the `frame` property, you can also use the `center` property, which sets the center of the view, also with respect to its superview. You usually use the `center` property when you are performing some animation and just want to change the position of a view.

PROGRAMMATICALLY ROTATING THE SCREEN

You've seen how your application can handle the changes in device orientation when the user rotates the device. There are times (such as when you are developing a game), however, when you want to force the application to display in certain rotations independently of the device's orientation.

There are two scenarios to consider:

➤ Rotating the screen orientation during runtime when your application is running

➤ Displaying the screen in a particular orientation when the View is loaded

Rotating During Runtime

During runtime, you can programmatically rotate the screen by using the `setOrientation:` method on an instance of the `UIDevice` class. Suppose you want the user to change the screen orientation when the user presses the Round Rect Button view. Using the project created earlier, You can code it as follows:

```
-(IBAction) btnClicked: (id) sender{
    [[UIDevice currentDevice] setOrientation:UIInterfaceOrientationLandscapeLeft];
}
```

The `setOrientation:` method takes in a single parameter specifying the orientation you want to change to.

 NOTE *After you have programmatically switched the orientation of your application, your application's rotation can still be changed when the device is physically rotated. The orientation that it can be changed to is dependent of what you set in the* `shouldAutorotateToInterfaceOrientation:` *method.*

Displaying the View in a Specific Orientation When Loading

When a View window is loaded, by default it is always displayed in the orientation that your device is in. If your application requires that you display the View window in a particular orientation when it is loaded, you can do so by setting the orientation of the status bar, like this:

```
- (void)viewDidLoad {

    [UIApplication sharedApplication].statusBarOrientation =
        UIInterfaceOrientationLandscapeRight;

    [super viewDidLoad];
}
```

It's interesting to note that the `setOrientation:` method described in the previous section cannot be used to change the orientation of the View during loading time:

```
- (void)viewDidLoad {
    //---does not work during View loading time---
    [[UIDevice currentDevice] setOrientation:UIInterfaceOrientationLandscapeLeft];

    [super viewDidLoad];
}
```

Likewise, setting the orientation of the status bar does not work during runtime (after the View has loaded):

```
//---does not work during run time---
[UIApplication sharedApplication].statusBarOrientation =
    UIInterfaceOrientationLandscapeLeft;
```

 NOTE *The orientation to which you are changing must first of all be specified in the* `shouldAutorotateToInterfaceOrientation:` *event.*

SUMMARY

This chapter explained how changes in screen orientations are handled by the various events in the View Controller class. Proper handling of screen orientations will make your application more useable and improve the user experience.

EXERCISES

1. Suppose you want your application to only support the landscape right and landscape left orientation. How should you modify your code?

2. What is the difference between the `frame` and `center` property of a view?

Answers to the Exercises can be found in Appendix A.

▶ **WHAT YOU LEARNED IN THIS CHAPTER**

TOPIC	KEY CONCEPTS
Handling device rotations	Implement the `shouldAutorotateToInterfaceOrientation:` method

Four orientations supported	`UIInterfaceOrientationPortrait`
	`UIInterfaceOrientationLandscapeLeft`
	`UIInterfaceOrientationLandscapeRight`
	`UIInterfaceOrientationPortraitUpsideDown`

Events fired when device is rotated	`willAnimateFirstHalfOfRotationToInterfaceOrientation:`
	`willAnimateSecondHalfOfRotationFromInterfaceOrientation:`
	`willRotateToInterfaceOrientation:`
	`willAnimateRotationToInterfaceOrientation:`

Properties for changing the position of a view	Use the `frame` property for changing the positioning and size of a view Use the `center` property for changing the positioning of a view

PART II
Displaying and Persisting Data?

Using the Table View

One of the most commonly used views in iPad applications is the Table view. It is used to display lists of items from which users can select, or they can tap it to display more information. Figure 7-1 shows a Table view in action in the Settings application.

In Chapter 4, you had your first taste of the Table view when you developed a Split View-based Application project. That chapter didn't fully dive into how the Table view works, and a lot of details were purposely left out. The Table view is such an important topic that it deserves a chapter on its own.

In this chapter, you examine the Table view in detail and explore the various building blocks that make it such a versatile view.

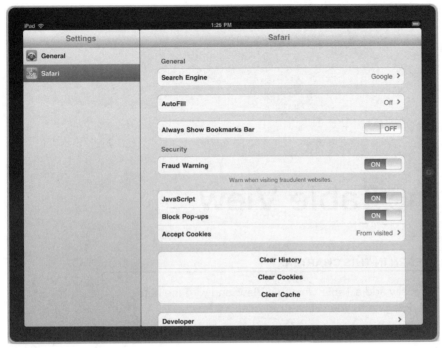

FIGURE 7-1

A SIMPLE TABLE VIEW

The best way to understand how to use a Table view in your application is to create a new View-based Application project and then manually add a Table view to the view and wire it to a View Controller. That way, you understand the various building blocks of the Table view.

Without further ado, use the following Try It Out to create a new project and see how to put a Table view together!

TRY IT OUT   Using a Table View

codefile TableViewExample.zip available for download at Wrox.com

1.   Create a new View-based Application project and name it `TableViewExample`.

2.   Double-click the `TableViewExampleViewController.xib` file to edit it in Interface Builder.

3.   Drag the `Table View` item from the Library and drop it onto the View window (see Figure 7-2).

4.   By default, the Table view fills up the entire View window. Resize the Table view to about a third of the width of the View window and set its Background color to a light yellow via the Attributes Inspector window (see Figure 7-3).

5. Right-click the Table view and connect the `dataSource` outlet to the `File's Owner` item (see Figure 7-4). Do the same for the `delegate` outlet (see Figure 7-5).

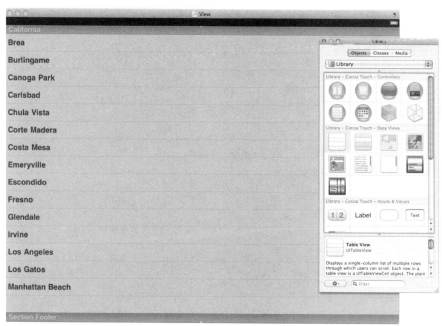

FIGURE 7-2

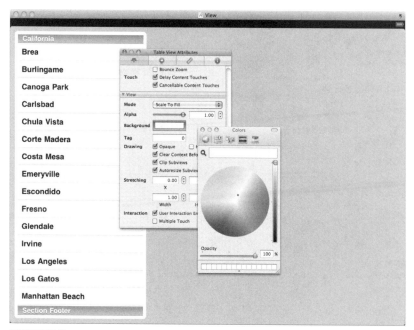

FIGURE 7-3

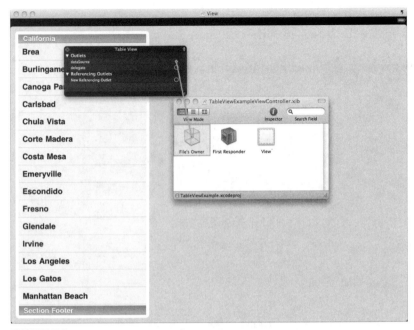

FIGURE 7-4

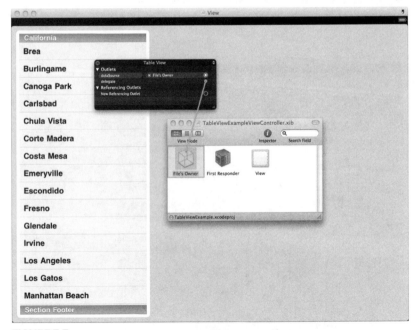

FIGURE 7-5

6. In the `TableViewExampleViewController.h` file, add the following bold statement:

```
#import <UIKit/UIKit.h>

@interface TableViewExampleViewController : UIViewController
    <UITableViewDataSource> {
}

@end
```

7. In the `TableViewExampleViewController.m` file, add the following statements that appear in bold:

```
#import "TableViewExampleViewController.h"

@implementation TableViewExampleViewController

NSMutableArray *listOfMovies;

//---insert individual row into the table view---
- (UITableViewCell *)tableView:(UITableView *)tableView
        cellForRowAtIndexPath:(NSIndexPath *)indexPath {

    static NSString *CellIdentifier = @"Cell";

    //---try to get a reusable cell---
    UITableViewCell *cell = [tableView
        dequeueReusableCellWithIdentifier:CellIdentifier];

    //---create new cell if no reusable cell is available---
    if (cell == nil) {
        cell = [[[UITableViewCell alloc]
                    initWithStyle:UITableViewCellStyleDefault
                  reuseIdentifier:CellIdentifier] autorelease];
    }

    //---set the text to display for the cell---
    NSString *cellValue = [listOfMovies objectAtIndex:indexPath.row];
    cell.textLabel.text = cellValue;

    return cell;
}

//---set the number of rows in the table view---
- (NSInteger)tableView:(UITableView *)tableView
 numberOfRowsInSection:(NSInteger)section {

    return [listOfMovies count];
}

- (void)viewDidLoad {

    //---initialize the array---
    listOfMovies = [[NSMutableArray alloc] init];

    //---add items---
```

```
        [listOfMovies addObject:@"Training Day"];
        [listOfMovies addObject:@"Remember the Titans"];
        [listOfMovies addObject:@"John Q."];
        [listOfMovies addObject:@"The Bone Collector"];
        [listOfMovies addObject:@"Ricochet"];
        [listOfMovies addObject:@"The Siege"];
        [listOfMovies addObject:@"Malcolm X"];
        [listOfMovies addObject:@"Antwone Fisher"];
        [listOfMovies addObject:@"Courage Under Fire"];
        [listOfMovies addObject:@"He Got Game"];
        [listOfMovies addObject:@"The Pelican Brief"];
        [listOfMovies addObject:@"Glory"];
        [listOfMovies addObject:@"The Preacher's Wife"];

        [super viewDidLoad];
    }

    - (void)dealloc {
        [listOfMovies release];
        [super dealloc];
    }
```

8. Press Command-R to test the application on the iPhone Simulator. Figure 7-6 shows the Table view displaying the list of movies.

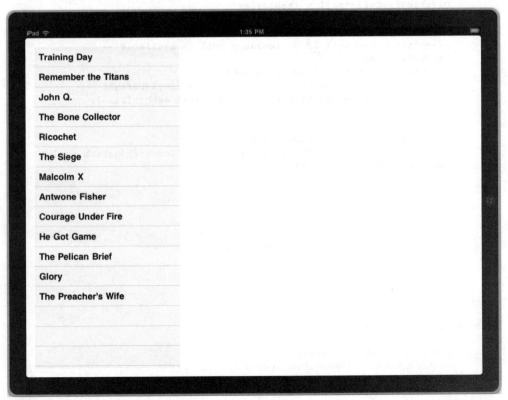

FIGURE 7-6

How It Works

You actually start the application in step 7 by creating an `NSMutableArray` object called `listOfMovies` containing a list of movie names. The items stored in this array will be displayed by the Table view.

```
- (void)viewDidLoad {

    //---initialize the array---
    listOfMovies = [[NSMutableArray alloc] init];

    //---add items---
    [listOfMovies addObject:@"Training Day"];
    [listOfMovies addObject:@"Remember the Titans"];
    [listOfMovies addObject:@"John Q."];
    [listOfMovies addObject:@"The Bone Collector"];
    [listOfMovies addObject:@"Ricochet"];
    [listOfMovies addObject:@"The Siege"];
    [listOfMovies addObject:@"Malcolm X"];
    [listOfMovies addObject:@"Antwone Fisher"];
    [listOfMovies addObject:@"Courage Under Fire"];
    [listOfMovies addObject:@"He Got Game"];
    [listOfMovies addObject:@"The Pelican Brief"];
    [listOfMovies addObject:@"Glory"];
    [listOfMovies addObject:@"The Preacher's Wife"];

    [super viewDidLoad];
}
```

To populate the Table view with items, you need to handle several events contained in the `UITableViewDataSource` protocol. Hence, you need to ensure that your view controller conforms to this protocol:

```
@interface TableViewExampleViewController : UIViewController
    <UITableViewDataSource> {
}
```

 NOTE *Strictly speaking, if you have connected the* `dataSource` *outlet to the* `File's Owner` *item, you don't need to add the preceding statement. However, doing both doesn't hurt anything. There is one advantage to adding the* `<UITableViewDataSource>` *protocol, though — the compiler will warn you if you forget to implement any mandatory methods in your code, helping to prevent errors.*

The `UITableViewDataSource` protocol contains several events that you can implement to supply data to the Table view. Two events handled in this example are:

➤   `tableView:numberOfRowsInSection:`

➤   `tableView:cellForRowAtIndexPath:`

The `tableView:numberOfRowsInSection:` event indicates how many rows you want the Table view to display. In this case, you set it to the number of items in the `listOfMovies` array:

```
//---insert individual row into the table view---
- (NSInteger)tableView:(UITableView *)tableView
 numberOfRowsInSection:(NSInteger)section {

    return [listOfMovies count];

}
```

The `tableView:cellForRowAtIndexPath:` event inserts a cell in a particular location of the Table view. This event is fired once for each row of the Table view.

Here, you retrieve the individual item from the array and insert it into the Table view:

```
- (UITableViewCell *)tableView:(UITableView *)tableView
        cellForRowAtIndexPath:(NSIndexPath *)indexPath {

    static NSString *CellIdentifier = @"Cell";

    //---try to get a reusable cell---
    UITableViewCell *cell = [tableView
        dequeueReusableCellWithIdentifier:CellIdentifier];

    //---create new cell if no reusable cell is available---
    if (cell == nil) {
        cell = [[[UITableViewCell alloc]
                initWithStyle:UITableViewCellStyleDefault
                reuseIdentifier:CellIdentifier] autorelease];
    }

    //---set the text to display for the cell---
    NSString *cellValue = [listOfMovies objectAtIndex:indexPath.row];
    cell.textLabel.text = cellValue;

    return cell;
}
```

Specifically, you use the `dequeueReusableCellWithIdentifier:` method of the `UITableView` class to obtain an instance of the `UITableViewCell` class. The `dequeueReusableCellWithIdentifier:` method returns a reusable Table view cell object. This is important because if you have a large table (say, with 10,000 rows) and you create a single `UITableViewCell` object for each row, you would generate a great performance and memory hit. Also, because a Table view displays only a fixed number of rows at any one time, reusing the cells that have been scrolled out of view would make more sense. This is exactly what the `dequeueReusableCellWithIdentifier:` method does. So, for example, if 10 rows are visible in the Table view, only 10 `UITableViewCell` objects are ever created — they always get reused when the user scrolls through the Table view.

> **NOTE** The `tableView:cellForRowAtIndexPath:` event is not fired continuously from start to finish. For example, if the Table view has 100 rows to be displayed, the event is fired continuously for the first, say, 10 rows that are visible. When the user scrolls down the Table view, the `tableView:cellForRowAt-IndexPath:` event is fired for the next couple of visible rows.

Adding a Header and Footer

You can display a header and footer for the Table view by simply implementing the following two methods in your View Controller:

```
- (NSString *)tableView:(UITableView *)tableView
titleForHeaderInSection:(NSInteger)section{

    //---display "Movie List" as the header---
    return @"Movie List";

}

- (NSString *)tableView:(UITableView *)tableView
titleForFooterInSection:(NSInteger)section {

    //---display "by Denzel Washington" as the footer---
    return @"by Denzel Washington";

}
```

Insert the preceding statements in the `TableViewExampleViewController.m` file and rerun the application; you'll see the header and footer of the Table view as shown in Figure 7-7.

Adding an Image

In addition to text, you can display an image next to the text of a cell in a Table view. Suppose you have an image named `apple.jpeg` in the `Resources` folder of your project (see Figure 7-8).

> **NOTE** You can simply drag and drop an image to the `Resources` folder of Xcode. When prompted, ensure that you save a copy of the image in your project.

To display an image next to the text of a cell, insert the following statements that appear in bold into the `tableView:cellForRowAtIndexPath:` method:

```
- (UITableViewCell *)tableView:(UITableView *)tableView
  cellForRowAtIndexPath:(NSIndexPath *)indexPath {
```

```objc
static NSString *CellIdentifier = @"Cell";

//---try to get a reusable cell---
UITableViewCell *cell = [tableView
    dequeueReusableCellWithIdentifier:CellIdentifier];

//---create new cell if no reusable cell is available---
if (cell == nil) {
    cell = [[[UITableViewCell alloc]
            initWithStyle:UITableViewCellStyleDefault
        reuseIdentifier:CellIdentifier] autorelease];
}

//---set the text to display for the cell---
NSString *cellValue = [listOfMovies objectAtIndex:indexPath.row];
cell.text = cellValue;

UIImage *image = [UIImage imageNamed:@"apple.jpeg"];
cell.imageView.image = image;

return cell;
}
```

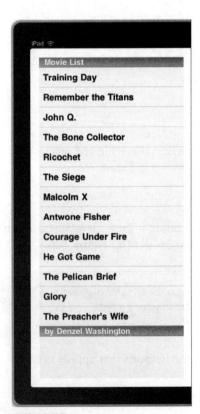

FIGURE 7-7

FIGURE 7-8

Press Command-R to test the application and you see that the image is displayed next to each row (see Figure 7-9).

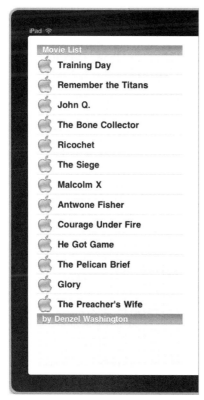

FIGURE 7-9

Notice that the UITableViewCell object already has the imageView property. All you need to do is to create an instance of the UIImage class and then load the image from the Resources folder of your project.

Displaying the Item Selected

So far, you have seen how to populate the Table view with items by ensuring that your View Controller conforms to the UITableViewDataSource protocol. This protocol takes care of populating the Table view, but if you want to select the items in a Table view, you need to conform to another protocol, UITableViewDelegate.

The UITableViewDelegate protocol contains events that allow you to manage selections, edit and delete rows, and display a header and footer.

To use the UITableViewDelegate protocol, modify the TableViewExampleViewController.h file by adding the bold statement as follows:

```
#import <UIKit/UIKit.h>

@interface TableViewExampleViewController : UIViewController
    <UITableViewDataSource, UITableViewDelegate>{

}

@end
```

Again, if you have connected the delegate outlet to the File's Owner item previously, you don't really need to add the preceding statement (UITableViewDelegate). However, doing both doesn't hurt.

The following Try It Out shows how you can allow users to make selections in a Table view.

TRY IT OUT Making a Selection in a Table View

1. Using the same project created earlier, add the following statements that appear in bold to the TableViewExampleViewController.m file:

```
#import "TableViewExampleViewController.h"

@implementation TableViewExampleViewController

NSMutableArray *listOfMovies;

- (void)tableView:(UITableView *)tableView
didSelectRowAtIndexPath:(NSIndexPath *)indexPath {

    NSString *movieSelected = [listOfMovies objectAtIndex:[indexPath row]];
    NSString *msg = [[NSString alloc] initWithFormat:@"You have selected %@",
                    movieSelected];

    UIAlertView *alert = [[UIAlertView alloc] initWithTitle:@"Movie selected"
                                                    message:msg
                                                    delegate:self
```

```
                                        cancelButtonTitle:@"OK"
                                        otherButtonTitles:nil];

        [alert show];
        [alert release];
        [movieSelected release];
        [msg release];
    }
```

2. Press Command-R to test the application on the iPhone Simulator.

3. Select a row by tapping it. An alert view displays the row you selected (see Figure 7-10).

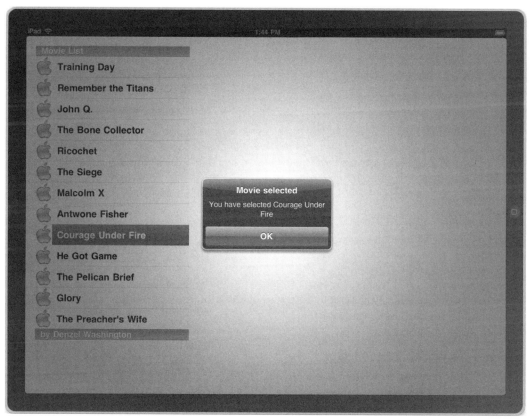

FIGURE 7-10

How It Works

One of the events in the `UITableViewDelegate` protocol is `tableView:didSelectRowAtIndexPath:`, which is fired when the user selects a row in the Table view. One of the parameters contained in the `tableView:didSelectRowAtIndexPath:` event is of the type `NSIndexPath`. The `NSIndexPath` class represents the path of a specific item in a nested array collection.

For this event, to know which row has been selected, you simply call the `row` property of the `NSIndexPath` object (`indexPath`) and then use the row number to reference against the `listOfMovies` array:

```
NSString *movieSelected = [listOfMovies objectAtIndex:[indexPath row]];
```

After the selected movie is retrieved, you simply display it using the `UIAlertView` class:

```
NSString *msg = [[NSString alloc] initWithFormat:@"You have selected %@",
                    movieSelected];

UIAlertView *alert = [[UIAlertView alloc] initWithTitle:@"Movie selected"
                                message:msg
                                delegate:self
                                cancelButtonTitle: @"OK"
                                otherButtonTitles:nil];
[alert show];
```

 NOTE The `row` property of the `NSIndexPath` class is one of the additions made by the UIKit framework to enable the identification of rows and sections in a Table view. So be aware that the original class definition of the `NSIndexPath` class does not contain the `row` property.

Indenting

Another event in the `UITableViewDelegate` protocol is `tableView:indentationLevelForRowAtIndexPath:`. When you handle this event, it is fired for every row that is visible on the screen. To set an indentation for a particular row, simply return an integer indicating the level of indentation:

```
- (NSInteger)tableView:(UITableView *)tableView
indentationLevelForRowAtIndexPath:(NSIndexPath *)indexPath {

    return [indexPath row] % 2;

}
```

In the preceding example, the indentation alternates between 0 and 1, depending on the current row number. Figure 7-11 shows how the Table view looks if you insert the preceding code in the `TableViewExampleViewController.m` file.

In real life, the Table view is often used with a Split View-based Application because it is very common for users to select an item from a Table view and then view the details of the item selected on the right side of the screen. For this reason, the Split View-based Application template in the iPhone SDK by default uses the `UITableViewController` class instead of the `UIViewController` class. In addition, you can group items in a Table view into sections so that you can add a header for each section.

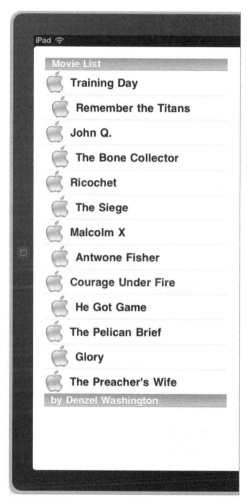

FIGURE 7-11

Using the Table View

In Chapter 4, you saw that a Split View-based Application project uses a Table view to display list of items on the left side of the screen. The RootViewController class programmatically fills up the Table view with rows of items; it did not make use of the Table view in Interface Builder. While it is perfectly alright to create a Table view from code, sometimes it is easier to customize the Table view from within Interface Builder. In particular, if you want to add a SearchBar to the Table view, it is much easier to do that in Interface Builder.

Hence in the following Try It Out, you learn how to use the Table view from within a Split View-based Application project and map it to a Table view in Interface Builder.

Mapping an XIB file to a View Controller

codefile TableView.zip available for download at Wrox.com

1. Create a new Split View-based Application project and name it `TableView`.

2. Examine the files in the `TableView` project, particularly the files created under the Classes and Resources folders (see Figure 7-12). Double-click the `MainWindow.xib` file to edit it in Interface Builder.

3. As shown in Chapter 4, the `MainWindow.xib` file contains a Split View Controller (see Figure 7-13).

The left side of the Split View Controller view is mapped to the `RootViewController` class (see Figure 7-14).

FIGURE 7-12

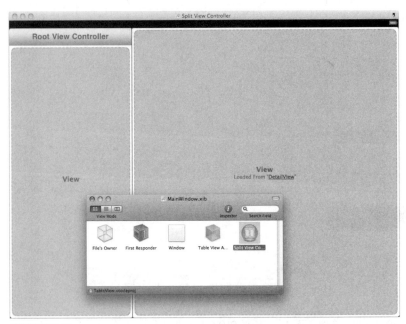

FIGURE 7-13

4. The `RootViewController` class uses the `UITableViewController` class (instead of the `UIViewController` class) and hence the left side of the Split View Controller will display a Table view:

```
#import <UIKit/UIKit.h>

@class DetailViewController;

@interface RootViewController : UITableViewController {
```

```
        DetailViewController *detailViewController;
}

@property (nonatomic, retain) IBOutlet DetailViewController
*detailViewController;

@end
```

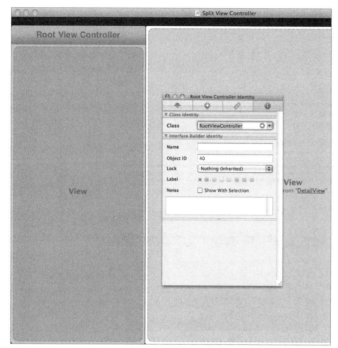

FIGURE 7-14

5. The content of the Table view is created programmatically, via the `RootViewController` class. However, you can also create an XIB file so that you can manipulate your Table view in Interface Builder. To do so, right-click the Resources folder and select Add ⇨ New File. Select the `User Interface` item listed under iPhone OS and then select the View XIB template (see Figure 7-15). Click Next. Name the XIB file as `RootView.xib`.

6. Double-click on the newly added `RootView.xib` file to edit it in Interface Builder. The `RootView.xib` window contains a `View` item. Delete it and add in a `Table View` from the Library instead (see Figure 7-16).

7. Right-click the `Table View` item and connect its `dataSource` and `delegate` outlets to the `File's Owner` item (see Figure 7-17).

8. Select the `File's Owner` item and view its Identity Inspector window. Set its Class property to `RootViewController` (see Figure 7-18).

FIGURE 7-15

FIGURE 7-16

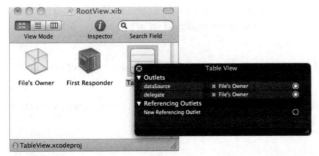

FIGURE 7-17

9. Control-click and drag the `File's Owner` item over the `Table View` (see Figure 7-19) and select `view`.

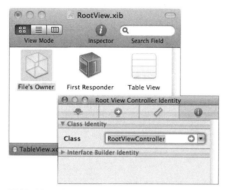

FIGURE 7-18

FIGURE 7-19

10. Finally, double-click on the `MainWindow.xib` file to edit it in Interface Builder. In the `MainWindow.xib` window, switch the View Mode to List view (see Figure 7-20). Select the `Root View Controller` item and view the Attributes Inspector window. Set the NIB Name property to `RootView`.

FIGURE 7-20

11. Save the files in Interface Builder.

12. In Xcode, press Command-R to test the application on the iPad Simulator. Figure 7-21 shows the Split View application.

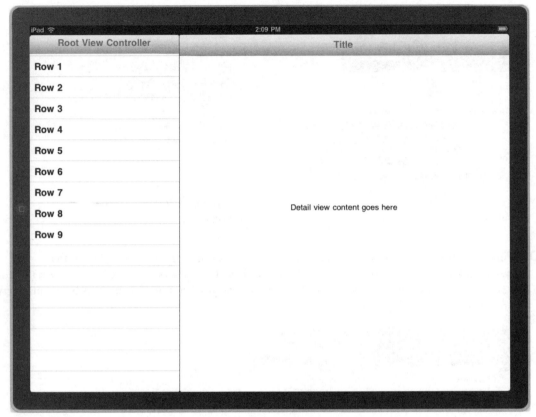

FIGURE 7-21

How It Works

The RootViewController class inherits from the UITableViewController class:

```
@interface RootViewController : UITableViewController {
```

This means that the class itself contains a Table view and that all the various method contained in the RootViewController.m file will be used to populate the Table view.

To connect the RootViewController class to an XIB file:

➤   You first created a View XIB file and then replaced the default View item with the Table View item.

➤   You also connected the dataSource and delegate outlets to the File's Owner item.

➤   The File's Owner item is then set to point to the RootViewController class.

➤   After that, you can connect the File's Owner item to the Table View item.

In the final step, you set the Root View Controller item in the Split View Controller to point to the newly created XIB file.

Up to this stage, you won't notice anything different — the Table view looks exactly as it was created using code. However, in the following sections, you will learn how to manipulate the Table view via Interface Builder.

Using a Property List

In this chapter, you've used an `NSMutableArray` object to hold a list of movie names. In real life, you might want to store the list in a property list. Storing the list of movie names in a property list allows you to organize the information, such as grouping them based on the release date and so on.

The following Try It Out shows how to store the movie names in a property list and then retrieve them to display in the Table view.

TRY IT OUT Display data from a Property List

1. Using the project created in the previous section, right-click the Resources folder and choose Add ➪ New File.

2. Select the `Resource` item under the Mac OS X category on the left of the New File dialog and select the Property List template on the right of the dialog (see Figure 7-22). Click Next.

FIGURE 7-22

3. Name the property list `Movies.plist`. The property list is now saved in the Resources folder of your project. Select it and create the list of items as shown in Figure 7-23.

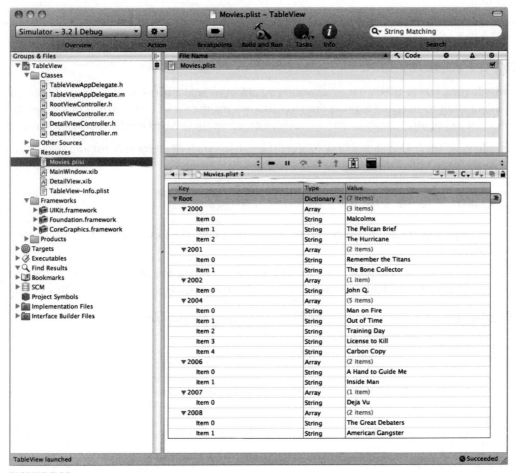

FIGURE 7-23

4. In the `RootViewController.h` file, add the following statements that appear in bold:

```
#import <UIKit/UIKit.h>

@class DetailViewController;

@interface RootViewController : UITableViewController {
    DetailViewController *detailViewController;

    NSDictionary *movieTitles;
    NSArray *years;
}

@property (nonatomic, retain) IBOutlet DetailViewController *detailViewController;
```

```
@property (nonatomic, retain) NSDictionary *movieTitles;
@property (nonatomic, retain) NSArray *years;

@end
```

5. In the `RootViewController.m` file, add the following statements that appear in bold:

```
#import "RootViewController.h"
#import "DetailViewController.h"

@implementation RootViewController

@synthesize detailViewController;

@synthesize movieTitles, years;

- (void)viewDidLoad {

    //---path to the property list file---
    NSString *path = [[NSBundle mainBundle] pathForResource:@"Movies"
                                                     ofType:@"plist"];

    //---load the list into the dictionary---
    NSDictionary *dic = [[NSDictionary alloc] initWithContentsOfFile:path];

    //---save the dictionary object to the property---
    self.movieTitles = dic;
    [dic release];

    //---get all the keys in the dictionary object and sort them---
    NSArray *array = [[movieTitles allKeys]
                        sortedArrayUsingSelector:@selector(compare:)];

    //---save the keys in the years property---
    self.years = array;

    [super viewDidLoad];
    self.clearsSelectionOnViewWillAppear = NO;
}

- (NSInteger)numberOfSectionsInTableView:(UITableView *)aTableView {
    // Return the number of sections.
    //return 1;
    return [years count];
}

- (NSInteger)tableView:(UITableView *)aTableView
 numberOfRowsInSection:(NSInteger)section {

    // Return the number of rows in the section.
    //return 10;

    //---check the current year based on the section index---
    NSString *year = [years objectAtIndex:section];

    //---returns the movies in that year as an array---
```

```
        NSArray *movieSection = [movieTitles objectForKey:year];

        //---return the number of movies for that year as the number of rows in that
        // section ---
        return [movieSection count];

    }
- (UITableViewCell *)tableView:(UITableView *)tableView
            cellForRowAtIndexPath:(NSIndexPath *)indexPath {

        static NSString *CellIdentifier = @"CellIdentifier";

        // Dequeue or create a cell of the appropriate type.
        UITableViewCell *cell = [tableView
            dequeueReusableCellWithIdentifier:CellIdentifier];

        if (cell == nil) {
            cell = [[[UITableViewCell alloc] initWithStyle:UITableViewCellStyleDefault
                        reuseIdentifier:CellIdentifier] autorelease];
            cell.accessoryType = UITableViewCellAccessoryNone;
        }

        // Configure the cell.
        //---get the year---
        NSString *year = [years objectAtIndex:[indexPath section]];

        //---get the list of movies for that year---
        NSArray *movieSection = [movieTitles objectForKey:year];

        //---get the particular movie based on that row---
        cell.textLabel.text = [movieSection objectAtIndex:[indexPath row]];

        return cell;
    }

- (NSString *)tableView:(UITableView *)tableView
titleForHeaderInSection:(NSInteger)section {

        //---get the year as the section header---
        NSString *year = [years objectAtIndex:section];
        return year;
    }

- (void)dealloc {
        [years release];
        [movieTitles release];
        [super dealloc];
    }
```

6. Press Command-R to test the application. You can now see the movies grouped into sections organized by year (see Figure 7-24).

FIGURE 7-24

7. You can also change the style of the Table view from `Plain` to `Grouped`. In the `RootView.xib` window, select the `Table View` item and open its Attributes Inspector window (see Figure 7-25). Set its Style property to `Grouped`.

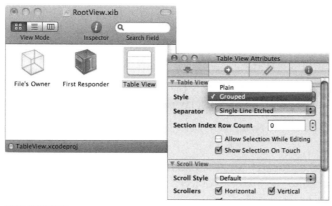

FIGURE 7-25

8.   Rerun the application, and you see that the Table view looks different (see Figure 7-26). When the application is displayed in Portrait mode, clicking the Root List button displays the Table view as shown in Figure 7-27.

FIGURE 7-26

How It Works

This project covers quite a number of concepts, and you will need some time to understand them all.

First, you created a property list and populated it with several key/value pairs. Essentially, you can visualize the key/value pairs stored in the property list as shown in Figure 7-28.

Each key represents a year, and the value for each key represents the movies released in that particular year. You will use the values stored in the property list and display them in the Table view.

Within the `RootViewController` class, you create two properties: `movieTitles` (an `NSDictionary` object) and `years` (an `NSArray` object).

When the view is loaded, you first locate the property list and load the list into the `NSDictionary` object, followed by retrieving all the years into the `NSArray` object:

```
- (void)viewDidLoad {

    //---path to the property list file---
```

```
    NSString *path = [[NSBundle mainBundle] pathForResource:@"Movies"
                                              ofType:@"plist"];

    //---load the list into the dictionary---
    NSDictionary *dic = [[NSDictionary alloc] initWithContentsOfFile:path];

    //---save the dictionary object to the property---
    self.movieTitles = dic;
    [dic release];

    //---get all the keys in the dictionary object and sort them---
    NSArray *array = [[movieTitles allKeys]
                    sortedArrayUsingSelector:@selector(compare:)];

    //---save the keys in the years property---
    self.years = array;

    [super viewDidLoad];
    self.clearsSelectionOnViewWillAppear = NO;
}
```

FIGURE 7-27

Key	Value
2000	"Malcom X', "The Pelican Brief", "The Hurricane"
2001	"Remember the Titans", "The Bone Collector"
2002	"John Q."
2004	"Man on Fire", "Out of Time", "Training Day", "License to Kill", "Carbon Copy"
2006	"A Hand to Guide Me", "Inside Man"
2007	"Deja Vu"
2008	"The Great Debaters", "American Gangster"

FIGURE 7-28

Because the Table view now displays the list of movies in sections, with each section representing a year, you need to tell the Table view how many sections are there. You do so by implementing the `numberOfSectionsInTableView:` method:

```
- (NSInteger)numberOfSectionsInTableView:(UITableView *)aTableView {
    // Return the number of sections.
    //return 1;
    return [years count];
}
```

After the Table view knows how many sections to display, it must also know how many rows to display in each section. You tell it that information by implementing the `tableView:numberOfRowsInSection:` method:

```
- (NSInteger)tableView:(UITableView *)aTableView
 numberOfRowsInSection:(NSInteger)section {

    // Return the number of rows in the section.
    //return 10;

    //---check the current year based on the section index---
    NSString *year = [years objectAtIndex:section];

    //---returns the movies in that year as an array---
    NSArray *movieSection = [movieTitles objectForKey:year];

    //---return the number of movies for that year as the number of rows in that
    // section ---
    return [movieSection count];

}
```

To display the movies for each section, you implement the `tableView:cellForRowAtIndexPath:`
method and extract the relevant movie titles from the `NSDictionary` object:

```
- (UITableViewCell *)tableView:(UITableView *)tableView
        cellForRowAtIndexPath:(NSIndexPath *)indexPath {

    static NSString *CellIdentifier = @"CellIdentifier";

    // Dequeue or create a cell of the appropriate type.
    UITableViewCell *cell = [tableView
        dequeueReusableCellWithIdentifier:CellIdentifier];

    if (cell == nil) {
        cell = [[[UITableViewCell alloc] initWithStyle:UITableViewCellStyleDefault
            reuseIdentifier:CellIdentifier] autorelease];
        cell.accessoryType = UITableViewCellAccessoryNone;
    }

    // Configure the cell.
    //---get the year---
    NSString *year = [years objectAtIndex:[indexPath section]];

    //---get the list of movies for that year---
    NSArray *movieSection = [movieTitles objectForKey:year];

    //---get the particular movie based on that row---
    cell.textLabel.text = [movieSection objectAtIndex:[indexPath row]];
    return cell;
}
```

Finally, you implement the `tableView:titleForHeaderInSection:` method to retrieve the year as the
header for each section:

```
- (NSString *)tableView:(UITableView *)tableView
titleForHeaderInSection:(NSInteger)section {

    //---get the year as the section header---
    NSString *year = [years objectAtIndex:section];
    return year;
}
```

Adding Indexing

The list of movies is pretty short, so scrolling through it is not too much of a hassle. However, imagine
that the list contains 10,000 titles spanning 100 years. In that case, scrolling from the top of the list
to the bottom of the list can take a long time. A very useful feature of the Table view is its capability
to display an index on the right side of the view. To add an index list to your Table view, you just need

to implement the `sectionIndexTitlesForTableView:` method and return the array containing the section headers, which is the `years` array in this case:

```
- (NSArray *)sectionIndexTitlesForTableView:(UITableView *)tableView {
    return years;
}
```

 NOTE *If the Table view's Style property is set to* `Grouped`, *the index will overlap with the layout of the Table view.*

Figure 7-29 shows the index displayed on the right side of the Table view.

FIGURE 7-29

Adding Search Capability

One very common function associated with the Table view is the capability to search the items contained within a Table view. For example, the Contacts application has the Search Bar at the top for easy searching of contacts.

In the following Try It Out, you will add search functionality to the Table view.

TRY IT OUT   **Adding a Search Bar to the Table View**

1.   Using the project created in the previous section, in Interface Builder drag a Search Bar from the Library and drop it onto the Table view (see Figure 7-30).

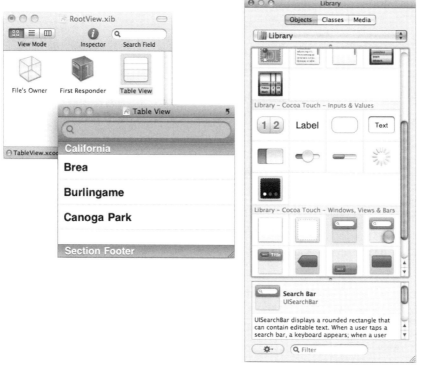

FIGURE 7-30

2.   Right-click the Search Bar and connect the `delegate` to the `File's Owner` item (see Figure 7-31).

FIGURE 7-31

3. In the `RootViewController.h` file, add the following statements that **appear in bold:**

```
#import <UIKit/UIKit.h>

@class DetailViewController;

@interface RootViewController : UITableViewController {
    DetailViewController *detailViewController;

    NSDictionary *movieTitles;
    NSArray *years;

    IBOutlet UISearchBar *searchBar;
}

@property (nonatomic, retain) IBOutlet DetailViewController
*detailViewController;

@property (nonatomic, retain) NSDictionary *movieTitles;
@property (nonatomic, retain) NSArray *years;

@property (nonatomic, retain) UISearchBar *searchBar;

@end
```

4. In Interface Builder, Control-click and drag the `File's Owner` item to the Search Bar and select `searchBar`.

5. In the `RootViewController.m` file, add the following statements that appear in bold:

```
#import "RootViewController.h"
#import "DetailViewController.h"
```

```objc
@implementation RootViewController

@synthesize detailViewController;

@synthesize movieTitles, years;

@synthesize searchBar;

- (void)viewDidLoad {

    //---path to the property list file---
    NSString *path = [[NSBundle mainBundle] pathForResource:@"Movies"
                                                     ofType:@"plist"];

    //---load the list into the dictionary---
    NSDictionary *dic = [[NSDictionary alloc] initWithContentsOfFile:path];

    //---save the dictionary object to the property---
    self.movieTitles = dic;
    [dic release];

    //---get all the keys in the dictionary object and sort them---
    NSArray *array = [[movieTitles allKeys]
                        sortedArrayUsingSelector:@selector(compare:)];

    //---save the keys in the years property---
    self.years = array;

    self.tableView.tableHeaderView = searchBar;
    searchBar.autocorrectionType = UITextAutocorrectionTypeYes;

    [super viewDidLoad];
    self.clearsSelectionOnViewWillAppear = NO;
}

- (void)dealloc {
    [searchBar release];
    [years release];
    [movieTitles release];
    [super dealloc];
}
```

6. Press Command-R to test the application on the iPad Simulator. Figure 7-32 shows the Search Bar displayed at the top of the Table view.

7. Back in Xcode again, edit the RootViewController.h file and add the following statements that appear in bold:

```objc
#import <UIKit/UIKit.h>

@class DetailViewController;

@interface RootViewController : UITableViewController {
```

```
        DetailViewController *detailViewController;

        NSDictionary *movieTitles;
        NSArray *years;

        IBOutlet UISearchBar *searchBar;

        BOOL isSearchOn;
        BOOL canSelectRow;
        NSMutableArray *listOfMovies;
        NSMutableArray *searchResult;
    }

    @property (nonatomic, retain) IBOutlet DetailViewController
    ^detailViewController;

    @property (nonatomic, retain) NSDictionary *movieTitles;
    @property (nonatomic, retain) NSArray *years;

    @property (nonatomic, retain) UISearchBar *searchBar;

    - (void) doneSearching: (id)sender;
    - (void) searchMoviesTableView;

    @end
```

8. In the `RootViewController.m` file, add the following methods:

```
    //---fired when the user taps on the searchbar---
    - (void)searchBarTextDidBeginEditing:(UISearchBar *)searchBar {
        isSearchOn = YES;
        canSelectRow = NO;
        self.tableView.scrollEnabled = NO;

        //---add the Done button at the top---
        self.navigationItem.rightBarButtonItem =
            [[[UIBarButtonItem alloc]
                 initWithBarButtonSystemItem:UIBarButtonSystemItemDone
                                      target:self action:@selector(doneSearching:)]
             autorelease];
    }

    //---done with the searching---
    - (void) doneSearching:(id)sender {
        isSearchOn = NO;
        canSelectRow = YES;
        self.tableView.scrollEnabled = YES;
        self.navigationItem.rightBarButtonItem = nil;

        //---hides the keyboard---
        [searchBar resignFirstResponder];
```

```
        //---refresh the TableView---
        [self.tableView reloadData];
}

//---fired when the user types something into the searchbar---
- (void)searchBar:(UISearchBar *)searchBar textDidChange:(NSString *)searchText
{

        //---if there is something to search for---
        if ([searchText length] > 0) {
            isSearchOn = YES;
            canSelectRow = YES;
            self.tableView.scrollEnabled = YES;
            [self searchMoviesTableView];
        }
        else {
            //---nothing to search---
            isSearchOn = NO;
            canSelectRow = NO;
            self.tableView.scrollEnabled = NO;
        }
        [self.tableView reloadData];
}

//---performs the searching using the array of movies---
- (void) searchMoviesTableView {
        //---clears the search result---
        [searchResult removeAllObjects];

        for (NSString *str in listOfMovies)
        {
            NSRange titleResultsRange = [str rangeOfString:searchBar.text
                                          options:NSCaseInsensitiveSearch];
            if (titleResultsRange.length > 0)
                [searchResult addObject:str];
        }
}

//---fired when the user taps the Search button on the keyboard---
- (void)searchBarSearchButtonClicked:(UISearchBar *)searchBar {
        [self searchMoviesTableView];
}

- (NSIndexPath *)tableView:(UITableView *)tableView
  willSelectRowAtIndexPath:(NSIndexPath *)indexPath {

        if (canSelectRow)
            return indexPath;
        else
            return nil;

}
```

FIGURE 7-32

9. Modify the following methods in bold in the `RootViewController.m` file:

```
- (void)viewDidLoad {
    //---path to the property list file---
    NSString *path = [[NSBundle mainBundle] pathForResource:@"Movies"
                                                ofType:@"plist"];

    //---load the list into the dictionary---
    NSDictionary *dic = [[NSDictionary alloc] initWithContentsOfFile:path];

    //---save the dictionary object to the property---
    self.movieTitles = dic;
    [dic release];

    //---get all the keys in the dictionary object and sort them---
```

```objc
        NSArray *array = [[movieTitles allKeys]
                        sortedArrayUsingSelector:@selector(compare:)];

    //---save the keys in the years property---
    self.years = array;

    //---Search---
    self.tableView.tableHeaderView = searchBar;
    searchBar.autocorrectionType = UITextAutocorrectionTypeYes;

    //---copy all the movie titles in the dictionary into the
    // listOfMovies array---
    listOfMovies = [[NSMutableArray alloc] init];
    for (NSString *year in array)    //---get all the years---
    {
        //---get all the movies for a particular year---
        NSArray *movies = [movieTitles objectForKey:year];
        for (NSString *title in movies) {
            [listOfMovies addObject:title];
        }
    }
    //---used for storing the search result---
    searchResult = [[NSMutableArray alloc] init];

    isSearchOn = NO;
    canSelectRow = YES;

    [super viewDidLoad];
    self.clearsSelectionOnViewWillAppear = NO;
}


- (NSInteger)numberOfSectionsInTableView:(UITableView *)aTableView {
    // Return the number of sections.
    //return 1;
    if (isSearchOn)
        return 1;
    else
        return [years count];
}

- (NSInteger)tableView:(UITableView *)aTableView
 numberOfRowsInSection:(NSInteger)section {

    // Return the number of rows in the section.
    //return 10;
    if (isSearchOn) {
        return [searchResult count];
    } else {
        //---check the current year based on the section index---
        NSString *year = [years objectAtIndex:section];
        //---returns the movies in that year as an array---
        NSArray *movieSection = [movieTitles objectForKey:year];
        //---return the number of movies for that year as the number
        //  of rows in that section ---
```

```objc
            return [movieSection count];
        }
    }

- (UITableViewCell *)tableView:(UITableView *)tableView
        cellForRowAtIndexPath:(NSIndexPath *)indexPath {

    static NSString *CellIdentifier = @"CellIdentifier";

    // Dequeue or create a cell of the appropriate type.
    UITableViewCell *cell = [tableView
        dequeueReusableCellWithIdentifier:CellIdentifier];

    if (cell == nil) {
        cell = [[[UITableViewCell alloc] initWithStyle:UITableViewCellStyleDefault
            reuseIdentifier:CellIdentifier] autorelease];
        cell.accessoryType = UITableViewCellAccessoryNone;
    }

    // Configure the cell.
    if (isSearchOn) {
        NSString *cellValue = [searchResult objectAtIndex:indexPath.row];
        cell.textLabel.text = cellValue;
    } else {
        //---get the year---
        NSString *year = [years objectAtIndex:[indexPath section]];
        //---get the list of movies for that year---
        NSArray *movieSection = [movieTitles objectForKey:year];
        //---get the particular movie based on that row---
        cell.textLabel.text = [movieSection objectAtIndex:[indexPath row]];
    }
    return cell;
}

- (NSString *)tableView:(UITableView *)tableView
titleForHeaderInSection:(NSInteger)section {
    //---get the year as the section header---
    NSString *year = [years objectAtIndex:section];
    if (isSearchOn)
        return nil;
    else
        return year;
}

- (NSArray *)sectionIndexTitlesForTableView:(UITableView *)tableView {
    if (isSearchOn)
        return nil;
    else
        return years;
}

- (void)dealloc {
```

```
        [listOfMovies release];
        [searchResult release];
        [searchBar release];
        [years release];
        [movieTitles release];
        [super dealloc];
    }
```

10. Press Command-R to test the application on the iPad Simulator.

11. Tap the Search Bar and the keyboard will appear (see Figure 7-33). Observe the following:

➤ As you type, the Table view displays the movies whose title contains the characters that you are typing (see Figure 7-34). You can select the search result by tapping it.

➤ When the keyboard appears and the Search Bar has no text in it, the Table view contains the original list and the rows are not searchable.

➤ When you click the Done button, the keyboard disappears and the original list appears.

FIGURE 7-33

FIGURE 7-34

How It Works

That is quite a lot of work, isn't it? But not to worry: It is actually quite easy to follow. First, you add an outlet to connect to the Search Bar:

```
IBOutlet UISearchBar *searchBar;
```

You define two Boolean variables so that you can track whether the search process is ongoing and whether the user can select the rows in the Table view:

```
BOOL isSearchOn;
BOOL canSelectRow;
```

You then define two NSMutableArray objects so that you can use one to store the list of movies and use another to temporarily store the result of the search:

```
NSMutableArray *listOfMovies;
NSMutableArray *searchResult;
```

When the view is first loaded, you first associate the Search Bar with the Table view and then copy the entire list of movie titles from the NSDictionary object into the NSMutableArray:

```
//---Search---
self.tableView.tableHeaderView = searchBar;
searchBar.autocorrectionType = UITextAutocorrectionTypeYes;

//---copy all the movie titles in the dictionary into the listOfMovies array---
listOfMovies = [[NSMutableArray alloc] init];
for (NSString *year in array)    //---get all the years---
{
    //---get all the movies for a particular year---
    NSArray *movies = [movieTitles objectForKey:year];
    for (NSString *title in movies)
    {
        [listOfMovies addObject:title];
    }
}

//---used for storing the search result---
searchResult = [[NSMutableArray alloc] init];

isSearchOn = NO;
canSelectRow = YES;
```

When the user taps the Search Bar, the searchBarTextDidBeginEditing: event (one of the methods defined in the UISearchBarDelegate protocol) fires. In this method, you add a Done button to the top-right corner of the screen. When the Done button is clicked, the doneSearching: method is called (which you define next).

```
//---fired when the user taps on the searchbar---
- (void)searchBarTextDidBeginEditing:(UISearchBar *)searchBar {
    isSearchOn = YES;
    canSelectRow = NO;
    self.tableView.scrollEnabled = NO;

    //---add the Done button at the top---
    self.navigationItem.rightBarButtonItem =
        [[[UIBarButtonItem alloc]
            initWithBarButtonSystemItem:UIBarButtonSystemItemDone
                                target:self action:@selector(doneSearching:)]
        autorelease];
}
```

The doneSearching: method makes the Search Bar resign its First Responder status (thereby hiding the keyboard). At the same time, you reload the Table view by calling the reloadData method of the Table view. This causes the various events associated with the Table view to be fired again.

```
//---done with the searching---
- (void) doneSearching:(id)sender {
    isSearchOn = NO;
    canSelectRow = YES;
```

```
        self.tableView.scrollEnabled = YES;
        self.navigationItem.rightBarButtonItem = nil;

        //---hides the keyboard---
        [searchBar resignFirstResponder];

        //---refresh the TableView---
        [self.tableView reloadData];
    }
```

As the user types into the Search Bar, the `searchBar:textDidChange:` event is fired for each character entered. In this case, if the Search Bar has at least one character, you call the `searchMoviesTableView` method (which you define next):

```
//---fired when the user types something into the searchbar---
- (void)searchBar:(UISearchBar *)searchBar textDidChange:(NSString *)searchText {

    //---if there is something to search for---
    if ([searchText length] > 0) {
        isSearchOn = YES;
        canSelectRow = YES;
        self.tableView.scrollEnabled = YES;
        [self searchMoviesTableView];
    }
    else {
        //---nothing to search---
        isSearchOn = NO;
        canSelectRow = NO;
        self.tableView.scrollEnabled = NO;
    }
    [self.tableView reloadData];
}
```

The `searchMoviesTableView` method performs the searching on the `listOfMovies` array. You use the `rangeOfString:options:` method of the `NSString` class to perform a case-insensitive search of each movie title using the specified string. The returning result is an `NSRange` object, which contains the location and length of the search string in the string being searched. If the length is more than zero, this means that a match has been found, and hence you add it to the `searchResult` array:

```
//---performs the searching using the array of movies---
- (void) searchMoviesTableView {
    //---clears the search result---
    [searchResult removeAllObjects];

    for (NSString *str in listOfMovies)
    {
        NSRange titleResultsRange = [str rangeOfString:searchBar.text
                                        options:NSCaseInsensitiveSearch];
        if (titleResultsRange.length > 0)
            [searchResult addObject:str];
    }
}
```

When the user taps the Search button (on the keyboard), you make a call to the `searchMoviesTableView` method:

```
//---fired when the user taps the Search button on the keyboard---
- (void)searchBarSearchButtonClicked:(UISearchBar *)searchBar {
    [self searchMoviesTableView];
}
```

The rest of the methods are straightforward. If the search is currently active (as determined by the `isSearchOn` variable), you display the list of titles contained in the `searchResult` array. If not, you display the entire list of movies.

Disclosures and Check Marks

Because users often select rows in a Table view to get more detailed information, rows in a Table view often sport images containing an arrow or a checkmark. Figure 7-35 shows an example of such arrows.

FIGURE 7-35

There are three types of images that you can display:

➤ Disclosure button

➤ Checkmark

➤ Disclosure indicator

To display one of these images, insert the following statement that appears in bold in the `tableView`
`:cellForRowAtIndexPath:` event:

```
- (UITableViewCell *)tableView:(UITableView *)tableView
cellForRowAtIndexPath:(NSIndexPath *)indexPath {

    static NSString *CellIdentifier = @"CellIdentifier";

    // Dequeue or create a cell of the appropriate type.
    UITableViewCell *cell = [tableView
        dequeueReusableCellWithIdentifier:CellIdentifier];
    if (cell == nil) {
        cell = [[[UITableViewCell alloc] initWithStyle:UITableViewCellStyleDefault
            reuseIdentifier:CellIdentifier] autorelease];
        cell.accessoryType = UITableViewCellAccessoryDetailDisclosureButton;
    }

    // Configure the cell.
    if (isSearchOn) {
        NSString *cellValue = [searchResult objectAtIndex:indexPath.row];
        cell.textLabel.text = cellValue;
    } else {
        //---get the year---
        NSString *year = [years objectAtIndex:[indexPath section]];
        //---get the list of movies for that year---
        NSArray *movieSection = [movieTitles objectForKey:year];
        //---get the particular movie based on that row---
        cell.textLabel.text = [movieSection objectAtIndex:[indexPath row]];
    }

    return cell;
}
```

You can use the following constants for the `accessoryType` property:

➤   `UITableViewCellAccessoryDetailDisclosureButton`

➤   `UITableViewCellAccessoryCheckmark`

➤   *`UITableViewCellAccessoryDisclosureIndicator`*

Figure 7-36 shows the different types of images corresponding to the three preceding constants.

Of the three image types, only the `UITableViewCellAccessoryDetailDisclosureButton` can handle a user's tap event. (The other two images are used for display only.) To handle the event when
the user taps the Disclosure button, you need to implement the `tableView:accessoryButton-`
`TappedForRowWithIndexPath:` method:

```
- (void)tableView:(UITableView *)tableView
accessoryButtonTappedForRowWithIndexPath:(NSIndexPath *)indexPath {

    //---insert code here---
    // e.g. navigate to another view to display detailed information, etc

}
```

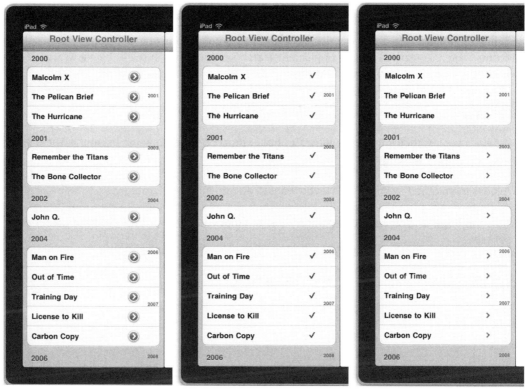

FIGURE 7-36

Figure 7-37 shows the two different events fired when a user taps the content of the cell as well as the Disclosure button.

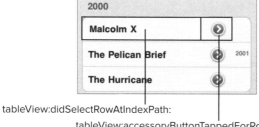

tableView:didSelectRowAtIndexPath:

tableView:accessoryButtonTappedForRowWithIndexPath:

FIGURE 7-37

Commonly, you use the Disclosure button to display detailed information about the selected row.

SUMMARY

This chapter explored the Table view and explained how to customize it to display items in the various forms. You also learned how to implement search functionality in the Table view, which is an essential function in real-world applications.

EXERCISES

1. Name the two protocols that your View Controller must conform to when using the Table view in your view. Briefly describe their uses.

2. Which is the method to implement if you want to add an index in a Table view?

3. Name the three disclosure and checkmark images that you can use. Which one of them handles user taps?

Answers to the Exercises can be found in Appendix A.

▶ **WHAT YOU LEARNED IN THIS CHAPTER**

TOPIC	KEY CONCEPTS
Add items to a Table view	Handle the various events in the `UITableViewDataSource` protocol.
Allow users to select rows in a Table view	Handle the various events in the `UITableViewDelegate` protocol.
Add images to rows in a Table view	Use the `imageView` property of the `UITableViewCell` class and set it to an instance of the `UIImage` class containing an image.

Use a property list with a Table view	Use the following code snippet to locate the property list:
	
	`NSString *path = [[NSBundle mainBundle]`
	`pathForResource:@"Movies"`
	`ofType:@"plist"];`
	
	Then use a combination of `NSDictionary` and `NSArray` objects to retrieve the key/value pairs stored in the property list.

Group items in a Table view in sections	Implement the following methods: ➤ `numberOfSectionsInTableView:` ➤ `tableView:numberOfRowsInSection:` ➤ `tableView:titleForHeaderInSection:`
Add an index to a Table view	Implement the `sectionIndexTitlesForTableView:` method.
Add disclosure and checkmark images to a row in a Table view	Set the `accessoryType` property of an `UITableViewCell` object to one of the following: ➤ `UITableViewCellAccessoryDetailDisclosureButton` ➤ `UITableViewCellAccessoryCheckmark` ➤ `UITableViewCellAccessoryDisclosureIndicator`
Implement a search in a Table view	Use the Search Bar view and handle the various events in the `UISearchBarDelegate` protocol.

8

Application Preferences

WHAT YOU WILL LEARN IN THIS CHAPTER:

➤ How to add application preferences to your application

➤ How to programmatically access the Settings values

➤ How to reset your application's preference settings

If you are a relatively seasoned Mac OS X user, you're likely familiar with the concept of application preferences. Almost every Mac OS X application has application-specific settings that are used for configuring the application's appearance and behavior. These settings are known as the *application preferences*.

In the iPhone OS, applications also have application preferences. In contrast to Mac OS X applications, however, whose application preferences are an integral part of the application, iPhone preferences are centrally managed by an application called Settings (see Figure 8-1).

The left side of the Settings application displays the preferences of system applications as well as third-party applications. Tapping any setting displays the details on the right side of the screen, where you can configure the preferences of an application.

In this chapter, you learn how to incorporate application preferences into your application and modify them programmatically during runtime.

CREATING APPLICATION PREFERENCES

Creating application preferences for your iPad application is a pretty straightforward process. The process involves adding a resource called the Settings Bundle to your project, configuring a property list file, and then deploying your application. When your application is deployed, the application preferences are automatically created for you in the Settings application.

The following Try It Out shows how to add application preferences to your iPad application project in Xcode.

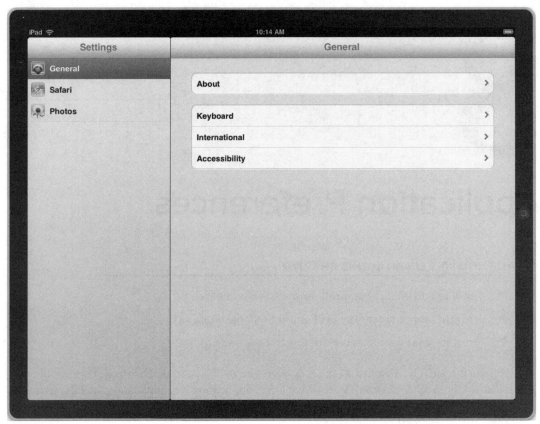

FIGURE 8-1

TRY IT OUT   Adding Application Preferences

1. Using Xcode, create a new View-based Application project and name it ApplicationSettings.

2. Right-click the project name in Xcode and add a new file. Select the Resource template category and click Settings Bundle (see Figure 8-2). Click Next.

3. When asked to name the file, use the default name of Settings.bundle and click Finish.

4. The Settings.bundle item should now be part of your project (see Figure 8-3). Click it and view the content of the Root.plist file using the default Property List editor.

5. Press Command-R to test the application on the iPhone Simulator. When the application is loaded on the Simulator, press the Home key to return to the main screen of the iPad. Tap the Settings application. You can now see a new Settings entry named ApplicationSettings (see Figure 8-4). When you click the ApplicationSettings entry, you see the default settings created for you.

FIGURE 8-2

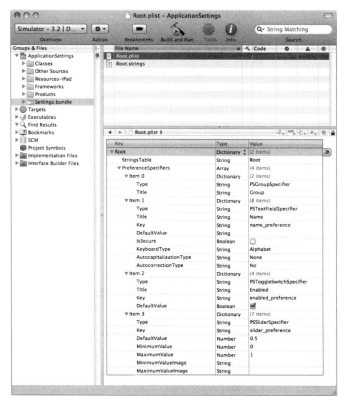

FIGURE 8-3

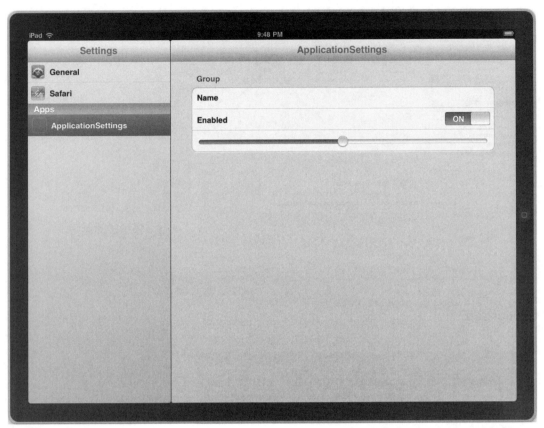

FIGURE 8-4

How It Works

It seems almost magical that without coding a single line, you have incorporated your application preferences into your application. The magic part is actually the Settings.bundle file that you have added to your project. It contains two files: Root.plist and Root.strings. The Root.plist file is an XML file that contains a collection of dictionary objects (key/value pairs). These key/value pairs are translated into the preferences entries you see in the Settings application.

Take a moment to understand the use of the various keys used in the Root.plist file. There are two root-level keys in the Root.plist file, as follows:

➤   StringsTable, which contains the name of the strings file associated with this file. In this case, it is pointing to Root.strings.

➤   PreferenceSpecifiers, which is of type Array and contains an array of dictionaries, with each item containing the information for a single preference.

Each preference is represented by an item (known as PreferenceSpecifiers), such as Item 0, Item 1, Item 2, and so on. Each item has a Type key, which indicates the type of data stored. It can be one of the following, as shown in Table 11-1.

TABLE 11-1: List of Preference Specifiers and Usage

ELEMENT TYPE	DESCRIPTION	USE FOR
PSTextFieldSpecifier	A text field preference. Displays an optional title and an editable text field.	Preferences that require the user to specify a custom string value.
PSTitleValueSpecifier	A read-only string preference.	Displaying preference values as formatted strings.
PSToggleSwitchSpecifier	A toggle switch preference.	Configuring a preference that can have only one of two values.
PSSliderSpecifier	A slider preference.	Preferences that represent a range of values. The value for this type is a real number whose minimum and maximum you specify.
PSMultiValueSpecifier	A multivalue preference.	Preferences that support a set of mutually exclusive values.
PSGroupSpecifier	A group item preference.	Organizing groups of preferences on a single page.
PSChildPaneSpecifier	A child pane preference.	Linking to a new page of preferences.

Each `PreferenceSpecifiers` key contains a list of subkeys that you can use. For example, the `PSTextFieldSpecifier` key provides `Type`, `Title`, `Key`, `DefaultValue`, `IsSecure`, `KeyBoardType`, `AutocapitalizationType`, and `AutocorrectionType` keys. You then set each key with its appropriate values.

Examine the `Root.plist` file in more detail. Note, for example, that `Item 2` has four keys under it: `Type`, `Title`, `Key`, and `DefaultValue`. The `Type` key specifies the type of information it is going to store. In this case, it is a `PSToggleSwitchSpecifier`, which means it will be represented visually as an ON/OFF switch. The `Title` key specifies the text that will be shown for this item (Item 2). The `Key` key is the identifier that uniquely identifies this key so that you can programmatically retrieve the value of this item in your application. Finally, the `DefaultValue` key specifies the default value of this item. In this case, it is checked, indicating that the value is ON.

 NOTE *The key/value pair in the* `Root.plist` *file is case sensitive. Hence, you need to be careful when modifying the entries. A typo can result in a nonfunctional application.*

In the next Try It Out, you modify the `Root.plist` file so that you can use it to store some user's credentials. This is very useful in cases where you are writing an application that requires users to log in to a server. When the user uses your application for the first time, he will supply his login credentials, such as username and password. Your application can then store the credentials in the application preferences so that the next time the user uses your application, the application can automatically retrieve the credentials without asking the user to supply them.

 NOTE *For more information on the use of each key, refer to Apple's "Settings Application Schema Reference" documentation. The easiest way to locate it is to do a Web search for the title. The URL is:* `http://developer.apple.com/iPhone/library/documentation/PreferenceSettings/Conceptual/SettingsApplicationSchemaReference/Introduction/Introduction.html`.

TRY IT OUT Modifying the Application Preferences

1. In Xcode, select the `Root.plist` file and remove all four items under the `PreferenceSpecifiers` key. You do so by selecting individual items under the `PreferenceSpecifiers` key and then pressing the Delete key.

2. To add a new item under the `PreferenceSpecifiers` key, select the `PreferenceSpecifiers` key and click the Add Child button (see Figure 8-5).

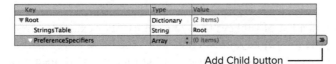

Add Child button ————

FIGURE 8-5

3. A new item is added for you. To add additional items, click the Add Sibling button (see Figure 8-6). Click the Add Sibling button three more times.

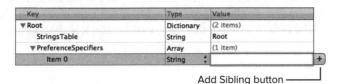

Add Sibling button ————

FIGURE 8-6

4. The `Root.plist` file should now look like Figure 8-7.

FIGURE 8-7

5. Change the Type of Item 0 to Dictionary and expand it by clicking the arrow displayed to the left of it (see Figure 8-8). Click the Add Child button to add a child to Item 0.

FIGURE 8-8

6. A new item is added under Item 0 (see Figure 8-9). Click the Add Sibling button to add another item under Item 0.

FIGURE 8-9

7. Remember, you use the Add Sibling button to add a new item within the same level. Use the Add Child button to add a new child item under the current level.

8. The Root.plist file should now look like Figure 8-10.

FIGURE 8-10

9. Modify the entire `Root.plist` file so that it looks like Figure 8-11. Ensure that the capitalization of each key and value pair is correct. Pay particular attention to the `Type` of each item.

Key	Type	Value
▼ Root	Dictionary	(2 items)
StringsTable	String	Root
▼ PreferenceSpecifiers	Array	(4 items)
▼ Item 0	Dictionary	(2 items)
Title	String	Account Information
Type	String	PSGroupSpecifier
▼ Item 1	Dictionary	(6 items)
Title	String	Login Name
Type	String	PSTextFieldSpecifier
Key	String	login_name
DefaultValue	String	login name
AutoCapitalizationType	String	None
AutocorrectionType	String	No
▼ Item 2	Dictionary	(5 items)
Title	String	Password
Type	String	PSTextFieldSpecifier
Key	String	password
DefaultValue	String	password
IsSecure	Boolean	☑
▼ Item 3	Dictionary	(6 items)
Title	String	Favorite Color
Type	String	PSMultiValueSpecifier
Key	String	color
DefaultValue	String	Red
▼ Values	Array	(3 items)
Item 0	String	Red
Item 1	String	Green
Item 2	String	Blue
▼ Titles	Array	(3 items)
Item 0	String	Red Color
Item 1	String	Green Color
Item 2	String	Blue Color

FIGURE 8-11

10. Save the project and press Command-R to test the application on the iPhone Simulator. Press the Home button and launch the Settings application again. Select the `ApplicationSettings` settings and observe the preferences shown (see Figure 8-12). Clicking on the Favorite Color setting will display a page for choosing your favorite color (see Figure 8-13).

11. Make some changes to the settings values and then press the Home button to return to the Home screen. The changes in the settings are automatically saved to the device. When you return to the Settings page again, the new values will be displayed.

How It Works

What you have done is basically modify the `Root.plist` file to store three preferences Login Name, Password, and Favorite Color. For the password field, you use the `IsSecure` key to indicate that the value must be masked when displaying it to the user. Of particular interest is the Favorite Color preference, for which you use the `Titles` and `Values` keys to display a list of selectable choices and their corresponding values to store on the iPad.

The following preference specifiers are used in this example:

➤ PSGroupSpecifier Used to display a group for the settings. In this case, all the settings are grouped under the Account Information group.

➤ PSTextFieldSpecifier Specifies a text field.

➤ PSMultiValueSpecifier Specifies a list of selectable values. The Titles item contains a list of visible text that users can select from. The Values item is the corresponding value for the text selected by the user. For example, if the user selects Blue Color as his favorite color, the value Blue will be stored on the iPhone.

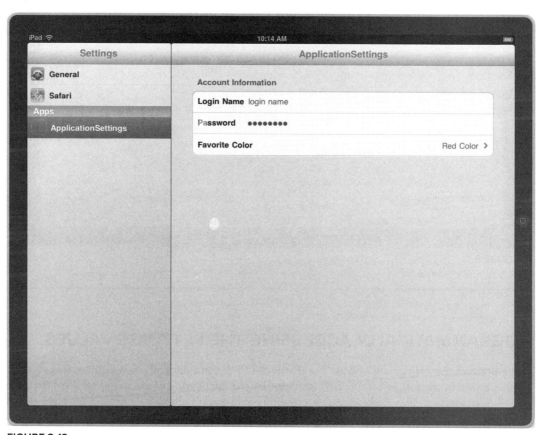

FIGURE 8-12

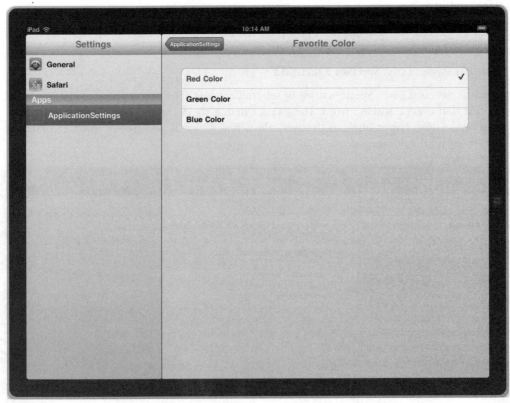

FIGURE 8-13

PROGRAMMATICALLY ACCESSING THE SETTINGS VALUES

The preferences settings are of little use if you can't programmatically access them from within your application. In the following sections, you modify the application so that you can load the preferences settings as well as make changes to them programmatically.

First, use the following Try It Out to prepare the UI by connecting the necessary outlets and actions.

TRY IT OUT   Preparing the UI

1.   Using the project created in the previous section, double-click the
ApplicationSettingsViewController.xib file to edit it in Interface Builder.

2.   Populate the View window with the following views (see Figure 8-14):

➤   Round Rect Button

➤   Label

➤ Text Field

➤ PickerView

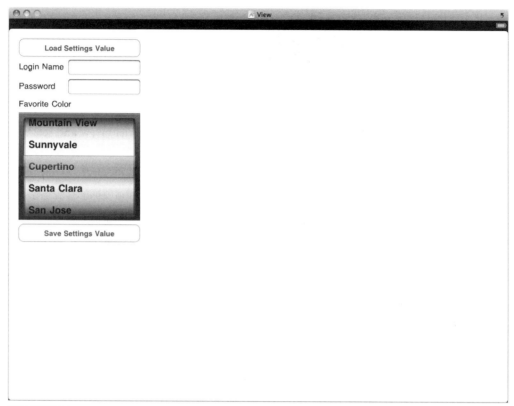

FIGURE 8-14

3. In Xcode, insert the following code that appears in bold into the ApplicationSettingsView-Controller.h file:

```
#import <UIKit/UIKit.h>

@interface ApplicationSettingsViewController : UIViewController
    <UIPickerViewDataSource, UIPickerViewDelegate> {

    IBOutlet UITextField *loginName;
    IBOutlet UITextField *password;
    IBOutlet UIPickerView *favoriteColor;
}

@property (nonatomic, retain) UITextField *loginName;
@property (nonatomic, retain) UITextField *password;
@property (nonatomic, retain) UIPickerView *favoriteColor;
```

```
-(IBAction) loadSettings: (id) sender;
-(IBAction) saveSettings: (id) sender;

@end
```

code snippet ApplicationSettingsViewController.h

4. In Interface Builder, connect the outlets and action to the various views. In the `ApplicationSettingsViewController.xib` window, do the following:

➤ Control-click and drag the File's Owner item to the first TextField view and select `loginName`.

➤ Control-click and drag the File's Owner item to the second TextField view and select `password`.

➤ Control-click and drag the File's Owner item to the Picker view and select `favoriteColor`.

➤ Control-click and drag the Picker view to the File's Owner item and select `dataSource`.

➤ Control-click and drag the Picker view to the File's Owner item and select `delegate`.

➤ Control-click and drag the Load Settings Value button to the File's Owner item and select `loadSettings:`.

➤ Control-click and drag the Save Settings Value button to the File's Owner item and select `saveSettings:`.

5. Right-click the File's Owner item to verify that all the connections are connected properly (see Figure 8-15).

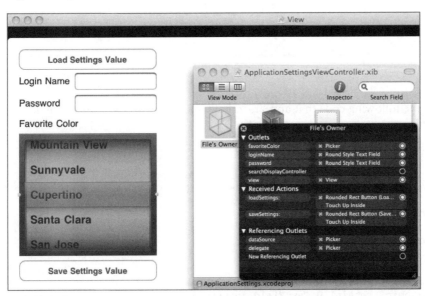

FIGURE 8-15

6. Save the project in Interface Builder.

7. In Xcode, add the following bold code to the `ApplicationSettingsViewController.m` file:

```objc
#import "ApplicationSettingsViewController.h"

@implementation ApplicationSettingsViewController

@synthesize loginName;
@synthesize password;
@synthesize favoriteColor;

NSMutableArray *colors;
NSString *favoriteColorSelected;

- (void)viewDidLoad {
    //---create an array containing the colors values---
    colors = [[NSMutableArray alloc] init];
    [colors addObject:@"Red"];
    [colors addObject:@"Green"];
    [colors addObject:@"Blue"];

    [super viewDidLoad];
}

//---number of components in the Picker view---
- (NSInteger)numberOfComponentsInPickerView:(UIPickerView *)thePickerView {
    return 1;
}

//---number of items(rows) in the Picker view---
- (NSInteger)pickerView:(UIPickerView *)thePickerView
numberOfRowsInComponent:(NSInteger)component {
    return [colors count];
}

//---populating the Picker view---
- (NSString *)pickerView:(UIPickerView *)thePickerView titleForRow:(NSInteger)row
            forComponent:(NSInteger)component {
    return [colors objectAtIndex:row];
}

//---the item selected by the user---
- (void)pickerView:(UIPickerView *)thePickerView
        didSelectRow:(NSInteger)row
          inComponent:(NSInteger)component {
    favoriteColorSelected = [colors objectAtIndex:row];
}

- (void)dealloc {
    [colors release];
    [favoriteColorSelected release];
    [loginName release];
    [password release];
```

```
[favoriteColor release];
[super dealloc];
}
```

8.   That's it! Press Command-R to test the application on the iPhone Simulator. Figure 8-16 shows the PickerView loaded with the three colors.

FIGURE 8-16

How It Works

So far, all the work that has been done prepares the UI for displaying the values retrieved from the preferences settings. In particular, you need to prepare the Picker view to display a list of colors from which the user can choose.

To load the Picker view with the three colors, ensure that the `ApplicationSettingsViewController` class conforms to the `UIPickerViewDataSource` and `UIPickerViewDelegate` protocols:

```
@interface ApplicationSettingsViewController : UIViewController
    <UIPickerViewDataSource, UIPickerViewDelegate> {
```

The `UIPickerViewDataSource` protocol defines the methods to populate the Picker view with items while the `UIPickerViewDelegate` protocol defines methods to enable users to select an item from the Picker view.

In the `ApplicationSettingsViewController.m` file, you first create an `NSMutableArray` object to store the list of colors available for selection, in the `viewDidLoad` method:

```
- (void)viewDidLoad {
    //---create an array containing the colors values---
    colors = [[NSMutableArray alloc] init];
```

```
[colors addObject:@"Red"];
[colors addObject:@"Green"];
[colors addObject:@"Blue"];

[super viewDidLoad];
}
```

To set the number of components (columns) in the Picker view, implement the `numberOfComponentsInPickerView:` method:

```
//---number of components in the Picker view---
- (NSInteger)numberOfComponentsInPickerView:(UIPickerView *)thePickerView {
    return 1;
}
```

To set the number of items (rows) you want to display in the Picker view, implement the `pickerView:numberOfRowsInComponent:` method:

```
//---number of items(rows) in the Picker view---
- (NSInteger)pickerView:(UIPickerView *)thePickerView
numberOfRowsInComponent:(NSInteger)component {
    return [colors count];
}
```

To populate the Picker view with the three colors, implement the `pickerView:titleForRow:forComponent:` method:

```
//---populating the Picker view---
- (NSString *)pickerView:(UIPickerView *)thePickerView
            titleForRow:(NSInteger)row
          forComponent:(NSInteger)component {
    return [colors objectAtIndex:row];
}
```

To save the color selected by the user in the Picker view, implement the `pickerView:didSelectRow:inComponent:` method:

```
//---the item selected by the user---
- (void)pickerView:(UIPickerView *)thePickerView didSelectRow:(NSInteger)row
    inComponent:(NSInteger)component {
    favoriteColorSelected = [colors objectAtIndex:row];
}
```

The color selected will now be saved in the `favoriteColorSelected` object.

Loading the Settings Values

With the user interface of the application ready, it is now time to see how you can programmatically load the values of the preference settings and then display them in your application. This display is useful because it gives your user a chance to view the values of the settings without needing to go to the Settings application.

TRY IT OUT Loading Settings Values

1. Using the project created in the previous section, insert the following method to the
`ApplicationSettingsController.m` file:

```
- (IBAction) loadSettings: (id) sender{

    NSUserDefaults *defaults = [NSUserDefaults standardUserDefaults];
    loginName.text = [defaults objectForKey:@"login_name"];
    password.text = [defaults objectForKey:@"password"];

    //---find the index of the array for the color saved---
    favoriteColorSelected = [[NSString alloc] initWithString:
                               [defaults objectForKey:@"color"]];

    int selIndex = [colors indexOfObject:favoriteColorSelected];

    //---display the saved color in the Picker view---
    [favoriteColor selectRow:selIndex inComponent:0 animated:YES];
}
```

code snippet ApplicationSettingsController.m

2. Press Command-R to test the application on the iPhone Simulator. When the application is loaded,
tap on the Load Settings Values button and you should see the settings values displayed in the Text
Field views and the PickerView (see Figure 8-17).

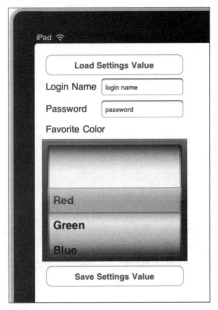

FIGURE 8-17

How It Works

To load the values of the preferences settings, you use a class known as the NSUserDefaults:

```
NSUserDefaults *defaults = [NSUserDefaults standardUserDefaults];
```

The preceding statement returns the one-and-only-one instance of the NSUserDefaults class. Think of NSUserDefaults as a common database that you can use to store your application preference settings.

To retrieve the values of the preference settings, you use the objectForKey: method and specify the name of the preference setting you want to retrieve:

```
loginName.text = [defaults objectForKey:@"login_name"];
password.text = [defaults objectForKey:@"password"];

//---find the index of the array for the color saved---
favoriteColorSelected = [[NSString alloc] initWithString:
                        [defaults objectForKey:@"color"]];
```

Resetting the Preference Settings Values

Sometimes you may want to reset the values of the preference settings of your application. This is especially true if you have made an error in the Root.plist file and want to reset all the settings. The easiest way to do this is to remove the application from the device or Simulator. To do so, simply tap and hold the application's icon, and when the icons start to wriggle, tap the X button to remove the application. The preference settings associated with the application will also be removed.

Another way to clear the values of the preference settings would be to navigate to the folder containing your application (on the iPhone Simulator). The applications on the iPhone Simulator are stored in the following folder: ~/Library/Application Support/iPhone Simulator>/<version_no>/ Applications/ (note that the tilde symbol (~) represents your home directory and not your root hard disk). Inside this folder, you need to find the folder containing your application. Within the application folder is a Library/Preferences folder. Delete the file ending with application_ name.plist (see Figure 8-18) and your preferences settings will now be reset.

FIGURE 8-18

Saving the Settings Values

Now that you have seen how to load the values of preferences settings, use the following Try It Out to see how to save the values back to the preferences settings. This allows users to directly modify their preferences settings from within your application, instead of using the Settings application to do so.

TRY IT OUT Saving Settings Values

1. Using the same project created in the previous section, insert the following method in the ApplicationSettingsViewController.m file:

```
-(IBAction) saveSettings: (id) sender {

    NSUserDefaults *defaults = [NSUserDefaults standardUserDefaults];
    [defaults setObject:loginName.text forKey:@"login name"];
    [defaults setObject:password.text forKey:@"password"];
    [defaults setObject:favoriteColorSelected forKey:@"color"];

    UIAlertView *alert = [[UIAlertView alloc]
                          initWithTitle:@"Settings Values Saved"
                          message:@"Settings Saved"
                          delegate:nil
                          cancelButtonTitle: @"Done"
                          otherButtonTitles:nil];
    [alert show];
    [alert release];
}
```

2. Press Command-R to test the application on the iPhone Simulator. Make some changes to the login name, password, and favorite color. When you click the Save Settings Value button, all the changes are made to the device (see Figure 8-19). When you restart the application, clicking the Load Settings Values button displays the updated settings values.

How It Works

You use the same approach to save the values back to the preferences settings as you do to retrieve those settings; that is, you use the NSUserDefaults class:

```
NSUserDefaults *defaults = [NSUserDefaults standardUserDefaults];
[defaults setObject:loginName.text forKey:@"login_name"];
[defaults setObject:password.text forKey:@"password"];
[defaults setObject:favoriteColorSelected forKey:@"color"];
```

Rather than use the objectForKey: method, you now use the setObject:forKey: method to save the values.

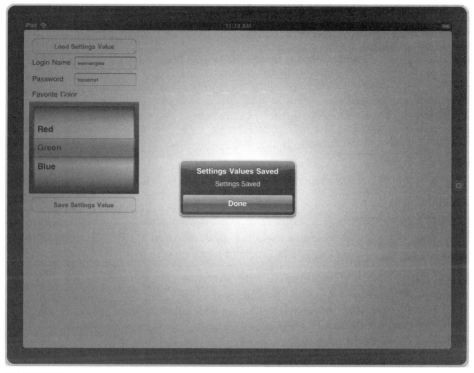

FIGURE 8-19

SUMMARY

This chapter explained how you can make use of the Application Preferences feature of the iPad to save your application's preferences to the Settings application. Doing so allows you to delegate most of the mundane tasks of saving and loading an application's preferences settings to the OS. All you need to do is to use the NSUserDefaults class to programmatically access the preferences settings.

1. You have learned that you can use the NSUserDefaults class to access the preferences settings values for your application. What are the methods for retrieving and saving the values?

2. What are the two ways in which you can remove the preferences settings for an application?

3. What is the difference between the Add Child button and the Add Sibling button in the Property List editor?

Answers to the Exercises can be found in Appendix A.

▶ **WHAT YOU LEARNED IN THIS CHAPTER**

TOPIC	KEY CONCEPTS
Adding application preferences to your application	Add a Settings Bundle file to your project and modify the `Root.plist` file.

Loading the value of a preference setting	`NSUserDefaults *defaults =`
	
	    `[NSUserDefaults standardUserDefaults];`
	
	`NSString *strLoginname =`
	
	    `[defaults objectForKey:@"login_name"];`

Resetting preference settings values	Either remove the entire application from the Home screen, or remove it via the iPhone Simulator folder on your Mac.

Saving the value of a preference setting	`NSUserDefaults *defaults =`
	
	    `[NSUserDefaults standardUserDefaults];`
	
	`[defaults setObject:loginName.text`
	
	    `forKey:@"login_name"];`

9

File Handling

WHAT YOU WILL LEARN IN THIS CHAPTER:

➤ Where your applications are stored on the iPad

➤ The various folders within your `Applications` folder

➤ How to read and write to files in the `Documents` and `tmp` folders

➤ How to use a property to store structured data

➤ How to programmatically retrieve values stored in a property list

➤ How to modify the values retrieved from a property list and save the changes to a file

➤ How to copy bundled resources to the application's folder during runtime

All the applications you have developed up to this point are pretty straightforward — the application starts, performs something interesting, and ends. In Chapter 8, you saw how you can make use of the application settings feature to save the preferences of your application to a central location managed by the Settings application. Sometimes, however, you simply need to save some data to your application's folder for use later. For example, rather than keep files you download from a remote server in memory, a more effective and memory efficient method is to save them in a file so that you can use them later (even after the application has shut down and restarted).

In this chapter, you learn more about how you can persist data in your application so that you can use it later. You learn the two available approaches: saving the data as files and as a property list. You also learn how to bundle resources such as text files and database files with your application so that when the application is installed on the user's device, the resources can be copied onto the local storage of the device and be used from there.

UNDERSTANDING THE APPLICATION FOLDERS

Your applications are stored in the iPad file system, so you'll find it useful to understand the folder structure of the iPad.

On the desktop, the content of the iPhone Simulator is stored in the `~/Library/Application Support/iPhone Simulator>/<version_no>/` folder.

> **NOTE** *The ~ (tilde) represents the current user's directory. Specifically, the preceding directory is equivalent to:*
>
> ```
> /Users/<username>/Library/Application Support/
> iPhone Simulator>/<version_no>/
> ```

Within this folder are five subfolders:

➤ Applications

➤ Library

➤ Media

➤ Root

➤ tmp

The `Applications` folder contains all your installed applications (see Figure 9-1). Within it are several folders with long filenames. These filenames are generated by Xcode to uniquely identify each of your applications. Each application's folder holds your application's executable file (the `.app` file, which includes all embedded resources), together with a few other folders, such as `Documents`, `Library`, and `tmp`. On the iPad, all applications run within their own sandboxed environments — that is, an application can access only the files stored within its own folder; it cannot access the folders of other applications.

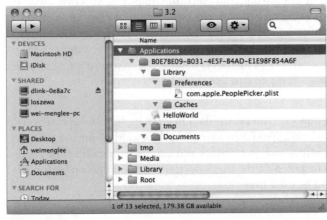

FIGURE 9-1

Using the Documents and Library Folders

The Documents folder is where you can store files used by your application, whereas the Library folder stores the application-specific settings. The tmp folder stores temporary data required by your application.

So how you do write to these folders? The following Try It Out provides an example of doing just that. You can download the indicated code files to work through the project.

TRY IT OUT   Writing and Reading from Files

codefile FilesHandling.zip available for download at Wrox.com

1.   Using Xcode, create a new View-based Application project and name it FilesHandling.

2.   In the FilesHandlingViewController.h file, add in the following bold statements:

```
#import <UIKit/UIKit.h>

@interface FilesHandlingViewController : UIViewController {

}

-(NSString *) documentsPath;
-(NSString *) readFromFile:(NSString *) filePath;
-(void) writeToFile:(NSString *) text withFileName:(NSString *) filePath;

@end
```

3.   In the FilesHandlingViewController.m file, add in the following bold statements:

```
#import "FilesHandlingViewController.h"

@implementation FilesHandlingViewController

//---finds the path to the application's Documents directory---
-(NSString *) documentsPath {
    NSArray *paths =
        NSSearchPathForDirectoriesInDomains(
            NSDocumentDirectory, NSUserDomainMask, YES);

    NSString *documentsDir = [paths objectAtIndex:0];
    return documentsDir;
}

//---write content into a specified file path---
-(void) writeToFile:(NSString *) text withFileName:(NSString *) filePath {
    NSMutableArray *array = [[NSMutableArray alloc] init];
    [array addObject:text];
    [array writeToFile:filePath atomically:YES];
    [array release];
}
```

```
//---read content from a specified file path---
-(NSString *) readFromFile:(NSString *) filePath {
    //---check if file exists---
    if ([[NSFileManager defaultManager] fileExistsAtPath:filePath]) {
        NSArray *array = [[NSArray alloc] initWithContentsOfFile: filePath];
        NSString *data = [NSString stringWithFormat:@"%@",
                                    [array objectAtIndex:0]];
        [array release];
        return data;
    }
    else
        return nil;
}

- (void)viewDidLoad {

    //---formulate filename---
    NSString *fileName =
        [[self documentsPath] stringByAppendingPathComponent:@"data.txt"];

    //---write something to the file---
    [self writeToFile:@"a string of text" withFileName:fileName];

    //---read it back---
    NSString *fileContent = [self readFromFile:fileName];

    //---display the content read in the Debugger Console window---
    NSLog(fileContent);

    [super viewDidLoad];
}
```

4. Press Command-R to test the application on the iPhone Simulator.

5. Go to Finder and navigate to the Documents folder of your application. The data.txt file is now visible (see Figure 9-2).

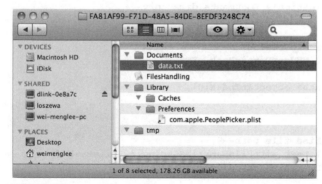

FIGURE 9-2

6. When you deploy the application, the location of the file on the real device is /private/var/mobile/Applications/<application_id>/Documents/data.txt.

7. Double-click the `data.txt` file to see its content as follows:

```
<?xml version="1.0" encoding="UTF-8"?>
<!DOCTYPE plist PUBLIC "-//Apple//DTD PLIST 1.0//EN"
    "http://www.apple.com/DTDs/PropertyList-1.0.dtd">
<plist version="1.0">
<array>
    <string>a string of text</string>
</array>
</plist>
```

8. Turn on the Debugger Console window (Shift-Command-R) and you see the application print the string `"a string of text"`.

How It Works

You first define the `documentsPath` method, which returns the path to the `Documents` directory:

```
//---finds the path to the application's Documents directory---
-(NSString *) documentsPath {
    NSArray *paths =
        NSSearchPathForDirectoriesInDomains(
            NSDocumentDirectory, NSUserDomainMask, YES);
    NSString *documentsDir = [paths objectAtIndex:0];
    return documentsDir;
}
```

Basically, you use the `NSSearchPathForDirectoriesInDomains()` function to create a list of directory search paths, indicating that you want to look for the `Documents` directory (using the `NSDocumentDirectory` constant). The `NSUserDomainMask` constant indicates that you want to search from the application's home directory, and the `YES` argument indicates that you want to obtain the full path of all the directories found.

To obtain the path to the `Documents` folder, simply extract the first item of the `paths` array (because there is one and only one `Documents` folder in an iPad application's folder). In fact, this block of code is derived from the Mac OS X API, where multiple folders might be returned. But in the case of the iPad, there can only be one `Documents` folder per application.

You next define the `writeToFile:withFileName:` method, which creates an `NSMutableArray` and adds the text to be written to file to it.

```
//---write content into a specified file path---
-(void) writeToFile:(NSString *) text withFileName:(NSString *) filePath {
    NSMutableArray *array = [[NSMutableArray alloc] init];
    [array addObject:text];
    [array writeToFile:filePath atomically:YES];
    [array release];
}
```

To persist the content (a process known as serialization) of the `NSMutableArray` to a file, you use its `writeToFile:atomically:` method. The `atomically:` parameter indicates that the file should first be written to a temporary file before it is renamed to the filename specified. This approach guarantees that the file will never be corrupted, even if the system crashes during the writing process.

To read the content from a file, you define the `readFromFile:` method:

```
//---read content from a specified file path---
-(NSString *) readFromFile:(NSString *) filePath {
    //---check if file exists---
    if ([[NSFileManager defaultManager] fileExistsAtPath:filePath]) {
        NSArray *array = [[NSArray alloc] initWithContentsOfFile: filePath];
        NSString *data = [NSString stringWithFormat:@"%@",
                                    [array objectAtIndex:0]];
        [array release];
        return data;
    }
    else
        return nil;
}
```

You first use an instance of the `NSFileManager` class to check to see whether the specified file exists. If it does, you read the content of the file into an `NSArray` object. In this case, because you know that the file contains a single line of text, you extract the first element in the array.

With all the methods in place, you are ready to make use of them. When the view is loaded, you create the pathname for a file that you want to save. You then write a string of text into the file and immediately read it back and print it in the Debugger Console window:

```
- (void)viewDidLoad {

    //---formulate filename---
    NSString *fileName =
        [[self documentsPath] stringByAppendingPathComponent:@"data.txt"];

    //---write something to the file---
    [self writeToFile:@"a string of text" withFileName:fileName];

    //---read it back---
    NSString *fileContent = [self readFromFile:fileName];

    //---display the content read in the Debugger Console window---
    NSLog(fileContent);

    [super viewDidLoad];
}
```

Storing Files in the Temporary Folder

In addition to storing files in the `Documents` directory, you can store temporary files in the `tmp` folder. Files stored in the `tmp` folder are not backed up by iTunes, so you need to find a permanent place for the files you want to be sure to keep. To get the path to the `tmp` folder, you can call the `NSTemporaryDirectory()` function, like this:

```
-(NSString *) tempPath{
    return NSTemporaryDirectory();
}
```

The following statement returns the path of a file (`"data.txt"`) to be stored in the `tmp` folder:

```
NSString *fileName = [[self tempPath]
    stringByAppendingPathComponent:@"data.txt"];
```

USING PROPERTY LISTS

In iPad programming, you can use property lists to store structured data using key/value pairs. Property lists are stored as XML files and are highly transportable across file systems and networks. For example, you might want to store a list of AppStore applications titles in your application. Because applications in the AppStore are organized into category, it would be natural to store this information using a property list employing the structure shown in the following table.

CATEGORY	TITLES
Games	`"Animal Park"`, `"Biology Quiz"`, `"Calculus Test"`
Entertainment	`"Eye Balls - iBlower"`, `"iBell"`, `"iCards Birthday"`
Utilities	`"Battery Monitor"`, `"iSystemInfo"`

In Xcode, you can create and add a property list in the Resources folder of your application and populate it with items using the built-in Property List Editor. The property list is deployed together with the application. Programmatically, you can retrieve the values stored in a property list using the `NSDictionary` class. More important, if you need to make changes to a property list, you can write the changes to a file so that subsequently you can refer to the file directly instead of the property list.

In the following Try It Out, you create a property list and populate it with some values. You then read the values from the property list during runtime, make some changes, and save the modified values to another property list file in the Documents directory.

> **NOTE** *To store application-specific settings that the user can modify outside your application, consider using the* `NSUserDefaults` *class to store the settings in the Settings application. Application Settings are discussed in Chapter 8.*

TRY IT OUT   Creating and Modifying a Property List

1. Using the same project created earlier, right-click the project name in Xcode and choose Add ⇨ New File.

2. Select the Resource item on the left of the New File dialog and select the Property List template on the right of the dialog (see Figure 9-3).

3. Name the property list as `Apps.plist`.

4. Populate `Apps.plist` as shown in Figure 9-4.

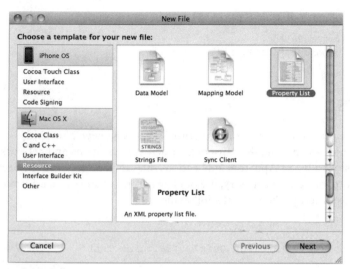

FIGURE 9-3

FIGURE 9-4

Add the following bold statements to the viewDidLoad method:- (void)viewDidLoad {

```
    //---formulate filename---
    NSString *fileName = [[self documentsPath]
```

```
                                stringByAppendingPathComponent:@"data.txt"];

//---write something to the file---
[self writeToFile:@"a string of text" withFileName:fileName];

//---read it back---
NSString *fileContent = [self readFromFile:fileName];

//---display the content read in the Debugger Console window---
NSLog(fileContent);

//---get the path to the property list file---
NSString *plistFileName =
    [[self documentsPath] stringByAppendingPathComponent:@"Apps.plist"];

//---if the property list file can be found---
if ([[NSFileManager defaultManager] fileExistsAtPath:plistFileName]) {
    //---load the content of the property list file into a NSDictionary
    // object---
    NSDictionary *dict = [[NSDictionary alloc]
                            initWithContentsOfFile:plistFileName];
    //---for each category---
    for (NSString *category in dict) {
        NSLog(category);
        NSLog(@"========");
        //---return all titles in an array---
        NSArray *titles = [dict valueForKey:category];
        //---print out all the titles in that category---
        for (NSString *title in titles) {
            NSLog(title);
        }
    }
    [dict release];
}
else {
    //---load the property list from the Resources folder---
    NSString *pListPath =
        [[NSBundle mainBundle] pathForResource:@"Apps" ofType:@"plist"];

    NSDictionary *dict =
        [[NSDictionary alloc] initWithContentsOfFile:pListPath];

    //---make a mutable copy of the dictionary object---
    NSMutableDictionary *copyOfDict = [dict mutableCopy];

    //---get all the different categories---
    NSArray *categoriesArray =
        [[copyOfDict allKeys] sortedArrayUsingSelector:@selector(compare:)];

    //---for each category---
    for (NSString *category in categoriesArray) {

        //---get all the app titles in that category---
        NSArray *titles = [dict valueForKey:category];

        //---make a mutable copy of the array---
```

```
        NSMutableArray *mutableTitles = [titles mutableCopy];

        //---add a new title to the category---
        [mutableTitles addObject:@"New App title"];

        //---set the array back to the dictionary object---
        [copyOfDict setObject:mutableTitles forKey:category];
        [mutableTitles release];
    }

    //---write the dictionary to file---
    fileName =
        [[self documentsPath] stringByAppendingPathComponent:@"Apps.plist"];

    [copyOfDict writeToFile:fileName atomically:YES];
    [dict release];
    [copyOfDict release];
}

[super viewDidLoad];
}
```

5. Press Command-R to test the application on the iPhone Simulator.

6. When you first run the application, you see that the application creates a new .plist file in the Documents directory of your application. Double-click the .plist file to view it using the Property List Editor; you see a new item named New App title for each category of applications (see Figure 9-5).

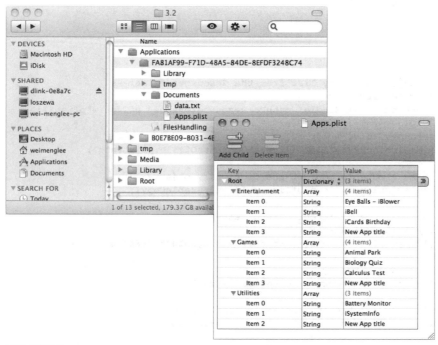

FIGURE 9-5

7. Run the application a second time and it prints the content of the `.plist` file in the `Documents` directory to the Debugger Console window (see Figure 9-6), proving the existence of the property list in the Documents folder.

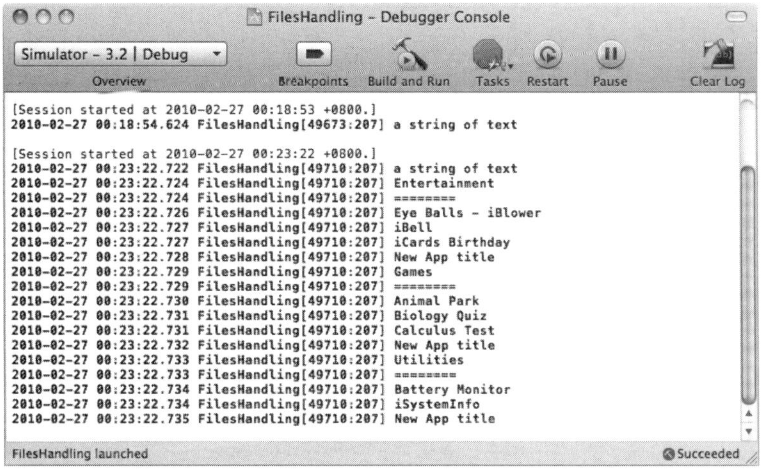

FIGURE 9-6

How It Works

The first part of this example shows how you can add a property list file to your application. In the property list file, you add three keys representing the category of applications in the AppStore: Entertainment, Games, and Utilities. Each category contains a list of application titles.

When the view is loaded, you look for a file named `Apps.plist` in the `Documents` directory of your application:

```
//---get the path to the property list file---
NSString *plistFileName =
    [[self documentsPath] stringByAppendingPathComponent:@"Apps.plist"];
```

If the file is found, you load its content into an `NSDictionary` object:

```
//---if the property list file can be found---
if ([[NSFileManager defaultManager] fileExistsAtPath:plistFileName]) {
    //---load the content of the property list file into a NSDictionary
    // object---
    NSDictionary *dict = [[NSDictionary alloc]
                          initWithContentsOfFile:plistFileName];
    //...
    //...
}
```

Next, you enumerate through all the keys in the dictionary object and print the title of each application in the Debugger Console window:

```
//---for each category---
for (NSString *category in dict) {
    NSLog(category);
```

```
        NSLog(@"=======");
        //---return all titles in an array---
        NSArray *titles = [dict valueForKey:category];
        //---print out all the titles in that category---
        for (NSString *title in titles) {
            NSLog(title);
        }
    }
    [dict release];
```

When the application is run for the first time, the Apps.plist file is not available, so you load it from the Resources folder:

```
else {
    //---load the property list from the Resources folder---
    NSString *pListPath =
        [[NSBundle mainBundle] pathForResource:@"Apps" ofType:@"plist"];

    NSDictionary *dict =
        [[NSDictionary alloc] initWithContentsOfFile:pListPath];
    //...
    //...
}
```

Because you are making changes to the dictionary object, you need to make a mutable copy of the dictionary object and assign it to an NSMutableDictionary object:

```
//---make a mutable copy of the dictionary object---
NSMutableDictionary *copyOfDict = [dict mutableCopy];
```

This step is important because the NSDictionary object is immutable, meaning that after the items are populated from the property list, you cannot add content to the dictionary object. Using the mutableCopy method of the NSDictionary class allows you to create a mutable instance of the dictionary object, which is NSMutableDictionary.

You then retrieve an array containing all the keys in the mutable dictionary object:

```
//---get all the different categories---
NSArray *categoriesArray =
    [[copyOfDict allKeys] sortedArrayUsingSelector:@selector(compare:)];
```

You use this array to loop through all the keys in the dictionary so that you can add some additional titles to each category:

```
//---for each category---
for (NSString *category in categoriesArray) {

}
```

Note that you cannot enumerate using the NSMutableDictionary object like this:

```
for (NSString *category in copyOfDict) {
    //...
}
```

That's because you cannot add items to the NSMutableDictionary object while it is being enumerated. Therefore, you need to loop using an NSArray object.

When you're inside the loop, you extract all the titles of the applications in each category and make a mutable copy of the array containing the titles of the applications:

```
//---get all the app titles in that category---
NSArray *titles = [dict valueForKey:category];

//---make a mutable copy of the array---
NSMutableArray *mutableTitles = [titles mutableCopy];
```

You can now add a new title to the mutable array containing the application titles:

```
//---add a new title to the category---
[mutableTitles addObject:@"New App title"];
```

After the additional item is added to the mutable array, set it back to the mutable dictionary object:

```
//---set the array back to the dictionary object---
[copyOfDict setObject:mutableTitles forKey:category];
[mutableTitles release];
```

Finally, you write the mutable dictionary object to a file using the writeToFile:atomically: method:

```
//---write the dictionary to file---
fileName =
    [[self documentsPath] stringByAppendingPathComponent:@"Apps.plist"];

[copyOfDict writeToFile:fileName atomically:YES];
[dict release];
[copyOfDict release];
```

COPYING BUNDLED RESOURCES

In the previous section, you saw how to embed a property list file into your application and then programmatically recreate the property list and save it onto the Documents folder during runtime. While that example showed the various ways to manipulate a property list, in general it is much easier to simply copy the resource (such as the property list) into the Documents folder directly.

All resources embedded within your application (commonly known as bundled resources) are read-only. If you need to make changes to them, you need to copy them onto the application's folders, such as the Documents or tmp folders. You can do so by copying the resource when the application starts up. The ideal location to perform this is in the application delegate. Using the preceding example, you could define the following copyFileInBundleToDocumentsFolder:withExtension: method in the FilesHandlingAppDelegate.m file:

Available for download on Wrox.com

```
- (void) copyFileInBundleToDocumentsFolder:(NSString *) fileName
                       withExtension:(NSString *) ext {

    //---get the path of the Documents folder---
```

```
    NSArray *paths = NSSearchPathForDirectoriesInDomains(
        NSDocumentDirectory, NSUserDomainMask, YES);
    NSString *documentsDirectory = [paths objectAtIndex:0];

    //---get the path to the file you want to copy in the Documents folder---
    NSString *filePath = [documentsDirectory stringByAppendingPathComponent:
                            [NSString stringWithString:fileName]];
    filePath = [filePath stringByAppendingString:@"."];
    filePath = [filePath stringByAppendingString:ext];
    [filePath retain];

    //---check if file is already in Documents folder,
    // if not, copy it from the bundle---
    NSFileManager *fileManger = [NSFileManager defaultManager];

    if (![fileManger fileExistsAtPath:filePath]) {
        //---get the path of the file in the bundle---
        NSString *pathToFileInBundle =
            [[NSBundle mainBundle] pathForResource:fileName ofType:ext];

        //---copy the file in the bundle to the Documents folder---
        NSError *error = nil;
        bool success =
            [fileManger copyItemAtPath:pathToFileInBundle
                                toPath:filePath error:&error];
        if (success) {
            NSLog(@"File copied");
        }
        else {
            NSLog([error localizedDescription]);
        }
    }
}
```

code snippet FilesHandlingAppDelegate.m

This method simply copies the specified file to the Documents folder if it is not already there.

To copy the property list when the application is starting up, call the copyFileInBundleToDocuments Folder:withExtension: method in the application:didFinishLaunchingWithOptions: event:

```
- (BOOL)application:(UIApplication *)application
didFinishLaunchingWithOptions:(NSDictionary *)launchOptions {

    //---copy the txt files to the Documents folder---
    [self copyFileInBundleToDocumentsFolder:@"Apps" withExtension:@"plist"];

    // Override point for customization after app launch
    [window addSubview:viewController.view];
    [window makeKeyAndVisible];

    return YES;
}
```

Doing so ensures that the property list is always copied to the Documents folder when the application starts running.

SUMMARY

This chapter demonstrated how to write a file to the file system of the iPhone and how to read it back. In addition, you saw how structured data can be represented using a property list and how you can programmatically work with a property list using a dictionary object. The next chapter shows you how to use databases to store more complex data.

EXERCISES

1. Describe the uses of the various folders within an application's folder.

2. What is the difference between the NSDictionary and NSMutableDictionary classes?

3. Name the paths of the Documents and tmp folders on a real device.

Answers to the Exercises can be found in Appendix A.

▶ **WHAT YOU LEARNED IN THIS CHAPTER**

TOPIC	KEY CONCEPTS
Subdirectories in each of the applications folders	`Documents`, `Library`, and `tmp`
Getting the path of the `Documents` directory	```NSArray *paths = NSSearchPathForDirectoriesInDomains(
NSDocumentDirectory,
NSUserDomainMask, YES);
NSString *documentsDir = [paths objectAtIndex:0];```
Getting the path of the `tmp` directory	```-(NSString *) tempPath {
return NSTemporaryDirectory();
}```
Check whether file exists	```if ([[NSFileManager defaultManager]
fileExistsAtPath:filePath]) {
}```
Load a property list from the `Resources` folder	```NSString *pListPath = [[NSBundle mainBundle]
pathForResource:@"Apps"
ofType:@"plist"];```
Create a mutable copy of an `NSDictionary` object	```NSDictionary *dict = [[NSDictionary alloc]
initWithContentsOfFile:pListPath];
NSMutableDictionary *copyOfDict = [dict mutableCopy];```
Using Bundled Resources in your application	Copy the resources onto the application's folders, such as `Documents` or `tmp`. You should copy the resources in the application's delegate when the application has just finished launching.

10

Database Storage Using SQLite3

For simple applications, you can write the data you want to persist to a simple text file. For more structured data, you can use a property list. For large and complex data, it is more efficient to store them using a database. The iPhone comes with the SQLite3 database library, which you can use to store your data. With your data stored in a database, your application can populate a Table view or store a large amount of data in a structured manner.

 NOTE *Besides using SQLite for data storage, developers can also use another framework for storage — Core Data. Core Data is part of the Cocoa API, which was first introduced in the iPhone SDK 3.0. It is basically a framework for manipulating data without worrying about the details of storage and retrieval. Core Data is beyond the scope of this book.*

This chapter shows you how to use the embedded SQLite3 database in your applications.

USING SQLITE3

To use a SQLite3 database in your application, you first need to add the `libsqlite3.dylib` library to your Xcode project. Use the following Try It Out to find out how. You will need to download the code files indicated for this and the rest of the Try It Out features in this chapter.

TRY IT OUT   Preparing Your Project to Use SQLite3

codefile Databases.zip available for download at Wrox.com

1. Using Xcode, create a new View-based Application project and name it `Databases`.

2. Right-click the `Frameworks` folder in your project and add the `libsqlite3.dylib` library to the project (see Figure 10-1).

FIGURE 10-1

3. In the `DatabasesViewController.h` file, declare a variable of type `sqlite3` as well as a method named `filePath` (see the code in bold):

```
#import <UIKit/UIKit.h>

#import "sqlite3.h"
```

```
@interface DatabasesViewController : UIViewController {
    sqlite3 *db;
}

-(NSString *) filePath;

@end
```

4. In the DatabasesViewController.m file, define the filePath method as shown in bold:

```
#import "DatabasesViewController.h"

@implementation DatabasesViewController

-(NSString *) filePath {
    NSArray *paths = NSSearchPathForDirectoriesInDomains(
                        NSDocumentDirectory, NSUserDomainMask, YES);
    NSString *documentsDir = [paths objectAtIndex:0];
    return [documentsDir stringByAppendingPathComponent:@"database.sql"];
}

- (void)viewDidLoad {
    [super viewDidLoad];
}

@end
```

How It Works

To work with SQLite3, you must link your application to a dynamic library called libsqlite3.dylib. The libsqlite3.dylib that you selected is an alias to the latest version of the SQLite3 library. On an actual iPad device, the libsqlite3.dylib is located in the /usr/lib/ directory.

To use a SQLite database, you need to create an object of type sqlite3:

```
sqlite3 *db;
```

The filePath method returns the full path to the SQLite database that will be created in the Documents directory on your iPad (within your application's sandbox):

```
-(NSString *) filePath {
    NSArray *paths = NSSearchPathForDirectoriesInDomains(
                        NSDocumentDirectory, NSUserDomainMask, YES);
    NSString *documentsDir = [paths objectAtIndex:0];
    return [documentsDir stringByAppendingPathComponent:@"database.sql"];
}
```

 NOTE *Chapter 9 discusses the various folders that you can access within your application's sandbox.*

CREATING AND OPENING A DATABASE

After the necessary library is added to the project, you can open a database for usage. You will use the various C functions included with SQLite3 to create or open a database, as demonstrated in the following Try It Out.

TRY IT OUT Opening a Database

1. Using the Databases project created previously, define the openDB method in the DatabasesViewController.m file:

```
#import "DatabasesViewController.h"

@implementation DatabasesViewController

-(NSString *) filePath {
    //...
}

-(void) openDB {
    //---create database---
    if (sqlite3_open([[self filePath] UTF8String], &db) != SQLITE_OK ) {
        sqlite3_close(db);
        NSAssert(0, @"Database failed to open.");
    }
}

- (void)viewDidLoad {
    [self openDB];
    [super viewDidLoad];
}

@end
```

How It Works

The sqlite3_open() C function opens a SQLite database whose filename is specified as the first argument:

```
[[self filePath] UTF8String]
```

In this case, the filename of the database is specified as a C string using the UTF8String method of the NSString class because the sqlite3_open() C function does not understand an NSString object.

The second argument contains a handle to the sqlite3 object, which in this case is db.

If the database is available, it opens the database. If the specified database is not found, a new database is created. If the database is successfully opened, the function will return a value of 0 (represented using the SQLITE_OK constant).

The following list from `http://www.sqlite.org/c3ref/c_abort.html` shows the result codes returned by the various SQLite functions:

```
#define SQLITE_OK            0     /* Successful result */
#define SQLITE_ERROR         1     /* SQL error or missing database */
#define SQLITE_INTERNAL      2     /* Internal logic error in SQLite */
#define SQLITE_PERM          3     /* Access permission denied */
#define SQLITE_ABORT         4     /* Callback routine requested an abort */
#define SQLITE_BUSY          5     /* The database file is locked */
#define SQLITE_LOCKED        6     /* A table in the database is locked */
#define SQLITE_NOMEM         7     /* A malloc() failed */
#define SQLITE_READONLY      8     /* Attempt to write a readonly database */
#define SQLITE_INTERRUPT     9     /* Operation terminated by sqlite3_interrupt()*/
#define SQLITE_IOERR         10    /* Some kind of disk I/O error occurred */
#define SQLITE_CORRUPT       11    /* The database disk image is malformed */
#define SQLITE_NOTFOUND      12    /* NOT USED. Table or record not found */
#define SQLITE_FULL          13    /* Insertion failed because database is full */
#define SQLITE_CANTOPEN      14    /* Unable to open the database file */
#define SQLITE_PROTOCOL      15    /* NOT USED. Database lock protocol error */
#define SQLITE_EMPTY         16    /* Database is empty */
#define SQLITE_SCHEMA        17    /* The database schema changed */
#define SQLITE_TOOBIG        18    /* String or BLOB exceeds size limit */
#define SQLITE_CONSTRAINT    19    /* Abort due to constraint violation */
#define SQLITE_MISMATCH      20    /* Data type mismatch */
#define SQLITE_MISUSE        21    /* Library used incorrectly */
#define SQLITE_NOLFS         22    /* Uses OS features not supported on host */
#define SQLITE_AUTH          23    /* Authorization denied */
#define SQLITE_FORMAT        24    /* Auxiliary database format error */
#define SQLITE_RANGE         25    /* 2nd parameter to sqlite3_bind out of range */
#define SQLITE_NOTADB        26    /* File opened that is not a database file */
#define SQLITE_ROW           100   /* sqlite3_step() has another row ready */
#define SQLITE_DONE          101   /* sqlite3_step() has finished executing */
```

Examining the Database Created

If the database is created successfully, it can be found in the `Documents` folder of your application's sandbox on the iPhone Simulator in the `~/Library/Application Support/iPhone Simulator/3.2/Applications/<App_ID>/Documents/` folder. Figure 10-2 shows the `database.sql` file.

FIGURE 10-2

Creating a Table

After the database is created, you can create a table to store some data. In the following Try It Out, you learn how to create a table with two text fields. For illustration purposes, create a table named `Contacts`, with two fields called `email` and `name`.

TRY IT OUT Creating a Table

This is a one-step process. Using the same `Databases` project, define the `createTableNamed:with-Field1:withField2:` method as follows:

```
#import "DatabasesViewController.h"

@implementation DatabasesViewController

-(NSString *) filePath {
    //...
}

-(void) openDB {
    //...
}

-(void) createTableNamed:(NSString *) tableName
           withField1:(NSString *) field1
           withField2:(NSString *) field2 {

    char *err;
    NSString *sql = [NSString stringWithFormat:
        @"CREATE TABLE IF NOT EXISTS '%@' ('%@' TEXT PRIMARY KEY, '%@' TEXT);",
        tableName, field1, field2];

    if (sqlite3_exec(db, [sql UTF8String], NULL, NULL, &err) != SQLITE_OK) {
        sqlite3_close(db);
        NSAssert(0, @"Tabled failed to create.");
    }
}

- (void)viewDidLoad {
    [self openDB];
    [self createTableNamed:@"Contacts" withField1:@"email" withField2:@"name"];
    [super viewDidLoad];
}

@end
```

code snippet DatabasesViewController.m

How It Works

The `createTableNamed:withField1:withField2:` method takes in three parameters: `tableName`, `field1`, and `field2`.

Using these parameters, you first formulate a SQL string and then create a table using the `sqlite3_exec()` C function, with the important arguments to this function being the `sqlite3` object, the SQL query string, and a pointer to a variable for error messages. If an error occurs in creating the database, you will use the `NSAssert` method to halt the application and close the database connection.

If the operation is successful, a table named `Contacts` with two fields (`email` and `name`) will be created.

 NOTE *For a jumpstart in the SQL language, check out the SQL tutorial at:* `http://w3schools.com/sql/default.asp.`

Inserting Records

After the table is created, you can insert some records into it. The following Try It Out shows you how to write three rows of records into the table created in the previous section.

TRY IT OUT Inserting Records

1. In the `Databases` project, define the `insertRecordIntoTableNamed:withField1:field1Value:andField2:field2Value:` method as follows and modify the `viewDidLoad` method as shown in bold:

Available for
download on
Wrox.com

```
#import "DatabasesViewController.h"

@implementation DatabasesViewController

-(NSString *) filePath {
    //...
}

-(void) openDB {
    //...
}

-(void) createTableNamed:(NSString *) tableName
         withField1:(NSString *) field1
         withField2:(NSString *) field2 {
    //...
}

-(void) insertRecordIntoTableNamed:(NSString *) tableName
                   withField1:(NSString *) field1
                   field1Value:(NSString *) field1Value
                   andField2:(NSString *) field2
                   field2Value:(NSString *) field2Value {

    NSString *sql = [NSString stringWithFormat:
        @"INSERT OR REPLACE INTO '%@' ('%@', '%@') VALUES ('%@','%@')",
```

```
            tableName, field1, field2, field1Value, field2Value];

    char *err;
    if (sqlite3_exec(db, [sql UTF8String], NULL, NULL, &err) != SQLITE_OK) {
        sqlite3_close(db);
        NSAssert(0, @"Error updating table.");
    }
}

- (void)viewDidLoad {
    [self openDB];
    [self createTableNamed:@"Contacts" withField1:@"email" withField2:@"name"];

    for (int i=0; i<=2; i++) {
        NSString *email = [[NSString alloc] initWithFormat:
                                @"user%d@learn2develop.net",i];
        NSString *name = [[NSString alloc] initWithFormat: @"user %d",i];
        [self insertRecordIntoTableNamed:@"Contacts"
            withField1:@"email" field1Value:email
            andField2:@"name" field2Value:name];
        [email release];
        [name release];
    }
    [super viewDidLoad];
}

@end
```

code snippet DatabasesViewController.m

How It Works

The code in this example is similar to that of the previous one; you formulate a SQL string and use the sqlite3_exec() C function to insert a record into the database:

```
NSString *sql = [NSString stringWithFormat:
    @"INSERT OR REPLACE INTO '%@' ('%@', '%@') VALUES ('%@','%@')",
    tableName, field1, field2, field1Value, field2Value];

char *err;
if (sqlite3_exec(db, [sql UTF8String], NULL, NULL, &err) != SQLITE_OK) {
    sqlite3_close(db);
    NSAssert(0, @"Error updating table.");
}
```

In the viewDidLoad method, you insert three records into the database by calling the insertRecord-IntoTableNamed:withField1:field1Value:andField2:field2Value: method:

```
for (int i=0; i<=2; i++) {
    NSString *email = [[NSString alloc] initWithFormat:
                            @"user%d@learn2develop.net",i];
    NSString *name = [[NSString alloc] initWithFormat: @"user %d",i];

    [self insertRecordIntoTableNamed:@"Contacts"
```

```
                    withField1:@"email" field1Value:email
                    andField2:@"name" field2Value:name];
}
```

Bind Variables

One of the common tasks involved in formulating SQL strings is the need to insert values into the query string and ensuring that the string is well formulated and contains no invalid characters. In the preceding section, you saw that to insert a row into the database, you had to formulate your SQL statement like this:

```
NSString *sql = [NSString stringWithFormat:
    @"INSERT OR REPLACE INTO '%@' ('%@', '%@') VALUES ('%@','%@')",
    tableName, field1, field2, field1Value, field2Value];

char *err;
if (sqlite3_exec(db, [sql UTF8String], NULL, NULL, &err) != SQLITE_OK) {
    sqlite3_close(db);
    NSAssert(0, @"Error updating table.");
}
```

SQLite supports a feature known as *bind variables* to help you formulate your SQL string. For example, the preceding SQL string can be formulated as follows using bind variables:

```
NSString *sqlStr = [NSString stringWithFormat:
    @"INSERT OR REPLACE INTO '%@' ('%@', '%@') VALUES (?,?)",
    tableName, field1, field2];

const char *sql = [sqlStr UTF8String];
```

Here, the ? is a placeholder for you to replace with the actual value of the query. In the preceding statement, assuming that `tableName` is Contacts, `field1` is email, and `field2` is name, the sql is now:

```
INSERT OR REPLACE INTO Contacts ('email', 'name') VALUES (?,?)
```

 NOTE *The ? can be inserted only into the VALUES and WHERE section of the SQL statement; you cannot insert it into a table name, for example. The following statement would be invalid:*

```
    INSERT OR REPLACE INTO ? ('email', 'name') VALUES (?,?)
```

To substitute the values for the ?, create a `sqlite3_stmt` object and use the `sqlite3_prepare_v2()` function to compile the SQL string into a binary form and then insert the placeholder values using the `sqlite3_bind_text()` function, like this:

```
sqlite3_stmt *statement;

if (sqlite3_prepare_v2(db, sql, -1, &statement, nil) == SQLITE_OK) {
```

```
            sqlite3_bind_text(statement, 1, [field1Value UTF8String], -1, NULL);
            sqlite3_bind_text(statement, 2, [field2Value UTF8String], -1, NULL);
    }
```

 NOTE *To bind integer values, use the* `sqlite3_bind_int()` *function.*

After the preceding call, the SQL string looks like this:

```
INSERT OR REPLACE INTO Contacts ('email', 'name') VALUES
    ('user0@learn2develop.net', 'user0')
```

To execute the SQL statement, you use the `sqlite3_step()` function, followed by the `sqlite3_finalize()` function to delete the prepared SQL statement:

```
        if (sqlite3_step(statement) != SQLITE_DONE)
            NSAssert(0, @"Error updating table.");

        sqlite3_finalize(statement);
```

 NOTE *In the previous section, you used the* `sqlite3_exec()` *function to execute SQL statements. In this example, you actually use a combination of* `sqlite3_prepare()`, `sqlite3_step()`, *and* `sqlite3_finalize()` *functions to do the same thing. In fact, the* `sqlite3_exec()` *function is actually a wrapper for these three functions. For non-query SQL statements (such as for creating tables, inserting rows, and so on), it is always better to use the* `sqlite3_exec()` *function.*

Retrieving Records

Now that the records have been successfully inserted into the table, it is time to get them out. This is a good way to ensure that they really have been saved. The following Try It Out shows you how to retrieve your records.

TRY IT OUT   **Retrieving the Records**

1.   In the `Databases` project, define the `getAllRowsFromTableNamed:` method as follows and modify the `viewDidLoad` method as shown in bold:

Available for download on Wrox.com

```
#import "DatabasesViewController.h"

@implementation DatabasesViewController

-(NSString *) filePath {
    //...
}
```

```objectivec
-(void) openDB {
    //...
}

-(void) createTableNamed:(NSString *) tableName
            withField1:(NSString *) field1
            withField2:(NSString *) field2 {
    //...
}

-(void) insertRecordIntoTableNamed:(NSString *) tableName
                      withField1:(NSString *) field1
                    field1Value:(NSString *) field1Value
                      andField2:(NSString *) field2
                    field2Value:(NSString *) field2Value {
    //...
}

-(void) getAllRowsFromTableNamed: (NSString *) tableName {

    //---retrieve rows---
    NSString *qsql = @"SELECT * FROM CONTACTS";
    sqlite3_stmt *statement;

    if (sqlite3_prepare_v2( db, [qsql UTF8String], -1, &statement, nil) ==
    SQLITE_OK) {
        while (sqlite3_step(statement) == SQLITE_ROW) {
            char *field1 = (char *) sqlite3_column_text(statement, 0);
            NSString *field1Str = [[NSString alloc] initWithUTF8String: field1];

            char *field2 = (char *) sqlite3_column_text(statement, 1);
            NSString *field2Str = [[NSString alloc] initWithUTF8String: field2];

            NSString *str = [[NSString alloc] initWithFormat:@"%@ - %@",
                                field1Str, field2Str];
            NSLog(str);

            [field1Str release];
            [field2Str release];
            [str release];
        }
        //---deletes the compiled statement from memory---
        sqlite3_finalize(statement);
    }
}

- (void)viewDidLoad {
    [self openDB];
    [self createTableNamed:@"Contacts" withField1:@"email" withField2:@"name"];

    for (int i=0; i<=2; i++) {
        NSString *email = [[NSString alloc] initWithFormat:
                            @"user%d@learn2develop.net",i];
```

```
            NSString *name = [[NSString alloc] initWithFormat: @"user %d",i];

            [self insertRecordIntoTableNamed:@"Contacts"
                withField1:@"email" field1Value:email
                andField2:@"name" field2Value:name];
        }

        [self getAllRowsFromTableNamed:@"Contacts"];
        sqlite3_close(db);
        [super viewDidLoad];
}

@end
```

code snippet DatabasesViewController.m

2. Press Command-R to test the application. In Xcode, press Command-Shift-R to display the Debugger Console window. When the application has loaded, the Debugger Console displays the records (see Figure 10-3), proving to you that the rows are indeed in the table.

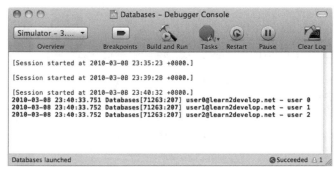

FIGURE 10-3

How It Works

To retrieve the records from the table, you first prepare the SQL statement and then use the `sqlite3_step()` function to execute the prepared statement. The `sqlite3_step()` function returns a value of 100 (represented by the `SQLITE_ROW` constant) if another row is ready. In this case, you call the `sqlite3_step()` function using a `while` loop, continuing as long as it returns a `SQLITE_ROW`:

```
if (sqlite3_prepare_v2( db, [qsql UTF8String], -1, &statement, nil) == SQLITE_OK) {
        while (sqlite3_step(statement) == SQLITE_ROW) {
            char *field1 = (char *) sqlite3_column_text(statement, 0);
            NSString *field1Str = [[NSString alloc] initWithUTF8String: field1];

            char *field2 = (char *) sqlite3_column_text(statement, 1);
            NSString *field2Str = [[NSString    alloc] initWithUTF8String: field2];

            NSString *str = [[NSString alloc] initWithFormat:@"%@ - %@",
                        field1Str, field2Str];
```

```
        NSLog(str);

        [field1Str release];
        [field2Str release];
        [str release];
    }
    //---deletes the compiled statement from memory---
    sqlite3_finalize(statement);
}
```

To retrieve the value for the first field in the row, you use the `sqlite3_column_text()` function by passing it the `sqlite3_stmt` object as well as the index of the field you are retrieving. For example, to retrieve the first field of the returned row, you use:

```
        char *field1 = (char *) sqlite3_column_text(statement, 0);
```

To retrieve an integer column (field), use the `sqlite3_column_int()` function.

BUNDLING SQLITE DATABASES WITH YOUR APPLICATION

While programmatically creating a SQLite database and using it during runtime is very flexible, most of the time you just need to create the database file during the designing stage of your development and bundle the database with your application so that it could be used during runtime. So instead of creating the database file using code, you need to create it in Mac OS X.

Fortunately, you can easily create a SQLite database file in Mac OS X by using the `sqlite3` application in Terminal. Figure 10-4 shows the command that you need to create a database named `mydata.sql`, containing a table named `Contacts` with two fields `email` and `name`. It also inserts a row into the table and then retrieves it out to verify that it is inserted properly.

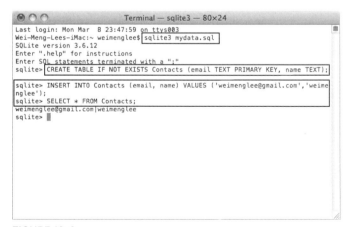

FIGURE 10-4

The commands are:

- ➤ `sqlite3 mydata.sql`

- ➤ `CREATE TABLE IF NOT EXISTS Contacts (email TEXT PRIMARY KEY, name TEXT);`

- ➤ `INSERT INTO Contacts (email, name) VALUES ('weimenglee@gmail.com', 'weimenglee');`

- ➤ `SELECT * FROM Contacts`

 NOTE *Remember to end each command with a semicolon (;).*

Also, by default when you launch Terminal, you are in your home directory. Hence, running the `sqlite3` *application will save your database file in your home directory.*

Even though you could use the `sqlite3` application to insert records into the database, it would be much easier to use a graphical tool to do that. For this, you can use the SQLite Database Browser, which you can download for free from `http://sourceforge.net/projects/sqlitebrowser/`. You can use the SQLite Database Browser (see Figure 10-5) to perform a wide variety of functions with the database file.

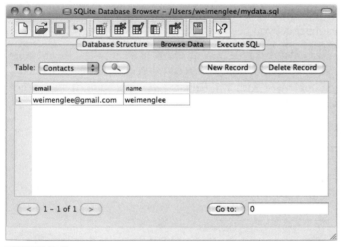

FIGURE 10-5

SUMMARY

This chapter provides a whirlwind introduction to the SQLite3 database used in the iPad. With SQLite3, you can now store all your structured data in an efficient manner and perform complex aggregations on your data.

EXERCISES Exercises

1. Explain the difference between the `sqlite3_exec()` function and the other three functions: `sqlite3_prepare()`, `sqlite3_step()`, and `sqlite3_finalize()`.

2. How do you obtain a C-style string from an `NSString` object?

3. Write the code segment to retrieve a set of rows from a table.

Answers to the Exercises can be found in Appendix A.

▶ **WHAT YOU LEARNED IN THIS CHAPTER**

TOPIC	KEY CONCEPTS
Use a SQLite3 database in your application	Need to add a reference to the `libsqlite3.dylib` library to your project.
Obtain a C-style string from a `NSString` object	Use the `UTF8String` method of the `NSString` class.
Create and open a SQLite3 database	Use the `sqlite3_open()` C function.
Execute a SQL query	Use the `sqlite3_exec()` C function.
Close a database connection	Use the `sqlite3_close()` C function.
Use bind variables	Create a `sqlite3_stmt` object. Use the `sqlite3_prepare_v2()` C function to prepare the statement. Use the `sqlite3_bind_text()` (or `sqlite3_bind_int()`, and so on) C function to insert the values into the statement. Use the `sqlite3_step()` C function to execute the statement. Use the `sqlite3_finalize()` C function to delete the statement from memory.
Retrieve records	Use the `sqlite3_step()` C function to retrieve each individual row.
Retrieve columns from a row	Use the `sqlite3_column_text()` (or `sqlite3_column_int()`, and so on) C function.

PART III
Advanced iPad Programming Techniques

11

Simple Animations

WHAT YOU WILL LEARN IN THIS CHAPTER:

➤ How to use the NSTimer class to create timers that will call methods at regular time intervals

➤ How to perform simple animations using the NSTimer class

➤ How to perform affine transformation on ImageView

➤ How to animate a series of images using ImageView

Up to this point, the applications you have written have all made use of the standard views provided by the iPhone SDK. As Apple has reiterated, the iPad is not just for serious work; it is also a gaming platform.

In this chapter, you can have some fun and create something visual. You learn how to perform some simple animations using a timer object and then perform some transformations on a view. Although it is beyond the scope of this book to show you how to create animations using OpenGL ES, this chapter does show you some interesting techniques that you can use to make your applications come alive!

USING THE NSTIMER CLASS

One of the easiest ways to get started with animation is to use the NSTimer class. The NSTimer class creates timer objects, which allow you to call a method at a regular time intervals. Using an NSTimer object, you can update an image at regular time intervals, thereby creating an impression that it is being animated.

In the following Try It Out, you learn how to display a bouncing ball on the screen using the NSTimer class. When the ball touches the sides of the screen, it bounces off in the opposite direction. You also learn how to control the frequency with which the ball animates. You need to download the code files indicated here for this and other Try It Out features within this chapter.

TRY IT OUT   Animating the Ball

---

codefile Animation.zip is available for download at Wrox.com

---

1.   Using Xcode, create a new View-based Application project and name it `Animation`.

2.   Drag and drop an image named `tennisball.jpg` to the `Resources` folder in Xcode. When the Add dialog appears, check the Copy Item into Destination Group's Folder (If Needed) option so that the image is copied into the project (see Figure 11-1).

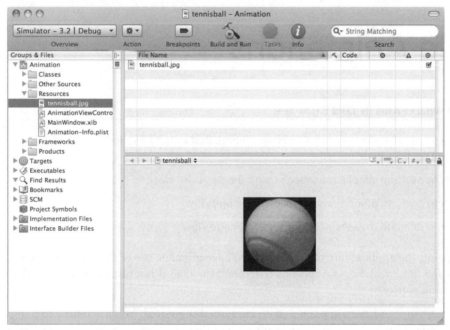

FIGURE 11-1

3.   Double-click the `AnimationViewController.xib` file to edit it in Interface Builder.

4.   Drag and drop an ImageView onto the View window and set its `Image` property to `tennisball.jpg` (see Figure 11-2).

Ensure that the size of the ImageView fits the entire tennis ball image. Later, you will move the ImageView on the screen, so it is important not to fill the entire screen with the ImageView.

5.   Select the View (outside the ImageView) and change the background color to black (see Figure 11-3).

6.   Add a Label and a Slider view from the Library onto the View window (see the lower left corner of Figure 11-4). Set the `Initial` property of the Slider view to `0.01`.

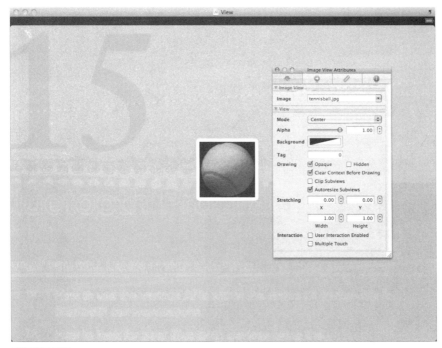

FIGURE 11-2

FIGURE 11-3

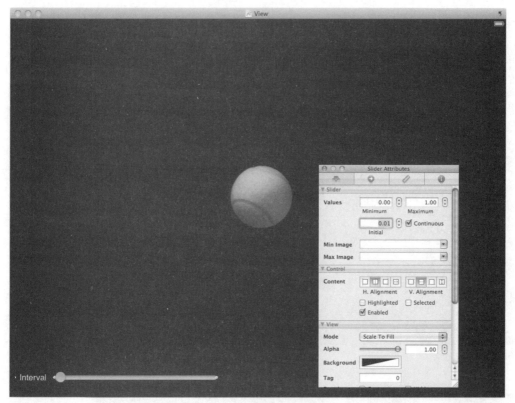

FIGURE 11-4

7. In the `AnimationViewController.h` file, declare the following outlets, fields, and actions:

```objc
#import <UIKit/UIKit.h>

@interface AnimationViewController : UIViewController {

    IBOutlet UIImageView *imageView;
    IBOutlet UISlider *slider;

    CGPoint delta;
    NSTimer *timer;

    float ballRadius;
}

@property (nonatomic, retain) UIImageView *imageView;
@property (nonatomic, retain) UISlider *slider;

-(IBAction) sliderMoved:(id) sender;

@end
```

8. Back in Interface Builder, connect the outlets and action as follows (see Figure 11-5 for the connections after all the outlets and action are connected):

➤ Control-click and drag the File's Owner item to the ImageView and select `imageView`.

➤ Control-click and drag the File's Owner item to the Slider view and select `slider`.

➤ Control-click and drag the Slider view to the File's Owner item and select `sliderMoved:`.

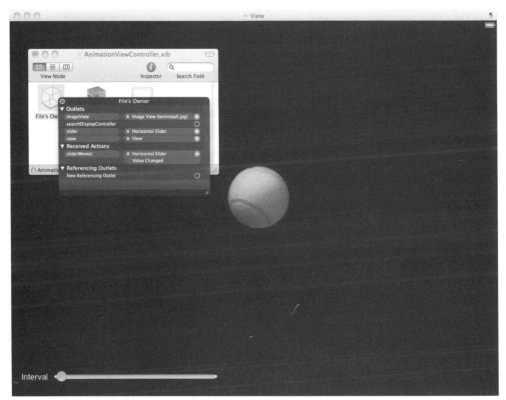

FIGURE 11-5

9. Add the following bold statements to the `AnimationViewController.m` file:

```
#import "AnimationViewController.h"

@implementation AnimationViewController

@synthesize imageView;
@synthesize slider;

-(void) onTimer {
    imageView.center = CGPointMake(imageView.center.x + delta.x,
                                   imageView.center.y + delta.y);
    if (imageView.center.x > self.view.bounds.size.width - ballRadius ||
        imageView.center.x < ballRadius)
```

```
                         delta.x = -delta.x;

           if (imageView.center.y > self.view.bounds.size.height - ballRadius ||
               imageView.center.y < ballRadius)
               delta.y = -delta.y;
       }

   - (void)viewDidLoad {

       ballRadius = imageView.frame.size.width / 2;
       [slider setShowValue:YES];
       delta = CGPointMake(12.0,4.0);

       timer = [NSTimer scheduledTimerWithTimeInterval:slider.value
                                       target:self
                                       selector:@selector(onTimer)
                                       userInfo:nil
                                        repeats:YES];
       [super viewDidLoad];
   }

   -(IBAction) sliderMoved:(id) sender {
       [timer invalidate];
       timer = [NSTimer scheduledTimerWithTimeInterval:slider.value
                                       target:self
                                       selector:@selector(onTimer)
                                       userInfo:nil
                                        repeats:YES];
   }

   - (void)didReceiveMemoryWarning {
       [super didReceiveMemoryWarning];
   }

   - (void)dealloc {
       [timer invalidate];
       [imageView release];
       [slider release];
       [super dealloc];
   }

   @end
```

10. Press Command-R to test the application on the iPhone Simulator. The tennis ball should now be animating on the screen (see Figure 11-6). Vary the speed of the animation by moving the slider to the right to slow it down and to the left to speed it up.

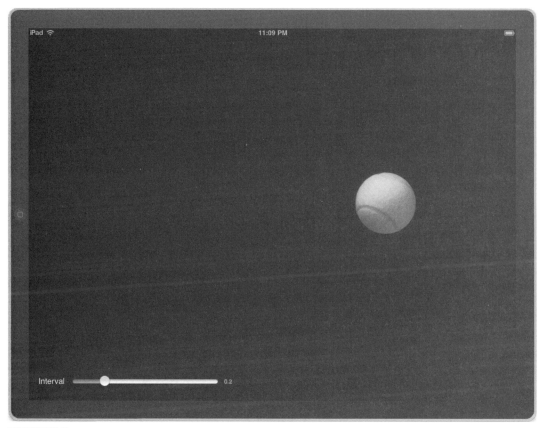

FIGURE 11-6

How It Works

When the view is loaded, the first thing you do is get the radius of the tennis ball, which in this case is half the width of the image:

```
ballRadius = imageView.frame.size.width / 2;
```

This value is used during the animation to check whether the tennis ball has touched the edges of the screen.

To set the slider to show its value, use the `setShowValue:` method:

```
[slider setShowValue:YES];
```

 NOTE *The* `setShowValue:` *method is undocumented, hence the compiler will sound a warning. Be forewarned that any use of undocumented methods may result in your application being rejected when you submit it to Apple for approval. In general, use undocumented methods only for debugging purposes.*

You also initialize the `delta` variable:

```
delta = CGPointMake(12.0,4.0);
```

The `delta` variable is used to specify how many pixels the image must move every time the timer fires. The preceding code tells it to move 12 pixels horizontally and 4 pixels vertically.

You next call the `scheduledTimerWithTimeInterval:target:selector:userInfo:repeats:` class method of the `NSTimer` class to create a new instance of the `NSTimer` object:

```
timer = [NSTimer scheduledTimerWithTimeInterval:slider.value
                             target:self
                           selector:@selector(onTimer)
                           userInfo:nil
                            repeats:YES];
```

The `scheduledTimerWithTimeInterval:` specifies the number of seconds between firings of the timer. Here, you set it to the value of the Slider view, which takes a value from 0.0 to 1.0. If the slider's value is 0.5, the timer object will fire every half-second.

The `selector:` parameter specifies the method to call when the timer fires, and the `repeats:` parameter indicates whether the timer object will repeatedly reschedule itself. In this case, when the timer fires, it calls the `onTimer` method, which you define next.

In the `onTimer` method, you change the position of the ImageView by setting its `center` property to a new value. After repositioning, you check whether the image has touched the edges of the screen; if it has, the value of the `delta` variable is negated:

```
-(void) onTimer {
    imageView.center = CGPointMake(imageView.center.x + delta.x,
                                   imageView.center.y + delta.y);

    if (imageView.center.x > self.view.bounds.size.width - ballRadius ||
        imageView.center.x < ballRadius)
        delta.x = -delta.x;

    if (imageView.center.y > self.view.bounds.size.height - ballRadius ||
        imageView.center.y < ballRadius)
        delta.y = -delta.y;
}
```

When you move the slider, the `sliderMoved:` method is called. In this method, first invalidate the timer object and then create another instance of the `NSTimer` class:

```
-(IBAction) sliderMoved:(id) sender {
    [timer invalidate];
    timer = [NSTimer scheduledTimerWithTimeInterval:slider.value
                                 target:self
                               selector:@selector(onTimer)
                               userInfo:nil
                                repeats:YES];
}
```

Moving the slider allows you to change the frequency at which the image is animated.

> **NOTE** *After an* NSTimer *object is started, you cannot change its firing interval. Therefore, the only way to change the interval is to invalidate the current one and create a new* NSTimer *object.*

Animating the Visual Change

You may have noticed that as you move the slider toward the right, the animation slows and becomes abrupt.

To make the animation smoother, you can animate the visual changes by using animation block. The start of the animation block is defined by the `beginAnimations:context:` class method of the `UIView` class:

```
[UIView beginAnimations:@"my_own_animation" context:nil];

//---animate for the duration of the slider value (time interval)---
[UIView setAnimationDuration:slider.value];

//---set the animation curve type---
[UIView setAnimationCurve:UIViewAnimationCurveLinear];

    imageView.center = CGPointMake(imageView.center.x + delta.x,
                                   imageView.center.y + delta.y);

[UIView commitAnimations];
```

To end an animation block, you call the `commitAnimations` class method of the `UIView` class. The preceding code animates the ImageView when it moves from one position to another (see Figure 11-7). This results in a much smoother animation than before.

FIGURE 11-7

TRANSFORMING VIEWS

You can use the `NSTimer` class to simulate some simple animation by constantly changing the position of the ImageView, but you can use the transformation techniques supported by the iPhone SDK to achieve the same effect.

Transforms are defined in Core Graphics, and the iPhone SDK supports standard affine 2D transforms. You can use the iPhone SDK to perform the following affine 2D transforms:

➤ Translation — Moves the origin of the view by the amount specified using the x and y axes

➤ Rotation — Moves the view by the angle specified

➤ Scaling — Changes the scale of the view by the x and y factors specified

NOTE *An affine transformation is a linear transformation that preserves co-linearity and ratio of distances. This means that all the points lying on a line initially will remain in a line after the transformation, with their respective ratio of distance between each other maintained.*

Figure 11-8 shows the effects of the various transformations.

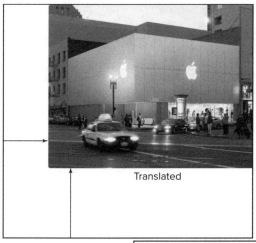

Translated

Rotated

Scaled

FIGURE 11-8

Translation

To perform an affine transform on a view, simply use its `transform` property. Recall that in the previous example, you set the new position of the view through its `center` property:

```
imageView.center = CGPointMake(imageView.center.x + delta.x,
                               imageView.center.y + delta.y);
```

Using 2D transformation, you can use its `transform` property and set it to a `CGAffineTransform` data structure returned by the `CGAffineTransformMakeTranslation()` function, like this:

```
//---in the AnimationviewController.h file---
CGPoint delta;
CGPoint translation;

//---in the viewDidLoad method---
delta = CGPointMake(12.0,4.0);
translation = CGPointMake(0.0,0.0);

-(void) onTimer {
    imageView.transform =
        CGAffineTransformMakeTranslation(translation.x, translation.y);

    translation.x += delta.x;
    translation.y += delta.y;

    if (imageView.center.x + translation.x >
        self.view.bounds.size.width - ballRadius ||
        imageView.center.x + translation.x < ballRadius)
        delta.x = -delta.x;

    if (imageView.center.y + translation.y >
        self.view.bounds.size.height - ballRadius ||
        imageView.center.y + translation.y < ballRadius)
        delta.y = -delta.y;
}
```

The `CGAffineTransformMakeTranslation()` function takes in two arguments — the value to move for the x axis and the value to move for the y axis.

The preceding code achieves the same effect as setting the `center` property of ImageView.

Rotation

The rotation transformation allows you to rotate a view using the angle you specify. In the following Try It Out, you modify the code from the previous example so that the tennis ball rotates as it bounces across the screen.

TRY IT OUT   Rotating the Tennis Ball

1.   In the `AnimationViewController.h` file, add the declaration for the `angle` variable:

```
#import <UIKit/UIKit.h>

@interface AnimationViewController : UIViewController {
    IBOutlet UIImageView *imageView;
    IBOutlet UISlider *slider;

    CGPoint delta;
```

```
    NSTimer *timer;

    float ballRadius;
    float angle;
}

@property (nonatomic, retain) UIImageView *imageView;
@property (nonatomic, retain) UISlider *slider;

-(IBAction) sliderMoved:(id) sender;

@end
```

2. In the `AnimationViewController.m` file, add the following bold statement:

 NOTE *If you have added the code to perform translation in the Translation section, be sure to remove it before adding the code outlined in the* `onTimer` *method.*

```
-(void) onTimer {

    //---rotation---
    imageView.transform = CGAffineTransformMakeRotation(angle);
    angle += 0.02;
    if (angle>6.2857) angle = 0;


    imageView.center = CGPointMake(imageView.center.x + delta.x,
                                   imageView.center.y + delta.y);

    if (imageView.center.x > self.view.bounds.size.width - ballRadius ||
        imageView.center.x < ballRadius)
        delta.x = -delta.x;

    if (imageView.center.y > self.view.bounds.size.height - ballRadius ||
        imageView.center.y < ballRadius)
        delta.y = -delta.y;
}



- (void)viewDidLoad {

    //---set the angle to 0---
```

```
        angle = 0;

        ballRadius = imageView.frame.size.width/2;
        [slider setShowValue:YES];
        delta = CGPointMake(12.0,4.0);
        timer = [NSTimer scheduledTimerWithTimeInterval:slider.value
                                                 target:self
                                               selector:@selector(onTimer)
                                               userInfo:nil
                                                repeats:YES];


        [super viewDidLoad];
    }
```

3. Press Command-R to test the application. The tennis ball now rotates as it bounces across the screen.

How It Works

To rotate a view, set its `transform` property using a `CGAffineTransform` data structure returned by the `CGAffineTransformMakeRotation()` function. The `CGAffineTransformMakeRotation()` function takes a single argument, which contains the angle to rotate (in radians). After each rotation, you increment the angle by 0.02:

```
        //---rotation---
        imageView.transform = CGAffineTransformMakeRotation(angle);
        angle += 0.02;
```

A full rotation takes 360 degrees, which works out to be 2p radian. If the angle exceeds 6.2857 (=2*3.142857), you reset `angle` to 0:

```
        if (angle>6.2857) angle = 0;
```

Scaling

For scaling of views, you use the `CGAffineTransformMakeScale()` function to return a `CGAffineTransform` data structure and set it to the `transform` property of the view:

```
        imageView.transform = CGAffineTransformMakeScale(angle,angle);
```

`CGAffineTransformMakeScale()` takes two arguments: the factor to scale for the x axis and the factor to scale for the y axis.

If you modify the previous Try It Out with the preceding statement, the tennis ball gets bigger as it bounces on the screen (see Figure 11-9). It then resets back to its original size and grows again.

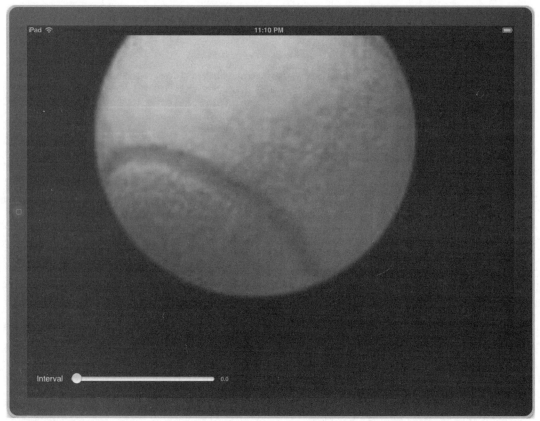

FIGURE 11-9

ANIMATING A SERIES OF IMAGES

So far, you have seen that you can use the ImageView to display a static image. In addition, you can use it to display a series of images and then alternate between them.

The following Try It Out shows how this is done using the ImageView.

TRY IT OUT Displaying a Series of Images

codefile Animations2.zip is available for download at Wrox.com

1. Using Xcode, create a new View-based Application project and name it `Animations2`.

2. Add a series of images to the `Resources` folder by dragging and dropping them into the `Resources` folder in Xcode. When the Add dialog appears, check the Copy Item into Destination Group's

Folder (If Needed) option so that each of the images will be copied into the project. Figure 11-10 shows the images added.

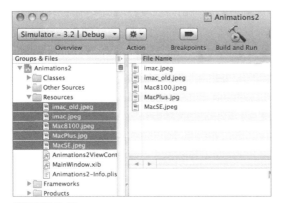

FIGURE 11-10

3. In the `Animations2ViewController.m` file, add the following bold statements:

```
- (void)viewDidLoad {

    NSArray *images = [NSArray arrayWithObjects:
                        [UIImage imageNamed:@"MacSE.jpeg"],
                        [UIImage imageNamed:@"imac.jpeg"],
                        [UIImage imageNamed:@"MacPlus.jpg"],
                        [UIImage imageNamed:@"imac_old.jpeg"],
                        [UIImage imageNamed:@"Mac8100.jpeg"],
                        nil];

    CGRect frame = CGRectMake(0,0,320,460);

    UIImageView *imageView = [[UIImageView alloc] initWithFrame:frame];
    imageView.animationImages = images;
    imageView.contentMode = UIViewContentModeScaleAspectFit;
    imageView.animationDuration = 3;     //---seconds to complete one set
                                         // of animation---
    imageView.animationRepeatCount = 0; //---continuous---
    [imageView startAnimating];
    [self.view addSubview:imageView];
    [imageView release];

    [super viewDidLoad];
}
```

4. Press Command-R to test the series of images on the iPhone Simulator. The images are displayed in the ImageView (see Figure 11-11), one at a time.

FIGURE 11-11

How It Works

You first create an NSArray object and initialize it with a few UIImage objects:

```
NSArray *images = [NSArray arrayWithObjects:
                       [UIImage imageNamed:@"MacSE.jpeg"],
                       [UIImage imageNamed:@"imac.jpeg"],
                       [UIImage imageNamed:@"MacPlus.jpg"],
                       [UIImage imageNamed:@"imac_old.jpeg"],
                       [UIImage imageNamed:@"Mac8100.jpeg"],
                       nil];
```

You then instantiate a UIImageView object:

```
CGRect frame = CGRectMake(0,0,320,460);
UIImageView *imageView = [[UIImageView alloc] initWithFrame:frame];
```

To get the ImageView to display the series of images, set its `animationImages` property to the `images` object. You also set the display mode of the ImageView:

```
imageView.animationImages = images;
imageView.contentMode = UIViewContentModeScaleAspectFit;
```

To control how fast the images are displayed, you set the `animationDuration` property to a value. This value indicates the number of seconds that the ImageView will take to display one complete set of images. The `animationRepeatCount` property enables you to specify how many times you want the animation to occur. Set it to 0 if you want it to display indefinitely:

```
imageView.animationDuration = 3;      //---seconds to complete one set
                                      // of animation---
imageView.animationRepeatCount = 0; //---continuous---
```

Finally, you start the animation by calling the `startAnimating` method. You also need to add the ImageView to the View window by calling the `addSubView:` method:

```
[imageView startAnimating];
[self.view addSubview:imageView];
```

SUMMARY

In this chapter, you have seen the usefulness of the `NSTimer` class and how it can help you perform some simple animations. You have also learned about the various affine transformations supported by the iPhone SDK. Last, you learned about the ability of the ImageView to animate a series of images at a regular time interval.

EXERCISES

1. Name the three affine transformations supported by the iPhone SDK.

2. How do you pause an `NSTimer` object and then make it continue?

3. What is the use of enclosing your block of code with the `beginAnimations` and `commitAnimations` methods of the `UIView` class?

```
[UIView beginAnimations:@"some_text" context:nil];
    //---code to effect visual change---
[UIView commitAnimations];
```

Answers to the Exercises can be found in Appendix A.

▶ **WHAT YOU LEARNED IN THIS CHAPTER**

TOPIC	KEY CONCEPTS
Using the `NSTimer` object to create timers	Create a timer object that will call the `onTimer` method every half-second: ```\nTimer = [NSTimer\nscheduledTimerWithTimeInterval:0.5\n target:self\n selector:@selector(onTimer)\n userInfo:nil\n repeats:YES];\n```
Stopping the `NSTimer` object	`[timer invalidate];`
Animating visual changes	```\n[UIView beginAnimations:@"some_text"\ncontext:nil];\n//---code to effect visual change---\n[UIView commitAnimations];\n```
Performing affine transformations	Use the `transform` property of the view.
Translation	Use the `CGAffineTransformMakeTranslation()` function to return a `CGAffineTransform` data structure and set it to the `transform` property.
Rotation	Use the `CGAffineTransformMakeRotation()` function to return a `CGAffineTransform` data structure and set it to the `transform` property.
Scaling	Use the `CGAffineTransformMakeScale()` function to return a `CGAffineTransform` data structure and set it to the `transform` property.
Animating a series of images using ImageView	Set the `animationImages` property to an array containing `UIImage` objects. Set the `animationDuration` property. Set the `animationRepeatCount` property. Call the `startAnimating` method.

12

Recognizing Gestures

WHAT YOU WILL LEARN IN THIS CHAPTER:

➤ How to use the six gesture recognizers to recognize commonly used gestures

➤ How to detect touches in your application

➤ How to differentiate between single and double taps

➤ How to implement the pinch gesture

➤ How to implement the drag gesture

One of the most important selling points of the iPad is its screen, which can detect multiple points of input. Multi-touch inputs allow for very natural interaction between users and your applications. Because of multi-touch, the mobile Safari Web browser is easily one of the most user-friendly Web browsers available on a smart phone. The iPad recognizes various multi-touch sequences, known as *gestures*, and performs the appropriate action associated with each.

In this chapter, you learn how to recognize gestures in your application and then implement some cool features that improve the interaction between the user and the application, such as a jigsaw puzzle application. By detecting touches, your application enables the user to rearrange the locations of the images on the screen, as well as change the size of the images using the pinching gesture.

RECOGNIZING GESTURES

iPhone SDK 3.2 introduces a new set of classes known as *gesture recognizers*. Gesture recognizers allow you to easily detect for gestures performed by the user. For example, the user may use two fingers to pinch the screen, indicating his intention to zoom in and out of an image. Instead of writing the code to detect the fingers movement, gesture recognizers provide an easy way for you to detect the various gestures supported by the iPad.

The iPhone SDK 3.2 supports six gesture recognizers:

➤ `UITapGestureRecognizer` — Detects tap(s) on a view

➤ `UIPinchGestureRecognizer` — Detects pinching in and out of a view

➤ `UIPanGestureRecognizer` — Detects panning or dragging of a view

➤ `UISwipeGestureRecognizer` — Detects swiping of a view

➤ `UIRotationGestureRecognizer` — Detects rotation of a view

➤ `UILongPressGestureRecognizer` — Detects long presses on a view (also known as "touch and hold")

All six gesture recognizers inherit from the `UIGestureRecognizer` base class. To get started with gesture recognizers, let's build an application that detects for taps on a view, and then progressively detects for other gestures.

Tapping

To use a gesture recognizer, all you need to do is to create an instance of the appropriate gesture recognizer, configure it accordingly, and then connect it to an event handler that will perform the required action when the gesture is recognized. The following Try It Out shows you how to detect taps on the iPad screen.

TRY IT OUT Recognizing Tapping

codefile Gestures.zip is available for download at Wrox.com

1. Using Xcode, create a new View-based Application project and name it `Gestures`.

2. Drag and drop the image named `architecture.jpg` onto the `Resources` folder of the Xcode project. When the Add dialog appears, check the Copy Item into Destination Group's Folder (If Needed) option so that the image is copied into the project (see Figure 12-1).

3. Double-click on the `GesturesViewController.xib` file located in the `Resources` folder to edit it in Interface Builder.

4. Add an ImageView from the Library to the View window.

5. Select the ImageView and view its Attributes Inspector window (Tools ⇨ Attributes Inspector). Set its properties as follows (see Figure 12-2):

➤ Image — `architecture.jpg`

➤ Mode — `Aspect Fit`

➤ Check the `User Interaction Enabled` option.

➤ Check the `Multiple Touch` option.

6. Save the file in Interface Builder.

FIGURE 12-1

7. Back in Xcode, edit the `GesturesViewController.h` file by adding the following bold statements:

```
#import <UIKit/UIKit.h>

@interface GesturesViewController : UIViewController {
    IBOutlet UIImageView *imageView;
}

@property (nonatomic, retain) UIImageView *imageView;

@end
```

8. In Interface Builder, connect the `imageView` outlet to the ImageView by control-clicking and dragging the File's Owner item over the ImageView. Select `imageView`.

9. In Xcode, edit the `GesturesViewController.m` file and add in the following bold statements:

```
#import "GesturesViewController.h"

@implementation GesturesViewController

@synthesize imageView;

- (void)viewDidLoad {

    //---tap gesture---
    UITapGestureRecognizer *tapGesture =
```

```
        [[UITapGestureRecognizer alloc]
            initWithTarget:self
                    action:@selector(handleTapGesture:)];

    tapGesture.numberOfTapsRequired = 2;
    [imageView addGestureRecognizer:tapGesture];
    [tapGesture release];

    [super viewDidLoad];
}

//---handle tap gesture---
-(IBAction) handleTapGesture:(UIGestureRecognizer *) sender {
    if (sender.view.contentMode == UIViewContentModeScaleAspectFit)
        sender.view.contentMode = UIViewContentModeCenter;
    else
        sender.view.contentMode = UIViewContentModeScaleAspectFit;
}

- (void)dealloc {
    [imageView release];
    [super dealloc];
}
```

FIGURE 12-2

10. To test the application on the iPhone Simulator, press Command-R.

11. Figure 12-3 shows the image displayed on the iPhone Simulator. When you double-click the image (which is double-tap on a real device), the image is enlarged (see Figure 12-4). When you double-click on the image again, it switches back to its original size.

FIGURE 12-3

How It Works

To detect for taps on a view, you first create an instance of the UITapGestureRecognizer class:

```
UITapGestureRecognizer *tapGesture =
    [[UITapGestureRecognizer alloc]
        initWithTarget:self
                action:@selector(handleTapGesture:)];
```

You set the current View Controller (self) to be the target of the gesture recognizer (which means you will handle all the messages sent when a gesture is detected in this current View Controller). The action: parameter specifies a selector that identifies the method name to handle the recognized gesture.

To recognize double-taps, set the numberOfTapsRequired property to 2:

```
tapGesture.numberOfTapsRequired = 2;
```

FIGURE 12-4

To attach the gesture recognizer to a view, in this case `imageView`, pass the `tapGesture` object to the `addGestureRecognizer:` method:

```
[imageView addGestureRecognizer:tapGesture];
```

Finally, release the `tapGesture` recognizer object:

```
[tapGesture release];
```

When a double-tap is detected by the application, the `handleTapGesture:` method will be invoked:

```
//---handle tap gesture---
-(IBAction) handleTapGesture:(UIGestureRecognizer *) sender {
    if (sender.view.contentMode == UIViewContentModeScaleAspectFit)
        sender.view.contentMode = UIViewContentModeCenter;
    else
        sender.view.contentMode = UIViewContentModeScaleAspectFit;
}
```

In `handleTapGesture:`, you can reference the view that has recognized the gesture, in this case `imageView`, by the `sender.view` object (alternatively, you can directly refer to the ImageView via `self.imageView`). This method is useful as you may have multiple views attached to the same gesture handler and `sender.view` will automatically refer to the view that recognized the gesture.

In this gesture handler, you toggle the image between the `UIViewContentModeScaleAspectFit` and `UIViewContentModeCenter` modes.

DISCRETE GESTURES AND CONTINUOUS GESTURES

There are two types of gestures — discrete and continuous. A discrete gesture sends a single message to the target when the gesture is recognized. For example, when you double-tap on a view and the gesture is detected, the target (method handling the gesture) is only invoked once. A continuous gesture, on the other hand, sends multiple messages to the target until the gesture ends. An example of a continuous gesture is the pinch gesture. As you put your fingers on the screen and pinch on a view, the target is called repeatedly, until you lift your fingers off your screen.

The `UITapGestureRecognizer`, `UISwipeGestureRecognizer`, and `UILongPressGestureRecognizer` are all discrete gesture recognizers. The `UIPinchGestureRecognizer`, `UIPanGestureRecognizer`, and `UIRotationGestureRecognizer` are all continuous gesture recognizers.

Pinching

The pinch gesture is very popular on the iPad (and on the iPhone and iPod touch). In the pinch gesture, you place two fingers on the screen and move them either apart or closer together to indicate your intention to zoom in or out of a view. The following Try It Out shows you how to recognize the pinch gesture in your application to change the size of an ImageView. Note, all the Try it Outs in this chapter use source code and images from the zip file you downloaded for the first Try it Out.

TRY IT OUT   Recognizing Pinching

1.   Using the same project created in the previous Try It Out, edit the `GesturesViewController.m` by adding the following bold statements:

```objc
#import "GesturesViewController.h"

@implementation GesturesViewController

@synthesize imageView;

CGFloat lastScaleFactor = 1;

- (void)viewDidLoad {

    //---tap gesture---
    UITapGestureRecognizer *tapGesture =
        [[UITapGestureRecognizer alloc]
            initWithTarget:self
                    action:@selector(handleTapGesture:)];

    tapGesture.numberOfTapsRequired = 2;
    [imageView addGestureRecognizer:tapGesture];
    [tapGesture release];

    //---pinch gesture---
    UIPinchGestureRecognizer *pinchGesture =
```

```
        [[UIPinchGestureRecognizer alloc]
            initWithTarget:self
                    action:@selector(handlePinchGesture:)];

    [imageView addGestureRecognizer:pinchGesture];
    [pinchGesture release];

    [super viewDidLoad];
}

//---handle pinch gesture---
-(IBAction) handlePinchGesture:(UIGestureRecognizer *) sender {

    CGFloat factor = [(UIPinchGestureRecognizer *) sender scale];

    if (factor > 1) {
        //---zooming in---
        sender.view.transform = CGAffineTransformMakeScale(
            lastScaleFactor + (factor-1),
            lastScaleFactor + (factor-1));
    } else {
        //---zooming out---
        sender.view.transform = CGAffineTransformMakeScale(
            lastScaleFactor * factor,
            lastScaleFactor * factor);
    }

    if (sender.state == UIGestureRecognizerStateEnded){
        if (factor > 1) {
            lastScaleFactor += (factor-1);
        } else {
            lastScaleFactor *= factor;
        }
    }
}
```

2.   To test the application on the iPhone Simulator, press Command-R.

3.   Press the Option button and you will be able to simulate the touch of two fingers on the screen. You will see two translucent white circle dots on the simulator. Click and drag the mouse to move them apart. Observe that the size of the image will change as you move the mouse (see Figure 12-5).

How It Works

As with the UITapGestureRecognizer, you first create an instance of the UIPinchGestureRecognizer and then connect it to a gesture handler:

```
        //---pinch gesture---
        UIPinchGestureRecognizer *pinchGesture =
            [[UIPinchGestureRecognizer alloc]
                initWithTarget:self
                        action:@selector(handlePinchGesture:)];

    [imageView addGestureRecognizer:pinchGesture];
    [pinchGesture release];
```

FIGURE 12-5

When a pinch gesture is recognized, the `handlePinchGesture:` method is invoked to handle it. Recall that the pinch gesture is a continuous gesture, and hence the `handlePinchGesture:` method will be called repeatedly as long as the fingers are on the screen.

To know whether this is a "zoom in" or "zoom out" gesture, you examine the `scale` property of the `UIPinchGestureRecognizer` object:

```
CGFloat factor = [(UIPinchGestureRecognizer *) sender scale];
```

If the fingers are moving apart, the value of `scale` is 1 or greater. If the fingers are moving closer, the value is smaller than 1. Every time you perform a pinch gesture, your application needs to remember the scale factor so that the next time you perform the gesture, you can resize the image based on its last drawn size. This is done when the pinch gesture ends (when the fingers are lifted off the screen). You examine the `sender.state` to see if the gesture has ended and then proceed to save the last scale factor:

```
if (sender.state == UIGestureRecognizerStateEnded){
    if (factor > 1) {
        lastScaleFactor += (factor-1);
    } else {
        lastScaleFactor *= factor;
    }
}
```

You change the size of the ImageView using the `CGAffineTransformMakeScale()` method.

```
if (factor > 1) {
    //---zooming in---
    sender.view.transform = CGAffineTransformMakeScale(
        lastScaleFactor + (factor-1),
        lastScaleFactor + (factor-1));
} else {
    //---zooming out---
    sender.view.transform = CGAffineTransformMakeScale(
        lastScaleFactor * factor,
        lastScaleFactor * factor);
}
```

Rotation

Another gesture that is supported by the iPhone SDK 3.2 is rotation. In the rotation gesture, you place two fingers on the screen and rotate them in a circular fashion. The following Try It Out shows how to use the `UIRotationGestureRecognizer` class to rotate the ImageView.

TRY IT OUT **Recognizing Rotation**

1. Using the same project created in the previous Try It Out, edit the `GesturesViewController.m` by adding the following bold statements:

```
#import "GesturesViewController.h"

@implementation GesturesViewController

@synthesize imageView;

CGFloat lastScaleFactor = 1;

CGFloat netRotation;

- (void)viewDidLoad {

    //---tap gesture---
    UITapGestureRecognizer *tapGesture =
        [[UITapGestureRecognizer alloc]
            initWithTarget:self
                action:@selector(handleTapGesture:)];

    tapGesture.numberOfTapsRequired = 2;
    [self.imageView addGestureRecognizer:tapGesture];
    [tapGesture release];

    //---pinch gesture---
    UIPinchGestureRecognizer *pinchGesture =
        [[UIPinchGestureRecognizer alloc]
            initWithTarget:self
                action:@selector(handlePinchGesture:)];
```

```
        [imageView addGestureRecognizer:pinchGesture];
        [pinchGesture release];

        //---rotate gesture---
        UIRotationGestureRecognizer *rotateGesture =
            [[UIRotationGestureRecognizer alloc]
                initWithTarget:self
                        action:@selector(handleRotateGesture:)];

        [imageView addGestureRecognizer:rotateGesture];
        [rotateGesture release];

        [super viewDidLoad];
    }

//---handle rotate gesture---
-(IBAction) handleRotateGesture:(UIGestureRecognizer *) sender {
    CGFloat rotation = [(UIRotationGestureRecognizer *) sender rotation];
    CGAffineTransform transform = CGAffineTransformMakeRotation(
                                        rotation + netRotation);
    sender.view.transform = transform;

    if (sender.state == UIGestureRecognizerStateEnded){
        netRotation += rotation;
    }
}
```

2. To test the application on the iPhone Simulator, press Command-R.

3. Press the Option button and you will be able to simulate two fingers touching on the screen. Click and drag the mouse in either the clockwise or counterclockwise direction. Observe that the ImageView rotates (see Figure 12-6).

How It Works

As usual, you create an instance of the UIRotationGestureRecognizer class and connect it to a handler method:

```
        //---rotate gesture---
        UIRotationGestureRecognizer *rotateGesture =
            [[UIRotationGestureRecognizer alloc]
                initWithTarget:self
                        action:@selector(handleRotateGesture:)];

        [imageView addGestureRecognizer:rotateGesture];
        [rotateGesture relcase];
```

When a rotation gesture is recognized, the handleRotateGesture: method is invoked. As the rotation gesture is a continuous gesture, this method will be called repeatedly.

To obtain the amount of rotation, you examine the rotation property of the UIRotationGestureRecognizer object:

```
        CGFloat rotation = [(UIRotationGestureRecognizer *) sender rotation];
```

FIGURE 12-6

The amount to rotate is represented in radians. To ensure that the ImageView rotates based on its last position, you save the angle of rotation when the rotation gesture is completed:

```
if (sender.state == UIGestureRecognizerStateEnded){
    netRotation += rotation;
}
```

Finally, you perform the rotation using the `CGAffineTransformMakeRotation()` method:

```
CGAffineTransform transform = CGAffineTransformMakeRotation(
                                rotation + netRotation);
sender.view.transform = transform;
```

Panning (or Dragging)

A very common gesture that most iPad users will encounter is the pan (or drag) gesture. Panning involves using the finger to touch on a view on the screen and then moving it while the finger is still on the screen. In the following Try It Out, you will use the `UIPanGestureRecognizer` to move the ImageView.

TRY IT OUT   Recognizing Panning

1. Using the same project created in the previous Try It Out, edit the `GesturesViewController.m` by adding the following bold statements:

```
#import "GesturesViewController.h"

@implementation GesturesViewController

@synthesize imageView;

CGFloat lastScaleFactor = 1;

CGFloat netRotation;

CGPoint netTranslation;

- (void)viewDidLoad {

    //---tap gesture---
    UITapGestureRecognizer *tapGesture =
        [[UITapGestureRecognizer alloc]
            initWithTarget:self
                    action:@selector(handleTapGesture:)];

    tapGesture.numberOfTapsRequired = 2;
    [self.imageView addGestureRecognizer:tapGesture];
    [tapGesture release];

    //---pinch gesture---
    UIPinchGestureRecognizer *pinchGesture =
        [[UIPinchGestureRecognizer alloc]
            initWithTarget:self
            action:@selector(handlePinchGesture:)];

    [imageView addGestureRecognizer:pinchGesture];
    [pinchGesture release];

    //---rotate gesture---
    UIRotationGestureRecognizer *rotateGesture =
        [[UIRotationGestureRecognizer alloc]
            initWithTarget:self
                    action:@selector(handleRotateGesture:)];

    [imageView addGestureRecognizer:rotateGesture];
    [rotateGesture release];

    //---pan gesture---
    UIPanGestureRecognizer *panGesture =
        [[UIPanGestureRecognizer alloc]
            initWithTarget:self
                    action:@selector(handlePanGesture:)];

    [imageView addGestureRecognizer:panGesture];
    [panGesture release];
```

```
        [super viewDidLoad];
    }

    //---handle pan gesture---
    -(IBAction) handlePanGesture:(UIGestureRecognizer *) sender {

        CGPoint translation = [(UIPanGestureRecognizer *) sender translationInView:imageView];

        sender.view.transform = CGAffineTransformMakeTranslation(
                                    netTranslation.x + translation.x,
                                    netTranslation.y + translation.y);

        if (sender.state == UIGestureRecognizerStateEnded){
            netTranslation.x += translation.x;
            netTranslation.y += translation.y;
        }
    }
```

2. To test the application on the iPhone Simulator, press Command-R.

3. Click the ImageView and move the mouse. Observe that the ImageView moves with your mouse (see Figure 12-7).

FIGURE 12-7

How It Works

You create an instance of the `UIPanGestureRecognizer` class and connect it to a handler method:

```
UIPanGestureRecognizer *panGesture =
    [[UIPanGestureRecognizer alloc]
        initWithTarget:self
                action:@selector(handlePanGesture:)];

[imageView addGestureRecognizer:panGesture];
[panGesture release];
```

When a panning gesture is recognized, the `handlePanGesture:` method is invoked. Panning is a continuous gesture, so this method is called repeatedly.

To obtain the amount of panning, you examine the `translation` property of the `UIPanGestureRecognizer` object:

```
CGPoint translation = [(UIPanGestureRecognizer *) sender translationInView:imageView];
```

To ensure that the ImageView can be moved from its last drawn position, you save the current panning amount when the gesture ends:

```
if (sender.state == UIGestureRecognizerStateEnded){
    netTranslation.x += translation.x;
    netTranslation.y += translation.y;
}
```

Finally, you move the ImageView using the `CGAffineTransformMakeTranslation()` method:

```
sender.view.transform = CGAffineTransformMakeTranslation(
                            netTranslation.x + translation.x,
                            netTranslation.y + translation.y);
```

Swiping

Another common gesture that you will encounter is the swipe. Using the swipe gesture, a user touches the screen with his finger, moves it in a particular direction, and then lifts it off the screen. The swipe gesture is commonly used for switching between views (such as viewing a series of photos in the Photos application).

The following Try It Out illustrates how to use the `UISwipeGestureRecognizer` to recognize the swipe gesture and then display different images in the ImageView.

TRY IT OUT   Recognizing Swiping

1. Using the same project created in the previous Try It Out, drag and drop the two images named `Buildings.jpeg` and `Bridge.jpeg` onto the `Resources` folder of the Xcode project. When the Add dialog appears, check the Copy Item into Destination Group's Folder (If Needed) option so that each image is copied into the project (see Figure 12-8).

FIGURE 12-8

2. Edit the GesturesViewController.m by adding the following bold statements:

```
#import "GesturesViewController.h"

@implementation GesturesViewController

@synthesize imageView;

CGFloat lastScaleFactor = 1;

CGFloat netRotation;

CGPoint netTranslation;

NSArray *images;
int imageIndex = 0;

- (void)viewDidLoad {

    //---tap gesture---
    UITapGestureRecognizer *tapGesture =
```

```
    [[UITapGestureRecognizer alloc]
        initWithTarget:self
        action:@selector(handleTapGesture:)];

tapGesture.numberOfTapsRequired = 2;
[self.imageView addGestureRecognizer:tapGesture];
[tapGesture release];

//---pinch gesture---
UIPinchGestureRecognizer *pinchGesture =
    [[UIPinchGestureRecognizer alloc]
        initWithTarget:self
        action:@selector(handlePinchGesture:)];

[imageView addGestureRecognizer:pinchGesture];
[pinchGesture release];

//---rotate gesture---
UIRotationGestureRecognizer *rotateGesture =
    [[UIRotationGestureRecognizer alloc]
        initWithTarget:self
                action:@selector(handleRotateGesture:)];

[imageView addGestureRecognizer:rotateGesture];
[rotateGesture release];

//---pan gesture---
UIPanGestureRecognizer *panGesture =
    [[UIPanGestureRecognizer alloc]
        initWithTarget:self
                action:@selector(handlePanGesture:)];
//---comment this out---
//[imageView addGestureRecognizer:panGesture];
[panGesture release];

//---swipe gesture---
images = [[NSArray alloc] initWithObjects:@"architecture.jpg",
                                          @"Buildings.jpeg",
                                          @"Bridge.jpeg", nil];

//---right swipe (default)---
UISwipeGestureRecognizer *swipeGesture =
    [[UISwipeGestureRecognizer alloc]
        initWithTarget:self
                action:@selector(handleSwipeGesture:)];

[imageView addGestureRecognizer:swipeGesture];
[swipeGesture release];

//---left swipe---
UISwipeGestureRecognizer *swipeLeftGesture =
    [[UISwipeGestureRecognizer alloc]
        initWithTarget:self
                action:@selector(handleSwipeGesture:)];
swipeLeftGesture.direction = UISwipeGestureRecognizerDirectionLeft;
```

```
        [imageView addGestureRecognizer:swipeLeftGesture];
        [swipeLeftGesture release];

        [super viewDidLoad];
    }

    //---handle swipe gesture---
    -(IBAction) handleSwipeGesture:(UIGestureRecognizer *) sender {

        UISwipeGestureRecognizerDirection direction =
            [(UISwipeGestureRecognizer *) sender direction];

        switch (direction) {
            case UISwipeGestureRecognizerDirectionUp:
                NSLog(@"up");
                break;
            case UISwipeGestureRecognizerDirectionDown:
                NSLog(@"down");
                break;
            case UISwipeGestureRecognizerDirectionLeft:
                imageIndex++;
                break;
            case UISwipeGestureRecognizerDirectionRight:
                imageIndex--;
                break;
            default:
                break;
        }

        imageIndex = (imageIndex < 0) ? ([images count] - 1):
                        imageIndex % [images count];
        imageView.image = [UIImage imageNamed:[images objectAtIndex:imageIndex]];
    }

    - (void)dealloc {
        [images release];
        [imageView release];
        [super dealloc];
    }
```

3. Test the application on the iPhone Simulator by pressing Command-R.

4. Click the ImageView and drag the mouse from left to right and then from right to left. The ImageView changes its image as you swipe it with your mouse.

How It Works

You first instantiate the images NSArray object with the names of the three images:

```
    //---swipe gesture---
    images = [[NSArray alloc] initWithObjects:@"architecture.jpg",
                                              @"Buildings.jpeg",
                                              @"Bridge.jpeg", nil];
```

By default, the UISwipeGestureRecognizer only recognizes right swipes (swiping from left to right). Hence, to recognize right swipes, you create an instance of the UISwipeGestureRecognizer class:

```
//---right swipe (default)---
UISwipeGestureRecognizer *swipeGesture =
    [[UISwipeGestureRecognizer alloc]
        initWithTarget:self
                action:@selector(handleSwipeGesture:)];

[imageView addGestureRecognizer:swipeGesture];
[swipeGesture release];
```

To recognize left swipes (swiping from right to left), you need to create another instance of the UISwipeGestureRecognizer class and configure its direction property, like this:

```
//---left swipe---
UISwipeGestureRecognizer *swipeLeftGesture =
    [[UISwipeGestureRecognizer alloc]
        initWithTarget:self
                action:@selector(handleSwipeGesture:)];

swipeLeftGesture.direction = UISwipeGestureRecognizerDirectionLeft;
[imageView addGestureRecognizer:swipeLeftGesture];
[swipeLeftGesture release];
```

When the swipe gestures are recognized, the handleSwipeGesture: method is invoked. Here, you examine the direction property of the UISwipeGestureRecognizer object to obtain the direction of the swipe.

```
UISwipeGestureRecognizerDirection direction =
    [(UISwipeGestureRecognizer *) sender direction];
```

Depending on the swipe direction, the image in the ImageView changes accordingly:

```
switch (direction) {
    case UISwipeGestureRecognizerDirectionUp:
        NSLog(@"up");
        break;
    case UISwipeGestureRecognizerDirectionDown:
        NSLog(@"down");
        break;
    case UISwipeGestureRecognizerDirectionLeft:
        imageIndex++;
        break;
    case UISwipeGestureRecognizerDirectionRight:
        imageIndex--;
        break;
    default:
        break;
}

imageIndex = (imageIndex < 0) ? ([images count] - 1):
                    imageIndex % [images count];
imageView.image = [UIImage imageNamed:[images objectAtIndex:imageIndex]];
```

NOTE *Remember to comment out the statements for the pan gesture recognizer. The swipe gesture recognizer will not work with the pan gesture recognizer.*

Long Press

Use the long press gesture recognizer to detect if the user is touching on a view and then holding onto it. A very common use of the long press gesture is when you want to save an image in the mobile Safari Web browser. When you long press on an image, an action sheet pops up, allowing you to save or copy that image.

The following Try It Out shows you how to recognize for long press using the `UILongPressGestureRecognizer`.

TRY IT OUT **Recognizing Long Presses**

1. Using the same project created in the previous Try It Out, edit the `GesturesViewController.m` by adding the following bold statements:

```
- (void)viewDidLoad {

    //---tap gesture---
    UITapGestureRecognizer *tapGesture =
        [[UITapGestureRecognizer alloc]
            initWithTarget:self
                action:@selector(handleTapGesture:)];

    tapGesture.numberOfTapsRequired = 2;
    [self.imageView addGestureRecognizer:tapGesture];
    [tapGesture release];

    //---pinch gesture---
    UIPinchGestureRecognizer *pinchGesture =
        [[UIPinchGestureRecognizer alloc]
            initWithTarget:self
                action:@selector(handlePinchGesture:)];

    [imageView addGestureRecognizer:pinchGesture];
    [pinchGesture release];

    //---rotate gesture---
    UIRotationGestureRecognizer *rotateGesture =
        [[UIRotationGestureRecognizer alloc]
            initWithTarget:self
                action:@selector(handleRotateGesture:)];

    [imageView addGestureRecognizer:rotateGesture];
```

```
    [rotateGesture release];

    //---pan gesture---
    UIPanGestureRecognizer *panGesture =
        [[UIPanGestureRecognizer alloc]
            initWithTarget:self
                action:@selector(handlePanGesture:)];
    //---comment this out---
    //[imageView addGestureRecognizer:panGesture];
    [panGesture release];

    //---swipe gesture---
    images = [[NSArray alloc] initWithObjects:@"architecture.jpg",
                                              @"Buildings.jpeg",
                                              @"Bridge.jpeg", nil];

    //---right swipe (default)---
    UISwipeGestureRecognizer *swipeGesture =
        [[UISwipeGestureRecognizer alloc]
            initWithTarget:self
                action:@selector(handleSwipeGesture:)];

    [imageView addGestureRecognizer:swipeGesture];
    [swipeGesture release];

    //---left swipe---
    UISwipeGestureRecognizer *swipeLeftGesture =
        [[UISwipeGestureRecognizer alloc]
            initWithTarget:self
                action:@selector(handleSwipeGesture:)];

    swipeLeftGesture.direction = UISwipeGestureRecognizerDirectionLeft;
    [imageView addGestureRecognizer:swipeLeftGesture];
    [swipeLeftGesture release];

    //---long press gesture---
    UILongPressGestureRecognizer *longpressGesture =
        [[UILongPressGestureRecognizer alloc]
            initWithTarget:self
                action:@selector(handleLongpressGesture:)];

    longpressGesture.minimumPressDuration = 1;
    longpressGesture.allowableMovement = 15;
    longpressGesture.numberOfTouchesRequired = 1;

    [imageView addGestureRecognizer:longpressGesture];
    [longpressGesture release];

    [super viewDidLoad];
}

//---handle long press gesture---
-(IBAction) handleLongpressGesture:(UIGestureRecognizer *) sender {
    UIActionSheet *actionSheet = [[UIActionSheet alloc]
```

```
                        initWithTitle:@"Image options"
                              delegate:self
                     cancelButtonTitle:nil
                destructiveButtonTitle:nil
                     otherButtonTitles:@"Save Image",
                                       @"Copy", nil];
    //---remember to implement the UIActionSheetDelegate protocol in your
    // view controller---
    [actionSheet showInView:self.view];
    [actionSheet release];
}
```

2. To test the application on the iPhone Simulator, press Command-R.

3. Click the ImageView and hold it there. Observe that a window pops up, asking you to either save the image or copy it (see Figure 12-9).

FIGURE 12-9

How It Works

As usual, you create an instance of the `UIPanGestureRecognizer` class and connect it to a handler method:

```
//---long press gesture---
UILongPressGestureRecognizer *longpressGesture =
    [[UILongPressGestureRecognizer alloc]
        initWithTarget:self
                action:@selector(handleLongpressGesture:)];
```

You configure the recognizer so that it only recognizes the long press when the user has clicked on the view using one finger, for one second, and does not move his finger more than 15 pixels from his original point of contact:

```
longpressGesture.minimumPressDuration = 1;
longpressGesture.allowableMovement = 15;
longpressGesture.numberOfTouchesRequired = 1;
```

You then attach the recognizer to the ImageView:

```
[imageView addGestureRecognizer:longpressGesture];
[longpressGesture release];
```

When a long press is detected, the `handleLongpressGesture:` method is invoked. Here, you simply print out an action sheet:

```
//---handle long press gesture---
-(IBAction) handleLongpressGesture:(UIGestureRecognizer *) sender {
    UIActionSheet *actionSheet = [[UIActionSheet alloc]
                          initWithTitle:@"Image options"
                               delegate:self
                      cancelButtonTitle:nil
                 destructiveButtonTitle:nil
                      otherButtonTitles:@"Save Image",
                                        @"Copy", nil];
    //---remember to implement the UIActionSheetDelegate protocol in your
    // view controller---
    [actionSheet showInView:self.view];
    [actionSheet release];
}
```

 NOTE *You need to implement the necessary action to perform when the user clicks on a button in your action sheet. The implementation details are not shown in this example. Remember to implement the* `UIActionSheetControllerDelegate` *protocol in your View Controller, though.*

DETECTING TOUCHES

While the gesture recognizers greatly simplify your life in detecting gestures, sometimes you simply want to detect touches on the screen and perform some custom action (such as writing a doodle application when the user can use his fingers to make a sketch).

To detect touches on the screen of the iPad, you need to acquaint yourself with a few events that handle the detection of touches. Through these events, you will know whether the user has single-tapped, double-tapped, or moved his fingers on your application and react accordingly. These events are:

➤ `touchesBegan:withEvent:` — Fires when one or more fingers touch down in a view or window

➤ `touchesMoved:withEvent:` — Fires when one or more fingers move within a view or window

➤ `touchesEnded:withEvent:` — Fires when one or more fingers are raised from a view or window

➤ `touchesCancelled:withEvent:` — Fires when a system event (such as low-memory warning) cancels the touch event

These events are defined in the `UIResponder` class, which is the superclass of `UIApplication`, `UIView`, and its subclasses. Hence, you can implement event handlers for these events in your View Controller.

 NOTE *The four touch events are the foundation events used by the gesture recognizers that you saw earlier in this chapter. To create your own custom gesture recognizers to recognize your own gestures (such as a figure-of-eight gesture), you need to implement your own event handlers for these four events. Creating your own custom gesture recognizer is beyond the scope of this book.*

Detecting Single Touch

Time to get the engine rolling! Make sure you download the code indicated here so you can work through the following Try It Out activity, in which you'll see how to detect when the user is tapping on the screen.

TRY IT OUT Detecting for Taps

codefile MultiTouch.zip is available for download at Wrox.com

1. Using Xcode, create a new View-based Application project and name it `MultiTouch`.

2. Drag and drop an image into the `Resources` folder. Figure 12-10 shows an image named `apple.jpeg` located in the `Resources` folder.

3. Double-click the `MultiTouchViewController.xib` file to edit it in Interface Builder.

4. Populate the View window with an ImageView. Ensure that the ImageView covers the entire View window.

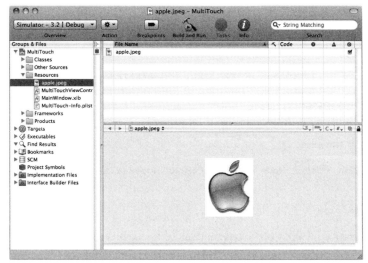

FIGURE 12-10

5. Select the ImageView and view its Attributes Inspector window (see Figure 12-11). Set its `Image` property to `apple.jpeg`.

6. In the `MultiTouchViewController.h` file, add the following statements that appear in bold:

```
#import <UIKit/UIKit.h>

@interface MultiTouchViewController : UIViewController {
    IBOutlet UIImageView *imageView;
}

@property (nonatomic, retain) UIImageView *imageView;

@end
```

7. Back in Interface Builder, Control-click and drag the File's Owner item to the ImageView. Select ImageView.

8. In the `MultiTouchViewController.m` file, add the following statements that appear in bold:

```
#import "MultiTouchViewController.h"

@implementation MultiTouchViewController

@synthesize imageView;

//---fired when the user finger(s) touches the screen---
-(void) touchesBegan: (NSSet *) touches withEvent: (UIEvent *) event {

    //---get all touches on the screen---
    NSSet *allTouches = [event allTouches];

    //---compare the number of touches on the screen---
```

```
    switch ([allTouches count])
    {
        //---single touch---
        case 1: {
            //---get info of the touch---
            UITouch *touch = [[allTouches allObjects] objectAtIndex:0];

            //---compare the taps---
            switch ([touch tapCount])
            {
                //---single tap---
                case 1: {
                    imageView.contentMode = UIViewContentModeScaleAspectFit;
                } break;

                //---double tap---
                case 2: {
                    imageView.contentMode = UIViewContentModeCenter;
                } break;
            }
        } break;
    }
}

- (void)dealloc {
    [imageView release];
    [super dealloc];
}
```

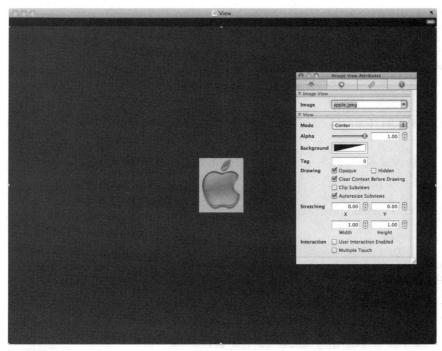

FIGURE 12-11

9. Press Command-R to test the application on the iPhone Simulator.

10. Single-tap the apple icon to enlarge it (see Figure 12-12). Double-tap it to return it to its original size.

FIGURE 12-12

How It Works

This application works by sensing the user's touch on the screen of the iPad. When the user touches the screen, the View or View Controller fires a series of events that you can handle. There are four such events:

➤   touchesBegan:withEvent:

➤   touchesEnded:withEvent:

➤   touchesMoved:withEvent:

➤   touchesCancelled:withEvent:

Take a closer look at the first event. The touchesBegan:withEvent: event is fired when at least one touch is sensed on the screen. In this event, you can know how many fingers are on the screen by calling the allTouches method of the UIEvent object (event):

```
//---get all touches on the screen---
NSSet *allTouches = [event allTouches];
```

The allTouches method returns an NSSet object containing a set of UITouch objects. To know how many fingers are on the screen, simply count the number of UITouch objects in the NSSet object using the count method. In this case, you are (at this moment) interested only in a single touch, therefore you implement only the case for one touch:

```
//---compare the number of touches on the screen---
switch ([allTouches count])
{
    //---single touch---
    case 1: {
        //---get info of the touch---
        UITouch *touch = [[allTouches allObjects] objectAtIndex:0];

        //---compare the taps---
        switch ([touch tapCount])
        {
            //---single tap---
            case 1: {
                imageView.contentMode = UIViewContentModeScaleAspectFit;
            } break;

            //---double tap---
            case 2: {
                imageView.contentMode = UIViewContentModeCenter;
            } break;
        }
    } break;
}
```

You extract details of the first touch by using the allObjects method of the NSSet object to return an NSArray object. You then use the objectAtIndex: method to obtain the first array item.

The UITouch object (touch) contains the tapCount property, which tells you whether the user has single-tapped the screen or performed a double tap (or more). If the user single-tapped the screen, you resize the image to fit the entire `ImageView` view using the `UIViewContentModeScaleAspectFit` constant. If it is a double-tap, you restore it to its original size using the `UIViewContentModeCenter` constant.

The other three events are not discussed in this section. The `touchesEnded:withEvent:` event is fired when the user's finger(s) is lifted from the screen. The `touchesMoved:withEvent:` event is fired continuously when the user's finger or fingers are touching and moving on the screen. Finally, if the application is interrupted while the user's finger is on the screen, the `touchesCancelled:withEvent:` event is fired.

 NOTE *In addition to detecting taps in the* `touchesBegan:withEvent:` *event, you can also detect them in the* `touchesEnded:withEvent:` *event.*

In the next section, you learn how to detect multi-touches in your application.

UNDERSTANDING MULTI-TAPPING

When a user performs a multi-tap on the screen, your application will fire the `touchesBegan:` and `touchesEnded:` events multiple times. For example, if the user taps on the screen once, the `touchesBegan:` and `touchesEnded:` events will be fired once, with the `tapCount` property of the `UITouch` object returning a value of 1. However, if the user taps the screen twice (in quick succession), then the `touchesBegan:` and `touchesEnded:` events will be fired twice; the first time these events are fired, the `tapCount` property will be 1, the second time the `tapCount` property will be 2.

Understanding the way multi-taps are detected is important because if you are detecting double-taps your application might redundantly execute blocks of code that are designed for single-tap. For example, in the preceding Try It Out, double-tapping on the image will first try to change the mode of the image to `UIViewContentModeScaleAspectFit` (which is what single-tap is supposed to do; in this case, because the image is already in the `UIViewContentModeScaleAspectFit` mode, the user won't notice any difference), then it changes back to the `UIViewContentModeCenter` mode (which is what double-tap is supposed to do). Ideally, it should not need to execute the block of code for single-tap.

To solve this problem, you have to write some code to check if a second tap is indeed coming:

➤ When a single-tap is detected, use a timer using an `NSTimer` object.

➤ When a double-tap is detected, stop the timer and check to see if the time difference between the second tap and the first tap is small enough (such as a fraction of a second) to constitute a double-tap. If it is, execute the code for double-tap. If it isn't, execute the code for single-tap.

If you are simply detecting for multi-taps in your application, the easiest method is to use the `UITapGestureRecognizer`, illustrated earlier.

Detecting Multi-touches

Detecting multi-touches is really very simple once you understand the concepts in the previous section. The capability to detect for multi-touches is very useful because you can use that to zoom in on views in your application.

The following Try It Out demonstrates how to detect multi-touches.

TRY IT OUT **Detecting Multi-touches**

1. Using the same project created in the previous section, modify the `touchesBegan:withEvent:` method by adding the following statements that appear in bold:

```
-(void) touchesBegan: (NSSet *) touches withEvent: (UIEvent *) event {

    //---get all touches on the screen---
    NSSet *allTouches = [event allTouches];

    //---compare the number of touches on the screen---
    switch ([allTouches count])
    {
        //---single touch---
        case 1: {
            //---get info of the touch---
            UITouch *touch = [[allTouches allObjects] objectAtIndex:0];

            //---compare the taps---
            switch ([touch tapCount])
            {
                //---single tap---
                case 1: {
                    imageView.contentMode = UIViewContentModeScaleAspectFit;
                } break;

                case 2: {
                    imageView.contentMode = UIViewContentModeCenter;
                } break;
            }
        } break;

        //---double-touch---
        case 2: {
            //---get info of first touch---
            UITouch *touch1 = [[allTouches allObjects] objectAtIndex:0];

            //---get info of second touch---
            UITouch *touch2 = [[allTouches allObjects] objectAtIndex:1];

            //---get the points touched---
            CGPoint touch1PT = [touch1 locationInView:[self view]];
            CGPoint touch2PT = [touch2 locationInView:[self view]];

            NSLog(@"Touch1: %.0f, %.0f", touch1PT.x, touch1PT.y);
            NSLog(@"Touch2: %.0f, %.0f", touch2PT.x, touch2PT.y);
```

```
            } break;
        }
    }
```

2. Press Command-R to test the application on the iPhone Simulator.

3. In the iPhone Simulator, press the Option key, and two circles should appear (see Figure 12-13). Clicking the screen simulates two fingers touching the screen of the device.

FIGURE 12-13

4. Open the Debugger Console window (press Command-Shift-R) and observe the output as you Option-click the screen of the iPhone Simulator multiple times (see Figure 12-14).

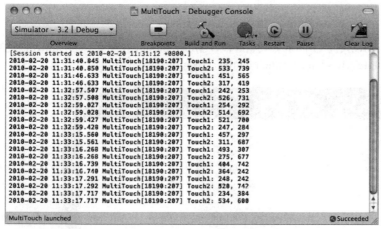

FIGURE 12-14

How It Works

As you do when detecting for single-touch, you check for multi-touches in the `touchesBegan:withEvent:` event. Rather than receive information about the first touch, you now obtain information for both the first and second touch:

```
//---get info of first touch---
UITouch *touch1 = [[allTouches allObjects] objectAtIndex:0];

//---get info of second touch---
UITouch *touch2 = [[allTouches allObjects] objectAtIndex:1];
```

To get the coordinates (represented as a `CGPoint` structure) of each touch, you use the `locationInView:` method of the `UITouch` class and pass it the view whose coordinate system you want the touch located:

```
//---get the points touched---
CGPoint touch1PT = [touch1 locationInView:[self view]];
CGPoint touch2PT = [touch2 locationInView:[self view]];
```

The coordinates returned by the `locationInView:` method are relative to the view specified. In the preceding snippet, the coordinates displayed are relative to the main View window.

The x and y coordinates of a `CGPoint` structure are represented using the `CGFloat` type, so you need to use the `%f` format specifier when printing them in the Debugger Console window:

```
NSLog(@"Touch1: %.0f, %.0f", touch1PT.x, touch1PT.y);
NSLog(@"Touch2: %.0f, %.0f", touch2PT.x, touch2PT.y);
```

To detect more than two touches, you simply extend the preceding code by getting information about the third touch, fourth touch, and so on.

NOTE *Using the iPhone Simulator, the coordinates for the two touches are often interchanged as you Option-click the same spot on the screen of the Simulator.*

Implementing the Pinch Gesture

You can combine the UIPinchGestureRecognizer, which you used earlier in this chapter, with what you've just learned about detecting for multi-touches to implement your own pinch gesture recognizer.

In the earlier pinch gesture example, you used the CGAffineTransformMakeScale() method to alter the size of the image. In this example, you will see another technique for changing the size of an image in the ImageView — you will alter the size of the image as it is being pinched.

In the following Try It Out, you learn how to implement the pinch gesture to zoom the image in and out in the ImageView.

TRY IT OUT **Zooming In and Out**

1. Using the same project created in the previous section, add the following statement that appears in bold to the MultiTouchViewController.h file:

```
#import <UIKit/UIKit.h>

@interface MultiTouchViewController : UIViewController {
    IBOutlet UIImageView *imageView;
}

@property (nonatomic, retain) UIImageView *imageView;

-(CGFloat) distanceBetweenTwoPoints: (CGPoint)fromPoint toPoint: (CGPoint)toPoint;

@end
```

2. In the MultiTouchViewController.m file, implement the distanceBetweenTwoPoints:toPoint: and touchesMoved:withEvent: methods and add the statements that appear in bold to the touchesBegan:withEvent: method:

```
#import "MultiTouchViewController.h"

@implementation MultiTouchViewController

@synthesize imageView;

CGFloat originalDistance;

-(CGFloat) distanceBetweenTwoPoints:(CGPoint)fromPoint toPoint:(CGPoint)toPoint {
    float lengthX = fromPoint.x - toPoint.x;
```

```objc
    float lengthY = fromPoint.y - toPoint.y;
    return sqrt((lengthX * lengthX) + (lengthY * lengthY));
}

-(void) touchesBegan: (NSSet *) touches withEvent: (UIEvent *) event {

    //---get all touches on the screen---
    NSSet *allTouches = [event allTouches];

    //---compare the number of touches on the screen---
    switch ([allTouches count])
    {
        //---single touch---
        case 1: {
            //---get info of the touch---
            UITouch *touch = [[allTouches allObjects] objectAtIndex:0];

            //---compare the taps---
            switch ([touch tapCount])
            {
                //---single tap---
                case 1: {
                    imageView.contentMode = UIViewContentModeScaleAspectFit;
                } break;

                case 2: {
                    imageView.contentMode = UIViewContentModeCenter;
                } break;
            }
        } break;

        //---double-touch---
        case 2: {
            //---get info of first touch---
            UITouch *touch1 = [[allTouches allObjects] objectAtIndex:0];
            //---get info of second touch---
            UITouch *touch2 = [[allTouches allObjects] objectAtIndex:1];

            //---get the points touched---
            CGPoint touch1PT = [touch1 locationInView:[self view]];
            CGPoint touch2PT = [touch2 locationInView:[self view]];

            NSLog(@"Touch1: %.0f, %.0f", touch1PT.x, touch1PT.y);
            NSLog(@"Touch2: %.0f, %.0f", touch2PT.x, touch2PT.y);

            //---record the distance made by the two touches---
            originalDistance = [self distanceBetweenTwoPoints:touch1PT
                                                      toPoint:touch2PT];

        } break;
    }
}

//---fired when the user moved his finger(s) on the screen---
```

```
-(void) touchesMoved: (NSSet *) touches withEvent: (UIEvent *) event {

    //---get all touches on the screen---
    NSSet *allTouches = [event allTouches];

    //---compare the number of touches on the screen---
    switch ([allTouches count])
    {
        //---single touch---
        case 1: {
        }  break;

        //---double-touch---
        case 2: {
            //---get info of first touch---
            UITouch *touch1 = [[allTouches allObjects] objectAtIndex:0];

            //---get info of second touch---
            UITouch *touch2 = [[allTouches allObjects] objectAtIndex:1];

            //---get the points touched---
            CGPoint touch1PT = [touch1 locationInView:[self view]];
            CGPoint touch2PT = [touch2 locationInView:[self view]];

            NSLog(@"Touch1: %.0f, %.0f", touch1PT.x, touch1PT.y);
            NSLog(@"Touch2: %.0f, %.0f", touch2PT.x, touch2PT.y);

            CGFloat currentDistance = [self distanceBetweenTwoPoints:touch1PT
                                                              toPoint:touch2PT];

            //---zoom in---
            if (currentDistance > originalDistance) {
                imageView.frame = CGRectMake(imageView.frame.origin.x - 2,
                                             imageView.frame.origin.y - 2,
                                             imageView.frame.size.width + 4,
                                             imageView.frame.size.height + 4);
            }
            else {
                //---zoom out---
                imageView.frame = CGRectMake(imageView.frame.origin.x + 2,
                                             imageView.frame.origin.y + 2,
                                             imageView.frame.size.width - 4,
                                             imageView.frame.size.height - 4);
            }
            originalDistance = currentDistance;
        } break;
    }
}
```

3. Press Command-R to test the application on the iPhone Simulator.

4. Single-tap the ImageView to enlarge. To zoom the image in and out, Option-click the image (see Figure 12-15).

NOTE *To use the pinch gesture on an image, you actually need to enlarge the image first. This is because the image can only be resized if its display mode is set to* UIViewContentModeScaleAspectFit. *Hence, in this case, you need to single-tap on the image (which actually sets the image mode to* UIViewContentModeScaleAspectFit*) before you can try the pinching effect.*

FIGURE 12-15

How It Works

To detect for the pinch gesture, you find the distance between the two fingers and constantly compare that distance so that you know whether the two fingers are moving toward or away from each other.

To find the distance between two fingers, you define the `distanceBetweenTwoPoints:toPoint:` method:

```
-(CGFloat) distanceBetweenTwoPoints:(CGPoint)fromPoint
                            toPoint:(CGPoint)toPoint {
    float lengthX = fromPoint.x - toPoint.x;
    float lengthY = fromPoint.y - toPoint.y;
    return sqrt((lengthX * lengthX) + (lengthY * lengthY));
}
```

This method takes in two `CGPoint` structures and then calculates the distance between them. No rocket science here — just the Pythagorean theorem in action.

When the two fingers first touch the screen, you record their distance in the `touchesBegan:withEvent:` method (see the code in bold):

```
-(void) touchesBegan: (NSSet *) touches withEvent: (UIEvent *) event {

    //...
    //---double-touch---
    case 2: {
        //---get info of first touch---
        UITouch *touch1 = [[allTouches allObjects] objectAtIndex:0];
        //---get info of second touch---
        UITouch *touch2 = [[allTouches allObjects] objectAtIndex:1];

        //---get the points touched---
        CGPoint touch1PT = [touch1 locationInView:[self view]];
        CGPoint touch2PT = [touch2 locationInView:[self view]];

        NSLog(@"Touch1: %.0f, %.0f", touch1PT.x, touch1PT.y);
        NSLog(@"Touch2: %.0f, %.0f", touch2PT.x, touch2PT.y);

        //---record the distance made by the two touches---
        originalDistance = [self distanceBetweenTwoPoints:touch1PT
                                                  toPoint:touch2PT];

    } break;
    }
}
```

As the two fingers move on the screen, you constantly compare their current distance with the original distance (see Figure 12-16).

FIGURE 12-16

If the current distance is greater than the original distance, this is a zoom-in gesture. If not, it is a zoom-out gesture:

```
//---fired when the user moved his finger(s) on the screen---
-(void) touchesMoved: (NSSet *) touches withEvent: (UIEvent *) event {

    //...
    //...
    //---double-touch---
    case 2: {
        //---get info of first touch---
        UITouch *touch1 = [[allTouches allObjects] objectAtIndex:0];

        //---get info of second touch---
        UITouch *touch2 = [[allTouches allObjects] objectAtIndex:1];

        //---get the points touched---
        CGPoint touch1PT = [touch1 locationInView:[self view]];
        CGPoint touch2PT = [touch2 locationInView:[self view]];

        NSLog(@"Touch1: %.0f, %.0f", touch1PT.x, touch1PT.y);
        NSLog(@"Touch2: %.0f, %.0f", touch2PT.x, touch2PT.y);

        CGFloat currentDistance =
            [self distanceBetweenTwoPoints:touch1PT
                                    toPoint:touch2PT];

        //---zoom in---
```

```
            if (currentDistance > originalDistance) {
                imageView.frame = CGRectMake(
                                    imageView.frame.origin.x - 2,
                                    imageView.frame.origin.y - 2,
                                    imageView.frame.size.width + 4,
                                    imageView.frame.size.height + 4);
            }
            else {
                //---zoom out---
                imageView.frame = CGRectMake(
                                    imageView.frame.origin.x + 2,
                                    imageView.frame.origin.y + 2,
                                    imageView.frame.size.width - 4,
                                    imageView.frame.size.height - 4);
            }
            originalDistance = currentDistance;
        } break;
    ...
    ...
```

Implementing the Drag Gesture

Another gesture that you can implement is the drag, in which you touch an item on the screen and then drag it by moving the finger. In the following Try It Out, you learn how to drag an ImageView on the screen by implementing the drag gesture.

TRY IT OUT   Dragging the ImageView

1. Using the `MultiTouch` project created earlier, resize the ImageView so that it fits the size of the image (see Figure 12-17).

2. Add the following statements that appear in bold to the `touchesMoved:withEvent:` method:

```
//---fired when the user moved his finger(s) on the screen---
-(void) touchesMoved: (NSSet *) touches withEvent: (UIEvent *) event {

    //---get all touches on the screen---
    NSSet *allTouches = [event allTouches];

    //---compare the number of touches on the screen---
    switch ([allTouches count])
    {
        //---single touch---
        case 1: {
            //---get info of the touch---
            UITouch *touch = [[allTouches allObjects] objectAtIndex:0];

            //---check to see if the image is being touched---
            CGPoint touchPoint = [touch locationInView:[self view]];

            if (touchPoint.x > imageView.frame.origin.x &&
```

```
                    touchPoint.x < imageView.frame.origin.x +
                                   imageView.frame.size.width &&
                    touchPoint.y > imageView.frame.origin.y &&
                    touchPoint.y <imageView.frame.origin.y +
                                   imageView.frame.size.height) {
                    [imageView setCenter:touchPoint];
            }
        } break;

        //---double-touch---
        case 2: {
            //---get info of first touch---
            UITouch *touch1 = [[allTouches allObjects] objectAtIndex:0];
            //---get info of second touch---
            UITouch *touch2 = [[allTouches allObjects] objectAtIndex:1];

            //...
            //...

        } break;
    }
}
```

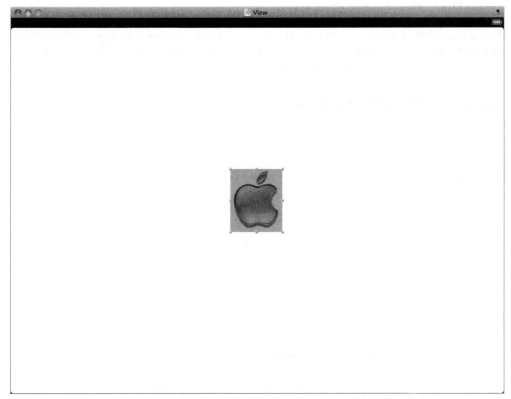

FIGURE 12-17

3. Press Command-R to test the application on the iPhone Simulator.

4. You can now tap the ImageView and then move the image anywhere on the screen simply by moving your finger (see Figure 12-18).

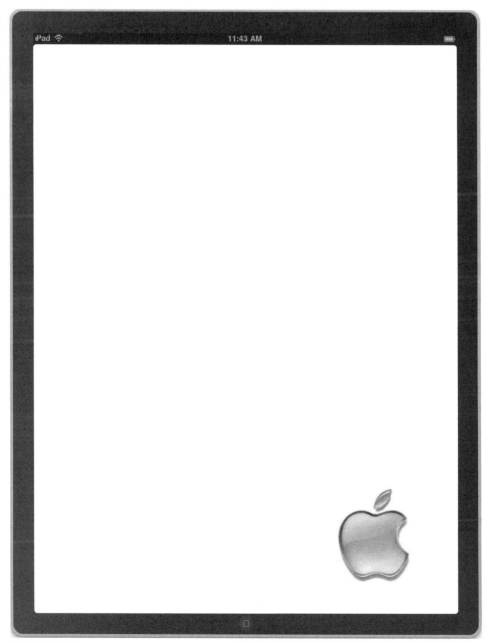

FIGURE 12-18

How It Works

The concept for this example is very simple. When a finger taps the screen, you check to see whether the position of the finger falls within the range of the ImageView:

```
CGPoint touchPoint = [touch locationInView:[self view]];

if (touchPoint.x > imageView.frame.origin.x &&
    touchPoint.x < imageView.frame.origin.x +
                    imageView.frame.size.width &&
    touchPoint.y > imageView.frame.origin.y &&
    touchPoint.y <imageView.frame.origin.y +
                    imageView.frame.size.height) {
    [imageView setCenter:touchPoint];
}
```

If it does, you simply reposition the ImageView by calling its `setCenter` property.

Using this technique, you can easily write a jigsaw puzzle application in which users can rearrange the different pieces of the jigsaw puzzle simply by dragging them on the screen.

SUMMARY

In this chapter, you saw the use of the various gesture recognizers included in the iPhone SDK 3.2 that allow you to easily recognize the gestures commonly performed on an iPad. In addition, you have seen the various events that you can handle if you want to perform your own tracking of the user's touch. Using these events, you can write your own routine to detect multiple touches in your application and use this knowledge to create some really interesting applications.

EXERCISES

1. Name the six gesture recognizers included in the iPhone SDK 3.2.

2. Name the gestures that are discrete and those that are continuous.

3. Name the four events for detecting touches in your application.

4. What is the difference between multi-taps and multi-touches?

5. How do you simulate multi-touch on the iPhone Simulator?

Answers to the Exercises can be found in Appendix A.

▶ **WHAT YOU LEARNED IN THIS CHAPTER**

TOPIC	KEY CONCEPTS
New gesture recognizers	* `UITapGestureRecognizer` * `UIPinchGestureRecognizer` * `UIPanGestureRecognizer` * `UISwipeGestureRecognizer` * `UIRotationGestureRecognizer` * `UILongPressGestureRecognizer`
Discrete gesture	A discrete gesture sends a single message to the target when the gesture is recognized.
Continuous gesture	A continuous gesture sends multiple messages to the target until the gesture ends.
Detect touches on the view	Handle the following event in the view or View Controller: * `touchesBegan:withEvent:` * `touchesEnded:withEvent:` * `touchesMoved:withEvent:` * `touchesCancelled:withEvent:`
Detect for taps (single, double, and so on)	You can detect for taps either in the `touchesBegan:withEvent:` or `touchesEnded:withEvent:` method.
Implement pinch gesture	Compare the distance made by the two touch points and deduce whether the gesture is zoom in or out.
Implement drag gesture	Ensure that the touch point falls within the area occupied by the view in question.

13

Accessing the Accelerometer

WHAT YOU WILL LEARN IN THIS CHAPTER:

➤ How to obtain accelerometer data from your iPad

➤ How to detect shakes to your device

iPad's built-in accelerometer allows your program to detect the orientation of the device and adapt the content to suit the new orientation. For example, when you rotate your device sideways, the Safari Web browser automatically switches the screen to landscape mode so that you now have a wider viewing space.

In this chapter, you learn how to access the accelerometer and how to use the Shake API to detect shakes to your iPad.

USING THE ACCELEROMETER

The accelerometer in iPad measures the acceleration of the device relative to freefall. A value of 1 indicates that the device is experiencing 1 g of force exerting on it (1 g of force being the gravitational pull of the earth, which your device experiences when it is stationary). The accelerometer measures the acceleration of the device in three different axes: X, Y, and Z. Figure 13-1 shows the different axes measured by the accelerometer.

Table 13-1 shows the readings of the three axes when the device is in the various positions. Bear in mind that you will never see the exact same values as these, because they are always fluctuating due to the sensitivity of the accelerometer.

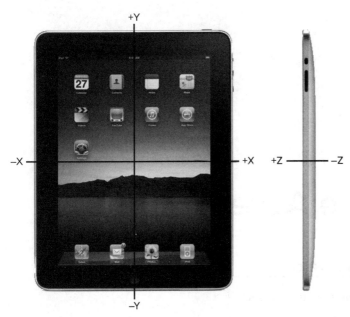

FIGURE 13-1

TABLE 13-1: The Various Readings of the X, Y, and Z Axes

POSITION	X	Y	Z
Vertical upright position	0.0	-1.0	0.0
Landscape Left	1.0	0.0	0.0
Landscape Right	-1.0	0.0	0.0
Upside Down	0.0	1.0	0.0
Flat Up	0.0	0.0	-1.0
Flat Down	0.0	0.0	1.0

If iPad is held upright and moved to the right quickly, the value of the X-axis will increase from 0 to a positive value. If it is moved to the left quickly, the value of the X-axis will decrease from 0 to a negative value. If the device is moved upward quickly, the value of the Y-axis will increase from -1.0 to a larger value. If the device is moved download quickly, the value of the Y-axis will decrease from -1.0 to a smaller value.

If the device is horizontal and then dropped, the value of the Z-axis will decrease from -1.0 to a smaller number. If it is moved upward, the value of the Z-axis will increase from -1.0 to a bigger number.

NOTE *The accelerometer used on the iPad gives a maximum reading of about +/- 2.3 g with a resolution of about 0.018 g.*

In the following Try it Out, you programmatically access the data returned by the accelerometer. Obtaining the accelerometer data allows you to build very interesting applications, such as a spirit level, as well as games that depend on motion detection.

TRY IT OUT **Accessing the Accelerometer Data**

codefile Accelerometer.zip available for download at Wrox.com

1. Using Xcode, create a new View-based Application project and name it `Accelerometer`.

2. Double-click the `AccelerometerViewController.xib` file to edit it in Interface Builder.

3. Populate the View window with the six Label views, as shown in Figure 13-2. Label the three labels on the left as X-axis, Y-axis, and Z-axis.

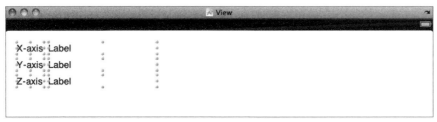

FIGURE 13-2

4. In the `AccelerometerViewController.h` file, add the following statements that appear in bold:

```
#import <UIKit/UIKit.h>

@interface AccelerometerViewController : UIViewController
    <UIAccelerometerDelegate> {

    IBOutlet UILabel *labelX;
    IBOutlet UILabel *labelY;
    IBOutlet UILabel *labelZ;
}

@property (nonatomic, retain) UILabel *labelX;
@property (nonatomic, retain) UILabel *labelY;
@property (nonatomic, retain) UILabel *labelZ;

@end
```

5. In Interface Builder, Control-click and drag the File's Owner item to each of the three Label views (on the right) and select `labelX`, `labelY`, and `labelZ`, respectively.

6. In the `AccelerometerViewController.m` file, add the following statements that appear in bold:

```
#import "AccelerometerViewController.h"

@implementation AccelerometerViewController

@synthesize labelX, labelY, labelZ;

- (void)viewDidLoad {
    UIAccelerometer *acc = [UIAccelerometer sharedAccelerometer];
    acc.delegate = self;
    acc.updateInterval = 1.0f/60.0f;
    [super viewDidLoad];
}

- (void)accelerometer:(UIAccelerometer *) acc
        didAccelerate:(UIAcceleration *) acceleration {

    NSString *str = [[NSString alloc] initWithFormat:@"%g", acceleration.x];
    labelX.text = str;

    str = [[NSString alloc] initWithFormat:@"%g", acceleration.y];
    labelY.text = str;

    str = [[NSString alloc] initWithFormat:@"%g", acceleration.z];
    labelZ.text = str;

    [str release];
}

- (void)dealloc {
    [labelX release];
    [labelY release];
    [labelZ release];

    [super dealloc];
}
```

7. Press Command-R to test the application on an iPad. Figure 13-3 shows the data displayed on the application when my iPad is resting flat on its back.

 NOTE For accelerometer data, you need a real device; the iPhone Simulator does not return any readings for accelerometer data.

iPad 🛜	10:10 PM	🔋

X-axis 0.0181122
Y-axis -0.0542266
Z-axis -0.977658

FIGURE 13-3

How It Works

To use the accelerometer in your iPad, you implement the `UIAccelerometerDelegate` protocol in your delegate (such as the View Controller):

```
@interface AccelerometerViewController : UIViewController
    <UIAccelerometerDelegate> {
```

When the view is loaded, you first obtain a single instance of the `UIAccelerometer` class using the `sharedAccelerometer` method. You then specify the delegate of the instance and the update interval in which you want to obtain accelerometer data:

```
- (void)viewDidLoad {
    UIAccelerometer *acc = [UIAccelerometer sharedAccelerometer];
    acc.delegate = self;
    acc.updateInterval = 1.0f/60.0f;
    [super viewDidLoad];
}
```

The `updateInterval` property specifies the interval in seconds — that is, the number of seconds between updates. In this case, you want the accelerometer data to be updated 60 times a second.

The `UIAccelerometerDelegate` protocol defines a single method that you need to implement to obtain accelerometer data: `accelerometer:didAccelerate:`. You then extract the values of the three axes and display them on the three Label views:

```
- (void)accelerometer:(UIAccelerometer *) acc
        didAccelerate:(UIAcceleration *) acceleration {

    NSString *str = [[NSString alloc] initWithFormat:@"%g",
                        acceleration.x];
    labelX.text = str;

    str = [[NSString alloc] initWithFormat:@"%g", acceleration.y];
    labelY.text = str;

    str = [[NSString alloc] initWithFormat:@"%g", acceleration.z];
    labelZ.text = str;

    [str release];
}
```

Detecting Shakes in iPad Using the Accelerometer

Using the accelerometer data, you can actually detect if a device is being shaken. You can do so by adding some code in the `accelerometer:didAccelerate:` event, like this:

```
#import "AccelerometerViewController.h"
#define kAccelerationThreshold 2.2
//...
//...
```

```
- (void)accelerometer:(UIAccelerometer *) acc
       didAccelerate:(UIAcceleration *)acceleration {

    if (fabsf(acceleration.x) > kAccelerationThreshold)
    {
        NSLog(@"Shake detected");
    }
}
```

The fabsf() function returns the absolute value of a floating-point number. In this case, if the X-axis value registers an absolute value of more than 2.2, it is deemed that the user is shaking the device.

USING SHAKE API TO DETECT SHAKES

Beginning with iPhone OS 3.0, Apple announced the availability of the new Shake API that helps you to detect shakes to the device. In reality, this API comes in the form of three events that you can handle in your code:

➤ motionBegan:

➤ motionEnded:

➤ motionCancelled:

These three events are defined in the UIResponder class, which is the super class of UIApplication, UIView, and its subclasses (including UIWindow). The following Try It Out shows you how to detect shakes to your device using these three events.

TRY IT OUT Using the Shake API

codefile Shake.zip available for download at Wrox.com

1. Using Xcode, create a new View-based Application project and name it Shake.

2. Double-click the ShakeViewController.xib file to edit it in Interface Builder.

3. Populate the View window with the following views, and you'll see Figure 13-4:

➤ TextField

➤ DatePicker

4. Insert the following statements that appear in bold into the ShakeViewController.h file:

```
#import <UIKit/UIKit.h>

@interface ShakeViewController : UIViewController {
    IBOutlet UITextField *textField;
    IBOutlet UIDatePicker *datePicker;
}

@property (nonatomic, retain) UITextField *textField;
```

```
@property (nonatomic, retain) UIDatePicker *datePicker;

-(IBAction) doneEditing: (id) sender;

@end
```

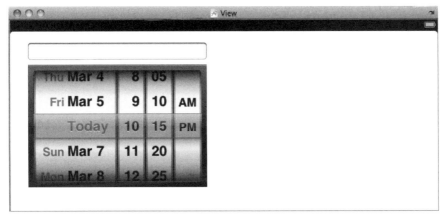

FIGURE 13-4

5. In Interface Builder:

   ➤ Control-click and drag the File's Owner item to the TextField view and select `textField`.

   ➤ Control-click and drag the File's Owner item to the DatePicker view and select `datePicker`.

6. Right-click the TextField view and connect its `Did End on Exit` event to the File's Owner item (see Figure 13-5). Select `doneEditing:`.

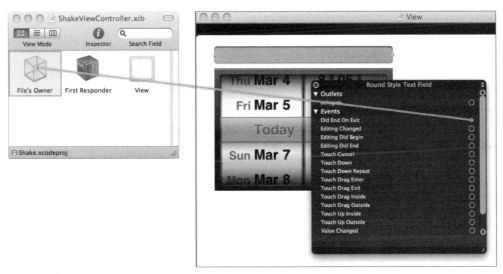

FIGURE 13-5

7. Insert the following statements that appear in bold to the ShakeViewController.m file:

```
#import "ShakeViewController.h"

@implementation ShakeViewController

@synthesize textField, datePicker;

- (void) viewDidAppear:(BOOL)animated {
    [self.view becomeFirstResponder];
    [super viewDidAppear:animated];
}

- (IBAction) doneEditing: (id) sender {
    //---when keyboard is hidden, make the view
    // the first responder
    // or else the Shake API will not work---
    [self.view becomeFirstResponder];
}

- (void)motionBegan:(UIEventSubtype)motion
        withEvent:(UIEvent *)event {
    if (event.subtype == UIEventSubtypeMotionShake) {
        NSLog(@"motionBegan:");
    }
}

- (void)motionCancelled:(UIEventSubtype)motion
        withEvent:(UIEvent *)event {
    if (event.subtype == UIEventSubtypeMotionShake) {
        NSLog(@"motionCancelled:");
    }
}

- (void)motionEnded:(UIEventSubtype)motion
        withEvent:(UIEvent *)event {
    if (event.subtype == UIEventSubtypeMotionShake) {
        NSLog(@"motionEnded:");
    }
}

- (void)dealloc {
    [textField release];
    [datePicker release];
    [super dealloc];
}
```

8. Right-click the Classes group in Xcode and choose Add ➪ New File. Choose the Cocoa Touch Class item on the left and select the Objective-C class template. Choose the UIView subclass (see Figure 13-6) and click Next.

9. Click Next and name the file ShakeView.m.

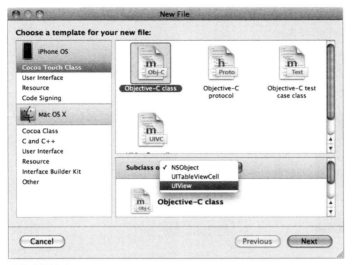

FIGURE 13-6

10. Insert the following statements in bold in `ShakeView.m`:

```objc
#import "ShakeView.h"

@implementation ShakeView

- (id)initWithFrame:(CGRect)frame {
    if ((self = [super initWithFrame:frame])) {
        // Initialization code
    }
    return self;
}

/*
// Only override drawRect: if you perform custom drawing.
// An empty implementation adversely affects
// performance during animation.
- (void)drawRect:(CGRect)rect {
    // Drawing code
}
*/

- (void)dealloc {
    [super dealloc];
}

- (BOOL)canBecomeFirstResponder {
    return YES;
}

@end
```

11. In Interface Builder, select the View window and view its Identity Inspector window. Select `ShakeView` as its class name (see Figure 13-7).

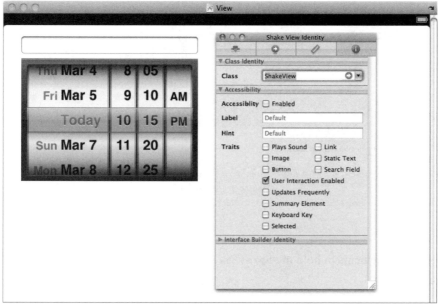

FIGURE 13-7

12. Save the file in Interface Builder.

13. Press Command-R to test the application on the iPhone Simulator. Open the Debugger Console window by pressing Command-Shift-R in Xcode.

14. With the application in the iPhone Simulator, choose Hardware ⇨ Shake Gesture to simulate shaking the device. Observe the information printed in the Debugger Console window (see Figure 13-8).

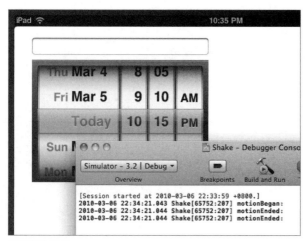

FIGURE 13-8

15. Tap the TextField view to make the keyboard appear. Choose Hardware ⇨ Shake Gesture to simulate shaking the device again. Observe the values printed in the Debugger Console window.

16. Close the keyboard by tapping the return key on the keyboard. Simulate shaking the simulator again and observe the output on the Debugger Console.

How It Works

Be aware that the three events used for monitoring shakes are fired only when there is a first responder in your View. Hence, the first thing you do when your View appears is to set it to become the first responder (in the `ShakeViewController.m` file):

```
- (void) viewDidAppear:(BOOL)animated {
    [self.view becomeFirstResponder];
    [super viewDidAppear:animated];
}
```

However, by default, the View cannot be a first responder, so you need to create a `UIView` subclass (`ShakeView.m`) so that you can override the default `canBecomeFirstResponder` method to return a `YES`:

```
- (BOOL)canBecomeFirstResponder {
    return YES;
}
```

Doing so allows your View to become a first responder. By default, Interface Builder wires your View with the `UIView` base class (with which you need not do anything most of the time). You now need to tell Interface Builder to use the newly created `ShakeView` subclass.

Next, you handle the three events in the `ShakeViewController.m` file:

```
- (void)motionBegan:(UIEventSubtype)motion
        withEvent:(UIEvent *)event {
    if (event.subtype == UIEventSubtypeMotionShake) {
        NSLog(@"motionBegan:");
    }
}

- (void)motionCancelled:(UIEventSubtype)motion
            withEvent:(UIEvent *)event {
    if (event.subtype == UIEventSubtypeMotionShake) {
        NSLog(@"motionCancelled:");
    }
}

- (void)motionEnded:(UIEventSubtype)motion
        withEvent:(UIEvent *)event {
    if (event.subtype == UIEventSubtypeMotionShake) {
        NSLog(@"motionEnded:");
    }
}
```

For each event, you first check that the motion is indeed a shake; then, print a debugging statement in the Debugger Console.

In the `doneEditing:` method (which is fired when the user dismisses the keyboard by tapping the return key), you make the View the first responder:

```
-(IBAction) doneEditing: (id) sender {
    //---when keyboard is hidden, make the view
        the first responder
    // or else the Shake API will not work---
    [self.view becomeFirstResponder];
}
```

If you don't do this, the three motion-sensing events are not fired. The key point to remember is that something must be the first responder.

The `motionBegan:` event is fired when the OS suspects that the device is being shaken. If eventually the OS determines that the action is not a shake, the `motionCancelled:` event is fired. When the OS finally determines that the action is a shake action, the `motionEnded:` event is fired.

Performing an Action When the Device Is Shaken

Now modify your project so that when the iPad is shaken, the DatePicker view is reset to today's date.

TRY IT OUT   Resetting the DatePicker when Shaken

1. In the `ShakeViewController.m` file, add the following statements that appear in bold:

```
- (void)ResetDatePicker {
    [datePicker setDate:[NSDate date]];
}

- (void)motionEnded:(UIEventSubtype)motion withEvent:(UIEvent *)event {
    if (event.subtype == UIEventSubtypeMotionShake) {
        NSLog(@"motionEnded:");
        [self ResetDatePicker];
    }
}
```

2. Press Command-R to test the application on the iPhone Simulator. Set the DatePicker view to some date. Choose Hardware ➪ Shake Gesture to simulate shaking the device. Notice that the DatePicker view now resets to today's date.

How It Works

In this example, you first added a `ResetDatePicker` method to reset the DatePicker view to today's date:

```
- (void)ResetDatePicker {
    [datePicker setDate:[NSDate date]];
}
```

When the device is shaken, you called the `ResetDatePicker` method to reset the DatePicker view to the current date:

```
- (void)motionEnded:(UIEventSubtype)motion withEvent:(UIEvent *)event {
    if (event.subtype == UIEventSubtypeMotionShake) {
        NSLog(@"motionEnded:");
        [self ResetDatePicker];
    }
}
```

SUMMARY

In this chapter, you have seen how to obtain the accelerometer data of your iPad. You also saw how to use the Shake API to help you determine if your device is being shaken. Combining all this knowledge allows you to create very compelling applications.

EXERCISES

1. Name the protocol that your delegate needs to conform to in order to use the accelerometer on your iPad.

2. Name the three events in the Shake API in iPhone SDK 3.0.

Answers to the Exercises can be found in Appendix A.

▶ **WHAT YOU LEARNED IN THIS CHAPTER**

TOPIC	KEY CONCEPTS
Accessing the accelerometer	Ensure that your View Controller conforms to the `UIAccelerometerDelegate` protocol and create an instance of the `UIAccelerometer` class.
	To listen to changes in acceleration, implement the `accelerometer:didAccelerate:` method.
Detecting shakes	You can cither use the accelerometer data or use the new Shake API in iPhone OS 3.0. For the Shake API, handle the following events: `motionBegan:`, `motionEnded:`, and `motionCancelled:`.

PART IV
Network Programming Techniques

14

Web Services

WHAT YOU WILL LEARN IN THIS CHAPTER:

➤ Understand the various ways to consume Web services in your iPad applications

➤ How to communicate with a Web service using SOAP, HTTP GET, and HTTP POST

➤ How to parse the result of a Web service call using the `NSXMLParser` class

Communicating with the outside world is one of the ways to make your iPad applications interesting and useful. This is especially true today when so many Web services provide so much useful functionality. However, consuming Web services in iPad is not for the faint-of-heart. Unlike other development tools (such as Microsoft Visual Studio), Xcode does not have built-in tools that make consuming Web services easy. Everything must be done by hand and you need to know how to form the relevant XML messages to send to the Web services and then parse the returning XML result.

This chapter explains how to communicate with XML Web services from within your iPad application. Using the examples in this chapter, you will have the solid foundation of consuming other Web services that you will need in your own projects.

 NOTE *For an introduction to XML Web services, check out this link:* `http://www.w3schools.com/webservices/ws_intro.asp`.

BASICS OF CONSUMING XML WEB SERVICES

Before you create an Xcode project to consume a Web service, it is good to examine a real Web service to see the different ways you can consume it. My favorite example is to use an ASMX XML Web service created using .NET. For discussion purposes, let's look at a Web service called IPToCountry, which allows you to supply an IP address and returns to you the country to which the IP address belongs.

The IPToCountry Web service is located at `http://www.ecubicle.net/iptocountry.asmx`. If you use Safari to load this URL, you will see that it exposes two Web methods as shown in Figure 14-1.

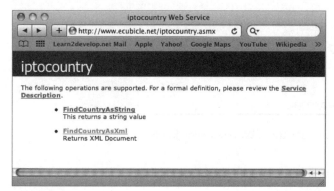

FIGURE 14-1

For this example, use the `FindCountryAsXml` method as an example, which returns the returning result (the country) as an XML string. Clicking the `FindCountryAsXml` link reveals the page shown in Figure 14-2.

The important parts are the sections following the Test section shown on the page. They detail the various ways in which you can consume the Web service — SOAP, HTTP GET, and HTTP POST. In the .NET world, accessing the Web service is a pretty straightforward affair — Visual Studio provides a built-in tool to create a Web proxy service object for the Web service simply by downloading the WSDL document. For iPad development, you need to get your hands dirty, so you must understand the underlying mechanics of how to consume a Web service.

Using SOAP 1.1

The first method to consume the Web service is using SOAP (Simple Object Access Protocol). When using SOAP, you need to use the POST method to send the following request to the Web service:

```
POST /iptocountry.asmx HTTP/1.1
Host: www.ecubicle.net
Content-Type: text/xml; charset=utf-8
Content-Length: length
SOAPAction: "http://www.ecubicle.net/webservices/FindCountryAsXml"

<?xml version="1.0" encoding="utf-8"?>
<soap:Envelope xmlns:xsi="http://www.w3.org/2001/XMLSchema-instance"
```

```
xmlns:xsd=http://www.w3.org/2001/XMLSchema
xmlns:soap="http://schemas.xmlsoap.org/soap/envelope/">
 <soap:Body>
    <FindCountryAsXml xmlns="http://www.ecubicle.net/webservices/">
      <V4IPAddress>string</V4IPAddress>
    </FindCountryAsXml>
  </soap:Body>
</soap:Envelope>
```

FIGURE 14-2

The bold italic words in the code are placeholders where you need to substitute the actual values.
A couple of important things to note in this example:

➤ The URL for the Web service is `"http://www.ecubicle.net/iptocountry.asmx"`. This
is the URL as shown in Figure 14-1.

➤ The URL for the SOAPAction is `"http://www.ecubicle.net/webservices/`
`FindCountryAsXml"`.

➤ The Content-Type for the request is text/xml; charset=utf-8.

➤ The HTTP method is POST.

➤ The SOAP request is:

```
<?xml version="1.0" encoding="utf-8"?>
<soap:Envelope xmlns:xsi="http://www.w3.org/2001/XMLSchema-instance"
xmlns:xsd="http://www.w3.org/2001/XMLSchema"
xmlns:soap="http://schemas.xmlsoap.org/soap/envelope/">
  <soap:Body>
    <FindCountryAsXml xmlns="http://www.ecubicle.net/webservices/">
      <V4IPAddress>string</V4IPAddress>
    </FindCountryAsXml>
  </soap:Body>
</soap:Envelope>
```

➤ The Content-Length of the SOAP request is the total number of characters of the SOAP request.

➤ The Web service will return the following response:

```
HTTP/1.1 200 OK
Content-Type: text/xml; charset=utf-8
Content-Length: length

<?xml version="1.0" encoding="utf-8"?>
<soap:Envelope xmlns:xsi="http://www.w3.org/2001/XMLSchema-instance"
xmlns:xsd="http://www.w3.org/2001/XMLSchema"
xmlns:soap="http://schemas.xmlsoap.org/soap/envelope/">
  <soap:Body>
    <FindCountryAsXmlResponse xmlns="http://www.ecubicle.net/webservices/">
      <FindCountryAsXmlResult>xml result</FindCountryAsXmlResult>
    </FindCountryAsXmlResponse>
  </soap:Body>
</soap:Envelope>
```

In particular, the result (country) will be enclosed within the block of XML results. You would need to extract it from the XML result.

Using SOAP 1.2

Using SOAP 1.2 is very similar to using SOAP 1.1. The following shows the SOAP request for SOAP 1.2:

```
POST /iptocountry.asmx HTTP/1.1
Host: www.ecubicle.net
Content-Type: application/soap+xml; charset=utf-8
Content-Length: length

<?xml version="1.0" encoding="utf-8"?>
<soap12:Envelope xmlns:xsi="http://www.w3.org/2001/XMLSchema-instance"
xmlns:xsd="http://www.w3.org/2001/XMLSchema"
xmlns:soap12="http://www.w3.org/2003/05/soap-envelope">
  <soap12:Body>
    <FindCountryAsXml xmlns="http://www.ecubicle.net/webservices/">
      <V4IPAddress>string</V4IPAddress>
    </FindCountryAsXml>
  </soap12:Body>
</soap12:Envelope>
```

The SOAP response for SOAP 1.2 would be:

```
HTTP/1.1 200 OK
Content-Type: application/soap+xml; charset=utf-8
Content-Length: length

<?xml version="1.0" encoding="utf-8"?>
<soap12:Envelope xmlns:xsi="http://www.w3.org/2001/XMLSchema-instance"
xmlns:xsd="http://www.w3.org/2001/XMLSchema"
xmlns:soap12="http://www.w3.org/2003/05/soap-envelope">
  <soap12:Body>
    <FindCountryAsXmlResponse xmlns="http://www.ecubicle.net/webservices/">
      <FindCountryAsXmlResult>xml result</FindCountryAsXmlResult>
    </FindCountryAsXmlResponse>
  </soap12:Body>
</soap12:Envelope>
```

Using HTTP GET

If you do not want to use SOAP, you could use the simpler HTTP GET method. Here is the format for sending the request:

```
GET /iptocountry.asmx/FindCountryAsXml?V4IPAddress=string HTTP/1.1
Host: www.ecubicle.net
HTTP/1.1 200 OK
Content-Type: text/xml; charset=utf-8
Content-Length: length
```

Take note of the following:

➤ The URL for the Web service is `http://www.ecubicle.net/iptocountry.asmx/`
`FindCountryAsXml?V4IPAddress=string`. This URL is formed by joining the Host name (on the second line) with the URL on the first line. The data to be sent is formatted as key/value pairs — `key1=value1&key2=value2&key3=value3`.

➤ The `Content-Type` for the request is `text/xml; charset=utf-8`.

➤ The `Content-Length` for the request is 0, since there is nothing you need to send separately (everything is sent through the query string).

➤ The HTTP Method is `GET`.

➤ The result will be returned in the following format:

```
<?xml version="1.0"?>
xml result
```

Using HTTP POST

In addition to using HTTP GET, you can also use HTTP POST. Here is the format for sending the request:

```
POST /iptocountry.asmx/FindCountryAsXml HTTP/1.1
```

```
Host: www.ecubicle.net
Content-Type: application/x-www-form-urlencoded
Content-Length: length

V4IPAddress=string
```

Take note of the following:

➤ The URL for the Web service is `http://www.ecubicle.net/iptocountry.asmx/` `FindCountryAsXml`. This URL is formed by joining the Host name (on the second line) with the URL on the first line.

➤ The `Content-Type` for the request is `application/x-www-form-urlencoded`.

➤ The `Content-Length` for the request is the length of `V4IPAddress=string`. The data to be sent is formatted as key/value pairs — *key1=value1&key2=value2&key3=value3*. Unlike HTTP GET, the data are not sent through the query string; it is sent after the HTTP headers.

➤ The HTTP Method is `POST`.

➤ The result will be returned in the following format:

```
HTTP/1.1 200 OK
Content-Type: text/xml; charset=utf-8
Content-Length: length

<?xml version="1.0"?>
xml result
```

CONSUMING WEB SERVICES USING SOAP, HTTP GET, AND HTTP POST

Now that you have seen the three ways of consuming Web services, which method should you use? Using HTTP GET (the simplest), you saw that all the information you need to pass to the Web service can be sent through the query string. However, the query string has a limit on its length, and is hence not suitable if you need to pass lots of data to the Web service. An alternative to this would be to use the HTTP POST method, which allows more data to be sent. However, HTTP POST has its limitations as well. As with HTTP GET, the data to be sent must be formatted as key/value pairs. But each key/value pair is limited in size to 1024 characters. The most versatile method is to use the SOAP method, which allows complex data types to be sent to the Web service through the SOAP request.

CONSUMING A WEB SERVICE IN YOUR IPAD APPLICATION

Now you're ready to tackle the exciting task of consuming a Web service in your iPad application! First, you learn how to communicate with the Web service using the SOAP method.

TRY IT OUT Consuming Web Services Using SOAP

1. Using Xcode, create a View-based Application project and name it `WebServices`.

2. Double-click the `WebServicesViewController.xib` file to edit it in Interface Builder.

3. Double-click the View item and populate the View window with the views as follows (see also Figure 14-3):

➤ Label

➤ Text Field

➤ Round Rect Button

➤ Activity Indicator

FIGURE 14-3

4. In Xcode, edit the `WebServicesViewController.h` file and add in the following bold statements:

```
#import <UIKit/UIKit.h>

@interface WebServicesViewController : UIViewController {
    IBOutlet UITextField *ipAddress;
    IBOutlet UIActivityIndicatorView *activityIndicator;

    NSMutableData *webData;
    NSMutableString *soapResults;
    NSURLConnection *conn;
}

@property (nonatomic, retain) UITextField *ipAddress;
@property (nonatomic, retain) UIActivityIndicatorView *activityIndicator;

- (IBAction)buttonClicked:(id)sender;

@end
```

5. Save the file and return to Interface Builder.

6. Perform the following actions:

➤ Control-click the File's Owner item and drag it over the Text Field view. Select `ipAddress`.

➤ Control-click the File's Owner item and drag it over the Activity Indicator view. Select `activityIndicator`.

➤ Control-click the Round Rect Button view and drag it over the File's Owner item. Select `buttonClicked:`.

7. Right-click the File's Owner item now and you should see the connections as shown in Figure 14-4.

FIGURE 14-4

8. In the `WebServicesViewController.m` file, add in the following bold statements:

```
import "WebServicesViewController.h"
@implementation WebServicesViewController

@synthesize ipAddress;
@synthesize activityIndicator;
```

9. Next, define the `buttonClicked:` method, which will formulate the SOAP request packet and send it over to the Web service:

```
- (IBAction)buttonClicked:(id)sender {

    NSString *soapMsg =
        [NSString stringWithFormat:
            @"<?xml version=\"1.0\" encoding=\"utf-8\"?>"
            "<soap:Envelope xmlns:xsi="
            "\"http://www.w3.org/2001/XMLSchema-instance\" "
            "xmlns:xsd=\"http://www.w3.org/2001/XMLSchema\" "
            "xmlns:soap=\"http://schemas.xmlsoap.org/soap/envelope/\">"
            "<soap:Body>"
            "<FindCountryAsXml xmlns=\"http://www.ecubicle.net/webservices/\">"
            "<V4IPAddress>%@</V4IPAddress>"
            "</FindCountryAsXml>"
            "</soap:Body>"
            "</soap:Envelope>",  ipAddress.text
```

```
        ];

    //---print it to the Debugger Console for verification---
    NSLog(soapMsg);

    NSURL *url = [NSURL URLWithString:
        @"http://www.ecubicle.net/iptocountry.asmx"];
    NSMutableURLRequest *req = [NSMutableURLRequest requestWithURL:url];

    //---set the various headers---
    NSString *msgLength = [NSString stringWithFormat:@"%d", [soapMsg length]];
    [req addValue:@"text/xml; charset=utf-8" forHTTPHeaderField:@"Content-Type"];
    [req addValue:@"http://www.ecubicle.net/webservices/FindCountryAsXml"
        forHTTPHeaderField:@"SOAPAction"];
    [req addValue:msgLength forHTTPHeaderField:@"Content-Length"];

    //---set the HTTP method and body---
    [req setHTTPMethod:@"POST"];
    [req setHTTPBody:[soapMsg dataUsingEncoding:NSUTF8StringEncoding]];

    [activityIndicator startAnimating];

    conn = [[NSURLConnection alloc] initWithRequest:req delegate:self];
    if (conn) {
        webData = [[NSMutableData data] retain];
    }
}
```

10. In the `WebServicesViewController.m` file, add the following methods:

```
-(void) connection:(NSURLConnection *) connection
didReceiveResponse:(NSURLResponse *) response {
    [webData setLength: 0];
}

-(void) connection:(NSURLConnection *) connection
    didReceiveData:(NSData *) data {
    [webData appendData:data];
}

-(void) connection:(NSURLConnection *) connection
  didFailWithError:(NSError *) error {
    [webData release];
    [connection release];
}

-(void) connectionDidFinishLoading:(NSURLConnection *) connection {
    NSLog(@"DONE. Received Bytes: %d", [webData length]);
    NSString *theXML = [[NSString alloc]
                        initWithBytes: [webData mutableBytes]
                        length:[webData length]
                        encoding:NSUTF8StringEncoding];
    //---shows the XML---
    NSLog(theXML);
```

```
    [theXML release];

    [activityIndicator stopAnimating];

    [connection release];
    [webData release];
}

-(void) dealloc {
    [ipAddress release];
    [activityIndicator release];
    [super dealloc];
}
```

11. Press Command-R to test the application on the iPhone Simulator. Enter the IP address **34.5.6.7** in the Text Field, and tap the Find Country button.

12. In Xcode, press Shift-Command-R to open the Debugger Console window. Observe that the following was sent to the Web service:

```
<?xml version="1.0" encoding="utf-8"?>
<soap:Envelope xmlns:xsi="http://www.w3.org/2001/XMLSchema-instance"
xmlns:xsd="http://www.w3.org/2001/XMLSchema"
xmlns:soap="http://schemas.xmlsoap.org/soap/envelope/">
    <soap:Body>
        <FindCountryAsXml xmlns="http://www.ecubicle.net/webservices/">
            <V4IPAddress>34.5.6.7</V4IPAddress>
        </FindCountryAsXml>
    </soap:Body>
</soap:Envelope>
```

13. The Web service responded with the following:

```
<?xml version="1.0" encoding="utf-8"?>
<soap:Envelope xmlns:soap="http://schemas.xmlsoap.org/soap/envelope/"
xmlns:xsi="http://www.w3.org/2001/XMLSchema-instance"
xmlns:xsd="http://www.w3.org/2001/XMLSchema">
    <soap:Body>
        <FindCountryAsXmlResponse xmlns="http://www.ecubicle.net/webservices/">
            <FindCountryAsXmlResult>
                <IPCountryService xmlns="">
                    <Country>United States</Country>
                </IPCountryService>
            </FindCountryAsXmlResult>
        </FindCountryAsXmlResponse>
    </soap:Body>
</soap:Envelope>
```

The response from the Web service indicates that you have managed to communicate with the Web service. The problem now is how to parse the XML to extract the relevant result that you want. In this case, the result you want is encapsulated in the <Country> element. In the next section you shall learn how to parse the XML response.

How It Works

Let's spend some time examining what you just did. First, you create the SOAP request packet:

```
NSString *soapMsg =
    [NSString stringWithFormat:
        @"<?xml version=\"1.0\" encoding=\"utf-8\"?>"
        "<soap:Envelope xmlns:xsi="
        "\"http://www.w3.org/2001/XMLSchema-instance\" "
        "xmlns:xsd=\"http://www.w3.org/2001/XMLSchema\" "
        "xmlns:soap=\"http://schemas.xmlsoap.org/soap/envelope/\">"
        "<soap:Body>"
        "<FindCountryAsXml xmlns=\"http://www.ecubicle.net/webservices/\">"
        "<V4IPAddress>%@</V4IPAddress>"
        "</FindCountryAsXml>"
        "</soap:Body>"
        "</soap:Envelope>",  ipAddress.text
    ];
```

Next, you create a URL load request object using an instance of the `NSMutableURLRequest` and `NSURL` objects:

```
NSURL *url = [NSURL URLWithString:@"http://www.ecubicle.net/iptocountry.asmx"];
NSMutableURLRequest *req = [NSMutableURLRequest requestWithURL:url];
```

You then populate the request object with the various headers, such as `Content-Type`, `SOAPAction`, and `Content-Length`. You also set the HTTP method and HTTP body:

```
NSString *msgLength = [NSString stringWithFormat:@"%d", [soapMsg length]];
[req addValue:@"text/xml; charset=utf-8" forHTTPHeaderField:@"Content-Type"];
[req addValue:@"http://www.ecubicle.net/webservices/FindCountryAsXml"
    forHTTPHeaderField:@"SOAPAction"];
[req addValue:msgLength forHTTPHeaderField:@"Content-Length"];

[req setHTTPMethod:@"POST"];
[req setHTTPBody: [soapMsg dataUsingEncoding:NSUTF8StringEncoding]];
```

Before you make the actual request to the Web service, you get the Activity Indicator view to start animating, providing a visual feedback to the user that the application is waiting for a response from the Web service:

```
[activityIndicator startAnimating];
```

To establish the connection with the Web service, you use the `NSURLConnection` class together with the request object just created:

```
conn = [[NSURLConnection alloc] initWithRequest:req delegate:self];
if (conn) {
    webData = [[NSMutableData data] retain];
}
```

The `NSURLConnection` object will now proceed to send the request to the Web service and asynchronously call the various methods (which you will define next) when responses are received from the Web service. The `data` method of the `NSMutableData` class returns an empty data object. The `NSMutableData` object represents a wrapper for byte buffers, which you will use to receive incoming data from the Web service.

When data starts streaming in from the Web service, the `connection:didReceiveResponse:` method will be called, which you need to implement here:

```
-(void) connection:(NSURLConnection *) connection
didReceiveResponse:(NSURLResponse *) response {
    [webData setLength: 0];
}
```

Here, you will initialize the length of `webData` to zero.

As the data progressively comes in from the Web service, the `connection:didReceiveData:` method will be called. Here, you will append the data received to the `webData` object:

```
-(void) connection:(NSURLConnection *) connection
    didReceiveData:(NSData *) data {
    [webData appendData:data];
}
```

If there is an error during the transmission, the `connection:didFailWithError:` method will be called:

```
-(void) connection:(NSURLConnection *) connection
  didFailWithError:(NSError *) error {
    [webData release];
    [connection release];
}
```

It is important that you handle the communication failure gracefully so that the user can try again later.

When the connection has finished and successfully downloaded the response, the `connectionDidFinishLoading:` method is called:

```
-(void) connectionDidFinishLoading:(NSURLConnection *) connection {
    NSLog(@"DONE. Received Bytes: %d", [webData length]);
    NSString *theXML = [[NSString alloc]
                        initWithBytes: [webData mutableBytes]
                        length:[webData length]
                        encoding:NSUTF8StringEncoding];
    //---shows the XML---
    NSLog(theXML);
    [theXML release];

    [activityIndicator stopAnimating];

    [connection release];
    [webData release];
}
```

Here, you simply print the XML response received from the Web service to the Debugger Console window and then stop the Activity Indicator view from animating.

Using HTTP POST to Talk to a Web Service

You can also use the HTTP POST method to communicate with the Web service. To talk to a Web service using HTTP POST, you just need to modify the `buttonClicked:` method, like this:

```
- (IBAction)buttonClicked:(id)sender {

    NSString *postString =
        [NSString stringWithFormat:@"V4IPAddress=%@", ipAddress.text];

    NSLog(postString);

    NSURL *url = [NSURL URLWithString:
        @"http://www.ecubicle.net/iptocountry.asmx/FindCountryAsXml"];
    NSMutableURLRequest *req = [NSMutableURLRequest requestWithURL:url];
    NSString *msgLength = [NSString stringWithFormat:@"%d", [postString length]];

    [req addValue:@"application/x-www-form-urlencoded"
        forHTTPHeaderField:@"Content-Type"];
    [req addValue:msgLength forHTTPHeaderField:@"Content-Length"];

    [req setHTTPMethod:@"POST"];
    [req setHTTPBody: [postString dataUsingEncoding:NSUTF8StringEncoding]];

    [activityIndicator startAnimating];

    conn = [[NSURLConnection alloc] initWithRequest:req delegate:self];
    if (conn) {
        webData = [[NSMutableData data] retain];
    }
}
```

Basically, you do away with forming the SOAP message and simply post a single string to the Web service, such as:

```
V4IPAddress=34.5.6.7
```

 NOTE Note that in order for HTTP POST to work, the Web service must support the HTTP POST method. Always refer to the documentation of the Web service (or the test page shown in Figure 14-2) to confirm if the Web service supports HTTP POST.

The result returned from the Web service will look like this:

```
<?xml version="1.0" encoding="utf-8"?>
<IPCountryService>
    <Country>United States</Country>
</IPCountryService>
```

Using HTTP GET to Talk to a Web Service

Using HTTP GET to talk to a Web service is even simpler than using HTTP POST because all the request information is passed via the query string. The following shows the modified `buttonClicked:` method to access the Web service using HTTP GET:

```
- (IBAction)buttonClicked:(id)sender {

    NSString *queryString =
        [NSString stringWithFormat:
    @"http://www.ecubicle.net/iptocountry.asmx/FindCountryAsXml?V4IPAddress=%@",
    ipAddress.text];

    NSURL *url = [NSURL URLWithString:queryString];
    NSMutableURLRequest *req = [NSMutableURLRequest requestWithURL:url];

    [req addValue:@"text/xml; charset=utf-8" forHTTPHeaderField:@"Content-Type"];
    [req addValue:0 forHTTPHeaderField:@"Content-Length"];

    [req setHTTPMethod:@"GET"];

    [activityIndicator startAnimating];

    conn = [[NSURLConnection alloc] initWithRequest:req delegate:self];
    if (conn) {
        webData = [[NSMutableData data] retain];
    }
}
```

Look at the Debugger Console when you run the modified application, and you should see the response like this:

```
<?xml version="1.0" encoding="utf-8"?>
<IPCountryService>
    <Country>United States</Country>
</IPCountryService>
```

> **NOTE** Note that in order for HTTP GET to work, the Web service must support the HTTP GET method. Always refer to the documentation of the Web service (or the test page shown in Figure 14-2) to confirm if the Web service supports HTTP GET.

PARSING THE XML RESPONSE

In the iPhone SDK, you can use the `NSXMLParser` object to parse an XML response returned by the Web service. The `NSXMLParser` class is an implementation of the Simple API for XML (SAX) mechanism, which parses an XML document serially.

An NSXMLParser object reads an XML document and scans it from beginning to end. As it encounters the various items in the document (such as elements, attributes, comments, and so on), it notifies its delegates so that appropriate actions can be taken (such as extracting the value of an element, etc).

TRY IT OUT   **Parsing the XML Result**

1. Using the WebServices project created in the previous section, add the following statements to the WebServicesViewController.h file to parse the response from the Web service:

```
#import <UIKit/UIKit.h>

@interface WebServicesViewController : UIViewController {
    IBOutlet UITextField *ipAddress;
    IBOutlet UIActivityIndicatorView *activityIndicator;

    NSMutableData *webData;
    NSMutableString *soapResults;
    NSURLConnection *conn;

    NSXMLParser *xmlParser;
    BOOL elementFound;
}

@property (nonatomic, retain) UITextField *ipAddress;
@property (nonatomic, retain) UIActivityIndicatorView *activityIndicator;

- (IBAction)buttonClicked:(id)sender;

@end
```

2. In the WebServicesViewController.m file, add in the following bold statements to the connec-tionDidFinishLoading: method:

```
-(void) connectionDidFinishLoading:(NSURLConnection *) connection {

    NSLog(@"DONE. Received Bytes: %d", [webData length]);
    NSString *theXML = [[NSString alloc]
                        initWithBytes: [webData mutableBytes]
                        length:[webData length]
                        encoding:NSUTF8StringEncoding];
    //---shows the XML---
    NSLog(theXML);
    [theXML release];

    [activityIndicator stopAnimating];

    if (xmlParser) {
        [xmlParser release];
    }

    xmlParser = [[NSXMLParser alloc] initWithData: webData];
    [xmlParser setDelegate: self];
```

```
    [xmlParser setShouldResolveExternalEntities:YES];
    [xmlParser parse];

    [connection release];
    [webData release];
}
```

3.   In the `WebServicesViewController.m` file, add in the following methods:

```
//---when the start of an element is found---
-(void) parser:(NSXMLParser *) parser
    didStartElement:(NSString *) elementName
      namespaceURI:(NSString *) namespaceURI
     qualifiedName:(NSString *) qName
         attributes:(NSDictionary *) attributeDict {

    if( [elementName isEqualToString:@"Country"]) {
        if (!soapResults) {
            soapResults = [[NSMutableString alloc] init];
        }
        elementFound = YES;
    }
}

//---when the text in an element is found---
-(void)parser:(NSXMLParser *) parser foundCharacters:(NSString *)string {
    if (elementFound) {
        [soapResults appendString: string];
    }
}

//---when the end of element is found---
-(void)parser:(NSXMLParser *)parser
    didEndElement:(NSString *)elementName
     namespaceURI:(NSString *)namespaceURI
    qualifiedName:(NSString *)qName {
    if ([elementName isEqualToString:@"Country"]) {
        //---displays the country---
        NSLog(soapResults);
        UIAlertView *alert = [[UIAlertView alloc] initWithTitle:@"Country found!"
                                                  message:soapResults
                                                  delegate:self
                                       cancelButtonTitle:@"OK"
                                       otherButtonTitles:nil];
        [alert show];
        [alert release];
        [soapResults setString:@""];
        elementFound = FALSE;
    }
}

-(void) dealloc {
    [soapResults release];
    [ipAddress release];
    [activityIndicator release];
```

```
        [super dealloc];
    }
```

4. Test the application on the iPhone Simulator by pressing Command-R. Enter an IP address and click the Find Country button. The application displays the result, as shown in Figure 14-5.

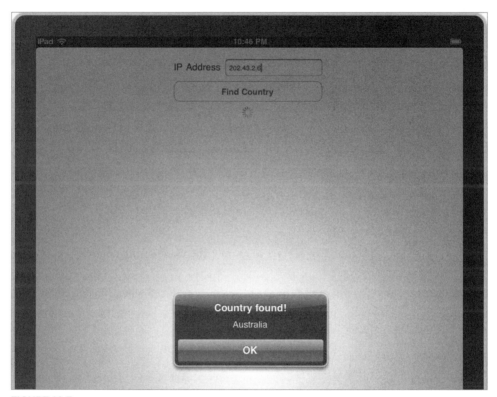

FIGURE 14-5

How It Works

To parse the XML result, you create an instance of the NSXMLParser class and then initialize it with the response returned by the Web service. The NSXMLParser is an implementation of the Simple APIs for XML (SAX) parser. It parses an XML document sequentially, in an event-driven manner. As the parser encounters the various elements, attributes, and so forth in an XML document, it raises events where you can insert your own event handlers to do your processing.

As the NSXMLParser object encounters the various items in the XML document, it will fire off several methods, which you need to define:

➤ parser:didStartElement:namespaceURI:qualifiedName:attributes: — Fired when the start tag of an element is found:

```
//---when the start of an element is found---
-(void) parser:(NSXMLParser *) parser
```

```
        didStartElement:(NSString *) elementName
          namespaceURI:(NSString *) namespaceURI
         qualifiedName:(NSString *) qName
            attributes:(NSDictionary *) attributeDict {

    if( [elementName isEqualToString:@"Country"]) {
        if (!soapResults) {
            soapResults = [[NSMutableString alloc] init];
        }
        elementFound = YES;
    }
}
```

Here, you check to see if the tag is <Country>. If it is, you will set the Boolean variable
elementFound to YES.

➤ parser:foundCharacters: — Fired when the text of an element is found:

```
-(void)parser:(NSXMLParser *) parser foundCharacters:(NSString *)string {
    if (elementFound) {
        [soapResults appendString: string];
    }
}
```

Here, if the <Country> tag is found, you start to extract the value of the Country element into the
soapResults object.

➤ parser:didEndElement:namespaceURI:qualifiedName: — Fired when the end of an element
is found:

```
//---when the end of element is found---
-(void)parser:(NSXMLParser *)parser
    didEndElement:(NSString *)elementName
     namespaceURI:(NSString *)namespaceURI
    qualifiedName:(NSString *)qName {
    if ([elementName isEqualToString:@"Country"]) {
        //---displays the country---
        NSLog(soapResults);
        UIAlertView *alert = [[UIAlertView alloc] initWithTitle:@"Country found!"
                                                        message:soapResults
                                                        delegate:self
                                              cancelButtonTitle:@"OK"
                                              otherButtonTitles:nil];
        [alert show];
        [alert release];
        [soapResults setString:@""];
        elementFound = FALSE;
    }
}
```

Here, you simply look for the </Country> tag so that you now know that the value of the Country
element has been correctly extracted. You then print out the value using a UIAlertView object.

SUMMARY

This chapter explored the various ways you can consume a Web service in your iPad applications — SOAP, HTTP GET, and HTTP POST. You also learned how to extract data from an XML document. Hopefully you now have a good idea of what is involved in consuming Web services.

EXERCISES

1. Name the three ways in which you can consume a Web service in your iPad applications.

2. Name the three key events you need to handle when using the NSURLConnection class.

3. Describe the steps in which the NSXMLParser class parses the content of an XML document.

Answers to the Exercises can be found in Appendix A.

▶ **WHAT YOU LEARNED IN THIS CHAPTER**

TOPIC	KEY CONCEPTS
Ways to consume a Web service	SOAP 1.1/1.2, HTTP GET, and HTTP POST
Formulating a URL request	Use the `NSMutableURLRequest` class
Establishing a URL connection	Use the `NSURLConnection` class
Class for storing byte buffers	Use the `NSMutableData` class

Events fired by the `NSURLConnection` class	`connection:didReceiveResponse:`
	`connection:didReceiveData:`
	`connection:didFailWithError:`
	`connectionDidFinishLoading:`

Parsing XML content	Use the `NSXMLParser` class

Events fired by the `NSXMLParser` class	`parser:didStartElement:namespaceURI:qualifiedName:attributes:`
	`parser:foundCharacters:`
	`parser:didEndElement:namespaceURI:qualifiedName:`

15

Bluetooth Programming

WHAT YOU WILL LEARN IN THIS CHAPTER:

➤ How to use the various APIs within the Game Kit framework for Bluetooth communications

➤ How to look for peer Bluetooth devices using the `GKPeerPickerController` class

➤ How to send and receive data from a connected device

➤ How to implement Bluetooth voice chat

The iPad comes with built-in Bluetooth functionality, allowing it to communicate with other Bluetooth devices, such as Bluetooth headsets, iPhone, iPod touch, and iPad. This chapter shows you how to write iPad applications that use Bluetooth to communicate with another device, performing tasks such as sending and receiving text messages, as well as voice chatting. Daunting as it may sound, Bluetooth programming is actually quite simple using the iPhone SDK. All the Bluetooth functionalities are encapsulated within the Game Kit framework.

 NOTE To test the concepts covered in this chapter, you need two devices — iPads, iPhones (3G or 3GS), or iPod touches (second generation or later) running iPhone OS 3.0 or later.

USING THE GAME KIT FRAMEWORK

One of the neat features available in the iPhone SDK is the Game Kit framework, which contains APIs that allow communications over a Bluetooth network. You can use these APIs to create peer-to-peer games and applications with ease. Unlike other mobile platforms, using

Bluetooth as a communication channel in the iPad is way easier than expected. In this section, you will learn how to build a simple application that allows two iPad (or iPhone and iPod touch) devices to communicate with each other.

Searching for Peer Devices

The first step to Bluetooth communication is for the devices to locate each other before any exchanges of data can take place. The following Try It Out shows you how to use the Game Kit framework to locate your Bluetooth peer.

TRY IT OUT Looking for Peer Devices

codefile Bluetooth.zip available for download at Wrox.com

1. Using Xcode, create a new View-based Application project and name it `Bluetooth`.

2. Add the GameKit framework to your project (see Figure 15-1).

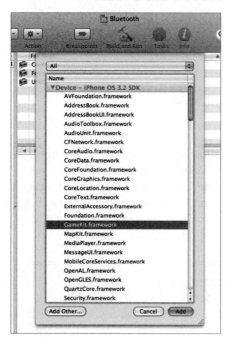

FIGURE 15-1

3. In the `BluetoothViewController.h` file, add in the following statements shown in bold:

```
#import <UIKit/UIKit.h>

#import <GameKit/GameKit.h>
```

```
@interface BluetoothViewController : UIViewController
    <GKSessionDelegate, GKPeerPickerControllerDelegate> {

    GKSession *currentSession;
    IBOutlet UITextField *txtMessage;
    IBOutlet UIButton *connect;
    IBOutlet UIButton *disconnect;

    GKPeerPickerController *picker;
}

@property (nonatomic, retain) GKSession *currentSession;
@property (nonatomic, retain) UITextField *txtMessage;
@property (nonatomic, retain) UIButton *connect;
@property (nonatomic, retain) UIButton *disconnect;

-(IBAction) btnSend:(id) sender;
-(IBAction) btnConnect:(id) sender;
-(IBAction) btnDisconnect:(id) sender;

@end
```

4. Double-click on `BluetoothViewController.xib` to edit it in Interface Builder. Add the following views to the View window (see Figure 15-2):

➤ Text Field

➤ Round Rect buttons (name them as Send, Connect, and Disconnect)

5. In the `BluetoothViewController.m` file, add in the following statements in bold:

```
#import "BluetoothViewController.h"

@implementation BluetoothViewController

@synthesize currentSession;
@synthesize txtMessage;
@synthesize connect;
@synthesize disconnect;
```

6. Back in Interface Builder, perform the following actions:

➤ Control-click on the File's Owner item and drag and drop it over the Text Field view. Select `txtMessage`.

➤ Control-click on the File's Owner item and drag and drop it over the Connect button. Select `connect`.

➤ Control-click on the File's Owner item and drag and drop it over the Disconnect button. Select `disconnect`.

➤ Control-click on the Send button and drag and drop it over the File's Owner item. Select `btnSend:`.

➤ Control-click on the Connect button and drag and drop it over the File's Owner item. Select `btnConnect:`.

➤ Control-click on the Disconnect button and drag and drop it over the File's Owner item. Select `btnDisconnect:`.

FIGURE 15-2

7. Right-click on the File's Owner item to verify that all the connections are made correctly (see Figure 15-3).

FIGURE 15-3

8. In Xcode, in the `BluetoothViewController.m` file, add in the following bold statements:

```
- (void)viewDidLoad {
    [connect setHidden:NO];
    [disconnect setHidden:YES];
    [super viewDidLoad];
}

-(IBAction) btnConnect:(id) sender {
    picker = [[GKPeerPickerController alloc] init];
    picker.delegate = self;
    picker.connectionTypesMask = GKPeerPickerConnectionTypeNearby;

    [connect setHidden:YES];
    [disconnect setHidden:NO];
    [picker show];
}

- (void)peerPickerController:(GKPeerPickerController *)pk
            didConnectPeer:(NSString *)peerID
                toSession:(GKSession *) session {

    self.currentSession = session;
    session.delegate = self;
    [session setDataReceiveHandler:self withContext:nil];

    picker.delegate = nil;
    [picker dismiss];
    [picker autorelease];
}
```

```
- (void)peerPickerControllerDidCancel:(GKPeerPickerController *)pk {
    picker.delegate = nil;
    [picker autorelease];

    [connect setHidden:NO];
    [disconnect setHidden:YES];
}

-(IBAction) btnDisconnect:(id) sender {
    [self.currentSession disconnectFromAllPeers];
    [self.currentSession release];
    currentSession = nil;

    [connect setHidden:NO];
    [disconnect setHidden:YES];
}

- (void)session:(GKSession *)session
            peer:(NSString *)peerID
 didChangeState:(GKPeerConnectionState)state {

    switch (state) {
        case GKPeerStateConnected:
            NSLog(@"connected");
            break;
        case GKPeerStateDisconnected:
            NSLog(@"disconnected");
            [self.currentSession release];
            currentSession = nil;

            [connect setHidden:NO];
            [disconnect setHidden:YES];
            break;
    }
}

- (void)dealloc {
    [txtMessage release];
    [currentSession release];
    [super dealloc];
}
```

9. Deploy the application onto two devices (either iPad, iPhone, or iPod touch). For deploying to a device other than the iPad, be sure to change the UI so that it fits the smaller screen.

10. Once the application is deployed onto two devices, launch the application on both devices. Tap the Connect button on each device. You will see the standard UI to discover other devices (see Figure 15-4).

11. After a few seconds, both devises should be able to find each other (see Figure 15-5). Tap on the name of the found device and the application attempts to connect to it.

12. When another device tries to connect to you, you see a popup as shown in Figure 15-6. Tap on Accept to connect and Decline to decline the connection.

FIGURE 15-4

FIGURE 15-5

FIGURE 15-6

How It Works

The GKSession object is used to represent a session between two connected Bluetooth devices. You use it to send and receive data between the two devices. Hence, you first create a variable of type GKSession:

```
GKSession *currentSession;
```

The GKPeerPickerController class provides a standard UI to let your application discover and connect to another Bluetooth device. This is the easiest way to connect to another Bluetooth device.

To discover and connect to another Bluetooth device, implement the btnConnect: method as follows:

```
-(IBAction) btnConnect:(id) sender {
    picker = [[GKPeerPickerController alloc] init];
    picker.delegate = self;
    picker.connectionTypesMask = GKPeerPickerConnectionTypeNearby;

    [connect setHidden:YES];
    [disconnect setHidden:NO];
    [picker show];
}
```

The connectionTypesMask property indicates the types of connections that the user can choose from. There are two types available: GKPeerPickerConnectionTypeNearby and GKPeerPickerConnectionTypeOnline. For Bluetooth communication, use the GKPeerPickerConnectionTypeNearby constant. The GKPeerPickerConnectionTypeOnline constant indicates an Internet-based connection.

When remote Bluetooth devices are detected and the user has selected and connected to one of them, the peerPickerController:didConnectPeer:toSession: method is called. It is implemented as follows:

```
- (void)peerPickerController:(GKPeerPickerController *)picker
            didConnectPeer:(NSString *)peerID
                toSession:(GKSession *) session {
    self.currentSession = session;
    session.delegate = self;
    [session setDataReceiveHandler:self withContext:nil];
    picker.delegate = nil;
```

```
    [picker dismiss];
    [picker autorelease];
}
```

When the user has connected to the peer Bluetooth device, you save the GKSession object to the currentSession property. This enables you to use the GKSession object to communicate with the remote device.

If the user cancels the Bluetooth Picker, the peerPickerControllerDidCancel: method is called. It's defined as follows:

```
- (void)peerPickerControllerDidCancel:(GKPeerPickerController *)picker {
    picker.delegate = nil;
    [picker autorelease];

    [connect setHidden:NO];
    [disconnect setHidden:YES];
}
```

To disconnect from a connected device, use the disconnectFromAllPeers method from the GKSession object:

```
-(IBAction) btnDisconnect:(id) sender {
    [self.currentSession disconnectFromAllPeers];
    [self.currentSession release];
    currentSession = nil;

    [connect setHidden:NO];
    [disconnect setHidden:YES];
}
```

When a device is connected or disconnected, the session:peer:didChangeState: method is called:

```
- (void)session:(GKSession *)session
           peer:(NSString *)peerID
  didChangeState:(GKPeerConnectionState)state {
    switch (state) {
        case GKPeerStateConnected:
            NSLog(@"connected");
            break;
        case GKPeerStateDisconnected:
            NSLog(@"disconnected");
            [self.currentSession release];
            currentSession = nil;

            [connect setHidden:NO];
            [disconnect setHidden:YES];
            break;
    }
}
```

Handling this event allows you to know when a connection is established or ended. For example, when the connection is established, you might want to immediately start sending data over to the other device.

Sending Data

Once two devices are connected via Bluetooth, you can start to send data to each other. The data are transmitted using the NSData object (which is actually a bytes buffer), so you are free to define your own data format to send any types of data (such as images, text files, binary files, and so on).

The following Try It Out shows how to send a simple text message to another Bluetooth-connected device.

TRY IT OUT   Sending Text to Another Device

1. Using the project created in the previous section, add the following methods to the BluetoothViewController.m file:

```
- (void) mySendDataToPeers:(NSData *) data {
    if (currentSession)
        [self.currentSession sendDataToAllPeers:data
                                  withDataMode:GKSendDataReliable
                                         error:nil];
}

-(IBAction) btnSend:(id) sender {
    //---convert an NSString object to NSData---
    NSData* data;
    NSString *str = [NSString stringWithString:txtMessage.text];
    data = [str dataUsingEncoding: NSASCIIStringEncoding];
    [self mySendDataToPeers:data];
}

- (void) receiveData:(NSData *)data
            fromPeer:(NSString *)peer
           inSession:(GKSession *)session
             context:(void *)context {

    //---convert the NSData to NSString---
    NSString* str;
    str = [[NSString alloc] initWithData:data encoding:NSASCIIStringEncoding];
    UIAlertView *alert = [[UIAlertView alloc] initWithTitle:@"Data received"
                                                    message:str
                                                   delegate:self
                                          cancelButtonTitle:@"OK"
                                          otherButtonTitles:nil];
    [alert show];
    [alert release];
}
```

2. Deploy the application onto two devices. Connect the devices using Bluetooth. Now enter some text and start sending to the other device. Data received from another device is shown in an alert view (see Figure 15-7).

FIGURE 15-7

How It Works

To send data to the connected Bluetooth device, use the sendDataToAllPeers: method of the GKSession object. The data that you send is transmitted via an NSData object.

The mySendDataToPeers: method is defined as follows:

```
- (void) mySendDataToPeers:(NSData *) data {
    if (currentSession)
        [self.currentSession sendDataToAllPeers:data
                             withDataMode:GKSendDataReliable
                                    error:nil];
}
```

> **NOTE** Note the use of the GKSendDataReliable constant. This constant means that the GKSession object continues to send the data until it is successfully transmitted or the connection times out. The data are delivered in the order they were sent. Use this constant when you need to ensure guaranteed delivery. On the other hand, the GKSendDataUnreliable constant indicates that the GKSession object sends the data once and does not retry if an error occurred. The data sent can be received out of order by recipients. Use this constant for small packets of data that must arrive quickly to be useful to the recipient.

The btnSend: method allows text entered by the user to be sent to the remote device:

```
-(IBAction) btnSend:(id) sender {
    //---convert an NSString object to NSData---
    NSData* data;
    NSString *str = [NSString stringWithString:txtMessage.text];
    data = [str dataUsingEncoding: NSASCIIStringEncoding];
    [self mySendDataToPeers:data];
}
```

When data is received from the other device, the receiveData:fromPeer:inSession:context: method is called:

```
- (void) receiveData:(NSData *)data
            fromPeer:(NSString *)peer
           inSession:(GKSession *)session
             context:(void *)context {

    //---convert the NSData to NSString---
    NSString* str;
    str = [[NSString alloc] initWithData:data
    encoding:NSASCIIStringEncoding];
    UIAlertView *alert =
    [[UIAlertView alloc] initWithTitle:@"Data received"
                               message:str
                               delegate:self
                      cancelButtonTitle:@"OK"
                      otherButtonTitles:nil];
```

```
            [alert show];
            [alert release];
}
```

Here, the received data is in the `NSData` format. To display it using the `UIAlertView` class, you convert it to an `NSString` object.

IMPLEMENTING VOICE CHATTING

Another cool feature of the Game Kit framework is the support for voice chat.

The Voice Chat service in the Game Kit allows two devices to establish a voice chat. The voice chat takes place over either an Internet or Bluetooth connection. This section shows you how to implement voice chatting over a Bluetooth communication channel.

TRY IT OUT Bluetooth Voice Chatting

codefile BluetoothChat.zip available for download at Wrox.com

1. Using Xcode, create a new View-based Application project and name it `BluetoothChat`.

2. Add the `GameKit` and `AVFoundation` frameworks to the Frameworks folder of the project (see Figure 15-8).

3. Add the following bold statements to the `BluetoothChatViewController.h` file:

```
#import <UIKit/UIKit.h>

#import <GameKit/GameKit.h>
#import <AVFoundation/AVFoundation.h>

@interface BluetoothChatViewController : UIViewController
    <GKVoiceChatClient> {

    GKSession *currentSession;

    IBOutlet UIButton *connect;
    IBOutlet UIButton *disconnect;

    GKPeerPickerController *picker;
}

@property (nonatomic, retain) GKSession *currentSession;
@property (nonatomic, retain) UIButton *connect;
@property (nonatomic, retain) UIButton *disconnect;

-(IBAction) btnMute:(id) sender;
-(IBAction) btnUnmute:(id) sender;
-(IBAction) btnConnect:(id) sender;
```

```
-(IBAction) btnDisconnect:(id) sender;
```

```
@end
```

4. Drag and drop a WAV file onto the Resources folder in Xcode (see Figure 15-9).

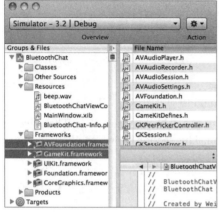

FIGURE 15-8

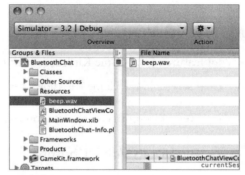

FIGURE 15-9

5. Double-click the `BluetoothViewController.xib` file to edit it in Interface Builder.

6. Populate the View window with three Round Rect Button views (see Figure 15-10). Name them as MUTE, Disconnect, and Connect.

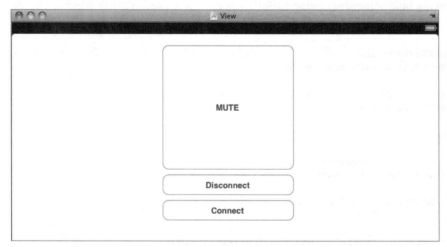

FIGURE 15-10

7. In the `BluetoothViewController.xib` window, perform the following connections:

➤ Control-click the File's Owner item and drag and drop it over the Connect button. Select `connect`.

➤ Control-click the File's Owner item and drag and drop it over the Disconnect button. Select `disconnect`.

➤ Control-click the Connect button and drag and drop it over the File's Owner item. Select `btnConnect:`.

➤ Control-click the Disconnect button and drag and drop it over the File's Owner item. Select `btnDisconnect:`.

➤ Right-click on the Mute button and connect the Touch Down event to the File's Owner item. Select `btnMute:`.

➤ Right-click on the Mute button and connect the Touch Up Inside event to the File's Owner item. Select `btnUnmute:`.

8. To verify that all the connections are made correctly, right-click on the File's Owner item and view its connections (see Figure 15-11).

FIGURE 15-11

9. Add the following bold statements to the `BluetoothViewController.m` file:

```
#import "BluetoothViewController.h"

@implementation BluetoothViewController

@synthesize currentSession;
@synthesize connect;
@synthesize disconnect;

NSString *recorderFilePath;

AVAudioPlayer *audioPlayer;

- (void)viewDidLoad {
    [connect setHidden:NO];
```

```objc
        [disconnect setHidden:YES];

        [super viewDidLoad];
}

-(IBAction) btnConnect:(id) sender {
        //---Select a nearby Bluetooth device---
        picker = [[GKPeerPickerController alloc] init];
        picker.delegate = self;
        picker.connectionTypesMask = GKPeerPickerConnectionTypeNearby;

        [connect setHidden:YES];
        [disconnect setHidden:NO];

        [picker show];
}

-(IBAction) btnDisconnect:(id) sender {
        //---disconnected from the other device---
        [self.currentSession disconnectFromAllPeers];
        [self.currentSession release];
        currentSession = nil;

        [connect setHidden:NO];
        [disconnect setHidden:YES];
}

-(void) peerPickerController:(GKPeerPickerController *)pk
              didConnectPeer:(NSString *)peerID
                   toSession:(GKSession *) session {
        self.currentSession = session;
        session.delegate = self;
        [session setDataReceiveHandler: self withContext:nil];
        picker.delegate = nil;
        [picker dismiss];
        [picker autorelease];
}

-(void) peerPickerControllerDidCancel:(GKPeerPickerController *)pk {
        picker.delegate = nil;
        [picker autorelease];

        [connect setHidden:NO];
        [disconnect setHidden:YES];
}

-(IBAction) btnMute:(id) sender {
        //---mute the voice chat---
        [GKVoiceChatService defaultVoiceChatService].microphoneMuted = YES;
}

-(IBAction) btnUnmute:(id) sender {
        //---unmute the voice chat---
        [GKVoiceChatService defaultVoiceChatService].microphoneMuted = NO;
}
```

```objc
//---returns a unique ID that identifies the local user---
-(NSString *) participantID {
    return currentSession.peerID;
}

-(void) voiceChatService:(GKVoiceChatService *) voiceChatService
              sendData:(NSData *) data
        toParticipantID:(NSString *)participantID {

    [currentSession sendData:data toPeers:
        [NSArray arrayWithObject:participantID]
        withDataMode:GKSendDataReliable error:nil];
}

-(void) session:(GKSession *)session
           peer:(NSString *)peerID
 didChangeState:(GKPeerConnectionState)state {

    switch (state) {
        case GKPeerStateConnected: {
            //---plays an audio file---
            NSString *soundFilePath = [[NSBundle mainBundle]
                pathForResource:@"beep" ofType:@"wav"];

            NSURL *fileURL = [[NSURL alloc]
                initFileURLWithPath: soundFilePath];

            AVAudioPlayer *audioPlayer =
                [[AVAudioPlayer alloc] initWithContentsOfURL:fileURL
                    error:nil];

            [fileURL release];
            [audioPlayer play];

            NSError *error;
            AVAudioSession *audioSession =
                [AVAudioSession sharedInstance];

            if (![audioSession
                setCategory:AVAudioSessionCategoryPlayAndRecord
                error:&error]) {
                NSLog(
                    @"Error setting category: %@",
                    [error localizedDescription]);
            }

            if (![audioSession setActive: YES error: &error]) {
                NSLog(@"Error activating audioSession: %@",
                    [error description]);
            }

            [GKVoiceChatService defaultVoiceChatService].client = self;

            //---initiating the voice chat---
```

```
            if (![[GKVoiceChatService defaultVoiceChatService]
                startVoiceChatWithParticipantID:peerID error:&error]) {
                NSLog(@"Error starting startVoiceChatWithParticipantID: %@",
                    [error userInfo]);
            }
        } break;

        case GKPeerStateDisconnected: {
            [[GKVoiceChatService defaultVoiceChatService]
                stopVoiceChatWithParticipantID:peerID];

            [self.currentSession release];
            currentSession = nil;

            [connect setHidden:NO];
            [disconnect setHidden:YES];
        } break;
    }
}

-(void) receiveData:(NSData *)data
        fromPeer:(NSString *)peer
       inSession:(GKSession *)session
         context:(void *)context {
    //---start the voice chat when initiated by the client---
    [[GKVoiceChatService defaultVoiceChatService]
        receivedData:data fromParticipantID:peer];
}

-(void)dealloc {
    if (currentSession) [currentSession release];
    [connect release];
    [disconnect release];

    [super dealloc];
}

@end
```

10. To test the application, deploy the application onto two devices. (For iPod touch, you need to connect it to an external microphone as it does not come with one.) Then run the application and press the Connect button to use Bluetooth to connect to each other. As soon as the two devices are connected, you can start chatting! To temporarily mute the conversation, press and hold the Mute button. When it is released, the conversation resumes. Have fun!

How It Works

When two Bluetooth devices are connected, you first play the beep sound and start the audio session (via the `session:peer:didChangeState:` method):

```
//---plays an audio file---
NSString *soundFilePath = [[NSBundle mainBundle]
    pathForResource:@"beep" ofType:@"wav"];
```

```
NSURL *fileURL = [[NSURL alloc]
    initFileURLWithPath: soundFilePath];

AVAudioPlayer *audioPlayer =
    [[AVAudioPlayer alloc] initWithContentsOfURL:fileURL
        error:nil];

[fileURL release];
[audioPlayer play];

NSError *error;
AVAudioSession *audioSession =
    [AVAudioSession sharedInstance];

if (![audioSession
    setCategory:AVAudioSessionCategoryPlayAndRecord
    error:&error]) {
    NSLog(
        @"Error setting category: %@",
        [error localizedDescription]);
}

if (![audioSession setActive: YES error: &error]) {
    NSLog(@"Error activating audioSession: %@",
        [error description]);
}

[GKVoiceChatService defaultVoiceChatService].client = self;
```

 WARNING *If you do not start the audio player, the voice chat will not work.*

You then retrieve a singleton instance of the GKVoiceChatService class and call its startVoiceChatWithParticipantID:error: method to start the voice chat:

```
if (![[GKVoiceChatService defaultVoiceChatService]
    startVoiceChatWithParticipantID:peerID error:&error]) {
    NSLog(@"Error starting startVoiceChatWithParticipantID: %@",
        [error userInfo]);
}
```

Calling the startVoiceChatWithParticipantID:error: method invokes the voiceChatService:sendData:toParticipantID: method (which is defined in the GKVoiceChatClient protocol), which makes use of the current Bluetooth session to send the configuration data to the other connected device:

```
-(void) voiceChatService:(GKVoiceChatService *) voiceChatService
            sendData:(NSData *) data
    toParticipantID:(NSString *)participantID {
    [currentSession sendData:data toPeers:
        [NSArray arrayWithObject:participantID]
```

```
            withDataMode:GKSendDataReliable error:nil];
}
```

When it has received the configuration data, the other device starts the Voice Chat service by calling the `receivedData:fromParticipantID:` method (also defined in the `GKVoiceChatClient` protocol):

```
- (void) receiveData:(NSData *)data
            fromPeer:(NSString *)peer
            inSession:(GKSession *)session
             context:(void *)context {
    [[GKVoiceChatService defaultVoiceChatService]
        receivedData:data fromParticipantID:peer];
}
```

The `GKVoiceChatService` uses the configuration information that was exchanged between the two devices and creates its own connection to transfer voice data.

You can mute the microphone by setting the `microphoneMuted` property to `YES`:

```
[GKVoiceChatService defaultVoiceChatService].microphoneMuted = YES;
```

SUMMARY

You have seen how easy it is to connect two iPads (or iPhones and iPod touches) using Bluetooth. Using the concepts shown in this chapter, you can build networked games and other interesting applications easily. You also saw how the Game Kit framework provides the `GKVoiceChatService` class that makes voice communication between two devices seamless. There is no need for you to know how the voices are transported between two devices — all you need to know is to call the relevant methods to initialize the chat. One important point you need to know, though — voice chat works not just over Bluetooth; it works over any communication channel. In fact, if you have two devices connected using TCP/IP, you can stream the voices over the wire.

EXERCISES

1. What is the class that you can use to locate peer Bluetooth devices?

2. Name the object that is responsible for managing the session between two connected Bluetooth devices.

3. Name the method from the `GKVoiceChatService` class that you need to call to establish a voice chat.

4. Name the two methods defined in the `GKVoiceChatClient` protocol that establishes a voice chat channel.

Answers to the Exercises can be found in Appendix A.

▶ **WHAT YOU LEARNED IN THIS CHAPTER**

TOPIC	KEY CONCEPTS
Looking for peer Bluetooth devices	Use the GKPeerPickerController class
Communicating between two Bluetooth devices	Use the GKSession class.
Establishing a voice chat	Call the startVoiceChatWithParticipantID:error: method from the GKVoiceChatService class
	On the initiator, call the voiceChatService:sendData:toParticipantID: method defined in the GKVoiceChatClient protocol
	On the receiver, call the receivedData:fromParticipantID: method defined in the GKVoiceChatClient protocol
Muting the microphone	[GKVoiceChatService defaultVoiceChatService] .microphoneMuted = YES;

16

Bonjour Programming

WHAT YOU WILL LEARN IN THIS CHAPTER:

➤ How to publish a service on the network using the NSNetService Class

➤ How to discover for services on the network using the NSNetServiceBrowser class

➤ How to resolve the IP addresses of services on the network so that you can communicate with them

Bonjour is Apple's implementation of the Zeroconf protocol, which enables the automatic discovery of computers, devices and services on an IP network. In this chapter, you will learn how to implement Bonjour on the iPad by using the NSNetService class to publish a service. You will also use the NSNetServiceBrowser class to discover services that have been published.

CREATING THE APPLICATION

The first thing you will do is to create the user interface for the application. You'll use a Table view to display the users that you have discovered on the network. As users are discovered, they will be added to the Table view.

TRY IT OUT   Creating the UI of the Application

1. Using Xcode, create a View-based Application project and name it Bonjour.

2. Double-click the BonjourViewController.xib file to edit it in Interface Builder. Populate the View window with the following views (see Figure 16-1):

➤ Label (set its text as "Discovered Users")

➤ Table View

➤ Text View

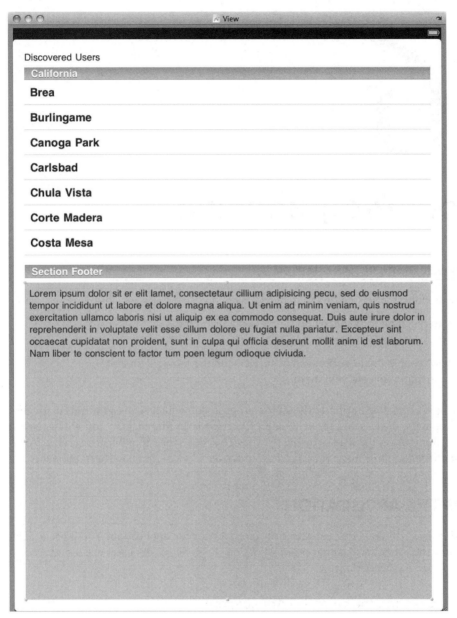

FIGURE 16-1

3. In the `BonjourViewController.h` file, add the following bold statements:

```
#import <UIKit/UIKit.h>

@interface BonjourViewController : UIViewController {
    //---outlets---
```

```
        IBOutlet UITableView *tbView;
        IBOutlet UITextView *debug;
}

//---expose the outlets as properties---
@property (nonatomic, retain) UITableView *tbView;
@property (nonatomic, retain) UITextView *debug;

@end
```

4. In the `BonjourViewController.xib` window, perform the following connections:

➤   Control-click the File's Owner item and drag and drop it over the Table view. Select `tbView`.

➤   Control-click the File's Owner item and drag and drop it over the Text view. Select `debug`.

➤   Right-click on the Table view and connect the `dataSource` outlet to the File's Owner item.

➤   Right-click on the Table view and connect the `delegate` outlet to the File's Owner item.

5. To verify that all the connections are made correctly, right-click on the File's Owner item and view its connections (see Figure 16-2).

FIGURE 16-2

How It Works

Because you'll use the Table view to display the list of users discovered on the network, you need to set the `dataSource` and `delegate` outlets to the File's Owner item. The TextView will be used to show the various things happening in the background. This is very useful for debugging your application and understanding what happens as services are discovered on the network.

PUBLISHING A SERVICE

With all the views and outlets wired up, you can publish a service using the `NSNetService` class. The following Try It Out shows you how.

TRY IT OUT Publishing a Service on the Network

1. Using the same project created in the previous section, add the following bold statements to the `BonjourAppDelegate.h` file:

```
#import <UIKit/UIKit.h>

@class BonjourViewController;

@interface BonjourAppDelegate : NSObject <UIApplicationDelegate> {
    UIWindow *window;
    BonjourViewController *viewController;

    //---use this to publish a service---
    NSNetService *netService;
}

@property (nonatomic, retain) IBOutlet UIWindow *window;
@property (nonatomic, retain) IBOutlet BonjourViewController *viewController;

@end
```

2. In the `BonjourAppDelegate.m` file, add the following statements in bold:

```
#import "BonjourAppDelegate.h"
#import "BonjourViewController.h"

@implementation BonjourAppDelegate

@synthesize window;
@synthesize viewController;

- (BOOL)application:(UIApplication *)application
didFinishLaunchingWithOptions:(NSDictionary *)launchOptions {

    // Override point for customization after app launch
    [window addSubview:viewController.view];
    [window makeKeyAndVisible];

    //---publish the service---
    netService = [[NSNetService alloc]
                initWithDomain:@""
                type:@"_MyService._tcp."
                name:@""
                port:9876];
    netService.delegate = self;
    [netService publish];
```

```
        return YES;
    }

    -(void)netService:(NSNetService *)aNetService
        didNotPublish:(NSDictionary *)dict {
        NSLog(@"Service did not publish: %@", dict);
    }

    - (void)applicationWillTerminate:(UIApplication *)application {
        //---stop the service when the application is terminated---
        [netService stop];
    }

    - (void)dealloc {
        [netService release];
        [viewController release];
        [window release];
        [super dealloc];
    }

    @end
```

How It Works

To publish a service on the network, you use the NSNetService class to advertise your presence on the network.

```
        NSNetService *netService;
```

Here, you advertise your presence on the network by publishing a network service when your application has finished launching (application:DidFinishLaunchingWithOptions:). You publish a network service by passing several parameters to the NSNetService class:

```
        netService = [[NSNetService alloc]
                        initWithDomain:@""
                                  type:@"_MyService._tcp."
                                  name:@""
                                  port:9876];
```

The first argument specifies the domain for the service. You use @"" to denote the default domain. The second argument indicates the service type and transport layer. In this example, you named the service as MyService and it uses TCP as the protocol. Note that you need to prefix the service name and protocol with an underscore (_) and end the protocol with a period (.). The third argument specifies the name of the service — you have used an empty string in this case. Finally, specify the port number on which the service is published via the fourth argument.

To publish the service, you use the publish method of the NSNetService class:

```
        [netService publish];
```

You also implemented the netService:didNotPublish: method so that in the event the service is not published successfully, you will write a message to the debugger console (or perhaps display an alert to the user).

When the application exits (`applicationWillTerminate:`) you will stop publishing the service:

```
- (void)applicationWillTerminate:(UIApplication *)application {
    //---stop the service when the application is terminated---
    [netService stop];
}
```

BROWSING FOR SERVICES

Now that you have seen how to publish a service, let's see how you can browse for services that have been published on the network. You will use the `NSNetServiceBrowser` class to discover services published on the network.

TRY IT OUT   Browsing for Services on the Network

1.   Using the `Bonjour` project from the previous Try it Out, add the following bold statements to the `BonjourViewController.h` file:

```
#import <UIKit/UIKit.h>

@interface BonjourViewController : UIViewController {
    IBOutlet UITableView *tbView;
    IBOutlet UITextView *debug;

    //---use for browsing services---
    NSNetServiceBrowser *browser;
    NSMutableArray *services;
}

-(void) resolveIPAddress:(NSNetService *)service;
-(void) browseServices;

@property (nonatomic, retain) UITableView *tbView;
@property (nonatomic, retain) UITextView *debug;

@property (readwrite, retain) NSNetServiceBrowser *browser;
@property (readwrite, retain) NSMutableArray *services;

@end
```

2.   In the `BonjourViewController.m` file, add the following bold statements:

```
#import "BonjourViewController.h"

#import <netinet/in.h>
#import <arpa/inet.h>
@implementation BonjourViewController

@synthesize tbView;
@synthesize debug;
```

```objc
@synthesize browser;
@synthesize services;

//---set the number of rows in the TableView---
- (NSInteger)tableView:(UITableView *)tableView
 numberOfRowsInSection:(NSInteger)section {
    return [services count];
}


//---display the individual rows in the TableView---
- (UITableViewCell *)tableView:(UITableView *)tableView
         cellForRowAtIndexPath:(NSIndexPath *)indexPath {

    static NSString *CellIdentifier = @"Cell";

    UITableViewCell *cell = [tableView
        dequeueReusableCellWithIdentifier:CellIdentifier];
    if (cell == nil) {
        cell = [[[UITableViewCell alloc]
            initWithStyle:UITableViewCellStyleDefault
            reuseIdentifier:CellIdentifier] autorelease];
    }

    //---display the hostname of each service---
    cell.textLabel.text = [[services objectAtIndex:indexPath.row] hostName];

    return cell;
}


//---browse for services---
-(void) browseServices {
    services = [NSMutableArray new];
    self.browser = [[NSNetServiceBrowser new] autorelease];
    self.browser.delegate = self;
    [self.browser searchForServicesOfType:@"_MyService._tcp." inDomain:@""];
}

-(void)viewDidLoad {
    debug.text = @"";
    [self browseServices];
    [super viewDidLoad];
}


//---services found---
-(void)netServiceBrowser:(NSNetServiceBrowser *)aBrowser
         didFindService:(NSNetService *)aService
              moreComing:(BOOL)more {

    [services addObject:aService];
    debug.text = [debug.text stringByAppendingString:
                    @"Found service. Resolving address...\n"];
    [self resolveIPAddress:aService];
}
```

```objc
//---services removed from the network---
-(void)netServiceBrowser:(NSNetServiceBrowser *)aBrowser
        didRemoveService:(NSNetService *)aService moreComing:(BOOL)more {
    [services removeObject:aService];
    debug.text = [debug.text stringByAppendingFormat:@"Removed: %@\n",
                        [aService hostName]];
    [self.tbView reloadData];
}


//---resolve the IP address(es) of a service---
-(void) resolveIPAddress:(NSNetService *)service {
    NSNetService *remoteService = service;
    remoteService.delegate = self;
    [remoteService resolveWithTimeout:0];
}


//---managed to resolve---
-(void)netServiceDidResolveAddress:(NSNetService *)service {
    NSString            *name = nil;
    NSData              *address = nil;
    struct sockaddr_in *socketAddress = nil;
    NSString            *ipString = nil;
    int                 port;

    //---get the IP address(es) of a service---
    for(int i=0;i < [[service addresses] count]; i++ ) {
        name = [service name];
        address = [[service addresses] objectAtIndex: i];
        socketAddress = (struct sockaddr_in *) [address bytes];
        ipString = [NSString stringWithFormat: @"%s",
            inet_ntoa(socketAddress->sin_addr)];
        port = socketAddress->sin_port;
        debug.text = [debug.text stringByAppendingFormat:
            @"Resolved: %@-->%@:%hu\n", [service hostName], ipString, port];
    }
    [self.tbView reloadData];
}


//---did not manage to resolve---
-(void)netService:(NSNetService *)service
    didNotResolve:(NSDictionary *)errorDict {

    debug.text = [debug.text stringByAppendingFormat:
                        @"Could not resolve: %@\n", errorDict];
}

- (void)dealloc {
    [tbView release];
    [debug release];
    [browser release];
    [services release];

    [super dealloc];
}

@end
```

3. That's it! Deploy the application onto at least two devices (one on the iPhone Simulator and one on a real device). When the application is running, it will search for all services published on the same network. As services are discovered, their names appear in the Table view. Figure 16-3 shows the Table view displaying the hostname of the devices it has discovered. In this example:

➤ "Wei-Meng-Lees-iMac.local" refers to the iPhone Simulator running the application.

➤ "Wei-Meng-Lees-iPod.local" refers to my iPod touch running the application.

➤ "Wei-Meng-Lees-iPhone.local" refers to my iPhone running the application.

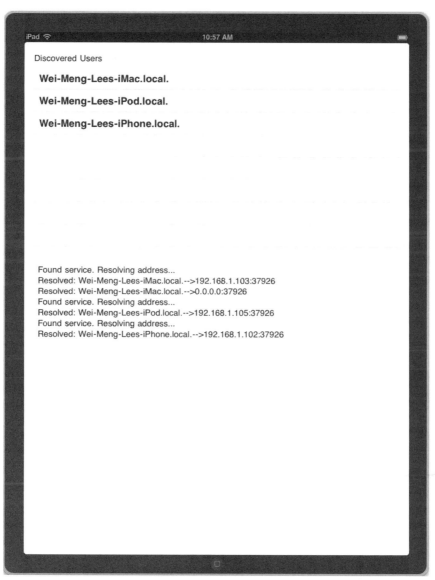

FIGURE 16-3

How It Works

There is quite a bit of coding involved here. So, let's take a more detailed look.

First, you defined the `browseServices` method, which uses the `NSNetServiceBrowser` class to search for the service named "`_MyService._tcp.`" in the default domain:

```
services = [NSMutableArray new];
self.browser = [[NSNetServiceBrowser new] autorelease];
self.browser.delegate = self;
[self.browser searchForServicesOfType:@"_MyService._tcp." inDomain:@""];
```

As services are discovered, the `netServiceBrowser:didFindService:moreComing:` method will be called. In this method, you add all the discovered services into the `services` mutable array:

```
-(void)netServiceBrowser:(NSNetServiceBrowser *)aBrowser
          didFindService:(NSNetService *)aService
              moreComing:(BOOL)more {

    [services addObject:aService];
    debug.text = [debug.text stringByAppendingString:
                    @"Found service. Resolving address...\n"];
    [self resolveIPAddress:aService];
}
```

You also try to resolve the IP address of the discovered service by calling the `resolveIPAddress:` method, which you will define.

The `resolveIPAddress:` method uses the `resolveWithTimeout:` method of the `NSNetService` instance (representing the service that was discovered) to obtain its IP addresses:

```
-(void) resolveIPAddress:(NSNetService *)service {
    NSNetService *remoteService = service;
    remoteService.delegate = self;
    [remoteService resolveWithTimeout:0];
}
```

If it managed to resolve the IP addresses of the service, the `netServiceDidResolveAddress:` method will be called. If it did not manage to resolve the IP address, the `netService:didNotResolve:` method will be called.

In the `netServiceDidResolveAddress:` method, you extract all the available IP addresses of the service and display them on the TextView. You then try to reload the Table view using the `reloadData` method of the `UITableView` class.

```
-(void)netServiceDidResolveAddress:(NSNetService *)service {
    NSString           *name = nil;
    NSData             *address = nil;
    struct sockaddr_in *socketAddress = nil;
    NSString           *ipString = nil;
    int                port;

    for(int i=0;i < [[service addresses] count]; i++ ) {
        name = [service name];
```

```
        address = [[service addresses] objectAtIndex: i];
        socketAddress = (struct sockaddr_in *) [address bytes];
        ipString = [NSString stringWithFormat: @"%s",
            inet_ntoa(socketAddress->sin_addr)];
        port = socketAddress->sin_port;
        debug.text = [debug.text stringByAppendingFormat:
            @"Resolved: %@-->%@:%hu\n", [service hostName], ipString, port];
    }
    [self.tbView reloadData];
}
```

When services are removed from the network, the `netServiceBrowser:didRemoveService:` method will be called, and hence in this method you will remove the service from the `services` mutable array:

```
-(void)netServiceBrowser:(NSNetServiceBrowser *)aBrowser
        didRemoveService:(NSNetService *)aService moreComing:(BOOL)more {
    [services removeObject:aService];
    debug.text = [debug.text stringByAppendingFormat:@"Removed: %@\n",
                    [aService hostName]];
    [self.tbView reloadData];
}
```

The rest of the code involves loading the Table view with the host name of the services that have been discovered. In particular, you display the host name of each service in the Table view:

```
//---display the individual rows in the TableView---
- (UITableViewCell *)tableView:(UITableView *)tableView
        cellForRowAtIndexPath:(NSIndexPath *)indexPath {

    static NSString *CellIdentifier = @"Cell";

    UITableViewCell *cell = [tableView
        dequeueReusableCellWithIdentifier:CellIdentifier];
    if (cell == nil) {
        cell = [[[UITableViewCell alloc]
            initWithStyle:UITableViewCellStyleDefault
            reuseIdentifier:CellIdentifier] autorelease];
    }

    //---display the hostname of each service---
    cell.textLabel.text = [[services objectAtIndex:indexPath.row] hostName];

    return cell;
}
```

With peers on the network discovered, what can you do next? You can use TCP/IP to connect with your peers on the network and send messages to them. Using TCP/IP for networking is beyond the scope of this book. However, interested users can download a working application from the author's website — http://www.learn2develop.net — that illustrates how to build a chat application using Bonjour.

SUMMARY

This chapter explained how to publish a service on the network using the NSNetService class and how to discover services on the local network using the NSNetServiceBrowser class. Once peers are discovered on the network, you can connect to them and initiate a peer-to-peer communication. A chat application is a good example of a Bonjour application.

EXERCISES

1. What is the class that you can use to publish a service on the network?

2. What is the class that you can use to discover services on the network?

3. Name the method that is called when a service is discovered.

4. Name the method that is called when a service is removed.

Answers to the Exercises can be found in Appendix A.

▶ WHAT YOU LEARNED IN THIS CHAPTER

TOPIC	KEY CONCEPTS
Publishing a service	Use the NSNetService class
Discovering services	Use the NSNetServiceBrowser class
Resolving the IP addresses of a service	Use the resolveWithTimeout: method of an NSNetService object
Getting the IP addresses of a service	Use the addresses method of an NSNetService object
Method that is called when a service is discovered	netServiceBrowser:didFindService:moreComing:
Method that is called when a service is removed	netServiceBrowser:didRemoveService:moreComing:

17

Apple Push Notification Services

WHAT YOU WILL LEARN IN THIS CHAPTER:

➤ Understand how to use the Apple Push Notification service

➤ How to generate a certificate request

➤ How to generate a development certificate

➤ How to create an App ID

➤ How to configure App ID for push notification

➤ How to create a provisioning profile

➤ How to provision a device

➤ How to deploy an iPad application onto a device

➤ How to use a push notification provider application

One of the key limitations of the iPad is its constraint on running applications in the background, which means that applications requiring a constant state of connectivity (such as social networking applications) will not be able to receive timely updates when the user switches to another application.

To overcome this limitation, Apple released the Apple Push Notification service (APNs). APNs allows your device to be constantly connected to Apple's push notification server. When you want to send a push notification to an application installed on the users' devices, you (the provider) can contact the APNs so that it can deliver a push message to the particular application installed on the intended device.

When your iPad application uses the Apple Push Notification service, the device remains connected to the APNs server using an open TCP/IP connection. To send notifications to your application running on iPad devices, you need to write a provider application that communicates with that server. Your provider application will send messages to the APNs server, which in turn relays the message to the various devices running your application by pushing the message to these devices through the TCP/IP connection.

While the steps for programming APNs are straightforward, there are several details that you need to perform to enable messages to be pushed successfully to the devices. In this chapter, you learn how to create an iPad application using the APNs. The following sections take you through the steps for APNs programming in more detail.

GENERATING A CERTIFICATE REQUEST

The first step to using the APNs is to generate a certificate request file so that you can use it to request for two development certificates — one for code signing your application and one to be used by your provider to send notifications to the APNs server. The following Try It Out shows you how to generate the certificate request.

TRY IT OUT Generating a Certificate Request

1. Launch the Keychain Access application in your Mac OS X (you can do so by typing "Keychain" in Spotlight).

2. Select Keychain Access ➪ Certificate Assistant ➪ Request a Certificate From a Certificate Authority (see Figure 17-1).

FIGURE 17-1

3. Enter the information required and select the "Saved to disk" option. Click Continue (see Figure 17-2).

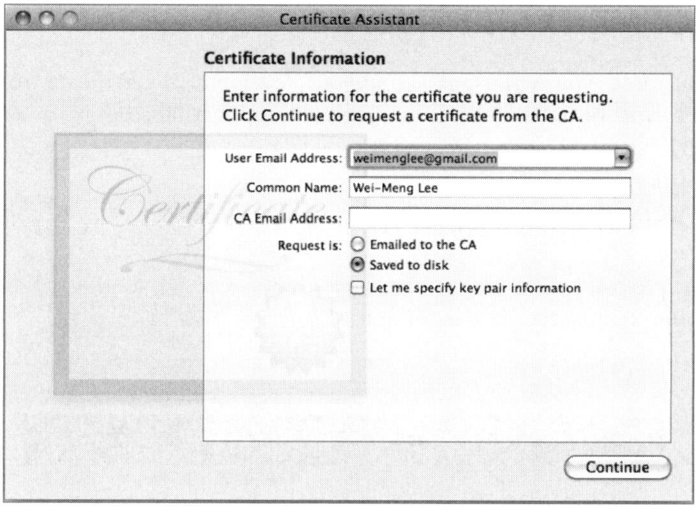

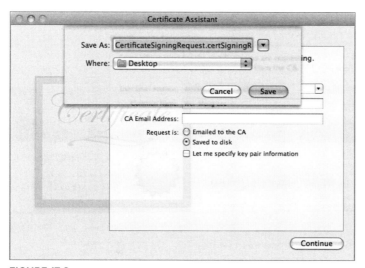

FIGURE 17-2

4. Save the certificate request using the suggested name and click Save (see Figure 17-3). Click Done in the next screen.

FIGURE 17-3

How It Works

This part is straightforward — use the Keychain Access application to generate a certificate request so that you can send it to Apple later to request for certificates.

GENERATING A DEVELOPMENT CERTIFICATE

Once the certificate request is generated, you will use it to request a development certificate from Apple. The development certificate will be used for code signing your application so that you can deploy your application on a real device.

TRY IT OUT   Generating a Development Request

1.   Sign in to the iPhone Developer Program at `http://developer.apple.com/iphone`. Click on the iPhone Provisioning Portal on the right of the page (see Figure 17-4).

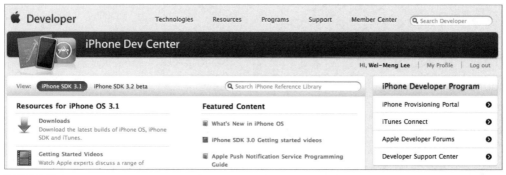

FIGURE 17-4

2.   The welcome page opens (see Figure 17-5).

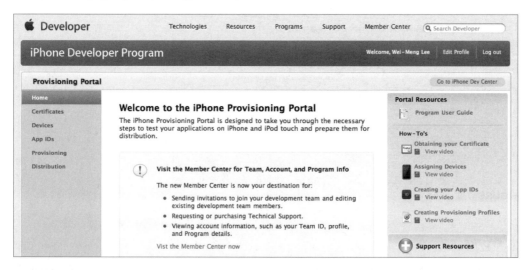

FIGURE 17-5

3.   Click on the Certificates tab on the left. The page shown in Figure 17-6 opens.

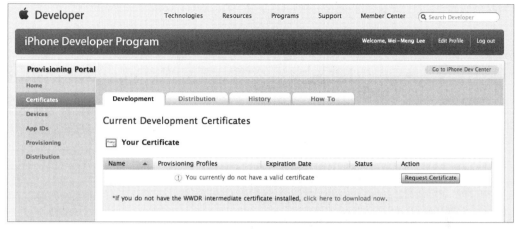

FIGURE 17-6

4. Click the Request Certificate button; the page shown in Figure 17-7 opens. Click the Choose File button and select the certificate request file that you created in the previous section. Click Submit.

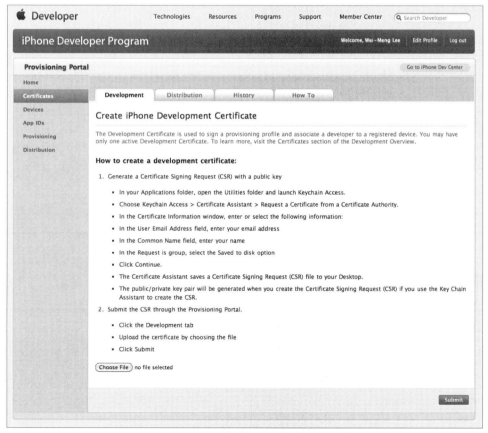

FIGURE 17-7

5. Your certificate is now pending approval. Click the Approve button (see Figure 17-8).

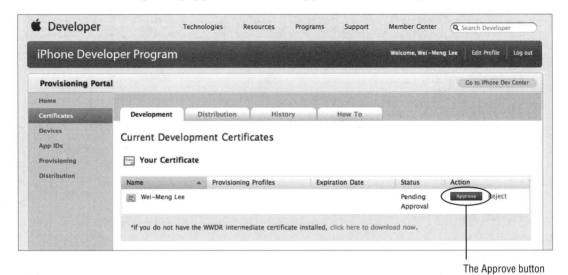

The Approve button

FIGURE 17-8

6. Refresh the page and after a few seconds the certificate will be ready and you can download it. Once the certificate is downloaded, double-click it to install it in the Keychain Access application. Figure 17-9 shows the development certificate installed in the Keychain Access application.

FIGURE 17-9

How It Works

This Try It Out generates the development certificate that you need to code sign your application so that it can be deployed to a real iPad for testing. The certificate installed in the Keychain Access application contains the private and public key pair. It is a good idea to back up the certificate at this juncture so that in the event you need to shift your development work to another computer, you can simply restore the certificate from the backup. Downloading the certificate from the iPhone Development portal and installing the certificate to another computer will not work because the certificate downloaded from Apple only contains the public key, and not the private key.

CREATING AN APP ID

Each iPad application that uses the APNs must have a unique application ID that identifies itself. In the following Try It Out, you create an App ID for push notification.

TRY IT OUT Creating an App ID for Your Application

1. In the iPhone Provisioning Portal, click on the App IDs tab on the left and then click the New App ID button (see Figure 17-10) based on other issues.

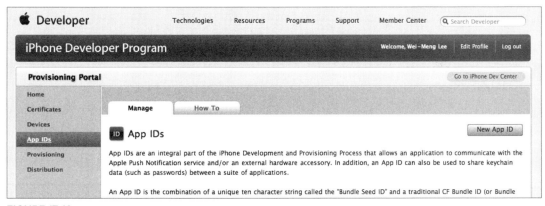

FIGURE 17-10

2. Enter `PushAppID` for the Description and select Generate New for the Bundle Seed ID. For the Bundle Identifier, enter `net.learn2develop.MyPushApp`. Click Submit (see Figure 17-11).

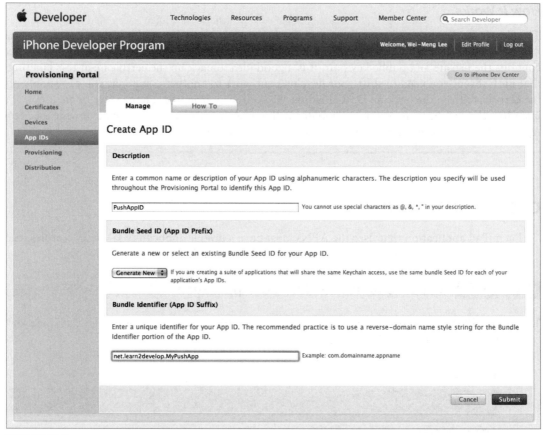

FIGURE 17-11

3. You should now see the App ID that you have created, together with those you may have previously created (see Figure 17-12).

Description	Apple Push Notification service	In App Purchase	Action
83F2FVK9TD.net.learn2develop.MyPush... PushAppID	⊘ Configurable for Development ⊘ Configurable for Production	⊘ Configurable	Configure

FIGURE 17-12

How It Works

For applications using the APNs, you need to specifically create an App ID to uniquely identify the application. The next section shows how to configure the new App ID for push notifications.

Configuring an App ID for Push Notifications

Once an App ID is created, you need to configure it for push notifications. The following Try It Out shows you how to do this.

TRY IT OUT   Configuring an App ID for Push Notifications

1. To configure an App ID for push notification, click the Configure link displayed to the right of the App ID. The Configure option (see Figure 17-13) becomes available.

FIGURE 17-13

2. Check the "Enable for Apple Push Notification service" option and click the Configure button displayed to the right of the Development Push SSL Certificate.

3. The Apple Push Notification service SSL Certificate Assistant screen opens. Click Continue.

4. Click the Choose File button to locate the certificate request file that you saved earlier, and then click Generate (see Figure 17-14).

FIGURE 17-14

5. Your SSL Certificate will now be generated. Click Continue (see Figure 17-15).

FIGURE 17-15

6. Click the Download Now button to download the SSL Certificate, and then click Done (see Figure 17-16).

FIGURE 17-16

7. The SSL Certificate you download is named `aps.developer.identity.cer`. Double-click it to install it in the Keychain Access application (see Figure 17-17). The SSL Certificate is used by your provider application in order to contact the APNs to send push notifications to your applications.

FIGURE 17-17

How It Works

When the App ID is configured for push notifications, you will need to upload the certificate signing request that you generated earlier to Apple so that you can obtain an SSL Certificate for your provider application. Once the SSL Certificate is downloaded, install it into your Keychain Access application.

Creating a Provisioning Profile

Next, you create a provisioning profile so that your application can be installed onto a real iPad device.

TRY IT OUT Creating a Provisioning Profile

1. In the iPhone Provisioning Portal, click the Provisioning tab and click the New Profile button (see Figure 17-18).

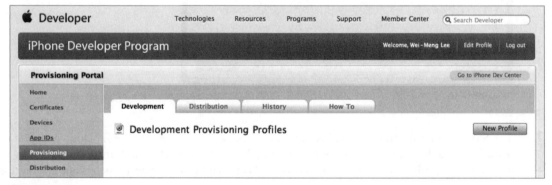

FIGURE 17-18

2. Type in `MyDevicesProfile` as the profile name. Select `PushAppID` as the App ID. Finally, check all the devices that you want to provision (you can register these devices with the iPhone Provisioning Portal through the Devices tab). Click Submit (see Figure 17-19).

3. The provisioning profile is now pending approval. After a few seconds, it appears (just refresh the browser if it is not ready). Click the Download button to download the provisioning profile (see Figure 17-20).

4. The downloaded provisioning profile is named `MyDevicesProfile.mobileprovision`.

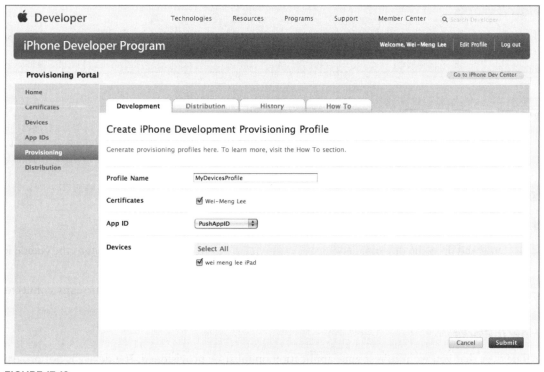

FIGURE 17-19

Download Button

FIGURE 17-20

How It Works

The provisioning profile associates one or more development certificates with one or more devices, and an App ID so that you can install your signed iPad application on a real iPad.

Provisioning a Device

With the provision profile created, you will now install it onto a real device. Once a device is provisioned, your signed iPad application will be able to run on your iPad.

TRY IT OUT   Provisioning a Device

1. Connect your iPad to your Mac.

2. Drag and drop the downloaded `MyDevicesProfile.mobileprovision` file onto the Xcode icon on the Dock.

3. Launch the Organizer application from within Xcode and select the device currently connected to your Mac. You should see the `MyDevicesProfile` installed on the device.

How It Works

All devices that you want to test your application on must be provisioned. If a device is not provisioned, you will not be able to install your application on it.

CREATING THE IPAD APPLICATION

Finally, you can write your iPad application to receive push notifications. The following Try It Out shows how you can programmatically receive notifications received from the APNs server.

TRY IT OUT   Creating an iPad Application

1. In Xcode, create a new View-based Application project and name it `ApplePushNotification`.

2. Drag and drop a WAV file (shown as `beep.wav` in this example) onto the Resources folder in Xcode (see Figure 17-21).

3. Expand on the Targets item in Xcode and select the `ApplePushNotification` item. Press Command-i. Then, in the info window, click the Properties tab (see Figure 17-22).

FIGURE 17-21

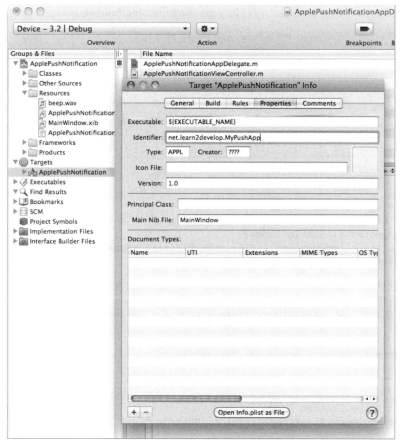

FIGURE 17-22

4. In the Identifier textbox, type `net.learn2develop.MyPushApp` (which is the Bundle Identifier you set in Figure 17-11).

5. Click on the Build tab and type `Code Signing` in the search box. In the Any iPhone OS Device item, select the profile as shown in Figure 17-23.

FIGURE 17-23

6. In the `ApplePushNotificationAppDelegate.m` file, type the following bold code:

```
#import "ApplePushNotificationAppDelegate.h"

#import "ApplePushNotificationViewController.h"

@implementation ApplePushNotificationAppDelegate

@synthesize window;
@synthesize viewController;

- (void)applicationDidFinishLaunching:(UIApplication *)application {
    [window addSubview:viewController.view];
    [window makeKeyAndVisible];

    NSLog(@"Registering for push notifications...");
    [[UIApplication sharedApplication]
        registerForRemoteNotificationTypes:
        (UIRemoteNotificationTypeAlert | UIRemoteNotificationTypeBadge |
         UIRemoteNotificationTypeSound)];
}

- (void)application:(UIApplication *)app
didRegisterForRemoteNotificationsWithDeviceToken:(NSData *)deviceToken {

    NSString *str = [NSString
        stringWithFormat:@"Device Token=%@",deviceToken];
    NSLog(str);
}

- (void)application:(UIApplication *)app
didFailToRegisterForRemoteNotificationsWithError:(NSError *)err {

    NSString *str = [NSString stringWithFormat: @"Error: %@", err];
    NSLog(str);
}

- (void)application:(UIApplication *)application
didReceiveRemoteNotification:(NSDictionary *)userInfo {

    for (id key in userInfo) {
        NSLog(@"key: %@, value: %@", key, [userInfo objectForKey:key]);
    }
}

- (void)dealloc {
    [viewController release];
    [window release];
    [super dealloc];
}

@end
```

7. Press Command-R to test the application on a real device. Press Shift-Command-R in Xcode to display the Debugger Console window. Carefully observe the device token that is printed. The device token is of the format: xxxxxxxx xxxxxxxx xxxxxxxx xxxxxxx xxxxxxxx xxxxxxxx xxxxxxxx

xxxxxxxx. Record this device token (you might want to cut and paste it into a text file). You will need it later for your provider application to uniquely identify the devices that will receive push notifications.

How It Works

To receive push notifications, you first need to configure your application with the App ID that you created earlier. You then configure your application so it is signed with the correct provisioning profile associated with your development certificate.

To register your application for push notification, you use the `registerForRemoteNotification-Types:` method of the `UIApplication` class:

```
[[UIApplication sharedApplication]
    registerForRemoteNotificationTypes:
    (UIRemoteNotificationTypeAlert | UIRemoteNotificationTypeBadge |
     UIRemoteNotificationTypeSound)];
```

This registers your application for the three types of notifications — alert, badge, and sound.

If the registration is successful, the `application:didRegisterForRemoteNotificationsWithDevice` `Token:` event will be called:

```
- (void)application:(UIApplication *)app
didRegisterForRemoteNotificationsWithDeviceToken:(NSData *)deviceToken {

    NSString *str = [NSString
        stringWithFormat:@"Device Token=%@",deviceToken];
    NSLog(str);
}
```

At this juncture, you print out the device token. In a real application, you should programmatically send the device token back to the provider application so that it can maintain a list of devices that needs to be sent the notifications. In fact, Apple recommends that every time your application starts up, you send the device token to the provider application to inform the provider that the application is still in use.

When the registration fails, the `application:didFailToRegisterForRemoteNotificationsWithError:` event is called:

```
- (void)application:(UIApplication *)app
didFailToRegisterForRemoteNotificationsWithError:(NSError *)err {

    NSString *str = [NSString stringWithFormat: @"Error: %@", err];
    NSLog(str);
}
```

If the application is running when it receives a push notification, the `application:didReceiveRemote` `Notification:` event is called:

```
- (void)application:(UIApplication *)application
didReceiveRemoteNotification:(NSDictionary *)userInfo {

    for (id key in userInfo) {
```

```
        NSLog(@"key: %@, value: %@", key, [userInfo objectForKey:key]);
    }
}
```

Here, you can examine the content of the message received. If the application is not running when it receives a push notification, the user will be prompted with an alert that looks like Figure 17-24.

Clicking the View button launches the application and fires the `application:didReceiveRemoteNotification:` event.

FIGURE 17-24

CREATING THE PUSH NOTIFICATION PROVIDER

A push notification provider is an application written by the application's developer to send push notifications to the iPad application through the APNs.

Here are the basic steps to send push notifications to your applications via the APNs server:

➤ Communicate with the APNs server using the SSL Certificate you created earlier.

➤ Construct the payload for the message you want to send.

➤ Send the push notification containing the payload to the APNs.

The APNs is a stream TCP socket that your provider can communicate with using a SSL secured communication channel. You send the push notification (containing the payload) as a binary stream. Once connected to the APNs, maintain the connection and send as many push notifications as you want within the duration of the connection.

 NOTE Refrain from opening and closing the connections to the APNs for each push notification that you want to send. Rapid opening and closing of connections to the APNs will be deemed a Denial-of-Service (DOS) attack and may prevent your provider from sending push notifications to your applications.

The format of a push notification message looks like Figure 17-25 (figure from Apple's documentation):

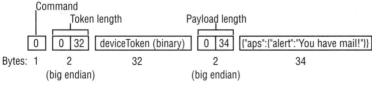

FIGURE 17-25

NOTE *For more details, please refer to Apple Push Notification Service Programming Guide. The full path to this guide is* `http://developer.apple.com/iphone/library/documentation/NetworkingInternet/Conceptual/RemoteNotificationsPG/Introduction/Introduction.html`.

The payload is a JSON-formatted string (maximum 256 bytes) carrying the information you want to send to your application. An example of a payload looks like this:

```
{
    "aps": {
        "alert" : "You got a new message!" ,
        "badge" : 5,
        "sound" : "beep.wav"},
    "acme1" : "bar",
    "acme2" : 42
}
```

To save yourself the trouble in developing a push notification provider from scratch, you can use the PushMeBaby application (for Mac OS X) written by Stefan Hafeneger (get it at `http://stefan.hafeneger.name/download/PushMeBabySource.zip`).

The following Try It Out shows how to modify the PushMeBaby application to send a notification to your application.

TRY IT OUT **Modifying the Provider Application**

1. Download the source of the PushMeBaby application and then open it in Xcode.

2. Right-click the Resources folder in Xcode and select Add Existing Files. Select the `aps.developer.identity.cer` file that you downloaded earlier (see Figure 17-26).

3. In the `ApplicationDelegate.m` file, modify the code as shown in bold, replacing the xxxxxxxx xxxxxxxx xxxxxxxx xxxxxxxx xxxxxxxx xxxxxxxx xxxxxxxx with the actual device token you obtained earlier:

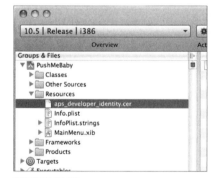

FIGURE 17-26

```
- (id)init {
    self = [super init];
    if(self != nil) {
        self.deviceToken =
        @"xxxxxxxx xxxxxxxx xxxxxxxx xxxxxxxx xxxxxxxx xxxxxxxx xxxxxxxx xxxxxxxx";

        self.payload = @"{\"aps\":{\"alert\":\"You got a new
message!\",\"badge\":5,\"sound\":\"beep.wav\"},\"acme1\":\"bar\",\"acme2\":42}";

        self.certificate = [[NSBundle mainBundle]
            pathForResource:@"aps_developer_identity" ofType:@"cer"];
    }
```

```
    return self;
}
```

4. Press Command-R to test the application. You will be asked to grant access to the certificate. Click Always Allow (see Figure 17-27).

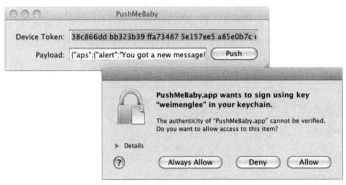

FIGURE 17-27

5. On the iPad, ensure that the `ApplePushNotification` application is not running. To send a message to the device, click the Push button. The server essentially sends the following message to the APNs:

```
{
    "aps": {
        "alert" : "You got a new message!" ,
        "badge" : 5,
        "sound" : "beep.wav"},
     "acme1" : "bar",
     "acme2" : 42
}
```

6. If the message is pushed correctly, you will see the notification as shown in Figure 17-28.

7. Debug the `ApplePushNotification` application by pressing Command-R and send a push message from the `PushMeBaby` application; the Debugger Console window will display the following outputs:

FIGURE 17-28

```
2010-03-24 21:11:49.182 ApplePushNotification[1461:207]
    key: acme1, value: bar
2010-03-24 21:11:49.187 ApplePushNotification[1461:207]
    key: aps, value: {
        alert = "You got a new message!";
        badge = 5;
        sound = "beep.wav";
    }
2010-03-24 21:11:49.191 ApplePushNotification[1461:207]
    key: acme2, value: 42
```

How It Works

Basically, the role of the provider is to send notifications to the APNs server for relaying to the devices. Hence, you are sending a message of the following format:

```
{
    "aps": {
        "alert" : "You got a new message!" ,
        "badge" : 5,
        "sound" : "beep.wav"},
    "acme1" : "bar",
    "acme2" : 42
}
```

Essentially, the `beep.wav` file name indicates to the client to play the `beep.wav` file when the notification is received.

SUMMARY

In this chapter, you have seen the various steps required to build an iPad application that utilizes the Apple Push Notification service. Take some time to go through the steps to obtain your development certificates and provisioning profile, for they commonly trip up a developer. But once you get it working, the effort is well worth it!

EXERCISES

1. Name the two certificates that you need to generate for using Apple Push Notification service.

2. Why is it recommended that you back up the development certificate in the Keychain Access application?

3. Name the method for registering for push notifications.

4. What is the use of the device token?

5. Name the event where you can obtain the notification pushed to your device.

Answers to the Exercises can be found in Appendix A.

▶ WHAT YOU LEARNED IN THIS CHAPTER

TOPIC	KEY CONCEPTS
Steps to using APNs	Generate a Certificate Request Generate a Development Certificate Create an App ID Configure App ID for Push Notification Create a Provisioning Profile Provision a device Create the iPad application Deploy the application onto a device Create the Push Notification Provider application
Development certificate	The certificate you download from Apple only contains the public key; the private key is saved in Keychain Access when you generated the certificate request. Recommended to backup the development certificate.
Provisioning profile	Specifies which devices can be allowed to deploy your applications.
Registering for push notifications	Use the `registerForRemoteNotificationTypes:` method of the `UIApplication` class.
Obtaining the device token	Obtainable from the `application:didRegisterForRemoteNotificationsWithDeviceToken:` event
Obtaining the push notification sent to the device	Obtainable from the `application:didReceiveRemoteNotification:` event

18

Displaying Maps

WHAT YOU WILL LEARN IN THIS CHAPTER:

➤ How to display Google Maps using the Map Kit framework

➤ How to obtain geographical data using the Core Location framework

➤ How to obtain directional data to rotate the map

➤ How to add annotations to a map

➤ How to perform reverse geocoding to obtain an address

With the advent of mobile devices, users are more and more accustomed to having access to locale information at their fingertips. In this chapter, you will learn how to use the Map Kit to give users that information quickly and easily.

DISPLAYING MAPS AND MONITORING CHANGES USING THE MAP KIT

The iPhone SDK 3.2 ships with the Map Kit framework, a set of libraries that work with the Google Mobile Maps Service. You can use the Map Kit to display maps within your iPad application, as well as to display your current location. In fact, you can enable the Map Kit to track your current location simply by setting a single property, and Map Kit will then automatically display your current location as you move.

In the following Try It Out, you will get started with the Map Kit. In particular, you will use the Map Kit to display your current location on the map.

Getting Started with Map Kit

codefile MapKit.zip available for download at Wrox.com

1. Using Xcode, create a View-based Application project and name it `MapKit`.

2. Add the `MapKit.framework` framework to the Frameworks folder of the project (see Figure 18-1).

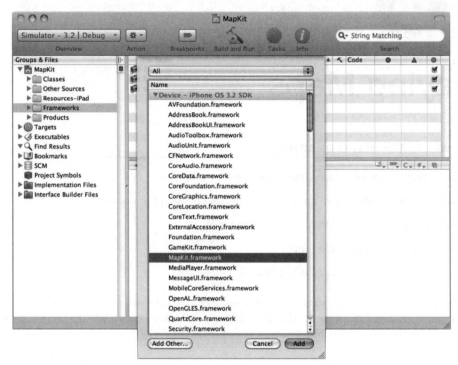

FIGURE 18-1

3. Double-click the `MapKitViewController.xib` file to edit it in Interface Builder.

4. Populate the View window with the following views (see Figure 18-2):

➤ MapView

➤ Round Rect Button (label it as Show My Location)

5. In the `MapKitViewController.h` file, add in the following bold statements:

```
#import <UIKit/UIKit.h>
```

#import <MapKit/MapKit.h>

```
@interface MapKitViewController : UIViewController {
```

```
    IBOutlet UIButton *btnShowLocation;
    IBOutlet MKMapView *mapView;
}

@property (nonatomic, retain) UIButton *btnShowLocation;
@property (nonatomic, retain) MKMapView *mapView;

-(IBAction) showLocation:(id) sender;

@end
```

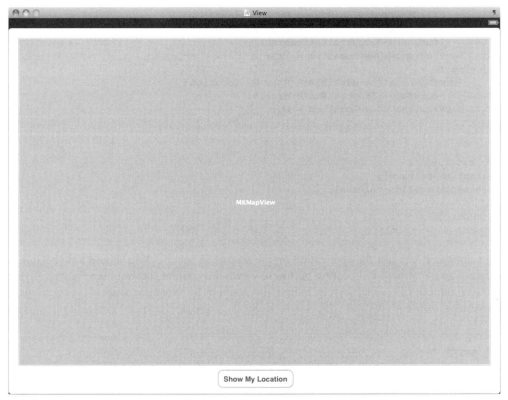

FIGURE 18-2

6. In Interface Builder, perform the following actions:

➤ Control-click and drag the File's Owner item and drop it over the MapView. Select `mapView`.

➤ Control-click and drag the File's Owner item and drop it over the Show My Location button. Select `btnShowLocation`.

➤ Control-click and drag the Show My Location button and drop it over the File's Owner item. Select `showLocation:`.

7. In the `MapKitViewController.m` file, add in the following bold statements:

```
#import "MapKitViewController.h"

@implementation MapKitViewController

@synthesize btnShowLocation;
@synthesize mapView;

-(IBAction) showLocation:(id) sender {

    if ([[btnShowLocation titleForState:UIControlStateNormal]
            isEqualToString:@"Show My Location"]) {
        [btnShowLocation setTitle:@"Hide My Location"
            forState:UIControlStateNormal];
        mapView.showsUserLocation = YES;
    } else {
        [btnShowLocation setTitle:@"Show My Location"
            forState:UIControlStateNormal];
        mapView.showsUserLocation = NO;
    }
}

- (void)dealloc {
    [mapView release];
    [btnShowLocation release];

    [super dealloc];
}
```

8. Press Command-R to test the application on the iPhone Simulator. You should now be able to see the map. Tap the Show My Location button to view your current location (see Figure 18-3). You can also zoom out of the map by pinching it and zoom in by spreading your two fingers apart on the screen.

 NOTE *The map may take up to 20 seconds to locate your current location. Also, the location that is displayed in the iPhone Simulator is locked on the Apple HQ in Cupertino, CA and not your actual location.*

How It Works

To show your current location on the map, you simply set the `showsUserLocation` of the `MKMapView` object to `YES`:

```
mapView.showsUserLocation = YES;
```

The map will automatically obtain the device's location using the Core Location framework (discussed in the second part of this chapter). As long as the `showsUserLocation` property is set to `YES`, the map will continually update to display the user's location.

Note that this property merely specifies whether the user's location is displayed on the map (represented as a throbbing blue circle); it does not center the map to display the user's location. Hence, if you are viewing the map of another location, your current location indicator may not be visible on the map.

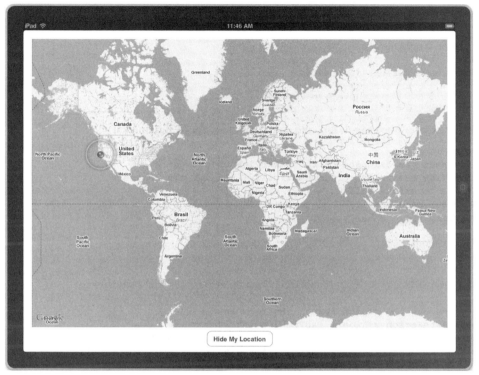

FIGURE 18-3

Observe that as you can pinch the map to zoom it in or out. As you change the zoom level of the map, it is important that you keep track of this information so that when the user restarts the application you can display the map using the previous zoom level.

In the following Try It Out, you keep track of the map zoom level as the user changes the zoom level.

TRY IT OUT   Printing Out the Zoom Level of the Map

1.   Using the `MapKit` project created in the previous section, edit the `MapKitViewController.h` file and add in the following bold statement:

```
#import <UIKit/UIKit.h>

#import <MapKit/MapKit.h>

@interface MapKitViewController : UIViewController
```

```
    <MKMapViewDelegate> {

    IBOutlet UIButton *btnShowLocation;
    IBOutlet MKMapView *mapView;
}

@property (nonatomic, retain) UIButton *btnShowLocation;
@property (nonatomic, retain) MKMapView *mapView;

-(IBAction) showLocation:(id) sender;

@end
```

2. In the `MapKitViewController.m` file, add in the following bold statements:

```
- (void)viewDidLoad {
    //---connect the delegate of the MKMapView object to
    // this view controller programmatically; you can also connect
    // it via Interface Builder---
    mapView.delegate = self;
    mapView.mapType = MKMapTypeHybrid;

    [super viewDidLoad];
}

-(void)mapView:(MKMapView *)mv regionWillChangeAnimated:(BOOL)animated {

    //---print out the region span - aka zoom level---
    MKCoordinateRegion region = mapView.region;
    NSLog([NSString stringWithFormat:@"%f",region.span.latitudeDelta]);
    NSLog([NSString stringWithFormat:@"%f",region.span.longitudeDelta]);

}
```

3. Press Command-R to test the application on the iPhone Simulator. Zoom in and out of the map and observe the values printed out on the Debugger Console window (see Figure 18-4).

How It Works

Whenever you change the zoom level of the map, the `mapView:regionWillChangeAnimated:` event will be fired. Hence, implement the event handler for this event if you want to know when a map is pinched. The `mapView:regionWillChangeAnimated:` event is defined in the `MKMapViewDelegate` protocol, so you need to implement this protocol in the View Controller:

```
@interface MapKitViewController : UIViewController
    <MKMapViewDelegate> {
```

The region displayed by the map is defined by the `region` property, which is a structure of type `MKCoordinateRegion`.

```
    //---print out the region span - aka zoom level---
    MKCoordinateRegion region = mapView.region;
```

FIGURE 18-4

The MKCoordinateRegion structure contains a member called center (of type CLLocationCoordinate2D) and another member called span, of type MKCoordinateSpan. The MKCoordinateSpan structure in turn contains two members — latitudeDelta and longitudeDelta (both of type CLLocationDegrees, which is a double):

```
NSLog([NSString stringWithFormat:@"%f",region.span.latitudeDelta]);
NSLog([NSString stringWithFormat:@"%f",region.span.longitudeDelta]);
```

Both members define the amount of distance to display for the map:

➤ latitudeDelta — One degree of latitude is approximately 111 kilometers (69 miles).

➤ longitudeDelta — One degree longitude spans a distance of approximately 111 kilometers (69 miles) at the equator but shrinks to 0 kilometers at the poles.

Examine the value of these two structures as you zoom in and out of the map — they are a good indicator for the zoom level of the map.

GETTING LOCATION DATA

Nowadays, mobile devices are commonly equipped with GPS receivers. Because of the many satellites orbiting the earth, courtesy of the U.S. government, you can use a GPS receiver to find your location easily. However, GPS requires a clear sky to work and hence does not work indoors.

Another effective way to locate your position is through cell tower triangulation. When a mobile phone is switched on, it is constantly in contact with base stations surrounding it. By knowing the identity of cell towers, it is possible to correlate this information into a physical location through the use of various databases containing the cell towers' identities and their exact geographical locations. Cell tower triangulation has its advantages over GPS because it works indoors, without the need to obtain information from satellites. However, it is not as precise as GPS because its accuracy depends on the area you are in. Cell tower triangulation works best in densely populated areas where the cell towers are closely located.

A third method of locating your position is to rely on Wi-Fi triangulation. Rather than connect to cell towers, the device connects to a Wi-Fi network and checks the service provider against databases to determine the location serviced by the provider. Of the three methods described here, Wi-Fi triangulation is the least accurate.

On the iPad, Apple provides the Core Location framework to help you determine your physical location. The beauty of this framework is that it makes use of all three approaches, and whichever method it uses is totally transparent to the developer. You simply specify the accuracy you need, and Core Location determines the best way to obtain the results for you.

Sound amazing? It is. The following Try It Out shows you how this is done in code.

TRY IT OUT   **Obtaining Location Coordinates**

codefile LBS.zip available for download at Wrox. com

1.   Using Xcode, create a View-based Application project and name it LBS.

2.   Add the `CoreLocation.framework` framework to the Frameworks folder (see Figure 18-5).

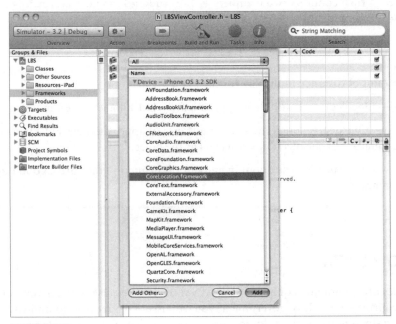

FIGURE 18-5

3. Double-click on `LBSViewController.xib` to edit it in Interface Builder. Populate the View window with the following views (see Figure 18-6):

➤ Label (name them Latitude, Longitude, and Accuracy)

➤ Text Field

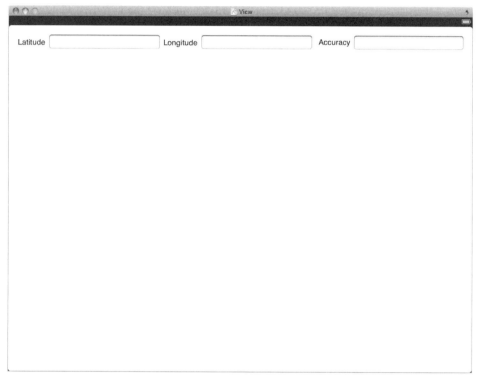

FIGURE 18-6

4. In the `LBSViewController.h` file, add the following statements appearing in bold:

```
#import <UIKit/UIKit.h>

#import <CoreLocation/CoreLocation.h>

@interface LBSViewController : UIViewController
    <CLLocationManagerDelegate> {

    IBOutlet UITextField *accuracyTextField;
    IBOutlet UITextField *latitudeTextField;
    IBOutlet UITextField *longitudeTextField;
    CLLocationManager *lm;
}

@property (retain, nonatomic) CLLocationManager *lm;
@property (retain, nonatomic) UITextField *accuracyTextField;
```

```
@property (retain, nonatomic) UITextField *latitudeTextField;
@property (retain, nonatomic) UITextField *longitudeTextField;

@end
```

5. In Interface Builder, perform the following actions:

➤ Control-click and drag the File's Owner item and drop it over the first Text Field view. Select `latitudeTextField`.

➤ Control-click and drag the File's Owner item and drop it over the second Text Field view. Select `longitudeTextField`.

➤ Control-click and drag the File's Owner item and drop it over the third Text Field view. Select `accuracyTextField`.

6. In the `LBSViewController.m` file, add the following statements appearing in bold:

```
#import "LBSViewController.h"

@implementation LBSViewController

@synthesize lm;
@synthesize latitudeTextField;
@synthesize longitudeTextField;
@synthesize accuracyTextField;

- (void) viewDidLoad {
    self.lm = [[CLLocationManager alloc] init];
    lm.delegate = self;
    lm.desiredAccuracy = kCLLocationAccuracyBest;
    lm.distanceFilter = kCLDistanceFilterNone;

    [lm startUpdatingLocation];

    [super viewDidLoad];
}

- (void) locationManager:(CLLocationManager *) manager
      didUpdateToLocation:(CLLocation *) newLocation
             fromLocation:(CLLocation *) oldLocation {

    //---display latitude---
    NSString *lat = [[NSString alloc] initWithFormat:@"%f",
                        newLocation.coordinate.latitude];
    latitudeTextField.text = lat;

    //---display longitude---
    NSString *lng = [[NSString alloc] initWithFormat:@"%f",
                        newLocation.coordinate.longitude];
    longitudeTextField.text = lng;

    //---display accuracy---
    NSString *acc = [[NSString alloc] initWithFormat:@"%f",
                        newLocation.horizontalAccuracy];
```

```
        accuracyTextField.text = acc;

        [acc release];
        [lat release];
        [lng release];

    }

- (void) locationManager:(CLLocationManager *) manager
          didFailWithError:(NSError *) error {

        NSString *msg = [[NSString alloc]
                            initWithString:@"Error obtaining location"];

        UIAlertView *alert = [[UIAlertView alloc]
                                initWithTitle:@"Error"
                                message:msg
                                delegate:nil
                                cancelButtonTitle: @"Done"
                                otherButtonTitles:nil];
        [alert show];
        [msg release];
        [alert release];

    }

- (void) dealloc{
        [lm release];
        [latitudeTextField release];
        [longitudeTextField release];
        [accuracyTextField release];

        [super dealloc];
    }

@end
```

7. Press Command-R to test the application on the iPhone Simulator. Observe the latitude, longitude, and accuracy reported (see Figure 18-7). The accuracy indicates the radius of uncertainty for the location, measured in meters.

FIGURE 18-7

 NOTE *You can test the application on the iPhone Simulator. Note that for the Simulator, the application will report the location of your Mac.*

How It Works

First, to use the CLLocationManager class, you need to implement the CLLocationManagerDelegate protocol in your View Controller:

```
@interface LBSViewController : UIViewController
    <CLLocationManagerDelegate> {
```

When the View is loaded, you create an instance of the CLLocationManager class:

```
- (void) viewDidLoad {

    self.lm = [[CLLocationManager alloc] init];
    lm.delegate = self;
    lm.desiredAccuracy = kCLLocationAccuracyBest;
    lm.distanceFilter = kCLDistanceFilterNone;

    [lm startUpdatingLocation];

    [super viewDidLoad];
}
```

You then proceed to specify the desired accuracy using the desiredAccuracy property. You can use the following constants to specify the accuracy that you want:

➤ kCLLocationAccuracyBest

➤ kCLLocationAccuracyNearestTenMeters

➤ kCLLocationAccuracyHundredMeters

➤ kCLLocationAccuracyKilometer

➤ kCLLocationAccuracyThreeKilometers

While you can specify the best accuracy that you want, the actual accuracy is not guaranteed. Also, specifying a location with greater accuracy takes a significant amount of time and your device's battery power.

The distanceFilter property allows you to specify the distance a device must move laterally before an update is generated. The unit for this property is in meters, relative to its last position. To be notified of all movements, use the kCLDistanceFilterNone constant.

Finally, you start the Location Manager using the startUpdatingLocation method. The user can enable/disable location services in the Settings application. If the service is not enabled and you go ahead with the location update, the application will ask the user if he or she would like to enable the location services.

To obtain location information, you need to handle two events:

➤ locationManager:didUpdateToLocation:fromLocation:

➤ locationManager:didFailWithError:

When a new location value is available, the `locationManager:didUpdateToLocation:fromLocation:` event is fired. If the location manager cannot determine the location, it fires the `locationManager:did FailWithError:` event.

When a location value is obtained, you display its latitude and longitude along with its accuracy using the `CLLocation` object:

```
- (void) locationManager:(CLLocationManager *) manager
     didUpdateToLocation:(CLLocation *) newLocation
            fromLocation:(CLLocation *) oldLocation {

    //---display latitude---
    NSString *lat = [[NSString alloc] initWithFormat:@"%f",
                        newLocation.coordinate.latitude];
    latitudeTextField.text = lat;

    //---display longitude---
    NSString *lng = [[NSString alloc] initWithFormat:@"%f",
                        newLocation.coordinate.longitude];
    longitudeTextField.text = lng;

    //---display accuracy---
    NSString *acc = [[NSString alloc] initWithFormat:@"%f",
                        newLocation.horizontalAccuracy];
    accuracyTextField.text = acc;

    [acc release];
    [lat release];
    [lng release];
}
```

The `horizontalAccuracy` property of the `CLLocation` object specifies the radius of accuracy in meters.

Displaying Location Using a Map

Obtaining the location value of a position is interesting, but it is not of much use if you cannot visually locate it on a map. Hence, the most ideal situation would be to use the location information and display it on a map. In the following Try it Out, you will use the Map Kit that you learned how to use in the first part of this chapter to display the map of the location coordinates returned by the Core Location framework. Also, you will see how to create the map programmatically, instead of creating it in Interface Builder.

TRY IT OUT Displaying the Location Using a Map

1. Using the LBS project that you just created, add the `MapKit.framework` to the Frameworks folder (see Figure 18-8).

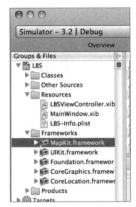

FIGURE 18-8

2. Add the following bold statements to the `LBSViewController.h` file:

```
#import <UIKit/UIKit.h>
#import <CoreLocation/CoreLocation.h>

#import <MapKit/MapKit.h>

@interface LBSViewController : UIViewController
    <CLLocationManagerDelegate,
      MKMapViewDelegate> {

    IBOutlet UITextField *accuracyTextField;
    IBOutlet UITextField *latitudeTextField;
    IBOutlet UITextField *longitudeTextField;
    CLLocationManager *lm;

    MKMapView *mapView;
}

@property (retain, nonatomic) CLLocationManager *lm;
@property (retain, nonatomic) UITextField *accuracyTextField;
@property (retain, nonatomic) UITextField *latitudeTextField;
@property (retain, nonatomic) UITextField *longitudeTextField;

@end
```

3. In the `LBSViewController.m` file, add the following bold statements:

```
- (void) viewDidLoad {

    self.lm = [[CLLocationManager alloc] init];
    lm.delegate = self;
    lm.desiredAccuracy = kCLLocationAccuracyBest;
    lm.distanceFilter = kCLDistanceFilterNone;
    [lm startUpdatingLocation];

    //---display the map in a region---
```

```
        mapView = [[MKMapView alloc]
                    initWithFrame:CGRectMake(10, 60, 1004, 678)];

        mapView.delegate = self;
        mapView.mapType = MKMapTypeHybrid;

        [self.view addSubview:mapView];

        [super viewDidLoad];
    }

- (void) locationManager:(CLLocationManager *) manager
        didUpdateToLocation:(CLLocation *) newLocation
              fromLocation:(CLLocation *) oldLocation {

    NSString *lat = [[NSString alloc] initWithFormat:@"%f",
                        newLocation.coordinate.latitude];
    latitudeTextField.text = lat;

    NSString *lng = [[NSString alloc] initWithFormat:@"%f",
                        newLocation.coordinate.longitude];
    longitudeTextField.text = lng;

    NSString *acc = [[NSString alloc] initWithFormat:@"%f",
                        newLocation.horizontalAccuracy];
    accuracyTextField.text = acc;

    [acc release];
    [lat release];
    [lng release];

    //---update the map---
    MKCoordinateSpan span;
    span.latitudeDelta=.001;
    span.longitudeDelta=.001;

    MKCoordinateRegion region;
    region.center = newLocation.coordinate;
    region.span = span;

    [mapView setRegion:region animated:TRUE];

    }

- (void) dealloc{
    [mapView release];

    [lm release];
    [latitudeTextField release];
    [longitudeTextField release];
    [accuracyTextField release];
    [super dealloc];
    }
```

4. Press Command-R to test the application on the iPhone Simulator. Observe the map displaying the location reported by the location manager (see Figure 18-9). The center of the map is the location reported.

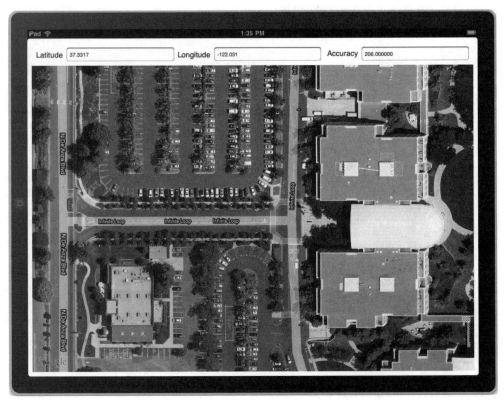

FIGURE 18-9

 NOTE *If you test the application on an iPad, you will see that the map updates itself dynamically when you move about.*

How It Works

To use the Map Kit in your application, you first need to add the `MapKit.framework` to your project.

Then, you implement the `MKMapViewDelegate` protocol in the View Controller to handle the various methods associated with the MapView:

```
@interface LBSViewController : UIViewController
    <CLLocationManagerDelegate,
    MKMapViewDelegate> {
```

When the view has loaded, you create an instance of the MKMapView class and set the map type (hybrid — map and satellite) to display:

```
//---display the map in a region---
mapView = [[MKMapView alloc]
               initWithFrame:CGRectMake(10, 60, 1004, 678)];

mapView.delegate = self;
mapView.mapType = MKMapTypeHybrid;

[self.view addSubview:mapView];
```

In this case, you specify the size of the map to display. You set the delegate property to self so that the view controller can implement all the method declared in the MKMapViewDelegate protocol.

To fill up the entire View window with the map, you would use the following statement:

```
//---fill up entire screen---
mapView = [[MKMapView alloc] initWithFrame:self.view.bounds];
```

When the location information is updated, you zoom into the location using the setRegion: method of the mapView object:

```
//---update the map---
MKCoordinateSpan span;
span.latitudeDelta=.001;
span.longitudeDelta=.001;

MKCoordinateRegion region;
region.center = newLocation.coordinate;
region.span = span;

[mapView setRegion:region animated:TRUE];
```

 NOTE *For more information on the* MKMapView *class, refer to Apple's documentation at* http://developer.apple.com/iphone/library/navigation/ Frameworks/CocoaTouch/MapKit/index.html.

Getting Directional Information

The iPad comes with a built-in compass. This Try It Out shows you how to programmatically obtain directional information using this new feature.

TRY IT OUT   Incorporating a Compass

You will need a real device (iPad) to test this application.

1.   Using the LBS project, add an image named Compass.gif to the Resources folder of the project (see Figure 18-10).

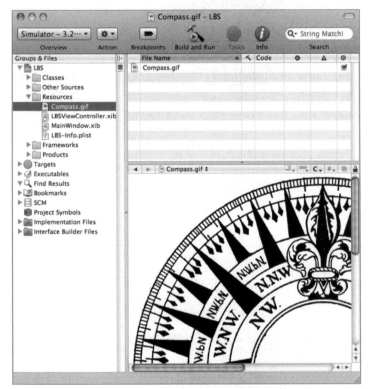

FIGURE 18-10

2.   In Interface Builder, drag and drop an ImageView to the View window and set its attributes in the Attributes Inspector window as follows (see also Figure 18-11):

> ➤   Image — Compass.gif

> ➤   Mode — Aspect Fit

3.   Add a Label view to the View window (see Figure 18-12).

4.   In the LBSViewController.h file, add the following bold statements:

```
#import <UIKit/UIKit.h>
#import <CoreLocation/CoreLocation.h>
#import <MapKit/MapKit.h>

@interface LBSViewController : UIViewController
    <CLLocationManagerDelegate,
```

```
    MKMapViewDelegate> {

    IBOutlet UITextField *accuracyTextField;
    IBOutlet UITextField *latitudeTextField;
    IBOutlet UITextField *longitudeTextField;
    CLLocationManager *lm;

    MKMapView *mapView;

    IBOutlet UIImageView *compass;
    IBOutlet UILabel *heading;
}

@property (retain, nonatomic) CLLocationManager *lm;
@property (retain, nonatomic) UITextField *accuracyTextField;
@property (retain, nonatomic) UITextField *latitudeTextField;
@property (retain, nonatomic) UITextField *longitudeTextField;

@property (nonatomic, retain) UIImageView *compass;
@property (nonatomic, retain) UILabel *heading;

@end
```

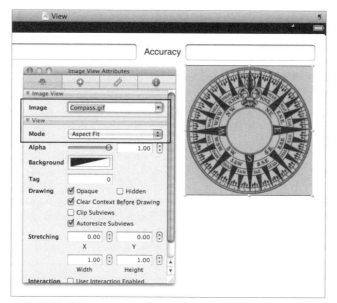

FIGURE 18-11

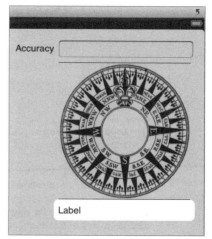

FIGURE 18-12

5. In Interface Builder, perform the following actions:

➤ Control-click and drag the File's Owner item and drop it over the ImageView. Select `compass`.

➤ Control-click and drag the File's Owner item and drop it over the Label view. Select `heading`.

6. In the `LBSViewController.m` file, add the following bold statements:

```
#import "LBSViewController.h"

@implementation LBSViewController

@synthesize lm;
@synthesize latitudeTextField;
@synthesize longitudeTextField;
@synthesize accuracyTextField;

@synthesize compass;
@synthesize heading;


- (void)viewDidLoad {
    self.lm = [[CLLocationManager alloc] init];
    lm.delegate = self;
    lm.desiredAccuracy = kCLLocationAccuracyBest;
    lm.distanceFilter = kCLDistanceFilterNone;

    [lm startUpdatingLocation];

    //---get the compass readings---
    [lm startUpdatingHeading];

    //---display the map in a region---
    mapView = [[MKMapView alloc]
                initWithFrame:CGRectMake(10, 60, 720, 678)];
    mapView.delegate = self;
    mapView.mapType = MKMapTypeHybrid;

    [self.view addSubview:mapView];

    [super viewDidLoad];
}

- (void)locationManager:(CLLocationManager *)manager
        didUpdateHeading:(CLHeading *)newHeading {

    heading.text = [NSString stringWithFormat:@"%f degrees",
                    newHeading.magneticHeading];

    //---headings is in degress---
    double d = newHeading.magneticHeading;

    //---convert degrees to radians---
    double radians = d/57.2957795;
    compass.transform = CGAffineTransformMakeRotation(-radians);
}

- (void)dealloc {
    [compass release];
    [heading release];
```

```
    [lm release];
    [latitudeTextField release];
    [longitudeTextField release];
    [accuracyTextField release];

    [super dealloc];
}
```

7. Press Command-R to test the application on an iPad. Observe the image as you turn the device (see Figure 18-13).

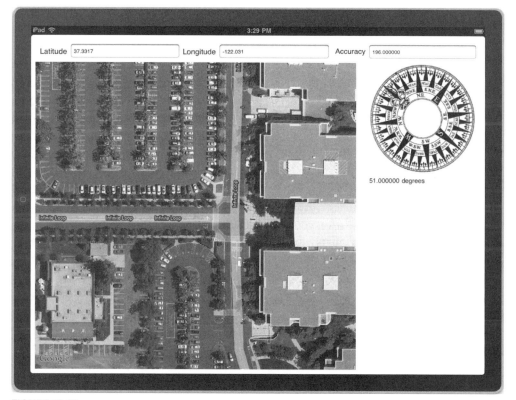

FIGURE 18-13

How It Works

Getting directional information is similar to getting location data you use the Core Location framework. Instead of calling the startUpdatingLocation method of the CLLocationManager object, you call the startUpdatingHeading method:

```
//---get the compass readings---
[lm startUpdatingHeading];
```

When directional information is available, the `locationManager:didUpdateHeading:` method will continually fire:

```
- (void)locationManager:(CLLocationManager *)manager
        didUpdateHeading:(CLHeading *)newHeading {

    heading.text = [NSString stringWithFormat:@"%f degrees",
                    newHeading.magneticHeading];

    //---headings is in degress---
    double d = newHeading.magneticHeading;

    //---convert degrees to radians---
    double radians = d/57.2957795;
    compass.transform = CGAffineTransformMakeRotation(-radians);
}
```

The `magneticHeading` property of the `CLHeading` parameter will contain the readings in degrees, with 0 representing magnetic North. The ImageView is then rotated based on the value of the heading. Note that you need to convert the degrees into radians for the `CGAffineTransformMakeRotation()` method.

Rotating the Map

The previous section showed how you can programmatically rotate the image of a compass based on the directional heading information you obtained from the Core Location framework. Using this concept, you could also rotate the map whenever the direction of your device changes. This is very useful when you are using the map for navigational purposes. By itself, the MapView does not support map rotation, but the following Try It Out shows how you can improvise.

TRY IT OUT Rotating the Map

1. Using the LBS project, double-click the `LBSViewController.xib` file to edit it in Interface Builder.

2. Drag and drop a View view from the Library and set its size and location via its Size Inspector window as follows (see also Figure 18-14):

➤ X:10

➤ Y: 60

➤ W: 720

➤ H: 678

3. In the Attributes Inspector window for the View, check the Clip Subviews option (see Figure 18-15).

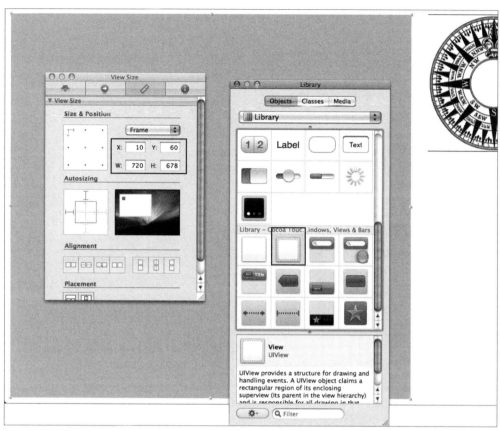

FIGURE 18-14

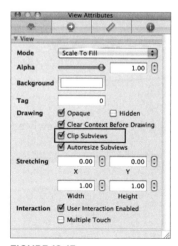

FIGURE 18-15

4. In Xcode, add the following bold statements to the `LBSViewController.h` file:

```
#import <UIKit/UIKit.h>
#import <CoreLocation/CoreLocation.h>
#import <MapKit/MapKit.h>
#import "MyAnnotation.h"
#import <MapKit/MKReverseGeocoder.h>

@interface LBSViewController : UIViewController
    <CLLocationManagerDelegate,
     MKMapViewDelegate,
     MKReverseGeocoderDelegate> {

    IBOutlet UITextField *accuracyTextField;
    IBOutlet UITextField *latitudeTextField;
    IBOutlet UITextField *longitudeTextField;
    CLLocationManager *lm;

    MKMapView *mapView;

    IBOutlet UIImageView *compass;
    IBOutlet UILabel *heading;

    MyAnnotation *annotation;

    NSString *location;
    MKReverseGeocoder *geocoder;

    IBOutlet UIView *viewForMap;
}

@property (retain, nonatomic) CLLocationManager *lm;
@property (retain, nonatomic) UITextField *accuracyTextField;
@property (retain, nonatomic) UITextField *latitudeTextField;
@property (retain, nonatomic) UITextField *longitudeTextField;

@property (nonatomic, retain) UIImageView *compass;
@property (nonatomic, retain) UILabel *heading;

@property (nonatomic, retain) IBOutlet UIView *viewForMap;

@end
```

5. In Interface Builder, Control-click and drag the File's Owner item and drop it over the newly added View view. Select `viewForMap`.

6. Add the following bold statements to the `LBSViewController.m` file:

```
@synthesize viewForMap;

- (void)viewDidLoad {
    self.lm = [[CLLocationManager alloc] init];

    if ([lm locationServicesEnabled]) {
        lm.delegate = self;
        lm.desiredAccuracy = kCLLocationAccuracyBest;
```

```
            lm.distanceFilter = kCLDistanceFilterNone;

            [lm startUpdatingLocation];

            //---get the compass readings---
            [lm startUpdatingHeading];
        }

        //---display the map---
        mapView = [[MKMapView alloc]
                    initWithFrame:CGRectMake(-140, -161, 1000,1000)];
                    //initWithFrame:CGRectMake(10, 60, 720, 678)];

        mapView.delegate = self;
        mapView.mapType = MKMapTypeHybrid;

        //[self.view addSubview:mapView];
        [self.viewForMap addSubview:mapView];

        [super viewDidLoad];
    }

    - (void)locationManager:(CLLocationManager *)manager
            didUpdateHeading:(CLHeading *)newHeading {

        heading.text = [NSString stringWithFormat:@"%f degrees",
                        newHeading.magneticHeading];

        //---headings is in degress---
        double d = newHeading.magneticHeading;

        //---convert degrees to radians---
        double radians = d/57.2957795;
        compass.transform = CGAffineTransformMakeRotation(-radians);

        //---rotate the map---
        mapView.transform = CGAffineTransformMakeRotation(-radians);
    }

    - (void)dealloc {
        [viewForMap release];

        [compass release];
        [heading release];
        [lm release];
        [latitudeTextField release];
        [longitudeTextField release];
        [accuracyTextField release];

        [super dealloc];
    }
```

7. Deploy the application to a real device. Observe that as you rotate the iPad, the map will rotate as well.

How It Works

How the map rotates is actually very simple. On first thought, the easiest way would be to apply the transformation to the mapView. However, doing not only rotates the map, it also rotates the entire rectangle (see Figure 18-16).

FIGURE 18-16

The trick is to embed the mapView within another View view and rotate it within the View. Hence, you added another View (viewForMap) in the View window and set it to Clip Subviews. Essentially, all the views added to this View will not display beyond its boundary.

Instead of displaying the map in the original size, you now need to set it to a minimum of 988.98 x 988.98 pixels (see Figure 18-17). This is the length of the diagonal of the viewable rectangle of the map. For simplicity, round it up to 1000 x 1000 pixels:

```
//---display the map---
mapView = [[MKMapView alloc]
            initWithFrame:CGRectMake(-140, -161, 1000,1000)];
```

The mapView is now added to viewForMap, instead of self.view:

```
//[self.view addSubview:mapView];
[self.viewForMap addSubview:mapView];
```

Recall that the initial position of the mapView was (10, 60):

```
            initWithFrame:CGRectMake(10, 60,720,678)];
```

But it must now be changed to (-140, -161):

```
            initWithFrame:CGRectMake(-140, -161, 1000,1000)];
```

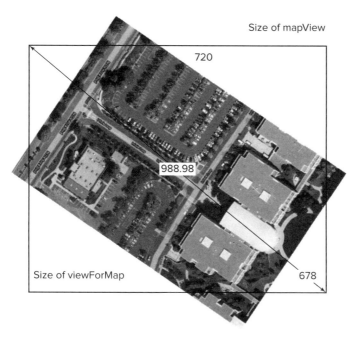

FIGURE 18-17

Figure 18-18 shows how the new coordinate of (-140, -161) was derived. Remember, when you try to add a view to another, the coordinate specified is always with respect to the view you are adding to. In this case, the reference point (0,0) is at `viewForMap`.

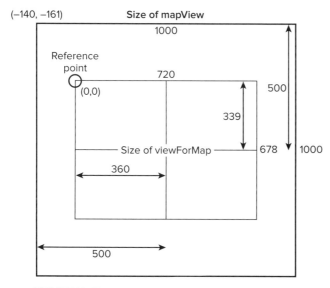

FIGURE 18-18

Finally, to rotate the map, apply the `CGAffineTransformMakeRotation()` method to the `mapView`:

```
//---rotate the map---
mapView.transform = CGAffineTransformMakeRotation(-radians);
```

Displaying Annotations

So far, you have used Core Location to report your current location and heading and then used the Map Kit to display a map representing your location. A visual improvement you can make to the project is to add a push pin onto the map, representing your current location.

In the following Try It Out, you learn how to add annotations to the map in Map Kit. Annotations enable you to display push pins on the map, denoting some locations.

TRY IT OUT   **Displaying a Push Pin**

1.   Continuing with the LBS project, add a new Objective-C Class file to the Classes folder of the project (see Figure 18-19).

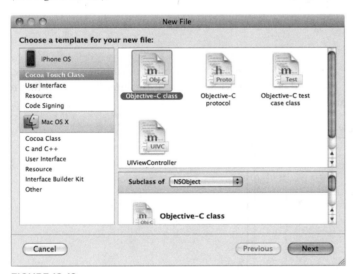

FIGURE 18-19

2.   Name it as `MyAnnotation.m`. Once it is added, you should see the `MyAnnotation.h` and `MyAnnotation.m` files under the Classes folder (see Figure 18-20).

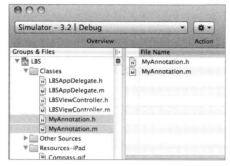

FIGURE 18-20

3. Populate the `MyAnnotation.h` file as follows:

```
#import <Foundation/Foundation.h>
#import <MapKit/MapKit.h>

@interface MyAnnotation : NSObject <MKAnnotation> {

    CLLocationCoordinate2D coordinate;
    NSString *title;
    NSString *subTitle;

}

@property (nonatomic, readonly) CLLocationCoordinate2D coordinate;
@property (nonatomic, retain) NSString *title;
@property (nonatomic, retain) NSString *subTitle;

-(id)initWithCoordinate:(CLLocationCoordinate2D) c
                  title:(NSString *) t
               subTitle:(NSString *) st;

-(void) moveAnnotation: (CLLocationCoordinate2D) newCoordinate;
-(NSString *)subtitle;
-(NSString *)title;

@end
```

4. Populate the `MyAnnotation.m` file as follows:

```
#import "MyAnnotation.h"

@implementation MyAnnotation

@synthesize coordinate;
@synthesize title;
@synthesize subTitle;

-(NSString *)subtitle {
    return subTitle;
}
```

```
-(NSString *)title {
    return title;
}

-(id)initWithCoordinate:(CLLocationCoordinate2D) c
                  title:(NSString *) t
               subTitle:(NSString *) st {

    coordinate = c;
    self.title = t;
    self.subTitle = st;
    return self;
}

-(void) moveAnnotation: (CLLocationCoordinate2D) newCoordinate {
    coordinate = newCoordinate;
}

- (void) dealloc{
    [title release];
    [subTitle release];
    [super dealloc];
}

@end
```

5. In the `LBSViewController.h` file, add the following bold statements:

```
#import <UIKit/UIKit.h>
#import <CoreLocation/CoreLocation.h>
#import <MapKit/MapKit.h>

#import "MyAnnotation.h"

@interface LBSViewController : UIViewController
    <CLLocationManagerDelegate, MKMapViewDelegate> {

    IBOutlet UITextField *accuracyTextField;
    IBOutlet UITextField *latitudeTextField;
    IBOutlet UITextField *longitudeTextField;
    CLLocationManager *lm;

    MKMapView *mapView;

    IBOutlet UIImageView *compass;
    IBOutlet UILabel *heading;

    MyAnnotation *annotation;
}
@property (retain, nonatomic) CLLocationManager *lm;
@property (retain, nonatomic) UITextField *accuracyTextField;
@property (retain, nonatomic) UITextField *latitudeTextField;
@property (retain, nonatomic) UITextField *longitudeTextField;

@property (nonatomic, retain) UIImageView *compass;
```

```
@property (nonatomic, retain) UILabel *heading;

@end
```

6. In the `LBSViewController.m` file, add the following bold statements:

```
- (void) locationManager:(CLLocationManager *) manager
      didUpdateToLocation:(CLLocation *) newLocation
            fromLocation:(CLLocation *) oldLocation {

    //---display latitude---
    NSString *lat = [[NSString alloc] initWithFormat:@"%f",
                    newLocation.coordinate.latitude];
    //latitudeTextField.text = lat;
    latitudeTextField.text = @"37.3317";

    //---display longitude---
    NSString *lng = [[NSString alloc] initWithFormat:@"%f",
                    newLocation.coordinate.longitude];
    //longitudeTextField.text = lng;
    longitudeTextField.text = @"-122.031";

    //---display accuracy---
    NSString *acc = [[NSString alloc] initWithFormat:@"%f",
                    newLocation.horizontalAccuracy];
    accuracyTextField.text = acc;

    [acc release];
    [lat release];
    [lng release];

    //---update the map---
    MKCoordinateSpan span;
    span.latitudeDelta=.001;
    span.longitudeDelta=.001;

    MKCoordinateRegion region;

    region.center = newLocation.coordinate;

    region.span = span;

    [mapView setRegion:region animated:TRUE];

    //---display an annotation here---
    if (annotation) {
        [annotation moveAnnotation:newLocation.coordinate];
    }
    else {
        annotation = [[MyAnnotation alloc]
                        initWithCoordinate:newLocation.coordinate
                                title:@"You are here"
                             subTitle:[NSString
                                stringWithFormat:@"Lat: %@. Lng: %@",
                                latitudeTextField.text,
```

```
                                                longitudeTextField.text]];
            [mapView addAnnotation:annotation];
        }
    }

    - (void)dealloc {
        [annotation release];

        [compass release];

        [lm release];
        [latitudeTextField release];
        [longitudeTextField release];
        [accuracyTextField release];

        [super dealloc];
    }
```

7. Press Command-R to test the application on the iPhone Simulator. You'll see the push pin inserted into the current position. When you tap on it, it displays the information in the annotation view as shown in Figure 18-21. Also observe that as you test it on a real device, the push pin will relocate on the map to represent your current location as you move.

FIGURE 18-21

How It Works

You first create the `MyAnnotation` class that inherits from the `MKAnnotation` base class. Within the `MyAnnotation` class, you implemented several properties (including `coordinate`, which specifies the center point of the annotation) and methods, in particular:

➤ `title` — Returns the title to be displayed on the annotation.

➤ `subtitle` — Returns the subtitle to be displayed on the annotation.

➤ `moveAnnotation:` — Changes the location of the annotation.

As the location of the device changes, you display an annotation to represent the current location:

```
//---display an annotation here---
if (annotation) {
    [annotation moveAnnotation:newLocation.coordinate];
}
else {
    annotation = [[MyAnnotation alloc]
                        initWithCoordinate:newLocation.coordinate
                                    title:@"You are here"
                             subTitle:[NSString
                                 stringWithFormat:@"Lat: %@. Lng: %@",
                                 latitudeTextField.text,
                                 longitudeTextField.text]];
    [mapView addAnnotation:annotation];
}
```

Note that if an annotation is already present, you simply move its position by calling the `moveAnnotation:` method.

Reverse Geocoding

While knowing your location coordinates is useful and displaying your location on the Google Maps is cool, the capability to know your current address is even cooler! The process of finding your address from a pair of latitude and longitude is known as *reverse geocoding*. The following Try It Out shows how to obtain the address of a location given its latitude and longitude. You will do so via the API exposed by the Map Kit.

TRY IT OUT Obtaining the Address

1. Continuing with the LBS project, add the following bold statements to the `LBSViewController.h` file:

```
#import <UIKit/UIKit.h>
#import <CoreLocation/CoreLocation.h>
#import <MapKit/MapKit.h>
#import "MyAnnotation.h"

#import <MapKit/MKReverseGeocoder.h>

@interface LBSViewController : UIViewController
    <CLLocationManagerDelegate,
     MKMapViewDelegate,
     MKReverseGeocoderDelegate> {

    IBOutlet UITextField *accuracyTextField;
    IBOutlet UITextField *latitudeTextField;
    IBOutlet UITextField *longitudeTextField;
    CLLocationManager *lm;
```

```
    MKMapView *mapView;

    IBOutlet UIImageView *compass;
    IBOutlet UILabel *heading;

    MyAnnotation *annotation;

    NSString *location;
    MKReverseGeocoder *geocoder;
}

@property (retain, nonatomic) CLLocationManager *lm;
@property (retain, nonatomic) UITextField *accuracyTextField;
@property (retain, nonatomic) UITextField *latitudeTextField;
@property (retain, nonatomic) UITextField *longitudeTextField;

@property (nonatomic, retain) UIImageView *compass;
@property (nonatomic, retain) UILabel *heading;

@end
```

2. In the `LBSViewController.m` file, add the following bold statements:

```
- (void) locationManager:(CLLocationManager *) manager
      didUpdateToLocation:(CLLocation *) newLocation
             fromLocation:(CLLocation *) oldLocation {

    //---perform reverse geocoding---
    if (!geocoder) {
       geocoder=[[MKReverseGeocoder alloc]
                initWithCoordinate:newLocation.coordinate];
       geocoder.delegate = self;
       [geocoder start];
    }

    //---display latitude---
    NSString *lat = [[NSString alloc] initWithFormat:@"%f",
                    newLocation.coordinate.latitude];
    latitudeTextField.text = lat;
    //...
    //...
    //...
}

- (void)reverseGeocoder:(MKReverseGeocoder *)geo
       didFailWithError:(NSError *)error{

    [geocoder release];
    geocoder = nil;

}

- (void)reverseGeocoder:(MKReverseGeocoder *)geo
       didFindPlacemark:(MKPlacemark *)placemark {
```

```
location = [NSString stringWithFormat:@"%@, %@",
              placemark.locality, placemark.country];
annotation.subTitle = location;

[geocoder release];
geocoder = nil;
}
```

3. Press Command-R to test the application on the iPhone Simulator. Notice that the Annotation view now displays the address of the location (see Figure 18-22).

FIGURE 18-22

How It Works

To perform reverse geocoding, use the MKReverseGeocoder class available in the Map Kit framework:

```
MKReverseGeocoder *geocoder;
```

When a location is obtained (via the locationManager:didUpdateToLocation:fromLocation: event), you instantiate the MKReverseGeocoder class by setting it to a location coordinate:

```
//---perform reverse geocoding---
if (!geocoder) {
    geocoder=[[MKReverseGeocoder alloc]
            initWithCoordinate:newLocation.coordinate];
    geocoder.delegate = self;
    [geocoder start];
}
```

The MKReverseGeocoder class works asynchronously, and will fire the reverseGeocoder:didFindPlacemark: event when an address has been found. Hence, you need to implement the MKReverseGeocoderDelegate protocol in the View Controller:

```
@interface LBSViewController : UIViewController
    <CLLocationManagerDelegate,
     MKMapViewDelegate,
     MKReverseGeocoderDelegate> {
```

When the address is found, you display the address as the subtitle of the annotation:

```
- (void)reverseGeocoder:(MKReverseGeocoder *)geo
        didFindPlacemark:(MKPlacemark *)placemark {

    location = [NSString stringWithFormat:@"%@, %@",
                    placemark.locality, placemark.country];
    annotation.subTitle = location;

    [geocoder release];
    geocoder = nil;
}
```

If the address cannot be found, the `reverseGeocoder:didFailWithError:` event will be fired:

```
- (void)reverseGeocoder:(MKReverseGeocoder *)geo
        didFailWithError:(NSError *)error{

    [geocoder release];
    geocoder = nil;

}
```

Displaying Disclosure Button

When displaying an annotation on the map, it is customary to have an option for the user to select the annotation so that more details on the location can be shown. For example, the user may want to know the detailed address of the location, or you can provide routing information for the selected location. In the Map Kit, you can add this option through a disclosure button. The following Try It Out shows how to display the disclosure button in an annotation.

TRY IT OUT **Displaying a Disclosure Button**

1. Continuing with the LBS project, add the following methods to the LBSViewController.m file:

```
- (MKAnnotationView *)mapView:(MKMapView *)aMapView
            viewForAnnotation:(id)ann {

    NSString *identifier = @"myPin";
    MKPinAnnotationView *pin =
        (MKPinAnnotationView *)[aMapView
            dequeueReusableAnnotationViewWithIdentifier:identifier];

    if (pin == nil) {
        pin = [[[MKPinAnnotationView alloc] initWithAnnotation:ann
                                    reuseIdentifier:identifier] autorelease];
    } else {
        pin.annotation = ann;
    }

    //---display a disclosure button on the right---
```

```
    UIButton *myDetailButton =
        [UIButton buttonWithType:UIButtonTypeDetailDisclosure];

    myDetailButton.frame = CGRectMake(0, 0, 23, 23);

    myDetailButton.contentVerticalAlignment =
        UIControlContentVerticalAlignmentCenter;

    myDetailButton.contentHorizontalAlignment =
        UIControlContentHorizontalAlignmentCenter;

    [myDetailButton addTarget:self action:@selector(checkButtonTapped:)
            forControlEvents:UIControlEventTouchUpInside];

    pin.rightCalloutAccessoryView = myDetailButton;

    pin.enabled = YES;
    pin.animatesDrop=TRUE;
    pin.canShowCallout=YES;

    return pin;
}

-(void) checkButtonTapped:(id) sender {
    //---know which button was clicked;
    // useful for multiple pins on the map---
    // UIControl *btnClicked = sender;

    UIAlertView *alert = [[UIAlertView alloc]
                        initWithTitle:@"Your Current Location"
                        message:location
                        delegate:self
                        cancelButtonTitle:@"OK"
                        otherButtonTitles:nil];
    [alert show];
    [alert release];
}
```

2. Press Command-R to test the application on the iPhone Simulator. The Annotation view now displays a disclosure button to the right of it (see Figure 18-23). Tapping on the button displays an alert view.

FIGURE 18-23

How It Works

What you did was override the `mapView:viewForAnnotation:` method (defined in the `MKMapViewDelegate` protocol), which is fired every time you add an annotation to the map.

Notice the block of code:

```
NSString *identifier = @"myPin";
MKPinAnnotationView *pin =
    (MKPinAnnotationView *)[aMapView
        dequeueReusableAnnotationViewWithIdentifier:identifier];

if (pin == nil) {
    pin = [[[MKPinAnnotationView alloc] initWithAnnotation:ann
                                        reuseIdentifier:identifier] autorelease];
} else {
    pin.annotation = ann;
}
```

It tries to reuse any annotation objects that are currently not visible on the screen. Imagine you have 10,000 annotations on the map; maintaining `MKPinAnnotationView` objects in memory is not a feasible option (too much memory is taken up). Hence, this code tries to reuse `MKPinAnnotationView` objects that are currently not visible on the screen.

The following code block displays a disclosure button next to the annotation:

```
//---display a disclosure button on the right---
UIButton *myDetailButton =
    [UIButton buttonWithType:UIButtonTypeDetailDisclosure];

myDetailButton.frame = CGRectMake(0, 0, 23, 23);

myDetailButton.contentVerticalAlignment =
    UIControlContentVerticalAlignmentCenter;

myDetailButton.contentHorizontalAlignment =
    UIControlContentHorizontalAlignmentCenter;

[myDetailButton addTarget:self action:@selector(checkButtonTapped:)
        forControlEvents:UIControlEventTouchUpInside];

pin.rightCalloutAccessoryView = myDetailButton;

pin.enabled = YES;
pin.animatesDrop=TRUE;
pin.canShowCallout=YES;
```

When the disclosure button is clicked, it fires the `checkButtonTapped:` method:

```
-(void) checkButtonTapped:(id) sender {
    //---know which button was clicked;
    // useful for multiple pins on the map---
    // UIControl *btnClicked = sender;

    UIAlertView *alert = [[UIAlertView alloc]
```

```
                              initWithTitle:@"Your Current Location"
                              message:location
                              delegate:self
                              cancelButtonTitle:@"OK"
                              otherButtonTitles:nil];
          [alert show];
          [alert release];
     }
```

In this case, you simply display an Alert view. You can also display another View window to show more detailed information.

SUMMARY

This chapter explained how to use the Map Kit framework to display the Google Maps in your iPad application. You also saw how to use the Core Location framework to help you obtain your location information. Combining the Map Kit and the Core Location frameworks enables you to create very compelling location-based services.

EXERCISES

1. Name the property of the MKMapView class that allows you to show your current location on the map.

2. Name the protocol that you need to implement in order to monitor for changes in your map.

3. Name the method that you need to call to start updating your location.

4. Name the method that you need to call to start updating your heading.

5. Name the class responsible for reverse geocoding.

Answers to the Exercises can be found in Appendix A.

▶ **WHAT YOU LEARNED IN THIS CHAPTER**

TOPIC	KEY CONCEPTS
Framework for displaying Google Maps	Map Kit
Framework for obtaining geographical location	Core Location
Class for displaying Google Maps	`MKMapView`
Showing current location on the map	`showsUserLocation`
Monitoring changes in the map	Implement the `MKMapViewDelegate` protocol
Changing the zoom level of the map	Set the `latitudeDelta` and `longitudeDelta` properties of the map
Monitoring changes in location	Implement the `CLLocationManagerDelegate` protocol
Getting location updates	Call the `startUpdatingLocation` method
Getting directional updates	Call the `startUpdatingHeading` method
Rotating the map	Embed the MapView in another View and rotate the MapView
Displaying annotations	Create a class that inherits from the `MKAnnotation` base class

PART V
Appendices

Answers to Exercises

This appendix provides the solutions for the end-of-chapter exercises located at the ends of Chapters 2–18 (there are no exercises in Chapter 1).

CHAPTER 2 EXERCISE SOLUTIONS

Answer to Question 1

The minimum image size you should design is 72×72 pixels. It is all right to design a larger image because the iPad automatically resizes it for you. In general, try to design a larger image because doing so prepares your application for the newer devices that Apple may roll out.

Answer to Question 2

You should implement the `shouldAutorotateToInterfaceOrientation:` method and code the appropriate statements to support the orientation you want. To support all orientations, simply return a `YES` in this method. The following code snippet supports the portrait and landscape left modes:

```
- (BOOL)shouldAutorotateToInterfaceOrientation:(UIInterfaceOrientation)
interfaceOrientation {
    // Return YES for supported orientations
    // return YES;
    return (interfaceOrientation==UIInterfaceOrientationPortrait ||
            interfaceOrientation==UIInterfaceOrientationLandscapeLeft);

}
```

Answer to Question 3

This is to ensure that the image is always copied into the Resources folder. If not, Xcode only makes a reference to the image and the image is not physically in the Resources folder.

CHAPTER 3 EXERCISE SOLUTIONS

Answer to Question 1

In the `.h` file:

```
//---declare an outlet---
IBOutlet UITextField *nameTextField;
//...
//...
//---expose the outlet as a property---
@property (nonatomic, retain) UITextField *nameTextField;
```

In the `.m` file:

```
@implementation BasicUIViewController

//---generate the getters and setters for the property---
@synthesize nameTextField;
- (void)dealloc {
    //---release the outlet---
    [nameTextField release];
    [super dealloc];
}
```

Answer to Question 2

In the `.h` file:

```
- (IBAction)btnClicked:(id)sender;
```

In the `.m` file:

```
@implementation BasicUIViewController
//...
//...
- (IBAction)btnClicked:(id)sender {
    //---your code for the action here---
}
```

Answer to Question 3

Use the Alert view when you simply want to notify the user when something happens. Use an action sheet when you need the user to make a selection, usually from a set of options.

Answer to Question 4

```
- (void)loadView {
    //---create a UIView object---
    UIView *view =
        [[UIView alloc] initWithFrame:[UIScreen mainScreen].applicationFrame];
```

```
    view.backgroundColor = [UIColor lightGrayColor];

    //---create a Button view---
    frame = CGRectMake(10, 70, 300, 50);
    UIButton *button = [UIButton buttonWithType:UIButtonTypeRoundedRect];
    button.frame = frame;
    [button setTitle:@"Click Me, Please!" forState:UIControlStateNormal];
    button.backgroundColor = [UIColor clearColor];
    button.tag = 2000;

    [button addTarget:self action:@selector(buttonClicked:)
        forControlEvents:UIControlEventTouchUpInside];

    [view addSubview:button];
    self.view = view;
}
```

CHAPTER 4 EXERCISE SOLUTIONS

Answer to Question 1

```
    mySecondViewController = [[MySecondViewController alloc]
                                initWithNibName:nil
                                bundle:nil];
```

Answer to Question 2

```
- (void)viewDidLoad {

    //---create a CGRect for the positioning---
    CGRect frame = CGRectMake(10, 10, 300, 50);

    //---create a Label view---
    label = [[UILabel alloc] initWithFrame:frame];
    label.textAlignment = UITextAlignmentCenter;
    label.font = [UIFont fontWithName:@"Verdana" size:20];
    label.text = @"This is a label";

    //---create a Button view---
    frame = CGRectMake(10, 250, 300, 50);
    button = [[UIButton buttonWithType:UIButtonTypeRoundedRect]
            initWithFrame:frame];
    [button setTitle:@"OK" forState:UIControlStateNormal];
    button.backgroundColor = [UIColor clearColor];

    [self.view addSubview:label];
    [self.view addSubview:button];

    [super viewDidLoad];
}
```

Answer to Question 3

```
        //---add the action handler and set current class as target---
        [button addTarget:self
            action:@selector(buttonClicked:)
            forControlEvents:UIControlEventTouchUpInside];

//...
//...
//...

-(IBAction) buttonClicked: (id) sender{
    //---do something here---
}
```

Answer to Question 4

In the `HelloWorldViewController.h` file, add in the following code in bold:

```
#import <UIKit/UIKit.h>

@interface HelloWorldViewController : UIViewController {

}

-(IBAction) btnClicked:(id) sender;

@end
```

In the `HelloWorldViewController.m` file, add in the following code:

```
-(IBAction) btnClicked:(id) sender{
    UIAlertView *alert = [[UIAlertView alloc]
                          initWithTitle:@"Button Clicked!"
                                message:@"Button was clicked!"
                               delegate:self
                      cancelButtonTitle:@"OK"
                      otherButtonTitles:nil];
    [alert show];
    [alert release];
}
```

In the `HelloWorldViewController.xib` file, control-click and drag the button and drop it over the File's Owner item. Select `btnClicked:`.

CHAPTER 5 EXERCISE SOLUTIONS

Answer to Question 1

First, handle the `Did End on Exit` event (or implement the `textFieldShouldReturn:` method in the View Controller). Then call the `resignFirstResponder` method of the `UITextField` object to release its first-responder status.

Answer to Question 2

Register for the notifications `UIKeyboardWillShowNotification` and `UIKeyboardWillHideNotification`.

Answer to Question 3

```
//---gets the size of the keyboard---
NSDictionary *userInfo = [notification userInfo];
NSValue *keyboardValue = [userInfo objectForKey:UIKeyboardBoundsUserInfoKey];
[keyboardValue getValue:&keyboardBounds];
```

CHAPTER 6 EXERCISE SOLUTIONS

Answer to Question 1

```
-(BOOL)shouldAutorotateToInterfaceOrientation:
(UIInterfaceOrientation)interfaceOrientation {

    return (interfaceOrientation == UIInterfaceOrientationLandscapeLeft ||
            interfaceOrientation == UIInterfaceOrientationLandscapeRight);

}
```

Answer to Question 2

The `frame` property defines the rectangle occupied by the view, with respect to its superview (the view that contains it). Using the `frame` property allows you to set the positioning and size of a view. Besides using the `frame` property, you can also use the `center` property, which sets the center of the view, also with respect to its superview. You usually use the `center` property when you are performing some animation and just want to change the position of a view.

CHAPTER 7 EXERCISE SOLUTIONS

Answer to Question 1

The two protocols are `UITableViewDataSource` and `UITableViewDelegate`.

The `UITableViewDataSource` protocol contains events in which you can populate the Table view with various items.

The `UITableViewDelegate` protocol contains events in which you can handle the selection of rows in a Table view.

Answer to Question 2

To add an index list to your Table view, you need to implement the `sectionIndexTitlesForTableView:` method.

Answer to Question 3

The three disclosure and checkmark images are as follows:

➤ `UITableViewCellAccessoryDetailDisclosureButton`

➤ `UITableViewCellAccessoryCheckmark`

➤ `UITableViewCellAccessoryDisclosureIndicator`

The `UITableViewCellAccessoryDetailDisclosureButton` image handles a user's tap event. The event name is `tableView:accessoryButtonTappedForRowWithIndexPath:`.

CHAPTER 8 EXERCISE SOLUTIONS

Answer to Question 1

For retrieving preferences settings values, you use the `objectForKey:` method. For saving preferences settings values, you use the `setObject:forKey:` method.

Answer to Question 2

You can either remove the application from the device or Simulator, or you can remove the file ending with *application_name*`.plist` in the application folder within the Simulator.

Answer to Question 3

The Add Child button is represented by three horizontal lines. It adds a child item to the currently selected item. The Add Sibling button, on the other hand, is represented by a plus sign (+). It adds an item on the same level as the currently selected item.

CHAPTER 9 EXERCISE SOLUTIONS

Answer to Question 1

The three folders are `Documents`, `Library`, and `tmp`. The `Documents` folder can be used by the developer to store application-related data. The `Library` stores application-specific settings, such as those used by the `NSUserDefaults` class. The `tmp` folder can be used to store temporary data that will not be backed up by iTunes.

Answer to Question 2

The `NSDictionary` class creates a dictionary object whose items are immutable; that is, after it is populated, you can no longer add items to it. The `NSMutableDictionary` class, on the other hand, creates a mutable dictionary object that allows items to be added to it after it is loaded.

Answer to Question 3

Location of the `Documents` directory on a real device:

```
/private/var/mobile/Applications/<application_id>/Documents/
```

Location of the `tmp` directory on a real device:

```
/private/var/mobile/Applications/<application_id>/tmp/
```

CHAPTER 10 EXERCISE SOLUTIONS

Answer to Question 1

The `sqlite3_exec()` function is actually a wrapper for the three functions: `sqlite3_prepare()`; `sqlite3_step()`; and `sqlite3_finalize()`. For nonquery SQL statements (such as for creating tables, inserting rows, and so on), it is always better to use the `sqlite3_exec()` function.

Answer to Question 2

To obtain a C-style string from an `NSString` object, use the `UTF8String` method from the `NSString` class.

Answer to Question 3

```objc
NSString *qsql = @"SELECT * FROM CONTACTS";
sqlite3_stmt *statement;

if (sqlite3_prepare_v2( db, [qsql UTF8String], -1, &statement, nil) ==
    SQLITE_OK) {

        while (sqlite3_step(statement) == SQLITE_ROW)
        {
            char *field1 = (char *) sqlite3_column_text(statement, 0);
            NSString *field1Str = [[NSString alloc] initWithUTF8String: field1];

            char *field2 = (char *) sqlite3_column_text(statement, 1);
            NSString *field2Str = [[NSString alloc] initWithUTF8String: field2];

            NSString *str = [[NSString alloc] initWithFormat:@"%@ - %@",
                            field1Str, field2Str];
```

```
        NSLog(str);

        [field1Str release];
        [field2Str release];
        [str release];
    }
    //---deletes the compiled statement from memory---
    sqlite3_finalize(statement);
}
```

CHAPTER 11 EXERCISE SOLUTIONS

Answer to Question 1

The three affine transformations are translation, rotation, and scaling.

Answer to Question 2

The only way to pause the NSTimer object is to call its invalidate method. To make it continue, you have to create a new NSTimer object.

Answer to Question 3

The beginAnimations and commitAnimations methods of the UIView class allow you to enclose blocks of code that cause visual changes so that the changes in visual appearance will be animated and not appear abruptly.

CHAPTER 12 EXERCISE SOLUTIONS

Answer to Question 1

The six gesture recognizers are:

➤ UITapGestureRecognizer for detecting tap(s) on a view.

➤ UIPinchGestureRecognizer for detecting pinching in and out of a view.

➤ UIPanGestureRecognizer for detecting panning or dragging of a view.

➤ UISwipeGestureRecognizer for detecting swiping of a view.

➤ UIRotationGestureRecognizer for detecting rotation of a view.

➤ UILongPressGestureRecognizer for detecting long presses on a view (also known as "touch and hold").

Answer to Question 2

Discrete Gestures:

➤ UITapGestureRecognizer

➤ UISwipeGestureRecognizer

➤ UILongPressGestureRecognizer

Continuous Gestures:

➤ UIPinchGestureRecognizer

➤ UIPanGestureRecognizer

➤ UIRotationGestureRecognizer

Answer to Question 3

The four events are:

➤ touchesBegan:withEvent:

➤ touchesEnded:withEvent:

➤ touchesMoved:withEvent:

➤ touchesCancelled:withEvent:

Answer to Question 4

When you multi-tap, you tap a single point in quick succession. This is similar to double-clicking in Mac OS X. When you multi-touch, on the other hand, you touch multiple contact points on the screen.

Answer to Question 5

Pressing the Option key allows you to simulate multi-touch on the iPhone Simulator.

CHAPTER 13 EXERCISE SOLUTIONS

Answer to Question 1

The protocol is UIAccelerometerDelegate.

Answer to Question 2

The three events are

- ➤ `motionBegan:`
- ➤ `motionEnded:`
- ➤ `motionCancelled:`

CHAPTER 14 EXERCISE SOLUTIONS

Answer to Question 1

The three ways are: SOAP 1.1/1.2, HTTP GET, and HTTP POST.

Answer to Question 2

The three key events are:

- ➤ `connection:didReceiveResponse:`
- ➤ `connection:didReceiveData:`
- ➤ `connectionDidFinishLoading:`

Answer to Question 3

The `NSXmlParser` class fires off the following events as it parses the content of an XML document:

- ➤ `parser:didStartElement:namespaceURI:qualifiedName:attributes:`
- ➤ `parser:foundCharacters:`
- ➤ `parser:didEndElement:namespaceURI:qualifiedName:`

CHAPTER 15 EXERCISE SOLUTIONS

Answer to Question 1

The class is `GKPeerPickerController`.

Answer to Question 2

The class is `GKSession`.

Answer to Question 3

Call the `startVoiceChatWithParticipantID:error:` method from the `GKVoiceChatService` class.

Answer to Question 4

On the initiator, call the `voiceChatService:sendData:toParticipantID:` method defined in the `GKVoiceChatClient` protocol.

On the receiver, call the `receivedData:fromParticipantID:` method defined in the `GKVoiceChatClient` protocol.

CHAPTER 16 EXERCISE SOLUTIONS

Answer to Question 1

The class is `NSNetService`.

Answer to Question 2

The class is `NSNetServiceBrowser`.

Answer to Question 3

The method name is `netServiceBrowser:didFindService:moreComing:`.

Answer to Question 4

The method name is `netServiceBrowser:didRemoveService:moreComing:`.

CHAPTER 17 EXERCISE SOLUTIONS

Answer to Question 1

The two certificates are the development certificate and the SSL certificate for the provider application.

Answer to Question 2

This is to ensure that you have the private and public key pair of the certificate.

Answer to Question 3

The method is `registerForRemoteNotificationTypes:`.

Answer to Question 4

The device token is used to uniquely identify the recipient of the push notification and is needed by the APNs server.

Answer to Question 5

The event is `application:didReceiveRemoteNotification:`.

CHAPTER 18 EXERCISE SOLUTIONS

Answer to Question 1

The property is `showsUserLocation`.

Answer to Question 2

The protocol is `MKMapViewDelegate`.

Answer to Question 3

The method is `startUpdatingLocation`.

Answer to Question 4

The method is `startUpdatingHeading`.

Answer to Question 5

The class is `MKReverseGeocoder`.

Getting Around in Xcode

Xcode is the integrated development environment (IDE) that Apple uses for developing Mac OS X, iPhone, and iPad applications. It is a suite of applications that includes a set of compilers, documentation, and Interface Builder (discussed in Appendix C).

Using Xcode, you can build your iPad applications from the comfort of an intelligent text editor, coupled with many different tools to help debug your iPad applications. If you are new to Xcode, this appendix can serve as a useful guide to get you started quickly. Appendix C covers the Interface Builder in more detail.

LAUNCHING XCODE

The easiest way to launch Xcode is to type **Xcode** in the textbox of Spotlight. Alternatively, you can launch Xcode by navigating to the `/Developer/Applications/` folder and double-clicking the Xcode icon.

 NOTE *For convenience, you can also drag the Xcode icon to the Dock so that in future you can launch it directly from the Dock.*

At the time of writing, the version of Xcode available is version 3.2.2.

Project Types Supported

Xcode supports the building of iPhone, iPad, and Mac OS X applications. When you create a new project in Xcode (which you do by choosing File ➪ New Project), you see the New Project dialog, as shown in Figure B-1.

As you can see, you have two main project types to create (iPhone OS and Mac OS X). Under the iPhone OS category, you have the Application and Library items.

FIGURE B-1

Select the Application item, and you will see all the different project types you can create, as follows:

➤   Navigation-based Application (iPhone only)

➤   OpenGL ES Application (iPhone and iPad)

➤   Split View-based Application (iPad only)

➤   Tab Bar Application (iPhone and iPad)

➤   Utility Application (iPhone only)

➤   View-based Application (iPhone and iPad)

➤   Window-based Application (iPhone and iPad)

For the Navigation-based Application, Split View-based Application, Utility Application, and Window-based project types, you have the option to use Core Data for storage.

   NOTE *Core Data is part of the Cocoa API that was first introduced to the iPhone SDK 3.0. It is basically a framework for manipulating data without worrying about the details of storage and retrieval. Core Data is beyond the scope of this book.*

Select the project type you want to create and click the Choose button. Then name the project.

When the project is created, Xcode displays all the files that make up your project (see Figure B-2).

Toolbar   Detail View

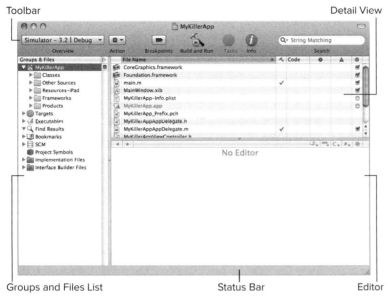

Groups and Files List   Status Bar   Editor

FIGURE B-2

The Xcode window is divided into five sections:

➤ **Toolbar**: Displays the buttons for commonly performed actions.

➤ **Groups and Files List**: Displays the files in a project. Files are grouped into folders and categories for better management.

➤ **Status Bar**: Displays the status information about the current action.

➤ **Detail View**: Displays the files contained in the folders and groups selected in the Groups and Files List section.

➤ **Editor**: Displays the appropriate editor showing the file currently selected.

To edit a code file, click the filename of a file to open the appropriate editor. For example, if you click an .h or .m file, the code editor in which you can edit your source code is displayed (see Figure B-3).

Click a .plist file, and the XML Property List editor launches (see Figure B-4).

Customizing the Toolbar

The Xcode window contains the toolbar section, in which you can place your favorite items for quick access. By default, the following items are placed in the toolbar:

➤ **Overview**: Enables you to select target settings such as the active SDK (iPhone OS version and device versus Simulator) as well as active configurations (Debug or Release).

➤ **Action**: Specifies the action you can perform with a selected item.

➤ **Breakpoints**: Toggles the Build and Run item (see next item) to Build and Debug so that you can attach a debugger to the application.

➤ **Build and Run:** Lets you build and deploy the application.

➤ **Tasks:** Stops any operation in progress.

➤ **Info:** Displays the detailed information of a selected item.

➤ **Search:** Filters the items currently displayed in the Detail View section.

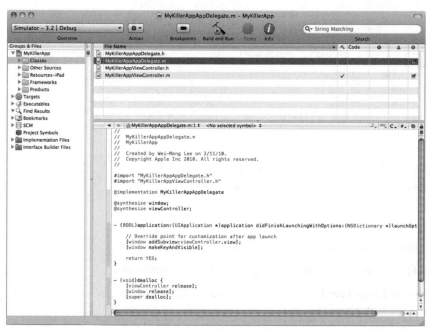

FIGURE B-3

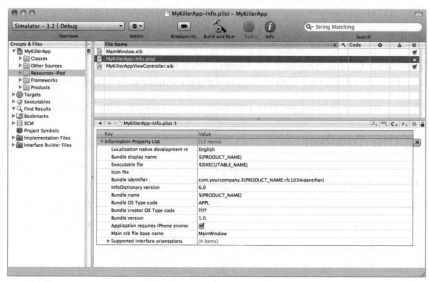

FIGURE B-4

You can add items to the toolbar by right-clicking the toolbar and selecting Customize Toolbar. A drop-down pane then shows all the items that you can add to the toolbar (see Figure B-5). To add an item to the toolbar, drag it directly onto the toolbar.

FIGURE B-5

Code Sense

One of the most common features of modern IDE is *code completion*, which makes the IDE automatically try to complete the statement you are typing based on the current context. In Xcode, the code-completion feature is known as Code Sense. For example, type the letters **uial** in a method, such as the `viewDidLoad()` method, and Code Sense automatically suggests the `UIAlertView` class (see Figure B-6; notice that the suggested characters are displayed in gray). To accept the suggested word, simply press the Tab or Enter key, or Ctrl-/.

FIGURE B-6

You can also invoke the Code Sense feature by pressing the Esc key (or press F5). Code Sense displays a list of words starting with the letters you have typed (see Figure B-7).

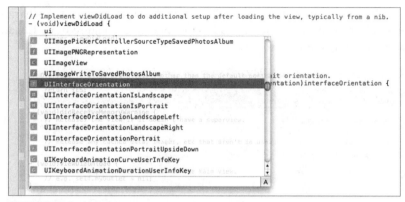

FIGURE B-7

Xcode automatically recognizes the code you are typing and inserts the relevant parameters' place-holders. For example, if you invoke the methods of an object, Xcode inserts the placeholders of the various parameters. Figure B-8 shows an example of the placeholders inserted for the UIAlertView object after you type **"i"**. To accept the placeholders for the various parameters, press the Tab key (you can also press the Enter key, or Ctrl-/).

```
// Implement viewDidLoad to do additional setup after loading the view, typically from a nib.
- (void)viewDidLoad {
    UIAlertView *alert = [[UIAlertView alloc] initWithTitle:(NSString *)title message:(NSString *)message delegate
    [super viewDidLoad];
}
```

FIGURE B-8

Press Ctrl-/ to move to each parameter placeholder and then enter a value. Alternatively, click each placeholder and type over it.

Running the Application

To execute an application, you first select the active SDK to use. You also choose whether you want to test it on a real device or use the included iPhone Simulator (the iPhone Simulator 3.2 emulates the iPad). You do so by selecting from the Overview list (see Figure B-9).

To run the application, press Command-R, and Xcode builds and deploys the application onto the selected device or simulator.

FIGURE B-9

DEBUGGING YOUR APPLICATIONS

Debugging your iPad applications is an essential part of your development journey. Xcode includes debugger utilities that help you trace and examine your code as you execute your application. The following sections show some of the tips and tricks that you can employ when developing your iPad applications.

Errors

When you try to run your application, Xcode first tries to build the project before it can deploy the application onto the real device or simulator. Any syntax errors that Xcode detects are immediately highlighted in red. Figure B-10 shows Xcode highlighting a syntax error. The error with the code block is the missing brace symbol ([) for the [[UIAlertView alloc] statement:

```
UIAlertView *alert = [UIAlertView alloc] initWithTitle:@"Hello World!"
                                               message:@"Hello, my World"
                                              delegate:self
                                       cancelButtonTitle:@"OK"
                                       otherButtonTitles:nil];
```

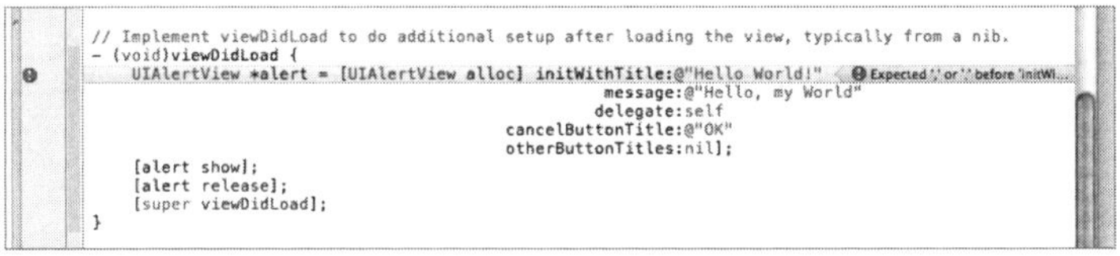

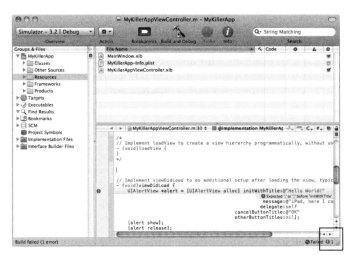

FIGURE B-10

You can also click the error icon located at the bottom right corner of the window to view the list of errors (see Figure B-11).

FIGURE B-11

Warnings

Objective-C is a case-sensitive language, and therefore one of the most common mistakes that beginners make is mixing up the capitalization for some of the method names. Consider the following:

```
- (void)viewDidLoad {
    UIAlertView *alert = [[UIAlertView alloc] initwithTitle:@"Hello World!"
                                            message:@"Hello, my World"
                                            delegate:self
                                    cancelButtonTitle:@"OK"
                                    otherButtonTitles:nil];

    [alert show];
    [alert release];
    [super viewDidLoad];
}
```

Can you spot the error? Syntactically, the preceding statements have no problem. However, one of the parameters appears with the wrong capitalization. It turns out that `initwithTitle:` was misspelled — it should be `initWithTitle:` (note the capital "W"). When you compile the program, Xcode will not flag the preceding code as an error; instead, it issues a warning message (see Figure B-12).

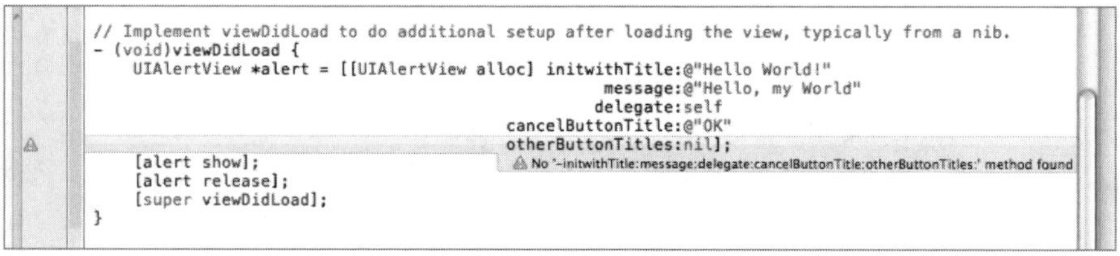

FIGURE B-12

Pay special attention to a warning message in Xcode, and check that the method name is spelled correctly, including the capitalization. Failing to do so may result in a runtime exception.

When a runtime exception occurs, the best way to troubleshoot the error is to open the Debugger Console window by pressing Shift-Command-R. The Debugger Console window displays all the debugging information that is printed when Xcode debugs your application. The window usually contains the clue that helps you determine exactly what went wrong behind the scenes. Figure B-13 shows the content of the Debugger Console window when an exception occurs. To find out the cause of the crash, scroll to the bottom of the window and look for the section displayed in bold. In this case, note the reason stated — the problem is with the `UIAlertView` object.

Setting Breakpoints

Setting breakpoints in your code is helpful in debugging your application. Breakpoints allow you to execute your code line by line and examine the values of variables so you can check that they perform as expected.

In Xcode, you set a breakpoint by clicking the left column of the code editor — a breakpoint arrow will appear (see Figure B-14).

FIGURE B-13

```
- (void)willRotateToInterfaceOrientation:(UIInterfaceOrientation)toInterfaceOrientation
                                duration:(NSTimeInterval)duration {

    if (toInterfaceOrientation == UIInterfaceOrientationPortrait) {
        btn.frame = CGRectMake(20,20,280,37);
    } else {
        btn.frame = CGRectMake(180,243,280,37);
    }
}
```

FIGURE B-14

 NOTE *You can toggle the state of a breakpoint by clicking it to enable or disable it. Breakpoints displayed in dark blue are enabled; those displayed in light blue are disabled. To remove a breakpoint, click on one and drag it out of its resting place. It will disappear into a puff of smoke!*

After you have set breakpoints in your application, press Command-Y to debug your application. The code will stop at your breakpoints.

 NOTE *If you press Command-R to run the application, your code will not stop at the breakpoints.*

When the application reaches the breakpoint you have set, Xcode indicates the current line of execution with a red arrow (see Figure B-15).

```
- (void)willRotateToInterfaceOrientation:(UIInterfaceOrientation)toInterfaceOrientation
                                duration:(NSTimeInterval)duration {

    if (toInterfaceOrientation == UIInterfaceOrientationPortrait) {
        btn.frame = CGRectMake(20,20,280,37);
    } else {
        btn.frame = CGRectMake(180,243,280,37);
    }
}
```

FIGURE B-15

At this juncture, you can do several things:

➤ Step Into (Shift-Command-I) — Step into the statements in a function/method.

➤ Step Over (Shift-Command-O) — Execute all the statements in a function /method and continue to the next statement.

➤ Step Out (Shift-Command-T) — Finish executing all the statements in a function or method and continue to the next statement after the function call.

➤ If you want to resume the execution of your application, press Option-Command-P.

➤ You can also examine the values of variables and objects by clicking the Show Debugger button (shown enclosed by the box in Figure B-16). You can also move your mouse over the objects and variables you are interested in to view their values.

FIGURE B-16

Using NSLog

In addition to setting breakpoints to trace the flow of your application, you can use the NSLog() function to print debugging messages to the Debugger Console window. The following statement prints a message to the Debugger Console window when the application changes orientation:

```
- (void)willRotateToInterfaceOrientation:
(UIInterfaceOrientation) toInterfaceOrientation
duration: (NSTimeInterval) duration {

    NSLog(@"In the willRotateToInterfaceOrientation:duration: event handler");

    UIInterfaceOrientation destOrientation = toInterfaceOrientation;
    if (destOrientation == UIInterfaceOrientationPortrait) {
        btn.frame = CGRectMake(20,20,280,37);
    }
    else {
        btn.frame = CGRectMake(180,243,280,37);
    }
}
```

Figure B-17 shows the output in the Debugger Console window (press Shift-Command-R to display it).

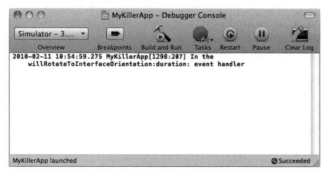

FIGURE B-17

Documentation

During the course of your development, you often need to check on the various methods, classes, and objects used in the iPhone SDK. The best way to check them out is to refer to the documentation. Xcode allows you to quickly and easily browse the definitions of classes, properties, and methods through the use of the Option key. To view the help documentation of an item, simply press the Option key. The cursor changes to a cross-hair. Double-click the item you want to check out, and a small window showing the summary of the selected item appears (see Figure B-18). Clicking on the icon on the top-right corner of the window displays the full Developer Documentation window.

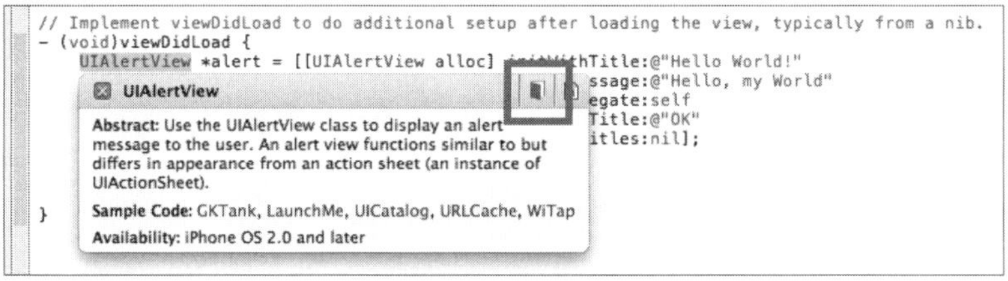

FIGURE B-18

Getting Around in Interface Builder

Interface Builder is one of the tools that comes with the iPhone SDK. It is a visual design tool that you can use to build the user interface of your iPad applications. Although not strictly required for the development of your iPad applications, Interface Builder plays an integral role in your journey of learning about iPad application development. This appendix covers some of the important features of Interface Builder.

.XIB WINDOW

The most direct way to launch Interface Builder is to double-click any of the .xib files in your Xcode project. For example, if you have created a View-based Application project, there are two .xib files in the Resources-iPad folder of Xcode. Double-clicking either of them launches Interface Builder.

When Interface Builder is launched, the first window that you see has the same name as your .xib file (see Figure C-1).

Within this window are several items, and depending on what you have double-clicked, you should see some of the following items:

➤ File's Owner

➤ First Responder

➤ View, Table View, Window, and so on

➤ Some View Controllers and delegates

FIGURE C-1

By default, the `.xib` window is displayed in icon mode. But you can also switch to list mode, where you can view some of the items in more detail. For example, Figure C-2 shows that when viewed in list mode, the View item displays a hierarchy of views contained within it.

FIGURE C-2

DESIGNING THE VIEW

To design the user interface of your application, you typically double-click the View (or Table view or other) item on the `.xib` window to visually display the window. To populate your View window with views, you drag and drop objects listed in the Library window (see the Library section for more information on the Library window). Figure C-3 shows a Label view being dropped onto the View window.

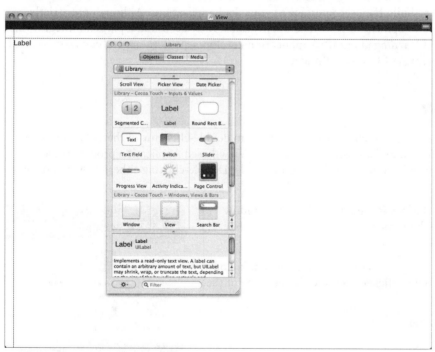

FIGURE C-3

As you position the view on the window, gridlines appear to guide you.

The View window also allows you to rotate the orientation of your view so that you can see how your view looks when it is rotated to the landscape orientation (see the box in Figure C-4; clicking on the arrow in the upper-right corner rotates the window).

FIGURE C-4

INTERFACE BUILDER KEYBOARD SHORTCUTS

As you add more views to the View window, you realize that you are spending a lot of time figuring out their actual sizes and locations with respect to other views. So here are some tips to make your life easier:

➤ To make a copy of a view on the View window, simply Option-click and drag a view.

➤ If a view is currently selected, pressing the Option key and then moving the mouse over the view displays that view's size information (see left of Figure C-5). If you move the mouse over another view, it displays the distance between that view and the selected view (see right of Figure C-5).

FIGURE C-5

INSPECTOR WINDOW

To customize the various attributes and properties of views, Interface Builder provides an Inspector window that is divided into four panes:

➤   Attributes Inspector

➤   Connection Inspector

➤   Size Inspector

➤   Identity Inspector

You can invoke the Inspector window by choosing Tools ➪ Library.

The following sections discuss each of the Inspector panes in more details.

Attributes Inspector Window

The Attributes Inspector window (see Figure C-6) is where you configure the attributes of views in Interface Builder. The window content is dynamic and changes depending on what is selected in the View window.

FIGURE C-6

You open the Attributes Inspector window by choosing Tools ⇨ Attributes Inspector.

Connections Inspector Window

The Connections Inspector window (see Figure C-7) is where you connect the outlets and actions to your View Controller in Interface Builder. Its content is dynamic and changes depending on what is selected in the View window.

Open the Connections Inspector window by choosing Tools ⇨ Connections Inspector.

Size Inspector Window

The Size Inspector window (see Figure C-8) is where you configure the size and positioning of views in Interface Builder.

Open it by selecting Tools ⇨ Size Inspector.

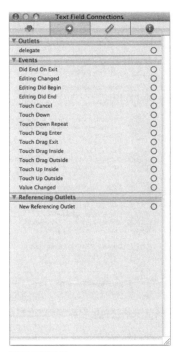

FIGURE C-7

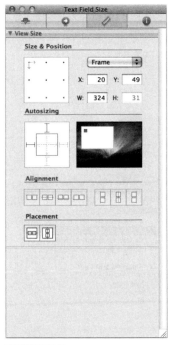

FIGURE C-8

FIGURE C-9

Identity Inspector Window

The Identity Inspector window (see Figure C-9) is where you configure the various properties of your selected view.

Open the Identity Inspector window by choosing Tools ⇨ Identity Inspector.

LIBRARY

The Library (Tools ⇨ Library) contains a set of views that you can use to build the user interface of your iPad applications. Figure C-10 shows part of the Library's set of views.

You can configure the Library to display its views in different modes (see Figure C-11):

➤ Icons

➤ Icons and Labels (which is the mode shown in Figure C-10)

➤ Icons and Descriptions

➤ Small Icons and Labels

Figure C-12 shows the Library displayed in the Icons and Descriptions mode.

FIGURE C-10

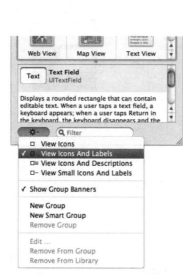

FIGURE C-11

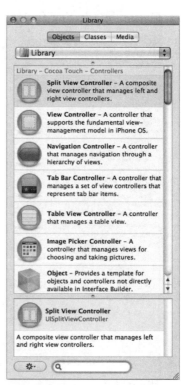

FIGURE C-12

OUTLETS AND ACTIONS

Outlets and actions are fundamental mechanisms in iPad programming through which your code can connect to the views in your user interface (UI). When you use outlets, your code can programmatically reference the views on your UI, with actions serving as event handlers that handle the various events fired by the various views.

Although you can write code to connect actions and outlets, Interface Builder simplifies the process by allowing you to use the drag-and-drop technique.

Creating Outlets and Actions

To create an action in Interface Builder, open the Library window and click the Classes tab. Select the View Controller that you are working on and then click the Actions tab at the lower part of the window (see Figure C-13; in this example the selected View Controller is `HelloWorldViewController`).

Click the plus sign (+) button and name your action. Remember to include the colon (:) character at the end of the action name if you want to pass additional arguments in to the action (useful when you have multiple views connecting to an action). The colon character allows the action to have an input parameter of type `id` (which you can change to other types), like this:

```
-(IBAction) myAction1:(id) sender;
```

Be sure to note that in Figure C-13 the action is listed under the `HelloWorldViewController.xib` header. This is because the action is defined within Interface Builder.

Likewise, click the Outlets tab to add an outlet to your View Controller. Click the plus sign (+) button in the Outlets section to create an outlet (see Figure C-14). It is always good to denote the specific type for the outlet that you are defining.

FIGURE C-13

FIGURE C-14

NOTE *You can delete outlets and actions that you have created in Interface Builder by clicking on the minus (–) button.*

Using the preceding sample, if you want the outlet to connect to a UITextField view, you should specify the type of myOutlet1 as UITextField rather than id.

After the outlet and action are created using Interface Builder, you still need to define them in the .h file, like this:

```
#import <UIKit/UIKit.h>

@interface HelloWorldViewController : UIViewController {

IBOutlet UITextField *myOutlet1;

}

-(IBAction) myAction1:(id) sender;

@end
```

 NOTE *Whether you are in Xcode or Interface Builder, be sure to save the file after you have modified it.*

In the Library window in Interface Builder, you can see that both the outlet and action are now listed under the HelloWorldViewController.h header (see Figure C-15). If you click the plus sign (+) button again, another outlet or action will be listed under the HelloWorldViewController.xib header until you define them in the .h file.

 NOTE *It is not strictly necessary to create your actions and outlets in Interface Builder. However, doing so allows you to connect the views before writing any code. This is useful if you have designers and developers working on different aspects of the project.*

 NOTE *Outlets and actions defined in the .h file cannot be deleted in the Library window by clicking the minus sign (–) button.*

Actually, a much simpler way is to define the outlets and actions directly in the .h files of your View Controllers first. That saves you the trouble of defining them in the Library window of the Interface Builder.

Alternatively, if you do not want to manually type in the declaration of the outlets and actions in your View Controller class, you can create the outlets and actions in Interface Builder (as just described), select the File's Owner item, and then choose File ➪ Write Class Files. Doing so causes Interface Builder to generate the code for the outlets and actions that you have added in the Library window. When you use this option, Interface Builder first asks whether you want to replace or merge with the View Controller files (if they are already present). Replacing the files causes the existing files to be replaced and all the changes you have made to the file will be gone. Hence, this is not the recommended option. Merging the files enables you to select the segments of code that you want to merge into your existing files. This is the safer option.

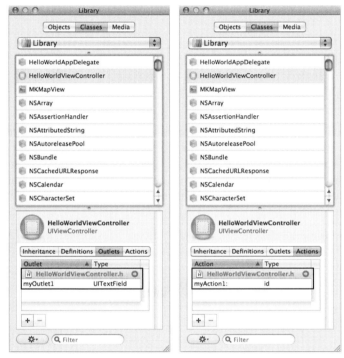

FIGURE C-15

Take note that for code generated by Interface Builder, the outlets will not be exposed as properties. You must manually add the code to expose the properties using the @property keyword and the @synthesize keyword to generate the getters and setters for the properties.

 NOTE In general, it is always easier to define the outlets and actions manually rather than have Interface Builder do it for you.

Connecting Outlets and Actions

You have two options for connecting the outlets and actions to the views; they are discussed in the following sections.

Method 1

For connecting outlets, Control-click and drag the File's Owner item to the view to which you want to connect (see Figure C-16).

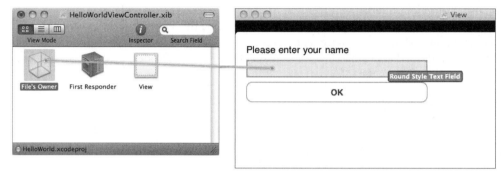

FIGURE C-16

When you release the mouse button, a list appears from which you can select the correct outlet. When defining your outlets (in the Library window, or in code), remember that you can specify the type of view your outlet is referring to. When you release the mouse button, Interface Builder lists only the outlets that match the type of view you have selected. For example, if you defined myOutlet1 as UIButton and you Control-click and drag the File's Owner item to a Text Field view on the View window, myOutlet1 does not appear in the list of outlets.

For connecting actions, Control-click and drag the view to the File's Owner item in the .xib window (see Figure C-17).

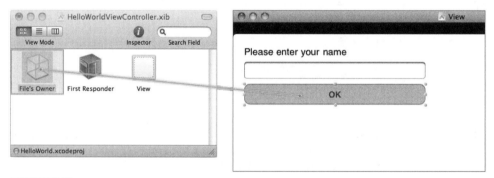

FIGURE C-17

When you release the mouse button, a list appears from which you can select the correct action.

When you have connected the outlets and actions, a good practice is to view all the connections in the File's Owner item by right-clicking it. Figure C-18 shows that the File's Owner item is connected to the Text Field view through the myOutlet1 outlet, and the Button's Touch Up Inside event is connected to the myAction1: action.

How does the Button know that it is the `Touch Up Inside` event (and not other events) that should be connected to the `myAction1:` action when you Control-click and drag the Button to the File's Owner item? Well, the `Touch Up Inside` event is such a commonly used event that it is the default event selected when you perform a Control-click and drag action. What if you want to connect other events other than the default event? The second method shows you how.

FIGURE C-18

Method 2

An alternative method for connecting outlets is to right-click the File's Owner item and connect the outlet to the view directly (see Figure C-19).

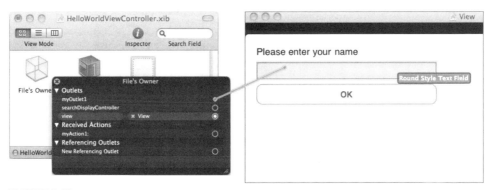

FIGURE C-19

For connecting actions, you can connect the relevant action with the views to which you want to connect (see Figure C-20). When you release the mouse button, the list of available events appears, and you can select the event you want.

Alternatively, you can right-click the view in question and connect the relevant events to the File's Owner item (see Figure C-21). When you release the mouse button, a list of actions appears. Select the action to which you want to connect.

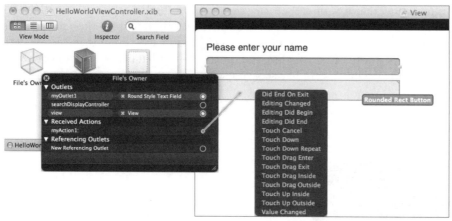

FIGURE C-20

FIGURE C-21

Crash Course in Objective-C

Objective-C is an object-oriented programming language used by Apple primarily for programming Mac OS X and iPhone/iPad applications. It is an extension to the standard ANSI C language and hence it should be an easy language to pick up if you are already familiar with the C programming language. This appendix assumes that you already have some background in C programming and focuses on the object-oriented aspects of the language. If you are coming from a Java or .NET background, many of the concepts should be familiar to you; you just have to understand the syntax of Objective-C and in particular pay attention to the section on memory management.

Objective-C source code files are contained in two types of files:

➤   .h — header files

➤   .m — implementation files

For the discussions that follow, assume that you have created a View-based Application project using Xcode and added an empty class named SomeClass to your project.

DIRECTIVES

If you observe the content of the SomeClass.h file, you will notice that at the top of the file is an #import statement:

```
#import <Foundation/Foundation.h>

@interface SomeClass : NSObject {

}

@end
```

The `#import` statement is known as a *preprocessor directive*. In C and C++, you use the `#include` preprocessor directive to include a file's content with the current source. In Objective-C, you use the `#import` statement to do the same, except that the compiler ensures that the file is included at most only once. To import a header file from one of the frameworks, you specify the header filename using angle brackets (`<>`) in the `#import` statement. To import a header file from within your project, you use the `"` and `"` characters, as in the case of the `SomeClass.m` file:

```
#import "SomeClass.h"

@implementation SomeClass

@end
```

CLASSES

In Objective-C, you will spend a lot of time dealing with classes and objects. Hence it is important that you understand how classes are declared and defined in Objective-C.

@interface

To declare a class, you use the `@interface` compiler directive, like this:

```
@interface SomeClass : NSObject {

}
```

This is done in the header file (`.h`) and the class declaration contains no implementation. The preceding code declares a class named `SomeClass`, and this class inherits from the base class named `NSObject`.

 NOTE *While you typically put your code declaration in an `.h` file, you can also put it inside an `.m` if need be. This is usually done for small projects.*

 NOTE *`NSObject` is the root class of most Objective-C classes. It defines the basic interface of a class and contains methods common to all classes that inherit from it. `NSObject` also provides the standard memory management and initialization framework used by most objects in Objective-C as well as reflection and type operations.*

In a typical View Controller class, the class inherits from the `UIViewController` class, such as in the following:

```
@interface HelloWorldViewController : UIViewController {

}
```

@implementation

To implement a class declared in the header file, you use the `@implementation` compiler directive, like this:

```
#import "SomeClass.h"

@implementation SomeClass

@end
```

This is done in a separate file from the header file. In Objective-C, you define your class in an `.m` file. Note that the class definition ends with the `@end` compiler directive.

 NOTE As mentioned earlier, you can also put your declaration inside an `.m` file. Hence, in your `.m` file you would then have both the `@interface` and `@implementation` directives.

@class

If your class references another class defined in another file, you need to import the header file of that file before you can use it. Consider the following example where you have defined two classes — `SomeClass` and `AnotherClass`. If you are using an instance of `AnotherClass` from within `SomeClass`, you need to import the `AnotherClass.h` file, as in the following code snippet:

```
//---SomeClass.h---
#import <Foundation/Foundation.h>
#import "AnotherClass.h"

@interface SomeClass : NSObject {
    //---an object from AnotherClass---
    AnotherClass *anotherClass;
}
@end

//---AnotherClass.h---
#import <Foundation/Foundation.h>
#import "SomeClass.h"

@interface AnotherClass : NSObject {
}

@end
```

However, if within `AnotherClass` you want to create an instance of `SomeClass`, you will not be able to simply import `SomeClass.h` in `AnotherClass`, like this:

```
//---SomeClass.h---
#import <Foundation/Foundation.h>
```

```
#import "AnotherClass.h"

@interface SomeClass : NSObject {
    AnotherClass *anotherClass;
}

@end

//---AnotherClass.h---
#import <Foundation/Foundation.h>
#import "SomeClass.h" //---cannot simply import here---

@interface AnotherClass : NSObject {
    SomeClass *someClass;  //---using an instance of SomeClass---
}

@end
```

Doing so results in circular inclusion. To prevent that, Objective-C uses the `@class` compiler directive as a forward declaration to inform the compiler that the class you specified is a valid class. You usually use the `@class` compiler directive in the header file, and in the implementation file you can use the `@import` compiler directive to tell the compiler more about the content of the class that you are using.

Using the `@class` compiler directive, the program now looks like this:

```
//---SomeClass.h---
#import <Foundation/Foundation.h>

@class AnotherClass;  //---forward declaration---

@interface SomeClass : NSObject {
    AnotherClass *anotherClass;
}
@end

//---AnotherClass.h---
#import <Foundation/Foundation.h>

@class SomeClass;      //---forward declaration---

@interface AnotherClass : NSObject {
    SomeClass *someClass;
}

@end
```

 NOTE Another notable reason to use forward declaration where possible is that it will reduce your compile times because the compiler does not need to traverse as many included header files and their includes, etc.

Class Instantiation

To create an instance of a class, you typically use the `alloc` keyword (more on this in the Memory Management section) to allocate memory for the object and then return it to a variable of the class type:

```
SomeClass *someClass = [SomeClass alloc];
```

In Objective-C, you need to prefix an object name with the `*` character when you declare an object. If you are declaring a variable of primitive type (such as `float`, `int`, `CGRect`, `NSInteger`, and so on), the `*` character is not required. Here are some examples:

```
CGRect frame;    //---CGRect is a structure---
int number;      //---int is a primitive type---
NSString *str    //---NSString is a class
```

Besides specifying the returning class type, you can also use the `id` type, like this:

```
id someClass = [SomeClass alloc];
id str;
```

The `id` type means that the variable can refer to any type of object and hence the `*` is implicitly implied.

Fields

Fields are the data members of objects. For example, the following code shows that `SomeClass` has three fields — `anotherClass`, `rate`, and `name`:

```
#import <Foundation/Foundation.h>

@class AnotherClass;

@interface SomeClass : NSObject {
    AnotherClass *anotherClass;
    float rate;
    NSString *name;
}

@end
```

Access Privileges

By default, the access privilege of all fields is `@protected`. However, the access privilege can also be `@public` or `@private`. The following list shows the various access privileges:

➤ `@private` — visible only to the class that declares it

➤ `@public` — visible to all classes

➤ `@protected` — visible to the class that declares it as well as to inheriting classes

Using the example shown in the previous section, if you now try to access the fields in `SomeClass` from another class, such as `AnotherClass`, you will not be able to see them:

```
SomeClass *someClass = [SomeClass alloc];
someClass->rate = 5;                //---rate is declared protected---
someClass->name = @"Wei-Meng Lee";  //---name is declared protected---
```

 NOTE *Observe that to access the fields in a class directly, you use the* `->` *operator.*

To make the `rate` and `name` visible outside the class, modify the `SomeClass.h` file by adding the `@public` compiler directive:

```
#import <Foundation/Foundation.h>

@class AnotherClass;

@interface SomeClass : NSObject {
    AnotherClass *anotherClass;

@public
    float rate;

@public
    NSString *name;
}

@end
```

The following two statements would now be valid:

```
someClass->rate = 5;                //---rate is declared protected---
someClass->name = @"Wei-Meng Lee";  //---name is declared protected---
```

Although you can access the fields directly, doing so goes against the design principles of object-oriented programming's rule of encapsulation. A better way is to encapsulate the two fields you want to expose in properties. Refer to the "Properties" section later in this appendix.

Methods

Methods are functions that are defined in a class. Objective-C supports two types of methods — instance methods and class methods.

Instance methods can be called only using an instance of the class. Instance methods are prefixed with the minus sign (-) character.

Class methods can be invoked directly using the class name and do not need an instance of the class in order to work. Class methods are prefixed with the plus sign (+) character.

NOTE *In some programming languages, such as C# and Java, class methods are known as static methods.*

The following code sample shows `SomeClass` with three instance methods and one class method declared:

```
#import <Foundation/Foundation.h>

@class AnotherClass;

@interface SomeClass : NSObject {
    AnotherClass *anotherClass;
    float rate;
    NSString *name;
}

//---instance methods---
-(void) doSomething;
-(void) doSomething:(NSString *) str;
-(void) doSomething:(NSString *) str withAnotherPara:(float) value;

//---class method---
+(void) alsoDoSomething;

@end
```

The following shows the implementation of the methods that were declared in the header file:

```
#import "SomeClass.h"

@implementation SomeClass

-(void) doSomething {
    //---implementation here---
}

-(void) doSomething:(NSString *) str {
    //---implementation here---
}

-(void) doSomething:(NSString *) str withAnotherPara:(float) value {
    //---implementation here---
}

+(void) alsoDoSomething {
    //---implementation here---
}

@end
```

To invoke the three instance methods, you first need to create an instance of the class and then call them using the instance created:

```
SomeClass *someClass = [SomeClass alloc];
[someClass doSomething];
[someClass doSomething:@"some text"];
[someClass doSomething:@"some text" withAnotherPara:9.0f];
```

Class methods can be called directly using the class name, as the following shows:

```
[SomeClass alsoDoSomething];
```

In general, you create instance methods when you need to perform some actions that are related to the particular instance of the class (that is, the object). For example, suppose you defined a class that represents the information of an employee. You may expose an instance method that allows you to calculate the overtime wage of an employee. In this case, you use an instance method because the calculation involves data specific to a particular employee object.

Class methods, on the other hand, are commonly used for defining helper methods. For example, you might have a class method called `GetOvertimeRate:` that returns the rates for working over-time. As all employees get the same rate for working overtime (assuming this is the case for your company), then there is no need to create instance methods and thus a class method will suffice.

The next section shows how to call methods with a varying number of parameters.

Message Sending (Calling Methods)

In Objective-C, you use the following syntax to call a method:

```
[object method];
```

Strictly speaking, in Objective-C you do not call a method; you send a message to an object. The message to be passed to an object is resolved during runtime and is not enforced at compile time. This is why the compiler does not stop you from running your program even though you may have misspelled the name of a method. It does try to warn you that the target object may not respond to your message, though, because the target object will simply ignore the message. Figure D-1 shows the warning by the compiler when one of the parameters for the `UIAlertView`'s initializer is misspelled (the `cancelButtonsTitle:` should be `cancelButtonTitle:`).

 NOTE *For the ease of understanding, I use the more conventional term of "calling a method" to refer to Objective-C's message sending mechanism.*

```
-(IBAction) buttonClicked: (id) sender{
    UIAlertView *alert = [[UIAlertView alloc] initWithTitle:@"Action invoked!"
                                                   message:@"Button clicked!"
                                                  delegate:self
                                         cancelButtonsTitle:@"OK"
                                          otherButtonTitles:nil];
        ⚠ warning: no '-initWithTitle:message:delegate:cancelButtonsTitle:otherButtonTitles:' method found
           (Messages without a matching method signature will be assumed to return 'id' and accept '...' as arguments.)
```

FIGURE D-1

Using the example from the previous section, the doSomething method has no parameter:

```
-(void) doSomething {
    //---implementation here---
}
```

Therefore, you can call it like this:

```
[someClass doSomething];
```

If a method has one or more inputs, you call it using the following syntax:

```
[object method:input1];                       //---one input---
[object method:input1 andSecondInput:input2]; //---two inputs---
```

The interesting thing about Objective-C is the way you call a method with multiple inputs. Using the earlier example:

```
-(void) doSomething:(NSString *) str withAnotherPara:(float) value {
    //---implementation here---
}
```

The name of the preceding method is doSomething:withAnotherPara:.

It is important to note the names of methods and to differentiate those that have parameters from those that do not. For example, doSomething refers to a method with no parameter, whereas doSomething: refers to a method with one parameter, and doSomething:withAnotherPara: refers to a method with two parameters. The presence or absence of colons in a method name dictates which method is invoked during runtime. This is important when passing method names as arguments, particularly when using the @selector (discussed in the Selectors section) notation to pass them to a delegate or notification event.

Method calls can also be nested, as the following example shows:

```
NSString *str = [[NSString alloc] initWithString:@"Hello World"];
```

Here, you first call the alloc class method of the NSString class and then call the initWithString: method of the returning result from the alloc method, which is of type id, a generic C type that Objective-C uses for an arbitrary object.

In general, you should not nest more than three levels because anything more than that makes the code difficult to read.

Properties

Properties allow you to expose your fields in your class so that you can control how values are set or returned. In the earlier example (in the Access Privileges section), you saw that you can directly access the fields of a class using the -> operator. However, this is not the ideal way and you should ideally expose your fields as properties.

Prior to Objective-C 2.0, programmers had to declare methods to make the fields accessible to other classes, like this:

```
#import <Foundation/Foundation.h>

@class AnotherClass;

@interface SomeClass : NSObject {
    AnotherClass *anotherClass;
    float rate;
    NSString *name;
}

//---expose the rate field---
-(float) rate;                          //---get the value of rate---
-(void) setRate:(float) value;          //---set the value of rate

//---expose the name field---
-(NSString *) name;                     //---get the value of name---
-(void) setName:(NSString *) value;     //---set the value of name---

@end
```

These methods are known as *getters* and *setters* (or sometimes better known as *accessors* and *mutators*). The implementation of these methods may look like this:

```
#import "SomeClass.h"

@implementation SomeClass

-(float) rate {
    return rate;
}

-(void) setRate:(float) value {
    rate = value;
}

-(NSString *) name {
    return name;
}

-(void) setName:(NSString *) value {
    [value retain];
    [name release];
    name = value;
}

@end
```

To set the value of these properties, you need to call the methods prefixed with the `set` keyword:

```
SomeClass *sc = [[SomeClass alloc] init];
[sc setRate:5.0f];
[sc setName:@"Wei-Meng Lee"];
```

Alternatively, you can use the dot notation introduced in Objective-C 2.0:

```
SomeClass *sc = [[SomeClass alloc] init];
sc.rate = 5;
sc.name = @"Wei-Meng Lee";
```

To obtain the values of properties, you can either call the methods directly or use the dot notation in Objective-C 2.0:

```
NSLog([sc name]); //---call the method---
NSLog(sc.name);   //---dot notation
```

To make a property read only, simply remove the method prefixed with the `set` keyword.

Notice that within the `setName:` method, you have various statements using the `retain` and `release` keywords. These keywords relate to memory management in Objective-C; you learn more about them in the "Memory Management" section, later in this appendix.

In Objective-C 2.0, you don't need to define getters and setters in order to expose fields as properties. You can do so via the `@property` and `@synthesize` compiler directives. Using the same example, you can use the `@property` to expose the `rate` and `name` fields as properties, like this:

```
#import <Foundation/Foundation.h>

@class AnotherClass;

@interface SomeClass : NSObject {
    AnotherClass *anotherClass;
    float rate;
    NSString *name;
}

@property float rate;
@property (retain, nonatomic) NSString *name;

@end
```

The first `@property` statement defines `rate` to be a property. The second statement defines `name` as a property as well, but it also specifies the behavior of this property. In this case, it indicates the behavior as `retain` and `nonatomic`, which you learn more about in the section on memory management later in this appendix. In particular, `nonatomic` means that the property is not accessed in a thread-safe manner. This is alright if you are not writing multi-threaded applications. Most of the time, you will use the `retain` and `nonatomic` combination when declaring properties.

In the implementation file, rather than define the getter and setter methods, you can simply use the `@synthesize` keyword to get the compiler to automatically generate the getters and setters for you:

```
#import "SomeClass.h"

@implementation SomeClass

@synthesize rate, name;

@end
```

As shown, you can combine several properties using a single `@synthesize` keyword. However, you can also separate them into individual statements:

```
@synthesize rate;
@synthesize name;
```

You can now use your properties as usual:

```
//---setting using setRate---
[sc setRate:5.0f];
[sc setName:@"Wei-Meng Lee"];

//---setting using dot notation---
sc.rate = 5;
sc.name = @"Wei-Meng Lee";

//---getting---
NSLog([sc name]); //---using the name method
NSLog(sc.name);   //---dot notation
```

To make a property read only, use the `readonly` keyword. The following statement makes the `name` property read only:

```
@property (readonly) NSString *name;
```

Initializers

When you create an instance of a class, you often initialize it at the same time. For example, in the earlier example (in the Class Instantiation section), you had this statement:

```
SomeClass *sc = [[SomeClass alloc] init];
```

The `alloc` keyword allocates memory for the object, and when an object is returned, the `init` method is called on the object to initialize the object. Recall that in `SomeClass`, you do not define a method named `init`. So where does the `init` method come from? It is actually defined in the `NSObject` class, which is the base class of most classes in Objective-C. The `init` method is known as an initializer.

If you want to create additional initializers, you can define methods that begin with the `init` word. (The use of the `init` word is more of a norm than a hard-and-fast rule.)

```
#import <Foundation/Foundation.h>

@class AnotherClass;

@interface SomeClass : NSObject {
    AnotherClass *anotherClass;
    float rate;
    NSString *name;
}

-(void) doSomething;
-(void) doSomething:(NSString *) str;
```

```
-(void) doSomething:(NSString *) str withAnotherPara:(float) value;

+(void) alsoDoSomething;

- (id)initWithName:(NSString *) n;
- (id)initWithName:(NSString *) n andRate:(float) r;

@property float rate;
@property (retain, nonatomic) NSString *name;

@end
```

The preceding example contains two additional initializers: `initWithName:` and `initWithName:andRate:`. You can provide the implementations for the two initializers as follows:

```
#import "SomeClass.h"

@implementation SomeClass

@synthesize rate, name;

- (id)initWithName:(NSString *) n {
    return [self initWithName:n andRate:0.0f];
}

- (id)initWithName:(NSString *) n andRate:(float) r {
    if (self = [super init]) {
        self.name = n;
        self.rate = r;
    }
    return self;
}

-(void) doSomething {
}

-(void) doSomething:(NSString *) str {
}

-(void) doSomething:(NSString *) str withAnotherPara:(float) value {
}

+(void) alsoDoSomething {
}

@end
```

Note that in the `initWithName:andRate:` initializer implementation, you first call the `init` initializer of the `super` (base) class so that its base class is properly initialized, which is necessary before you can initialize the current class:

```
- (id)initWithName:(NSString *) n andRate:(float) r {
    if (self = [super init]) {
        //...
```

```
        //...
    }
    return self;
}
```

The rule for defining an initializer is simple: If a class is initialized properly, it should return a reference to `self` (hence the `id` type). If it fails, it should return `nil`.

For the `initWithName:` initializer implementation, notice that it calls the `initWithName:andRate:` initializer:

```
- (id)initWithName:(NSString *) n {
    return [self initWithName:n andRate:0.0f];
}
```

In general, if you have multiple initializers, each with different parameters, you should chain them by ensuring that they all call a single initializer that performs the call to the super class's `init` initializer. In Objective-C, the initializer that performs the call to the super class's `init` initializer is called the *designated initializer*.

 NOTE As a general guide, the designated initializer should be the one with the greatest number of parameters.

To use the initializers, you can now call them during instantiation time:

```
SomeClass *sc1 = [[SomeClass alloc] initWithName:@"Wei-Meng Lee" andRate:35];
SomeClass *sc2 = [[SomeClass alloc] initWithName:@"Wei-Meng Lee"];
```

MEMORY MANAGEMENT

Memory management in Objective-C programming (especially for iPad) is a very important topic that every iPad developer needs to be aware of. As do all other popular languages, Objective-C supports garbage collection, which helps to remove unused objects when they go out of scope and hence releases memory that can be reused. However, because of the severe overhead involved in implementing garbage collection, the iPad does not support garbage collection. This leaves you, the developer, to manually allocate and de-allocate the memory of objects when they are no longer needed.

This section discusses the various aspects of memory management on the iPad.

Reference Counting

To help you allocate and de-allocate memory for objects, the iPhone OS uses a scheme known as *reference counting* to keep track of objects to determine whether they are still needed or can be disposed of. Reference counting basically uses a counter for each object, and as each object is created, the count increases by 1. When an object is released, the count decreases by 1. When the count reaches 0, the memory associated with the object is reclaimed by the OS.

In Objective-C, a few important keywords are associated with memory management. The following sections take a look at each of them.

alloc

The `alloc` keyword allocates memory for an object that you are creating. You have seen it in almost all exercises in this book. An example is as follows:

```
NSString *str = [[NSString alloc] initWithString:@"Hello"];
```

In this example, you are creating an `NSString` object and instantiating it with a default string. When the object is created, the reference count of that object is 1. Because you are the one creating it, the object belongs to you, and it is your responsibility to release the memory when you are done with it.

 NOTE *See the "release" section for information on how to release an object.*

So how do you know when an object is owned, and by whom? Consider the following example:

```
NSString *str = [[NSString alloc] initWithString:@"Hello"];
NSString *str2 = str;
```

In this example, you use the `alloc` keyword for `str`, so you own `str`. Therefore, you need to release it when you no longer need it. However, `str2` is simply pointing to `str`, so you do not own `str2`, meaning that you need not release `str2` when you are done using it.

new

Besides using the `alloc` keyword to allocate memory for an object, you can also use the `new` keyword, like this:

```
NSString *str = [NSString new];
```

The `new` keyword is functionally equivalent to

```
NSString *str = [[NSString alloc] init];
```

As with the `alloc` keyword, using the `new` keyword makes you the owner of the object, so you need to release it when you are done with it.

retain

The `retain` keyword increases the reference count of an object by 1. Consider the previous example:

```
NSString *str = [[NSString alloc] initWithString:@"Hello"];
NSString *str2 = str;
```

In that example, you do not own `str2` because you do not use the `alloc` keyword on the object. When `str` is released, the `str2` will no longer be valid.

> **NOTE** How do you release `str2`, then? Well, it is autoreleased. See the
> "Convenience Method and Autorelease" section for more information.

If you want to make sure that `str2` is available even if `str` is released, you need to use the
`retain` keyword:

```
NSString *str = [[NSString alloc] initWithString:@"Hello"];
NSString *str2 = str;
[str2 retain];
[str release];
```

In the preceding case, the reference count for `str` is now 2. When you release `str`, `str2` will still be
valid. When you are done with `str2`, you need to release it manually.

> **NOTE** As a general rule, if you own an object (using `alloc` or `retain`), you
> need to release it.

release

When you are done with an object, you need to manually release it by using the `release` keyword:

```
NSString *str = [[NSString alloc] initWithString:@"Hello"];

//...do what you want with the object...

[str release];
```

When you use the `release` keyword on an object, it causes the reference count of that object to
decrease by 1. When the reference count reaches 0, the memory used by the object is released.

One important aspect to keep in mind when using the `release` keyword is that you cannot release
an object that is not owned by you. For example, consider the example used in the previous section:

```
NSString *str = [[NSString alloc] initWithString:@"Hello"];
NSString *str2 = str;
[str release];
[str2 release];  //---this is not OK as you do not own str2---
```

Attempting to release `str2` will result in a runtime error because you cannot release an object not
owned by you. However, if you use the `retain` keyword to gain ownership of an object, you do
need to use the `release` keyword:

```
NSString *str = [[NSString alloc] initWithString:@"Hello"];
NSString *str2 = str;
[str2 retain];
[str release];
[str2 release];  //---this is now OK as you now own str2---
```

Recall that earlier in the section on properties, you defined the `setName:` method, where you set the value of the `name` field:

```
-(void) setName:(NSString *) value {
    [value retain];
    [name release];
    name = value;
}
```

Notice that you first had to retain the `value` object, followed by releasing the `name` object and then finally assigning the `value` object to `name`. Why do you need to do that as opposed to the following?

```
-(void) setName:(NSString *) value {
    name = value;
}
```

Well, if you were using garbage collection, the preceding statement would be valid. However, because iPhone OS does not support garbage collection, the preceding statement will cause the original object referenced by the `name` object to be lost, thereby causing a memory leak. To prevent that leak, you first retain the `value` object to indicate that you wish to gain ownership of it; then you release the original object referenced by `name`. Finally, assign `value` to `name`:

```
[value retain];
[name release];
name = value;
```

Convenience Method and Autorelease

So far, you learned that all objects created using the `alloc` or `new` keywords are owned by you. Consider the following case:

```
NSString *str = [NSString stringWithFormat:@"%d", 4];
```

In this statement, do you own the `str` object? The answer is no, you don't. This is because the object is created using one of the *convenience methods* — static methods that are used for allocating and initializing objects directly. In the preceding case, you create an object but you do not own it. Because you do not own it, you cannot release it manually. In fact, objects created using this method are known as *autorelease* objects. All autorelease objects are temporary objects and are added to an *autorelease pool*. When the current method exits, all the objects contained within it are released. Autorelease objects are useful for cases in which you simply want to use some temporary variables and do not want to burden yourself with allocations and de-allocations.

The key difference between an object created using the `alloc` (or `new`) keyword and one created using a convenience method is that of ownership, as the following example shows:

```
NSString *str1 = [[NSString alloc] initWithFormat:@"%d", 4];
[str1 release]; //---this is ok because you own str1---

NSString *str2 = [NSString stringWithFormat:@"%d", 4];
[str2 release]; //---this is not ok because you don't own str2---
//---str2 will be removed automatically when the autorelease pool is activated---
```

UNDERSTANDING REFERENCE COUNTING USING AN ANALOGY

When you think of memory management using reference counting, it is always good to use a real-life analogy to put things into perspective.

Imagine a room in the library that you can reserve for studying purposes. Initially, the room is empty and hence the lights are off. When you reserve the room, the librarian increases a counter to indicate the number of persons using the room. This is similar to creating an object using the `alloc` keyword.

When you leave the room, the librarian decreases the counter, and if the counter is now 0, this means that the room is no longer being used and the lights can thus be switched off. This is similar to using the `release` keyword to release an object.

There may be times when you have booked the room and are the only one in the room (hence, the counter is 1) until a friend of yours comes along. He may simply come and visit you and therefore doesn't register with the librarian. Hence, the counter does not increase. Because he is just visiting you and hasn't booked the room, he has no rights to decide whether the lights should be switched off. This is similar to assigning an object to another variable without using the `alloc` keyword. In this case, if you leave the room (release), the lights will be switched off and your friend will have to leave.

Consider another situation in which you are using the room and another person also booked the room and shares it with you. In this case, the counter is now 2. If you leave the room, the counter goes down to 1, but the lights are still on because another person is in the room. This situation is similar when you create an object and assign it to another variable that uses the `retain` keyword. In such a situation, the object is released only when both objects release it.

If you want to take ownership of an object when using a convenience method, you can do so using the `retain` keyword:

```
NSString *str2 = [[NSString stringWithFormat:@"%d", 4] retain];
```

To release the object, you can use either the `autorelease` or `release` keyword. You learned earlier that the `release` keyword immediately decreases the reference count by 1 and that the object is immediately de-allocated from memory when the reference count reaches 0. In contrast, the `autorelease` keyword promises to decrease the reference count by 1, not *immediately*, but sometime later. It is like saying, "Well, I still need the object now, but later on I can let it go." The following code makes it clear:

```
NSString *str = [[NSString stringWithFormat:@"%d", 4] retain];
[str autorelease];   //you don't own it anymore; still available
NSlog(str);          //still accessible for now
```

 NOTE *After you have autoreleased an object, do not release it anymore.*

Note that the statement

```
NSString *str2 = [NSString stringWithFormat:@"%d", 4];
```

has the same effect as

```
NSString *str2 = @"4";
```

Although autorelease objects seem to make your life simple by automatically releasing objects that are no longer needed, you have to be careful when using them. Consider the following example:

```
for (int i=0; i<=99999; i++){
    NSString *str = [NSString stringWithFormat:@"%d", i];
    //...
    //...
}
```

You are creating an NSString object for each iteration of the loop. Because the objects are not released until the function exits, you may well run out of memory before the autorelease pool (see next section) can kick in to release the objects.

One way to solve this dilemma is to use an autorelease pool, as discussed in the next section.

REFERENCE COUNTING: THE ANALOGY CONTINUES

Continuing with our analogy of the room in the library, imagine that you are about to sign out with the librarian when you realize that you have left your books in the room. You tell the librarian that you are done with the room and want to sign out now, but because you left your books in the room, you tell the librarian not to switch off the lights yet so that you can go back to get the books. At a later time, the librarian can switch off the lights at his or her own choosing. This is the behavior of autoreleased objects.

Autorelease Pools

All autorelease objects are temporary objects and are added to an *autorelease pool*. When the current method exits, all the objects contained within it are released. However, sometimes you want to control how the autorelease pool is emptied, rather than wait for it to be called by the OS. To do so, you can create an instance of the NSAutoreleasePool class, like this:

```
for (int i=0; i<=99999; i++){
    NSAutoreleasePool *pool = [[NSAutoreleasePool alloc] init];
    NSString *str1 = [NSString stringWithFormat:@"%d", i];
    NSString *str2 = [NSString stringWithFormat:@"%d", i];
    NSString *str3 = [NSString stringWithFormat:@"%d", i];
    //...
    //...
    [pool release];
}
```

In this example, for each iteration of the loop, an `NSAutoreleasePool` object is created, and all the autorelease objects created within the loop — `str1`, `str2`, and `str3` — go into it. At the end of each iteration, the `NSAutoreleasePool` object is released so that all the objects contained within it are automatically released. This ensures that you have at most three autorelease objects in memory at any one time.

dealloc

You have learned that by using the `alloc` or the `new` keyword, you own the object that you have created. You have also seen how to release the objects you own using the `release` or `autorelease` keyword. So when is a good time for you to release them?

As a rule of thumb, you should release the objects as soon as you are done with them. So if you created an object in a method, you should release it before you exit the method. For properties, recall that you can use the `@property` compiler directive together with the `retain` keyword:

```
@property (retain, nonatomic) NSString *name;
```

Because the values of the property will be retained, it is important that you free it before you exit the application. A good place to do so is in the `dealloc` method of a class (such as a View Controller):

```
-(void) dealloc {
    [self.name release];    //---release the name property---
    [super dealloc];
}
```

The `dealloc` method of a class is fired whenever the reference count of its object reaches 0. Consider the following example:

```
SomeClass *sc1 = [[SomeClass alloc] initWithName:@"Wei-Meng Lee" andRate:35];
//...do something here…
[sc1 release];  //---reference count goes to 0; dealloc will be called---
```

The preceding example shows that when the reference count of `sc1` goes to 0 (when the `release` statement is called), the `dealloc` method defined within the class will be called. If you do not define this method in the class, its implementation in the base class will be called.

Memory Management Tips

Memory management is a tricky issue in iPad programming. Although there are tools that you can use to test for memory leaks, this section presents some simple things you can do to detect memory problems that might affect your application.

First, ensure that you implement the `didReceiveMemoryWarning` method in your View Controller:

```
- (void)didReceiveMemoryWarning {
    //---insert code here to free unused objects---
    [super didReceiveMemoryWarning];
}
```

The `didReceiveMemoryWarning` method will be called whenever your iPad runs out of memory. You should insert code in this method so that you can free resources/objects that you do not need.

In addition, you should also handle the `applicationDidReceiveMemoryWarning:` method in your application delegate:

```
- (void)applicationDidReceiveMemoryWarning:(UIApplication *)application {
    //---insert code here to free unused objects---
    [[ImageCache sharedImageCache] removeAllImagesInMemory];
}
```

In this method, you should stop all memory-intensive activities, such as audio and video playback. You should also remove all images cached in memory.

PROTOCOLS

In Objective-C, a *protocol* declares a programmatic interface that any class can choose to implement. A protocol declares a set of methods, and an adopting class may choose to implement one or more of its declared methods. The class that defines the protocol is expected to call the methods in the protocols that are implemented by the adopting class.

The easiest way to understand protocols is to examine the `UIAlertView` class. As you have experienced in the various chapters in this book, you can simply use the `UIAlertView` class by creating an instance of it and then calling its `show` method:

```
UIAlertView *alert = [[UIAlertView alloc]
                         initWithTitle:@"Hello"
                              message:@"This is an alert view"
                             delegate:self
                     cancelButtonTitle:@"OK"
                     otherButtonTitles:nil];
    [alert show];
```

The preceding code displays an alert view with one button — OK. Tapping the OK button automatically dismisses the alert view. If you want to display additional buttons, you can set the `otherButtonTitles:` parameter like this:

```
UIAlertView *alert = [[UIAlertView alloc]
                         initWithTitle:@"Hello"
                              message:@"This is an alert view"
                             delegate:self
                     cancelButtonTitle:@"OK"
                     otherButtonTitles:@"Option 1", @"Option 2", nil];
```

The alert view now displays three buttons — OK, Option 1, and Option 2. But how do you know which button was tapped by the user? You can determine this by handling the relevant method(s) that will be fired by the alert view when the buttons are clicked. This set of methods is defined by the `UIAlertViewDelegate` protocol. This protocol defines the following methods:

➤   `alertView:clickedButtonAtIndex:`

➤   `willPresentAlertView:`

➤   didPresentAlertView:

➤   alertView:willDismissWithButtonIndex:

➤   alertView:didDismissWithButtonIndex:

➤   alertViewCancel:

If you want to implement any of the methods in the UIAlertViewDelegate protocol, you need to ensure that your class, in this case the View Controller, conforms to this protocol. A class conforms to a protocol using angle brackets (<>), like this:

```
@interface UsingViewsViewController : UIViewController
    <UIAlertViewDelegate> {  //---this class conforms to the UIAlertViewDelegate
                             // protocol---
    //...
}
```

> **NOTE** *To conform to more than one delegate, separate the protocols with commas, such as <UIAlertViewDelegate, UITableViewDataSource>.*

After the class conforms to a protocol, you can implement the method in your class:

```
- (void)alertView:(UIAlertView *)alertView
clickedButtonAtIndex:(NSInteger)buttonIndex {

    NSLog([NSString stringWithFormat:@"%d", buttonIndex]);

}
```

Delegate

In Objective-C, a delegate is just an object that has been assigned by another object as the object responsible for handling events. Consider the case of the UIAlertView example that you have seen previously:

```
UIAlertView *alert = [[UIAlertView alloc]
                        initWithTitle:@"Hello"
                            message:@"This is an alert view"
                        delegate:self
                    cancelButtonTitle:@"OK"
                    otherButtonTitles:nil];
```

The initializer of the UIAlertView class includes a parameter called the delegate. Setting this parameter to self means that the current object is responsible for handling all the events fired by this instance of the UIAlertView class. If you don't need to handle events fired by this instance, you can simply set it to nil:

```
UIAlertView *alert = [[UIAlertView alloc]
                        initWithTitle:@"Hello"
```

```
                        message:@"This is an alert view"
                      delegate:nil
              cancelButtonTitle:@"OK"
              otherButtonTitles:nil];
```

If you have multiple buttons on the alert view and want to know which button was tapped, you need to handle the methods defined in the UIAlertViewDelegate protocol. You can either implement it in the same class in which the UIAlertView class was instantiated (as shown in the previous section), or create a new class to implement the method, like this:

```
//---SomeClass.m---
@implementation SomeClass

- (void)alertView:(UIAlertView *)alertView
clickedButtonAtIndex:(NSInteger)buttonIndex {

    NSLog([NSString stringWithFormat:@"%d", buttonIndex]);

}

@end
```

To ensure that the alert view knows where to look for the method, create an instance of SomeClass and then set it as the delegate:

```
SomeClass *myDelegate = [[SomeClass alloc] init];

UIAlertView *alert = [[UIAlertView alloc]
                         initWithTitle:@"Hello"
                             message:@"This is an alert view"
                           delegate:myDelegate
                      cancelButtonTitle:@"OK"
                      otherButtonTitles:@"Option 1", @"Option 2", nil];
[alert show];
```

SELECTORS

In Objective-C, a selector is the name used to select a method to execute for an object. It is used to identify a method. You have seen the use of a selector in some of the chapters in this book. Here is one of them:

```
//---create a Button view---
CGRect frame = CGRectMake(10, 50, 300, 50);
UIButton *button = [UIButton buttonWithType:UIButtonTypeRoundedRect];
button.frame = frame;
[button setTitle:@"Click Me, Please!" forState:UIControlStateNormal];
button.backgroundColor = [UIColor clearColor];
[button addTarget:self action:@selector(buttonClicked:)
    forControlEvents:UIControlEventTouchUpInside];
```

The preceding code shows that you are dynamically creating a `UIButton` object. In order to handle the event (for example, the `Touch Up Inside` event) raised by the button, you need to call the `addTarget:action:forControlEvents:` method of the `UIButton` class:

```
[button addTarget:self action:@selector(buttonClicked:)
    forControlEvents:UIControlEventTouchUpInside];
```

The `action:` parameter takes in an argument of type `SEL` (selector). In the preceding code, you pass in the name of the method that you have defined — `buttonClicked:` — which is defined within the class:

```
-(IBAction) buttonClicked: (id) sender {
    //...
}
```

Alternatively, you can create an object of type `SEL` and then instantiate it by using the `NSSelectorFromString` function (which takes in a string containing the method name):

```
NSString *nameOfMethod = @"buttonClicked:";
SEL methodName = NSSelectorFromString(nameOfMethod);
```

The call to the `addTarget:action:forControlEvents:` method now looks like this:

```
[button addTarget:self action:methodName
forControlEvents:UIControlEventTouchUpInside];
```

 NOTE *When naming a selector, be sure to specify the full name of the method. For example, if a method name has one or more parameters, you need to add a ":" in the sector, such as:*

```
NSString *nameOfMethod = @"someMethod:withPara1:andPara2:";
```

 NOTE *Because Objective-C is an extension of C, it is common to see C functions interspersed throughout your Objective-C application. C functions use the parentheses () to pass in arguments for parameters.*

CATEGORIES

A category in Objective-C allows you to add methods to an existing class without the need to subclass it. You can also use a category to override the implementation of an existing class.

 NOTE *In some languages (such as C#), a category is known as an extension method.*

As an example, imagine that you want to test whether a string contains a valid email address. You can add an `isEmail` method to the `NSString` class so that you can call the `isEmail` method on any `NSString` instance, like this:

```
NSString *email = @"weimenglee@gmail.com";
if ([email isEmail]) {
    //...
}
```

To do so, you can simply create a new class file and code it as follows:

```
//---utils.h---
#import <Foundation/Foundation.h>

//---NSString is the class you are extending---
@interface NSString (stringUtils)

//---the method you are adding to the NSString class---
- (BOOL) isEmail;

@end
```

Basically, it looks the same as declaring a new class except that it does not inherit from any other class. The `stringUtils` is a name that identifies the category you are adding, and you can use any name you want.

Next, you need to implement the method(s) you are adding:

```
//---utils.m---
#import "Utils.h"

@implementation NSString (Utilities)

- (BOOL) isEmail {
    NSString *emailRegEx =
        @"(?:[a-z0-9!#$%\\&'*+/=?\\^_`{|}~-]+(?:\\.[a-z0-9!#$%\\&'*+/=?\\^_`{|}"
        @"~-]+)*|\"(?:[\\x01-\\x08\\x0b\\x0c\\x0e-\\x1f\\x21\\x23-\\x5b\\x5d-\\"
        @"x7f]|\\\\[\\x01-\\x09\\x0b\\x0c\\x0e-\\x7f])*\")@(?:(?:[a-z0-9](?:[a-"
        @"z0-9-]*[a-z0-9])?\\.)+[a-z0-9](?:[a-z0-9-]*[a-z0-9])?|\\[(?:(?:25[0-5"
        @"]|2[0-4][0-9]|[01]?[0-9][0-9]?)\\.){3}(?:25[0-5]|2[0-4][0-9]|[01]?[0-"
        @"9][0-9]?|[a-z0-9-]*[a-z0-9]:(?:[\\x01-\\x08\\x0b\\x0c\\x0e-\\x1f\\x21"
        @"-\\x5a\\x53-\\x7f]|\\\\[\\x01-\\x09\\x0b\\x0c\\x0e-\\x7f])+)\\])";

    NSPredicate *regExPredicate = [NSPredicate
                                      predicateWithFormat:@"SELF MATCHES %@",
                                      emailRegEx];
    return [regExPredicate evaluateWithObject:self];
}

@end
```

NOTE *The code for validating an email address using regular expression is adapted from* `http://cocoawithlove.com/2009/06/verifying-that-string-is-email-address.html`.

You can then test for the validity of an email address using the newly added method:

```
NSString *email = @"weimenglee@gmail.com";
if ([email isEmail])
    NSLog(@"Valid email");
else
    NSLog(@"Invalid email");
```

INDEX

INDEX

K

N